TENDING THE TALKING WIRE

To Ed, my Friend

Charlie

11/96

ENJOY

TENDING THE TALKING WIRE

A Buck Soldier's View of Indian Country
1863 - 1866

Edited by

WILLIAM E. UNRAU

University of Utah Press
Salt Lake City, Utah

Volume twelve of the University of Utah Publications
in the American West, under the editorial direction of
the Center for Studies of the American West.
S. Lyman Tyler, Director
Brigham D. Madsen, General Editor

Frontispiece: Henry F. Farney, "The Song of the Talking Wire,"
courtesy of the Taft Museum, Cincinnati, Ohio.

To Deb and Bill

A Couple of Wild Westerners

Contents

ILLUSTRATIONS

MAPS

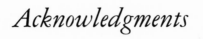

Acknowledgments

Hervey Johnson's letters from Indian country were first brought to the editor's attention by Michael Heaston, former Curator of Special Collections at Wichita State University's Ablah Library, and by Hal Ottaway, a professional anthropologist with an abiding interest in the American West. Through their efforts, which the editor gratefully acknowledges, a meeting was arranged with John J. Wassal, Jr., who discovered the Johnson letters among property he purchased in 1959 from the Omar Aley estate in Wichita, Kansas. An avid collector with a more than casual interest in history, Mr. Wassal cooperated to the fullest extent, and his permission to publish the letters in their original form is hereby recognized. While not wholly successful, his efforts to locate the heirs of Hervey Johnson were unrelenting, and his interest in the substance of the correspondence belies the notion that only professionally trained persons can appreciate the importance of primary. documents.

Others who provided invaluable assistance were Charles C. Sharp, late Superintendent of the Fort Laramie National Historic Site; Douglas C. McChristian, Acting Superintendent of the Fort Laramie National Historic Site; B. Franklin Cooling, United States Army Military Research Collection, Carlisle Barracks; Robert G. Athearn of the University of Colorado; T. A. Larson, Charles Roundy, and E. B. Long of the University of Wyoming; Craig Miner and John Narnsberger of Wichita State University; Elmer Parker and George Chalou of the National Archives; Carl N. Tyson; Henry P. Walker of Tucson, Arizona; Joseph Snell of the Kansas State Historical Society; Joseph Gambone of Topeka, Kansas; Maxine Benson of the Colorado State Historical Society; Frank Levstik of the Ohio Historical Society; Katherine Halverson of the Wyoming State Archives and Historical Department; Martin F. Schmidt of the Louisville Free Public Library; Michael Sievers of the Fort Worth Museum of Science and History; Katherine Hanna of the Taft Museum; Wolfgang Stoddard of New York City; James Nottage, Curator of the Kansas State Historical Society; and James F. Bentley of the Filson Club.

Miriam Schreer's hard work and cheerful disposition made this project an unforgettable experience. The staff of the University of Utah Press, particularly Norma Mikkelsen and Peggy Lee, warrant special recognition for their professionalism and many personal kindnesses. The editor also wishes to acknowledge the cooperation of Paul Magelli, Dean of Fairmont College of Liberal Arts and Sciences, Wichita State University, and financial assistance provided by the Wichita State University Faculty Research Committee.

William E. Unrau

The American soldier enters the army voluntarily, and at once applies himself to become proficient in his new profession. . . . There are no requirements asked of him that he is not always ready to comply with. . . . His officers are not compelled to drive him continually, but he is himself anxious to become a leader.

Twenty Years among our Hostile Indians, 1889
Captain James Lee Humfreville

They think it a "big thing" to be a commissioned officer. . . . All the orders that have been sent here for us have been of no avail, and we don't look for any better respect to be paid to future orders. . . . I'm afraid it wont be healthy for some of our "Shoulder strap Men" to be along with us when we do start east. I believe half of them are afraid of us now.

Corporal Hervey Johnson
Company G, Eleventh Ohio Volunteer Cavalry
Fort Laramie, April 1, 1866

Introduction

A visit to the Western Americana division of most major libraries prompts the conclusion that the military frontier of the trans-Missouri West after 1850 has captured the attention of a large portion of the reading public. Memoirs, diaries, books, and articles have been published in quantities that overwhelm readers, and publication of much of this material has been urged on by the notion that here, in almost archetypal form, may be discovered the very essence of Indian resistance to the white invader. The specialist may wonder if anything of value is left to be said or interpreted.

There is, if it is understood that the West of the mid-nineteenth century was a region of unusual diversity and importance to the nation at large, and that its history has often been oversimplified. Virtually everything was in a state of flux beyond the Big Muddy, as the Missouri River came to be known. The raw setting, the political immaturity, and especially the region's remarkable potential for economic development and exploitation fired the imaginations of even the most conservative-minded Americans. Indeed, the bumptious adolescence of the trans-Missouri West suggests a striking analogy with the trans-Appalachian West of the Jacksonian era. Side by side, roughhewn adventurers and more sophisticated types (at least so they thought) were attracted to this latest style American Arcadia, very much like their predecessors had been drawn to the Midwest and New South after the War of 1812. The rush to the California mines following the Mexican War confirmed mobility as an irrevocable characteristic of the mass culture, as did the emerging belief that Americans somehow were manifestly destined to prevail over less fortunate creatures, whether they be Bretons, Mexicans, Orientals, or Indians.[1]

It was, of course, an ethnocentric ideal not critically perceived by the majority of its participants. Nevertheless, this missionary-like zeal was real, for the westward-bound emigrant seldom took his trek lightly. Responding to a pervasive national psychology of expansion, he saw himself as extending the area of freedom or reducing the wilderness to a garden

---

[1] For the alternative interpretations of Manifest Destiny see Albert K. Weinberg, *Manifest Destiny: A Study in Nationalist Expansionism in American History*; Frederick Merk, *Manifest Destiny and Mission in American History: A Reinterpretation*; and William H. Goetzmann, *When the Eagle Screamed: The Romantic Horizon in American Diplomacy, 1800–1860*.

or bringing civilization to the sanctuary of the "savage." At a more practical level, however, the thrust into the trans-Missouri West inevitably involved physical confrontation for the simple reason that most of the land was claimed by Indians — Indians who by the decade of the 1860's had been prompted to believe that the national government was committed to preserving the integrity of their traditional domain. In this the military resources of the United States were obliged to assume an important role; but it was not a very popular one, as some foreign observers were quick to point out.

Charles Joseph LaTrobe — English traveler, philanthropist, occasional servant of Whitehall, and outspoken critic of British native policy in Australia — toured frontier America in the years 1832–1833. In company with Washington Irving, he visited Fort Snelling, Fort Armstrong, Prairie du Chien, Fort Gibson, and a number of Indian agencies west of the Missouri. He came to appreciate the unenviable role the military was expected to play in the conflict of cultures, and he was especially impressed with the developing cleavage between the officer class and the more egalitarian-minded men of enlisted ranks:

> The dislike to personal subordination in which the youth of the country are nutured from childhood, and the possibility of every man who has character making his way in a more credible manner, prevent the [military] ranks being filled with better subjects; and degraded indeed is the class of men whom the young officer must toil to bring into sober subordination. Desertion, which is stated to prevail to the annual extent of one half of the whole army — always keeps up the call for new recruits, and the recommencement of his labours. Added to this and the frequently complete utter state of exile from good society consequent upon the service, at an age when that is absolutely necessary for the formation of the character of the young and ardent — the post of an officer on the frontiers is by no means either an enviable, or in the idea of many of his fellow-citizens, an honourable one. . . . The officer on the frontiers is now called to defend the Indian against the citizen, and then to protect the citizen against the Indian; and in enforcing the orders of the executive against the encroachments and nefarious dealings of the loose inhabitant of the boundary, he is sure to win the hatred of the latter, who, as a citizen, will always meet

4

with a sympathy, which, however just the cause, will rarely be accorded the officer.[2]

LaTrobe's defense of the officer was matched by Richard Burton's subsequent defense of the enlisted man. Commenting on the basis of his overland journey to the Mormon settlements in 1860, the famous British traveler countered:

I heard more of army grievances during my second stay at Camp Floyd [Fort Crittenden, Utah Territory]. The term of a soldier's [regular] enlistment, five years, is too short, especially for the cavalry branch, and the facilities for desertion are enormous. Between the two, one-third of the army disappears every year. . . . The soldier has no time to learn his work; he must drive wagons, clear bush, make roads, and build huts and stables. When thoroughly drilled, he can take his discharge, and having filled a purse out of his very liberal pay ($11 per mensem), he generally buys ground and becomes a landed proprietor. The officers are equally well salaried, but marching, counter-marching, and contingent expenses are heavy enough to make the profession little better than it is in France.[3]

Unfortunately, such divergence of opinion is not clarified by the uncritical character of Western military history in general. At best, much of the material weighing heavily on the library shelves is repetitious, romanticized, and grounded on a flagrant disregard for serious research. Compare, for example, Robert G. Athearn's knowledgeable portrayal of General Sherman as a Western military commander with J. P. Dunn's misguided conclusions regarding the army and the Indian. Or consider William Leckie's account of warfare on the southern Plains in contradistinction to Samuel Crawford's biased version of the same events. Dunn and Crawford were writers who by background, training, and the immediacy of their experiences were unable to engage themselves in the research techniques expected of modern historians. Yet, like Eugene F. Ware's per-

[2] Charles Joseph LaTrobe, *The Rambler in North America: 1832–1833*, vol. 2, pp. 319–20.

[3] Sir Richard F. Burton, *The City of the Saints and Across the Rocky Mountains to California*, p. 499.

ception of the military frontier around Fort Laramie in 1864 or De Benneville R. Keim's account of General Sheridan in the West,[4] Dunn and Crawford developed their narratives with conviction. Their conclusions take on a special significance when generalized within the framework of contemporary scholarship. Indeed, the serious student does himself a disservice if he ignores the work of these "primitive" historians.

There is, perhaps, a more critical problem involved in the writing of Western military history (or, for that matter, virtually all military history). It stems from the occupational position of those recording the so-called facts. Circumstances underlying the decision-making process, the nature of discipline and morale in a given company or regiment, accounts of what really happened in the field of battle, and analyses of immediate and long-range consequences are available to the historian primarily in the form of orders, reports, and correspondence prepared by the officer class. Even a casual survey of the monumental *Official Records of the Union and Confederate Armies*,[5] the massive manuscript collections in the Military Division of the National Archives,[6] or the seemingly endless supply of frontier newsprint warrants the conclusion that with few exceptions the available "documents" were processed through the memoranda mill of the military elite. Here and there, by way of an occasional diary, letter to a friend or relative back home, or official investigation, the enlisted man's view entered the picture, but by comparison to the paper avalanche generated by the officer class, these kinds of records are too

---

[4] Robert G. Athearn, *William Tecumseh Sherman and the Settlement of the West*; Jacob P. Dunn, Jr., *Massacres of the Mountains: A History of the Indian Wars of the Far West, 1815–1875*; William H. Leckie, *The Military Conquest of the Southern Plains*; Samuel J. Crawford, *Kansas in the Sixties*; Captain Eugene F. Ware, *The Indian War of 1864*; and De Benneville R. Keim, *Sheridan's Troopers on the Borders: A Winter Campaign on the Plains*.

[5] *The War of the Rebellion: A Compilation of the Official Records of the Union and Confederate Armies*, 128 vols.

[6] The most important records in the Military Archives Division, National Archives (hereinafter cited as NA), for the western military frontier are Records of the Adjutant General's Office, RG 94; Records of the Office of the Secretary of War, RG 107; Records of the Office of Judge Advocate General, Army, RG 153; Records of the Office of Inspector General, RG 159; Records of the War Department General Staff, RG 165; and Records of United States Army Continental Commands, 1821–1920, RG 393.

few and far between.[7] It is, then, like finding a desert oasis to discover the letters of an enlisted man — an uncelebrated nobody whose perception and criticism of and sensitivity to the larger framework of military involvement in Indian country were recorded in great detail, on a regular basis, and over an extended period of time. Such is the contribution of Corporal Hervey Johnson, Company G, Eleventh Regiment of Ohio Volunteer Cavalry. That he was literate, given to detailed accounts, and especially anxious to demonstrate that Indian fighting was no great adjustment for a maturing Buckeye volunteer with a family tradition of pacifism makes his correspondence all the more significant.

Hervey Johnson was born of Quaker stock in Leesburgh, Highland County, Ohio, on June 13, 1839. Following the Quaker migration to southwestern Ohio from the Piedmont Region of Virginia and North Carolina that began in the closing years of the eighteenth century, Hervey's great-grandfather, "Governor" James Johnson, brought his large family from Bedford County, Virginia, to Fairfield Township in northern Highland County, Ohio, in 1812. Here he purchased several hundred acres of bottom land and laid out the townsite of "Old Leesburgh." Apparently his efforts at town promotion were abortive almost from the start, since he soon became involved in unsuccessful litigation with the promoters of nearby "New Leesburgh."[8]

---

[7] Examples of some of the better published accounts are Robert S. Bliss, "Journal of [Sgt.] Robert S. Bliss, with the Mormon Battalion," *Utah Historical Quarterly*, vol. 4, nos. 3 and 4 (1931), pp. 67–96, 110–28; George F. Brimlow, ed., "Two Cavalrymen's Diaries of the Bannock War, 1878," *Oregon Historical Quarterly*, vol. 68, nos. 3 and 4 (1967), pp. 221–58, 293–316; John M. Ellis and Robert E. Stowers, eds. and annots., "The Nevada Uprising of 1860 as Seen by Private Charles A. Scott," *Arizona and the West*, vol. 3, no. 4 (1961), pp. 355–76. Gene M. Gressley, ed., "A Soldier with Crook: The Letters of Henry Porter," *Montana, the Magazine of Western History*, vol. 8, no. 3 (1958), pp. 33–47; Myra E. Hull, ed., "Soldiering on the High Plains, the Diary of Lewis Byram Hull, 1864–1866," *Kansas Historical Quarterly*, vol. 7, no. 1 (1938), pp. 3–53; Ben Innis, ed., "The Fort Buford Diary of Pvt. Wilmot P. Sanford," *North Dakota History*, vol. 33, no. 4 (1966), pp. 335–78; and Francis Paul Prucha, ed., "An Army Private at Fort Snelling in 1849," *Minnesota History*, vol. 36, no. 1 (1958), pp. 13–17. The paucity of these records is in sharp contrast to the voluminous memoirs, recollections, and autobiographies of such western military giants as Frémont, Sherman, Sheridan, Miles, Carrington, Forsyth, Crook, and Custer.

[8] Rev. J. W. Klise, *The County of Highland*, pp. 77–79; *History of Ross and Highland Counties, Ohio*, pp. 402–9.

Little is known about Hervey's grandfather John except that he was a farmer in the Clear Creek community not far from Leesburgh, that he remained a faithful Quaker, and that he had at least one son, Gerrard, who married Mary Coffin in 1838. To this union were born six children — Hervey, Warren, Semira, Abi, Sybil, and Orpah — of whom Hervey was the eldest. Following the pioneering tradition of his grandfather, Gerrard Johnson migrated to New London, Howard County, Indiana, sometime after 1851, where he and his family were associated with the Honey Creek Monthly Meeting, and where he continued the agricultural pursuits of his forefathers until his untimely death in 1856. The responsibility for the relatively large and unaffluent family then fell heavily on Hervey, a young man of seventeen, and his younger brother Warren. Tragic memories of their late father were not easily forgotten, and the prospect of remaining on the sparsely populated prairie-plains of north-central Indiana was so dismal that the following year the Johnson family returned to their modest Ohio farm.[9] Four years later their relatively uneventful life was interrupted by the beginning of the Civil War.

Southern Ohio in the early months of the Civil War was a turbulent area. Heavily populated by southern emigrants whose loyalties vacillated between Union and Confederate persuasions, and whose farmsteads had some of the poorest soil in the entire Midwest, the region was especially susceptible to the agricultural depression precipitated by Lincoln's closing of the southern markets in 1861. It was a hotbed of Copperheadism, Negrophobia, and the political machinations of northerners with southern sympathies. Union defeats during the first two years of war caused grave concern among the settlements just north of the Ohio River, and the fear was repeatedly expressed that Confederate raiders might shortly ravage the countryside.[10]

Fortunately, Ohio provided enough volunteer regiments under the Draft of 1862 to prevent enforcement of the much-feared policy of conscription. In light of their traditional position of nonviolence, the Quakers

---

[9] Corporal Hervey Johnson, Company G, Consolidated Military and/or Pension Files (hereinafter cited as CMPF); Compiled Records Showing Service of Military Units in Volunteer Union Organizations, NA.

[10] Frank L. Klement, *The Copperheads in the Middle West*, pp. 16, 25–26, 73–77.

in the southern counties viewed the future with guarded optimism, but as the Union cause worsened in the critical months following the Emancipation Proclamation (January 1, 1863), and as the principle of federal conscription was written into law in March 1863, it became apparent that the inability to find or afford an acceptable replacement was tantamount to obligatory military service in one manner or another, regardless of one's ideology or religious convictions. All things considered, and especially for most young Quaker men, enlisting in a volunteer regiment under the direction of neighbors and friends was by far the more desirable course of action. The possibility that one might be sent to less critical areas of conflict was an added inducement.

Anticipating the conscription law of March 1863, the leading paper of Highland County reported, on February 4, 1863, that trouble was brewing with Indians on the far-western border. It was believed that the situation was especially grave in Utah, for military intelligence had it that "secession agents [were] operating among the Indians." [11] Earlier, in the summer of 1861, William O. Collins, father of Caspar Collins and a prominent resident and lawyer of Hillsboro (the county seat of Highland County) had received authority from Washington to recruit a regiment of cavalry, to be denominated the Ohio Seventh. Four companies, A, B, C, and D, were enrolled, but on December 1 the recruiting was halted under an order requiring that all "incomplete organizations" be consolidated. Consequently, the various companies of the Sixth and Seventh Cavalry were formed into one regiment, which was designated the Sixth. Companies A, B, C, and D — those largely enrolled from Highland County — were then numbered the First Battalion of the Sixth Regiment, which was

---

[11] *The Highland Weekly News*, Hillsboro, Ohio, February 4, 1863. The *News* doubtlessly was responding to official reports coming from the Military District of Utah. On December 20, 1862, for example, Colonel Patrick Edward Connor reported: "I am reliably informed that the so-called President [of the Church of Jesus Christ of Latter-day Saints, Brigham] Young, is making active preparations indicating a determination on his part to oppose the Government of the United States in the spring, provided Utah is not admitted into the Union as a State, or in case of a foreign war or serious reverse to our arms. . . . Brigham Young is now engaged in mounting cannon for the purpose of resisting the Government, has had reports circulated, which have reached the ears of those highest in authority in order to mature his plans, gain time and prepare his cannon." Connor to Lieutenant R. C. Drum, December 20, 1862, *The War of the Rebellion*, series I, vol. 48, pt. 2, p. 257.

ordered to Camp Dennison, Ohio. On March 13, 1862, this battalion was detached from the Sixth, ordered to report to General Henry W. Halleck at Benton Barracks, St. Louis, and make preparations for the long journey to Indian country. Marching by way of Forts Leavenworth and Kearny, the battalion arrived at Fort Laramie, Dakota Territory, on May 30, 1862, and shortly thereafter was permanently deatched from the Sixth Regiment and designated the "First Independent Battalion of Ohio Volunteer Cavalry." Until September of that same year it provided protection for the overland emigrants and guarded the newly constructed Pacific Telegraph from a log cabin installation near South Pass known as Pacific Springs, and thereafter had as its permanent headquarters Fort Laramie, some 300 miles to the east.[12]

On August 10, 1857, in a significant compromise designed to delineate the regional communication monopolies of the nation, as well as in anticipation of the strategy accompanying the planning and completion of the Union Pacific Railroad, the American Telegraph Company, the Atlantic and Ohio Telegraph Company, the New York, Albany and Buffalo Telegraph Company, the Western Union Telegraph Company, the New Orleans and Ohio Telegraph Lessees, and the Illinois and Mississippi Telegraph Company forged an economic alliance that established the necessary political foundation for passage, on June 16, 1860, of the Pacific Telegraph Act. The Act provided a ten-year subsidy at $40,000 per annum for construction of a line from the Missouri River to Carson City, Nevada, to be completed within two years from July 31, 1860. As well, the Act granted to the successful bidder the right-of-way and plots, not to exceed 160 acres with an average of one every fifteen miles, for the construction of repeater or repair stations. For such generosity the government was allowed priority use of the line and the right to make connections with any military posts in the United States. The contract between Carson City and Salt Lake City was awarded to the Overland Telegraph Company, with a capitalization of $1,250,000; the Omaha–Salt Lake City contract went to

---

[12] Compiled Records Showing Service of Military Units in Volunteer Union Organizations, Ohio, Sixth through Twelfth Cavalry, Records of the Adjutant General's Office, RG 94, M 594, R 141, NA; *Official Roster of the Soldiers of the State of Ohio in the War of the Rebellion, 1861–1866*, pp. 547–48; *History of Ross and Highland Counties, Ohio*, pp. 138–39.

With completion of the transcontinental telegraph in 1861, communication between East and West was cut from the minimum ten days required by Pony Express to a matter of minutes. The mystified Indians referred to the telegraph as the talking or singing wire, but soon realized that it provided the white invaders with a tremendous military advantage and attacked it with a vengeance. *From "The Overland Pony Express," photographed by Savage, Salt Lake City, from a painting by George M. Ottinger,* Harper's Weekly, *vol. 11, no. 566 (November 2, 1867), p. 693.*

the Pacific Telegraph Company, with a capitalization of $1,000,000. The latter firm was easily dominated by such Western Union magnates as Hiram Sibley, Jeptha H. Wade, and Samuel L. Selden. Under the expert guidance of surveyor and construction superintendent Edward Creighton, the Omaha–Salt Lake City line was completed on October 1, 1861, well ahead of schedule. Six days later, under the guidance of James Gamble, the Overland construction crews reached Salt Lake and for the first time the continent was connected by telegraphic wire.[13]

With the Indians increasingly restive in the face of the mysterious talking wire and massive white migrations to Montana, Oregon, and California, it was not difficult for Lieutenant Colonel Collins to make a strong case in Washington for bringing his meager force up to regimental strength, even though it had been involved in only two official engagements with Indians up to that time. More persuasive was the fear that the transcontinental telegraph might be permanently disrupted. When it was first completed in late 1861, the mystified Indians variously referred to the telegraph as the "talking wire," the "singing wire," or the "humming messenger wire." In time they came to understand that the wire provided the white invader with a tremendous advantage on the field of battle, and they attacked the telegraph with a vengeance. To protect, repair, and even operate the remote repeater stations required a good deal of manpower — the kind of manpower that could be best provided by the military.[14]

On June 1, 1863, the Provost General for Ohio began enforcing the Conscription Act in Highland County.[15] Three days later the *Highland News* reported that "Lt. Col. Collins has recently returned from Washington, where he has obtained authority to recruit men for an additional battalion to the one now under his command."[16] Shortly thereafter, the

---

[13] Robert Luther Thompson, *Wiring A Continent, The History of the Telegraph Industry in the United States, 1832–1866*, pp. 314, 348–72.

[14] *Official Roster of the Soldiers of the State of Ohio*, p. 548. For the Indian threat to the telegraph see Major-General Grenville M. Dodge, *The Battle of Atlanta and Other Campaigns, Addresses, Etc.*, pp. 63–77.

[15] E. A. Parrott to J. A. Sinnett, June 1, 1863, Letters from A. A. Provost Marshall General for Ohio to Captain John A. Sinnett, U.S. Provost General for Ohio, Official Circulars and Local Letters, 13th District, 1863–1865, Archives Division, Ohio Historical Society, Columbus.

[16] *Highland Weekly News*, June 4, 1863.

News advised that "he [Collins] is getting men quite rapidly. . . . Volunteering is quite active again, in anticipation of the 'draft' being at hand. Now is your time, boys, delays are dangerous." [17]

Hervey Johnson heeded the editor's advice. Within two weeks the young farmer from Leesburgh presented himself at Hillsboro, where, on July 11, 1863, he enlisted for a three-year tour of duty with what came to be designated the Eleventh Regiment of Ohio Volunteer Cavalry.[18] His enlistment bounty amounted to $100, with $25 paid to him at the time of his enlistment and the remainder due when he should be mustered out. He was twenty-four years old and on his official Muster Roll was described as five feet ten inches tall with blue eyes, brown hair, and a light complexion. Of the sixty-four men who were eventually enrolled in Captain Levi Rinehart's Company G, Hervey was the thirty-first to enlist. Happily, a significant number of men from his own community were placed in Company G, including several of his closest friends.[19]

Three years and 100 letters later, Corporal Hervey Johnson was mustered out at Fort Leavenworth, Kansas. His return to Ohio with the other men of the Eleventh Ohio was an unheralded event, unaccompanied by the traditional pomp and circumstance celebrations prepared for heroes returning from the field of battle.[20] In the meantime, the young Quaker soldier had matured a great deal and undoubtedly was considerably wiser. He had learned that an enlisted man's essential business was to obey, not to question. He had learned to dislike Indians, Mormons, and especially the overland emigrants. He had come to despise commissioned officers, their duplicity, and the red tape that allowed them to maintain their positions of authority. He had learned that getting ahead in orthodox American style was far more attractive to the average westerner than getting back to the fundamentals of nature and discovering personal freedom at

[17] *Ibid.*, June 18, 1863.

[18] Johnson, CMPF.

[19] *Ibid.*; Muster Roll of Captain Levi M. Rinehart, Company G, Eleventh Ohio Volunteer Cavalry (hereinafter cited as Eleventh OVC), United States Army, Lieutenant Colonel William O. Collins, Commander, May 20–June 15, 1863, Archives Division, Ohio Historical Society, Columbus.

[20] Johnson, CMPF; *Highland Weekly News*, April 5, July 26, August 9, 1866.

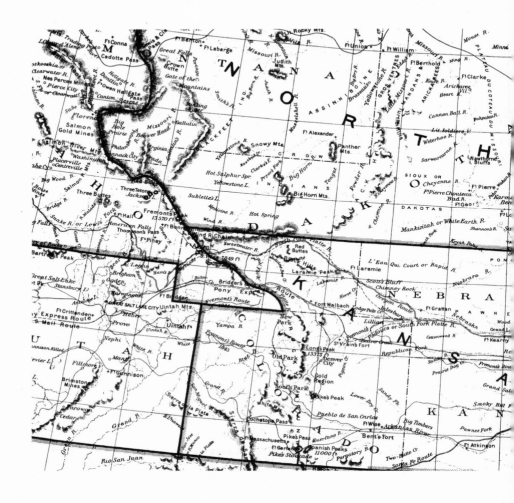

Section from a military map of the United States showing the boundaries of the Union and Confederate divisions and departments, June 30, 1864. *From* Atlas to Accompany the Official Records of the Union and Confederate Armies, *p. 169, plate CLXIX. Washington, D.C.: U.S. Government Printing Office, 1891–95.*

the so-called cutting edge of the frontier. He had come to appreciate the debilitating consequences of monotony and boredom, as well as the personal satisfaction that could be derived from exploring and reflecting on the natural wonders of the great West. And he had learned how difficult it was to pass the lonely days and weeks before he could return to the life of a civilian.

During Johnson's nearly three years of service in Indian country he witnessed significant changes in the face of the West, as is evident from the altering datelines of his letters. When the young Quaker cavalryman arrived at Fort Laramie in early October 1863, the region where his official duties were to take him was part of the Idaho Territory, created on March 3, 1863, out of eastern Washington Territory and the western flank of the Nebraska Territory. A combination of factors contributed to Idaho's political birth, not the least of which were important gold strikes on the Clearwater branch of the Snake River in 1859, on the Salmon fork in 1861, and in the Boise basin in 1862. Understandably, Washington territorial leaders fought to retain their ore-rich country but were no match for separatist-minded miners, agricultural entrepreneurs, and a Union Congress aware of the region's potential for state-making. Within a few months comparable developments in other quarters brought yet another change of address to Johnson's camps of operation—Fort Laramie, Sweetwater Station, Deer Creek Station, and Platte Bridge — as well as other military telegraph installations along the route to Oregon, Salt Lake City, and California. Pay dirt, the universal catalyst for uninhibited mobility in the West, was found on the Beaverhead branch of the Jefferson River, Montana, in 1862. The following spring a major strike was made on Alder Creek east of Bannack City; and in the spring of 1864, Last Chance Gulch near the future site of Helena yielded gold in quantities sufficient to attract a human stampede on the model of the 1859 rush to Colorado. Once again the pressure for political organization could not be contained, and on May 26, 1864, Montana Territory was created at the expense of an unrealistically large Idaho Territory. At the same time most of present Wyoming was attached to the Dakota Territory, established as early as 1861, so that when Johnson dispatched letters in the late spring of 1864, he addressed them from Dakota Territory — a remote and uncertain place

16

where, in the meantime, relations between the Sioux Indians and the white invaders had greatly deteriorated. Had the young Ohioan remained in this inhospitable setting beyond the span of his official enlistment, his letters might very well have recorded yet another change in address. Wyoming Territory was established in 1868, leaving the once massive Dakota Territory no greater than the present states of North and South Dakota.[21]

If these paper boundaries were not always comprehended by Johnson, they surely were uncertain to emigrants pursuing an American utopia with reckless abandon. Certainly they were confusing and suggestive to his family back in Ohio. Indeed, to the average Easterner, urged on by the land-office model of a prolific, fee-simple empire, the West of Hervey Johnson was taking on the parameters of a romantic construction, with villains (Indians) and victims (ranchers and cavalrymen) confronting one another over not very certain spoils. That Johnson, in a limited but nevertheless profound manner, attempted to challenge this oversimplification is important, for, in the final analysis, no more effective antidote to uncritical imagery may be found than that based on an honest, candid account of personal experience.

From a different but complementary perspective, the drawings of Charles Frederick Moellmann add a graphic dimension to the correspondence of Johnson. Moellmann was a Prussian emigrant who settled in the southern Ohio neighborhood where Johnson came to his maturity, and who enlisted in the Eleventh Ohio on July 17, 1863, less than a week after Johnson had cast his lot with the military. Moellmann was designated bugler of Company G (Johnson's Company) and saw service at virtually every military post between Scott's Bluff and South Pass. During his three years of duty, which included an important assignment as cartographer at District Headquarters in Omaha, Moellmann produced at least sixty pencil, crayon, and watercolor drawings of Indian and military life on the Oregon Trail. Those reproduced in this volume reveal the work of an amateur artist with an eye for detail and, like the letters of Johnson, a

---

[21] Hubert Howe Bancroft, *History of Washington, Idaho, and Montana, 1845–1889*, pp. 442–46. See also James H. Hawley, ed., *History of Idaho, The Gem of the Mountains*, pp. 134–37; K. Ross Toole, *Montana, An Uncommon Land*, chs. IV–V, VII; Taft A. Larson, *History of Wyoming*, chs. 2–4.

perception that something historically significant was taking place that should be recorded for posterity.[22]

Following his honorable discharge in the summer of 1866, Hervey Johnson married Elizabeth Engle, a pre-war sweetheart from Samantha, Ohio, a small village not far from Hervey's own community at Leesburgh. The Johnsons remained in Highland County until 1878. From there they moved to Laurener County, Tennessee, in 1878, to Mahaska County, Iowa, in 1882, and to Sedgwick County, Kansas, in 1889. Here, in the city of Wichita, Hervey was employed as a flagman for the Santa Fe Railroad until his death on March 12, 1923. He was survived by his widow and three children, Edgar, Alberta, and Azaylia. Thirty-six years later, in 1959, the letters that follow were discovered as part of the property purchased by Mr. John J. Wassal, Jr., from the Omar Aley estate at 1515 Fairview Street, Wichita, Kansas. All efforts to determine how or under what circumstances the letters came into the possession of the Aley family have failed, but that they are authentic is unquestionable.[23]

Because Hervey Johnson wrote with surprising sophistication, and because it is the editor's belief that punctuation and syntax for a particular period are of more than casual interest, the principal changes made are those deemed absolutely essential. Johnson's letters contain many run-on sentences with no punctuation or capitalization to indicate where one thought ends and another begins, and no paragraphs. For ease of reading, some punctuation, capitalization, and paragraphing have been added, but only where necessary, with the original style being retained as much as possible. Spelling follows Johnson's original, but obvious thoughtless slips and repetitions have been corrected without special notation. Ma-

---

[22] Charles Frederick Moellmann, CMPF, NA; James H. Nottage, "A Centennial History of Artist Activities in Wyoming, 1837–1937," *Annals of Wyoming*, vol. 48, no. 1 (Spring 1976), p. 86. Like other writers, Nottage uses the spelling Moellman, which is the spelling found in most of Moellmann's official military file. However, Moellmann clarified the record after he was mustered out of the service by pointing out that the mustering officer had made the error at the time of his enlistment. See Moellmann to United States Commissioner of Pensions, December 16, 1896, Moellmann CMPF, NA.

[23] Johnson CMPF; *The Wichita Eagle*, Wichita, Kansas, March 13, 1923. Interview with Mr. John J. Wassal, Jr., Wichita, Kansas, November 12, 1971, and interview with Mrs. Elizabeth Holcomb, Wichita, Kansas, December 15, 1971.

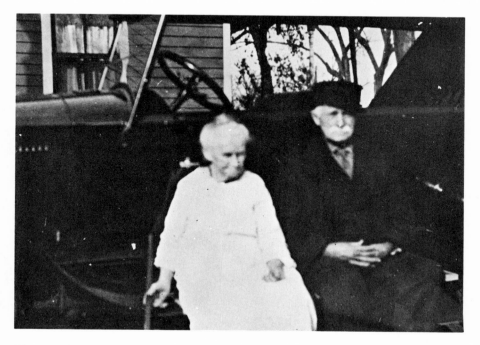

Hervey Johnson and his wife, Elizabeth Engle Johnson. This photograph was taken at their home in Wichita, Kansas, shortly before his death in 1923. *Courtesy of Mrs. Elizabeth Holcomb, Hervey Johnson's granddaughter by marriage, and Mr. Warren Holcomb, Hervey Johnson's great grandson.*

terial of a highly personal nature and of no apparent interest except to the immediate circle of Johnson's close relatives and friends has been deleted. These deletions are indicated by the traditional use of ellipses. Additions for the purposes of clarity have been bracketed.

En Route to Indian Country

July 18, 1863 — September 20, 1863

Indian country during the Civil War decade was a loosely defined area west of the Missouri River. But it had not always been that way. Prior to the Texas and Oregon annexations (1845–1846) and the massive Mexican Cession (1848), the national government during the Jacksonian period had designated the area west of the Mississippi River, west and north of Missouri, and west of the Arkansas Territory as the permanent abode of the American Indians. Here, in accordance with treaties ostensibly negotiated in good faith, the northeastern Indians and so-called Five Civilized Tribes from the south (the Creeks, Seminoles, Cherokees, Chocktaws, and Chickasaws) were to live and let live in peaceful bliss. Removed from the corrupting influences of the Anglo-American frontiersmen, and with the assistance of missionaries and government agents, the Native Americans were to proceed with the manifestly destined business of learning the white man's way of life.

For awhile the plan seemed to be working. But Uncle Sam's explosive expansion to the shores of the Pacific brought thousands of additional Indians into contact with migratory Americans and dictated significant modifications in Indian policy. The veritable horde of miners, ranchers, farmers, and speculators who rushed to the Far West following the Mexican War simply could not be contained. They were determined to strike it rich or reduce the wilderness to a ranch or garden, and they saw no reason why "savage" Indians should not be required to accept more limited living space. Mostly accommodating at first, the Indians of the Great Plains and Intermontane Plateau regions soon challenged the new dispensation.

For the Dakota people, who inhabited the strategically situated north central Plains, the Fort Laramie Treaty of 1851 was the beginning of the end. Not then fully aware of the ultimate consequences, they accepted more precise delineations of their traditional domains and granted to the government the right to construct roads and military posts within their territories — which, as they understood it, were to be as much for their benefit as for that of the invaders. By the late 1850's faced with relinquishing their traditional domains, the Brulé, Oglala, and Teton Sioux were encouraged to demonstrate a more obstinate posture.

As he affixed his signature to his enlistment papers in the midsummer of 1863, it is doubtful if Hervey Johnson perceived the essence of the

23

unfolding drama. His knowledge of Indians and the vast expanses of the trans-Missouri West were limited by the agrarian milieu of his southern Ohio home. His Quaker heritage, in juxtaposition to the ominous implications of the Civil War on the border, undoubtedly excited a feeling of apprehension and fear concerning the months and years ahead. On the other hand, it should be remembered that Johnson was an exceptionally curious person — a man ready for new experiences and obviously conditioned by the uncritical images most "settled folk" of the Midwest entertained about distant Indian country. Thus, his candid and on occasion almost swaggering descriptions of his experiences provide the perceptive reader with unique insights regarding the molding of a genuine frontier cavalryman.

En route to Indian country Private Hervey Johnson learned a great deal about the environmental diversity of western America. Marching with the Eleventh Ohio Volunteers along the route that thousands of adventurers before him had followed to Oregon, California, and the various mining camps, he was impressed with the immense distances, with the stark nakedness of the setting, with the natural wonders that so often were ignored by the routine migrant, and, most important of all, with the potential that at least some of the region offered for future development. He also had a brief opportunity to participate in military maneuvers on the Kansas–Missouri border at a time when Missouri "border ruffians" and New England abolitionists were engaged in a microcosmic version of the impending Civil War. By the time he reached Fort Laramie in the late summer of 1863, the young cavalryman from Ohio surely viewed himself as a seasoned "westerner."

Camp Dennison [Ohio][1]
July 18th/63

Sister Sibil[2]

I have at last found an opportunity to write a letter home. The reason I have not written sooner is because we were expecting to start west almost every day, and I did not want to write till we were about ready. I am pretty well now the most of the boys are the same, there is but one of our company in the hospital. he got his ankle dislocated by being thrown from his horse while on a scouting expedition. I went to see Uncle John Lynches the day I left Hillsboro. Dick Johnson was with me. we got leave of the captain and changed cars at Loveland and went to Henia [Ohio], went to Jamestown on the Bus[3] and rode out on a wagon to Uncles. we found all well but Jane She was down with something like the dyptheria, but getting better Matilda and Aunt had both been down with the same thing but were well. we staid second day night and went back to Henia next day took the seven o'clock train and arrived in camp some time after dark. I found where our company was quartered and crawled into the bunk with Albert and Sam Engle[4] but I did not sleep much the boards were too hard I thought morning would never come the night was twenty four hours long and a heap of time in an hour, but I am getting accustomed to camp life now and can stand it pretty well.

We were expecting to leave this place last thursday, it having been set to start on some time before. but last first day just after we had eaten

---

[1] Camp Dennison was near Miamisville, Hamilton County, Ohio. Francis B. Heitman, *Historical Register and Dictionary of the United States Army*, vol. 2, p. 495.

[2] Hervey spells his sister's name variously as Sibil, Sibyl, or Sybil.

[3] This was a military ambulance outfitted for troop transportation.

[4] Private Samuel Engle, a brother of Hervey Johnson's future wife Elizabeth, enlisted in Company G, Eleventh OVC, on June 27, 1863, at Hillsboro, Ohio. Following confinement for pneumonia in the Fort Kearny and Fort Laramie hospitals from October 1863 until April 1864, he served on detached service as a teamster at such points on the Overland Trail as Platte Bridge, Sweetwater Station, and South Pass. He also served with the stable police at Fort Laramie prior to his honorable discharge in July 1866. Private Samuel Engle, CMF. Efforts to obtain the official records of Albert Johnson were unsuccessful. Military Service Records Division, NA, to the editor, February 24, 1973. See postscript to letter of December 1, 1863, in which Albert's family is identified.

Bird's-eye lithograph of Camp Dennison, Ohio, where in 1863 Hervey Johnson was mustered as a private in the Eleventh Regiment of Ohio Volunteer Cavalry. *Courtesy of the Ohio Historical Society.*

our dinner and while we were signing our names to the pay roll, an Officer rode up with a dispatch for the captain.[5] I heard him order the cooks to prepare three days rations, the boys smell a mice when they heard that. they thought there was something up but no person could tell what. In a short time we were ordered to get our horses ready for a march. the boys were astonished we had no saddles bridles arms or anything else any how every fellow got his horse and very soon some fifteen or twenty cases of saddles and the accouterments were unloaded before our quarters we rigged up in short style and started off about six in the after noon we knew not where to but in a southern direction we marched six or seven miles and halted in a town called madison [Ohio] for water we started in a few minutes again, and about two in the night found ourselves in cincinnati. we put our horses up at the government stables and went to the soldiers home. I threw myself on a bench and with my hat for a pillow I went to sleep waked up in the morning and had a good breakfast saddled up our horses and started on the march. we went out about seven miles below the city to a place I called the seven mile house which was to be our headquarters. this is on the cincinnati and harrison pike. we fed our horses and ate a bite ourselves and then the captain detailed about twenty five men to go on a scouting expedition for the purpose of ascertaining the whereabouts of morgan[6] I was among them.

---

[5] Captain Levi M. Rinehart, commander of Company G, Eleventh OVC, enlisted at Columbus, Ohio, on May 23, 1863. He was placed under arrest by order of General Robert B. Mitchell in September 1864, and while awaiting trial under a general court-martial at Fort Laramie, was permitted to "lead a party against Indians at Laprelle Creek," where on February 13, 1865, he was "killed by Indians." Such, at least, was the official account of Rinehart's untimely death. However, according to Corporal Hervey Johnson's private correspondence — and contrary to Agnes W. Spring's friendly version of the affair — Rinehart's performance as a company commander was anything but responsible, and his death came under questionable circumstances. See Captain Levi M. Rinehart's CMF; Record of Current Events in the Military History of 'G' Co., Eleventh OVC for the Eight Months Ending October 1, 1865, Consolidated Morning Reports, Letters, and Endorsements, 11th OVC, Records of the Adjutant General's Office, 1780's–1917, RG 94, NA; Agnes W. Spring, *Caspar Collins, The Life and Exploits of an Indian Fighter of the Sixties*, pp. 71–72; and Hervey Johnson to his sister Sibil, October 23, 1864, and February 19, 1865. "It will suffice to say," wrote Johnson, "that when a Captain gets to paying attention to emigrants and *squaws* to the neglect of his duty to his men, it is time that the men should take matters in hand."

[6] General John Hunt Morgan, a leader of the abortive Confederate "Ohio Raid" in the summer of 1863, was a native of Huntsville, Alabama, veteran of the Mexican

We started of inquiring of every one we met if morgan was close about. we went on towards harrison [Ohio] and presently met two men coming in a buggy they said that morgan was at Harrison stealing all the horses in the country and that he had tried to catch them

we spurred our horses forward and soon arrived in miamitown on the big miami [River] we had three men sent on ahead to reconnoitre we followed on across the river for about a mile the captain sent me on ahead, I rode on about a hundred yards, and the command stopped I soon saw a man riding towards me in a gallop he stopped and told me that morgans men were camped back the road some distance I called the captain up and told him and while we were talking about what would be best to do two of the boys who had been sent on ahead came running back at full speed and said that they run right on to the rebels before they knew it they said they had captured tom king[7] he was one of the three who went in the advance. on hearing this the captain drew us up in line across the pike for action we waited a little and presently heard the sound of horses hoofs coming towards us on the pike and voices calling to some one to halt, we thought from the dust they kicked up that there were two many of them for us, so we fell back to the bridge where we had left a dozen or more men. Finding that they were not disposed to follow us we went back and instead of following the pike round the hill we went straight up to the top through a defile, from the top we could see the rebs showing themselves in the pike just where it made from behind the hill we exchanged a few shots with them when they began to retire behind the hill. we then went back to the bridge crossed the river alighted and hitched our horses and prepared to defend the bridge if they should attempt to cross on it. but they did not follow us. They showed

War, and subsequent resident of Lexington, Kentucky. Morgan led an army of 2,500 mounted infantry through southern Indiana, through the present suburbs of Cincinnati, and headed east on the north side of the Ohio River. He was finally captured near Blennerhassett Island, imprisoned, escaped in November 1863, and was killed near Greenville, Tennessee, in September 1864. See Basil W. Duke, *A History of Morgan's Cavalry*, pp. 18–19, 407–62; James G. Randall and David Donald, *The Civil War and Reconstruction*, p. 412.

[7] A native of Fremont, Ohio, Sergeant Thomas E. King was mustered in the Eleventh OVC on July 20, 1863. Following detached service with Company G at Platte Bridge, Sweetwater Station, South Pass, and Fort Laramie, he was mustered out on July 10, 1866. Sergeant Thomas E. King, CMF.

Hervey Johnson's first military assignment was to join a scouting expedition
pursuing General John Hunt Morgan, leader of the abortive Confederate "Ohio Raid"
in the summer of 1863. *From John S. C. Abbott's "Heroic Deeds of Heroic Men,"*
Harper's New Monthly Magazine, *vol. 31, no. 183 (August 1865), p. 289.*

themselves however about a hundred of them drawn up in line along the pike about three hundred yards distant from us. but came no nearer   they evidently supposed we had a large force and that we were trying to draw them in to ambush   Our captain concluded that we had no business with so many men and we began to retire slowly along the road towards quarters we got back within a mile of there   we were scattered about on different roads on picket duty. that was the hardest thing I had to do for after two thirds of the night before I had to sit on my saddle all night again. However we met no enemy that night. But I must confess that it made me feel curious to stand in the middle of the road in a dark night and halt any person who may be coming towards me. once in the night I heard the sound of horses approaching me. there were near forty, I stood still awaiting with feelings that may be better imagined than described their near approach when within hailing distance I halted them, they stopped and I found them to be some of our own men but belonging to another company   Several persons were stopped and turned back during the night   also several wagons going to the city to market were turned back

well the night wore away at last, and after eating a piece of bread and butter all I had had since the morning befor and all I got till that day at noon and feeding my mare some corn we started about sunrise on another expedition   we (privates) knew not where. we had gone perhaps eight miles when a citizen who had gone on with the advance guard came back at full speed   he told us that morgans men were just a little way ahead   that the advance had captured one of them. we were all electrified by this piece of news and flew forward at our utmost speed   every man tried to get before, as we were passing near a farm house I heard the report of a pistol from the bushes in a fence corner, some one had shot at Dave Cook[8] but missed him. We rode on to Beever's Tavern twelve miles from Cincinnati on the Colerein pike   we found that the main army had about twelve miles the start of us, so we set ourselves to catching straglers of which the country was full they having scattered on our approach. men were immediately sent to all the houses and barns in the neighborhood to search them   we caught one

---

[8] A native of Hillsboro, Ohio, Private David Cook was mustered in the Eleventh OVC on July 20, 1863. Following detached service with Company G as cook, teamster, and stable policeman, he was discharged November 25, 1865, on a surgeon's certificate of disability. Private David Cook, CMF.

lieutenant and some ten or a dozen privates   one of our boys took two himself. he ran towards them and when they prepared to fire at him he halted till they discharged their pieces then ran at them with his revolver ready and told them to give up their arms or he would shoot them which they did. we remained about there a short time when the advance of Gen'l Hobson's[9] forces came up, he had about thirteen regiments all mounted besides several peices of artilery. He had been pursuing Morgan for fifteen days but had not been able to overtake him on account of Morgan having fresh horses all the time that he had taken from the people through where he had passed.

Well after Hobsons forces had passed we returned towards quarters and while going along the pike as it wound through a defile among the hills on the east side of the river we were told by some citizens that there were fifty rebels back over the hill. we turned about formed in line sent out feelers and soon found it was a false alarm. we got on to headquarters and were there informed that morgan had gone back to harrison which we soon found was another false alarm caused by the return through harrison of some Indian soldiers that hobson had sent home.

we had a good supper of bread beef butter and coffee   after the tables were cleared I laid down on a bench in the dining room with my hat for a pillow and my arms by my side but did not sleep much on account of the guards coming off and going on duty   well early in the morning a scout came in and told us that the pickets were firing   we were up saddled our horses put on our equipments in short order. a Sergeant and twelve men went to see what was the matter and found it a false report. well we rested easy that day. we went about among the farmers got our breakfasts and horses fed. went some where else got our dinners, some where else, staid all night and got breakfast. then started on the march for carthage [Ohio]. the citizens brought us plenty of provisions. we scouted round the most of the day and at night started for Camp Dennison   got there about three in the morning. found Tom King the boy whom Morgan capptured at home

[9] Brigadier General Edward Henry Hobson, a veteran of the Mexican War, became colonel of the Thirteenth Kentucky Regiment on January 1, 1862, was promoted to the position of brigadier general of volunteers on November 29, 1862, and, ironically, was captured by Morgan at Cynthiana, Kentucky, in the late spring of 1864. He was mustered out of the Union Army on August 24, 1865. Heitman, *Historical Register*, vol. 1, p. 533; Duke, *A History of Morgan's Cavalry*, p. 526.

paroled. we were mustered in today get our pay tomorrow dont know
when we start west I may come home if I can get off.

Hervey

St. Louis [Missouri]
August 5th 1863

Sister Sibil

It may cause a little surprise to recieve a letter from this place, But here
I am and have been since evening before last. We left Camp Dennison last
seventh day morning. We were so busy packing up that I had not time to
write before we started. We got to the city about three in the evening, (we
went horseback,) and loaded our horses on the cars and started about nine
at night We arrived at Vincennes [Indiana] on first day at twelve, we unloaded, watered, and fed and loaded again our horses and were soon across
the Wabash. traveled all night again and arrived at the mississippi about
twelve on second day. we staid about the ferry till nearly night and then
started for Benton Barracks[10] where we arrived about eight at night this is
a very large camp there are several thousand soldiers here most of them
paroled prisoners. this is a very pretty camp a great deal nicer than Camp
Dennison with the exception of the hospitals. I have been round among
them some since I came here and they look quite cheerless compared with
those of Camp Dennison the health of the company is good, not a man in
the hospital.

The most of the company take the boat this evening for fort Leavenworth I expect to start tomorrow with some others that were left. I got out

---

[10] "Camp of Instruction, Benton Barracks," was built just west of the St. Louis
fairgrounds in the summer of 1861 under order of General John C. Frémont. By
April 1862, over 23,000 troops were quartered there. Floyd Calvin Shoemaker, *Missouri and Missourians*, vol. 1, p. 901. Contrary to Corporal Johnson's rather idyllic
description, Anthony Trollope, on the basis of a visit to Benton Barracks during the
winter of 1862, stated, "Never in my life before had I been in a place so horrid to the
eyes and nose. . . . The whole space between the two rows of sheds was a field of
mud. . . . The soldiers were mud stained from head to foot. These volunteer soldiers
are in their nature dirty, as must be all men brought together in numerous bodies without special appliances for cleanliness, or control and discipline as to their personal
habits." Anthony Trollope, *North America*, vol. 2, p. 109.

my horse to start this evening but there was enough for a boat load without me I got acquainted yesterday with a soldier from oskaloosa [Iowa] he has two brothers living there with whom I was acquainted his name is Tom Freddick.[11] Semira knows his brother. he lived at Uncle Bens. Tom was at Oskaloosa[12] last Spring. he says that uncle Ben was much in want of money, but that there was a good deal coming to him from the government. I think I must write to Uncle Ben this evening if I have time. I am writing in the grove in Camp Benton with a board leaned against a tree for a desk and the ground for a seat so I must be excused for bad writing. I have to be here because I am one of the stable guards and must be in hearing of the corporal when he wants me to go on guard. Sam Engle went on the boat this evening Al Johnson[13] and Dick have gone down in town I might have gone if I had kept out of the way of the sergeant when he detailed the guards. us soldiers see, and do, and bear, agreat many things that I might tell you if I had time. for want of time and paper I must close.

Hervey

Steamer Sioux City
Aug 13th/63

Dear Sister

I have again taken my pen for the purpose of writing to thee. We left St Louis last seventh day, about four in the afternoon. there are only about forty of our company along the rest went sometime ago. We passed Lexing-

---

[11] Efforts to locate the official military and/or pension files of Thomas Freddick were unsuccessful. Military Service Records Division, NA, to the editor, February 24, 1973.

[12] Oskaloosa College, Oskaloosa, Iowa. Founded in 1855 by Reverend Aaron Chatterton and incorporated in 1858, classes were not organized in this Church of Christ (Christian) school until 1861. The Iowa Yearly Meeting (Friends) maintained a Boarding School at the Spring Creek Meetinghouse located about two-and-one-half miles northeast of Oskaloosa. The school, which burned in 1863 and subsequently became the nucleus of William Penn College, may have been the institution Freddick attended. William Heiss to the editor, July 3, 1972, and Leonard F. Parker, "Higher Education in Iowa," in Herbert B. Adams, ed., *Contributions to American Educational History, No. 17*, p. 136.

[13] See letter of July 18, 1863, n. 4.

ton [Missouri] yesterday evening the place where Col. Muligan[14] surrendered to Price.[15] There are a great many ruins of Buildings there, almost all the towns along the river show that the torch has been there. Large brick factories, warehouses and machine shops have all shared alike   we passed some places that had been burned only a few days previous. We passed Kansas City this morning stopped and unloaded arms and ammunition for the eleventh Kansas, about a mile further up lays Wyandot City [Kansas].[16] We have been five days now on the Missouri River, and we expect to land at ft Leavenworth this afternoon whence we will start across the plains after resting a week or two.

I like this manner of travelling very well but I would prefer the spring or fall season for river travelling   We get no water to drink but river water and that is very unhealthy to those who are not accustomed to it. The use of it has given a great many of the boys the diarrhea and my self among them though I have not be unable for duty yet. I reported on the sick roll this morning in order to get some medicine. The doctor gave me some pills but I dont know yet how they will act

The river is very low now, so low that we ran aground several times on our trip, once we were about two hours getting off a sand bar which was done by prizing the boats up   I cannot describe the manner in [which] it was done so that you could understand it. Two or three days ago we en-

---

[14] Colonel James Adelbert Mulligan, a native of New York, was promoted to Brevet Brigadier General of Volunteers for gallant service at the Battle of Winchester, Virginia, in 1864, died July 23, 1864, from wounds sustained at Winchester. At the Battle of Lexington his force numbered 3,000 as opposed to Price's 15,000. Heitman, *Historical Register*, vol. 1, p. 735; Edwin C. McReynolds, *Missouri: A History of the Crossroads State*, p. 230.

[15] General Sterling Price was the Confederate victor and hero of Wilson's Creek, Missouri, August 10, 1861. See Robert E. Shalhope, *Sterling Price: Portrait of a Southerner*, pp. 174–78.

[16] Wyandot (or Wyandotte) was located on the north side of the Kansas River just below its confluence with the Missouri River. Named after Wyandot Indians, who were removed from the Sandusky region of Ohio in 1843, the townsite was part of the Wyandot reservation and was surveyed in 1857 shortly after an assignment of land had been made to three white and three Wyandot promoters. The town had over 1,400 residents by January 1859 and eventually was recognized as the urban nucleus from which present Kansas City, Kansas, developed. *Wyandotte County and Kansas City, Kansas*, pp. 388–89; A. T. Andreas, *History of the State of Kansas*, pp. 1226–27, 1230–31.

countered a storm just at night   the wind blew terrifically and the rain fell in torrents. we ran in and tied to a tree on the south shore, and laid there till morning   the morning was fair and everything except the corn, (which was pretty flat) looked as if there had been no storm, the timber was so scrubby that storms would have very little effect on it   we are just now passing Sparksburg on the missouri shore

We soldiers fare pretty hard on the boat. we are not allowed to go in the cabin with out special permission from the Officers. The rooms where we principly stay is on the hurricane deck, with clouds and sky for our only shelter   it is the nicest place to ride if the sun did not shine so hot. I think we must mak quite a mixed up appearance to the inhabitants along the river, think of two hundred men with saddles, blankets, guns, sabres, pistols and every thing else pertaining to soldiers equipments all in mixed confusion on the upper deck of a boat and one may have some idea of how we look.

Our guns were loaded yesterday in anticipation of an attack from the guerrillas who infest western missouri. We also had two mountain howitzers brought out on the boiler deck and loaded with canister shot,[17] yet not a rebel did we see though there may have been a thousand looking at us.

The scenery of the Missouri river is very beautiful. The high shelving rocks, and jutting crags and cavernous sides contrast strangely with the broad woody bottoms with prairie here and there extending as far as the eye can reach. We have met very few boats going down the river. we passed the Sam Gatz yesterday and the Wyandot river packet this morning. Two or three mornings ago we passed a boat fast on a sand bar. I am writing in the cabin and the passengers are just eating their dinner   it makes me feel like I would [want] to be at [home] and get one more good meal. I have not eaten any thing scarcely since yesterday morning when I spent my last cent for a pie. I would give half a dollar now if I had it for such a dinner as

---

[17] These howitzers were bronze twelve pounders patterned after cannons used by the French in the mountains of Algiers and northern Spain. They were first cast for the War Department at the cannon foundry of Cyrus Alger & Company in South Boston, Massachusetts, after October 1836. Because Lieutenant John C. Frémont took one of these weapons on his well-publicized exploring expedition of 1843–1844, they are sometimes referred to as "Frémont mountain howitzers." They could fire either cannister or round shells, and because the barrel, ammunitions chests, and carriage could be easily disassembled for packing on horses, they were especially popular in the mountain West. See Carl P. Russell, *Guns on the Early Frontier*, pp. 269–78.

I see on the table here. they have every thing that a farmer has without it is milk there are potatoes green corn apples carrots cabbages beets onions tomatoes cornbread fresh beef and other things too numerous to mention. I must content myself with Uncle Sam's fare for awhile yet I hope that we will soon be able to have fresh meat of our own killing [letter ends.]

[Hervey]

Fort Leavenworth Kansas
Aug 18th/63

Dear Sister Sibil

I was just preparing to write thee a letter this morning, when one of my comerades told me he had a letter for me. I thought I would wait then till I had read it before I wrote. I was very glad to hear from home again. this is the first letter I have recieved since I enlisted. It came up last night on the packet Emile. There is great stir and confusion in the camp this morning caused by preparations to go after some guerrillas who are prowling in the vicinity, twenty men were detailed from each company to go. I would have gone if I had not intended to write, enough volunteered to go without me anyhow.

We arrived at this place last fifth day about four o'clock. I was sick when we got here had been ever since we embarked at St. Louis, and was for two or three days after we got here. We got our [enlistment] bounty (twenty seven dollars) the next day after our arrival, I soon got well then, for then I could buy something fit for a sick man to eat. We live well here the peddlers bring in vegetables every day such as green corn, cabbage, onions, tomatoes, beans, cucumbers butter, milk, icecream, and other luxuries, fresh tomatoes cured me completely. I would buy them at five cents a dozen and eat a dozen at a time, pretty good sized ones too. There are several of the company sick now, one or two in the hospital, the general complaint is diarrhea.

I recon I must tell something about the country here. Fort Leavenworth[18] lays on a high bluff on the west side of the Missouri River, it com-

---

[18] Fort Leavenworth was established May 18, 1827, by Colonel Henry Leavenworth, Third U.S. Infantry, after whom the post was named. Its location was (and

36

mands the river for some miles both above and below, but why it is called a fort is something curious to me, it is a kind of soldiers town with no walls or guns mounted. the only sign of a fort that I have seen is an old ridge of dirt and a row or two of posts set close together The Government buildings here are mostly of brick, the Barracks for soldiers are very comfortable, they are all two story brick. We are living at present in the open air, we have tents but the most of the boys would rather sleep on their blankets outside. I have got so that I can sleep any where or any how. The weather has been very fine since we came here almost hot enough to melt a person, this is why the boys prefer to sleep out doors. Our Captain got badly hurt last night, he went down to Leavenworth City[19] about two miles below here and some how or other his horse got drunk and coming through a bridge on his way back the bridge broke or something happened that the captain got off his horse and had to be carried to his tent. I dont think his horse will get drunk again soon as he dont allow any body to ride him out but himself. Sam Engle is sitting by me writing to some one at home.

I dont know when we will leave this place. We were to have left to day but it is three o'clock now and we have not started yet. We may start tomorrow and may not this week but before this reaches its destination we will have set out on our seven hundred miles horsebackride It seems hard to look ahead and think of it, and we will no doubt endure many privations and hardships, but I hope we will get through it all. I have a nice little bey mare that I think will carry me through, I call her fanny She is as spunky and as big a fool as old bet was, but, I think I can manage her. I have not heard yet whether there was any draft in Ohio or not I would like to hear

---

is) on the right bank of the Missouri River roughly twenty-three miles above the mouth of the Kansas River. During the 1860's it was a major supply depot for nearly all military posts in the Rocky Mountain region. Robert W. Frazer, *Forts of the West*, p. 56.

[19] Located just south of Fort Leavenworth, and presently the county seat of Leavenworth County, Kansas, the town site was staked by General George W. Gist, John C. Gist, and Samuel Farnandis in June 1854. An "official plat" was filed in the Surveyor General's Office at Fort Leavenworth on December 24, 1854, and by the early 1860's Leavenworth was the largest and most sophisticated city in the new state of Kansas. Prior to the land cession treaty of May 6, 1854, the site of future Leavenworth was part of the Delaware Reservation. Jess A. Hall and Leroy T. Hand, *History of Leavenworth County, Kansas*, pp. 116–17.

if there was and who of my acquaintance drew [military draft] tickets. It seems to me that there are no young men about there almost all the boys I know are either here or in the twenty fourth Battery. It must be very lonesome to those who are at home I think. Sam will not stay at home when he gets home from Earlham[20] I know it will be so lonesome to him. You folks at home have no idea what we soldiers have to endure, but it is not soldierly to complain so we say nothing and console ourselves with the thoughts that it would have been worse had we been drafted and sent south especially at this time of year. Two Kansas boys have enlisted in our company here They are both in the same tent with me their names are George Sebastian[21] and Hervey Merwin.[22] Hervey has been in the western country eight years he says we will have nothing to do out there in the mountains he dont know what they want so many men out there for. he has been out there and I suppose he knows the natives. I hope what he says will be true.

I want you to take care of my clothes put them where the moths wont get at them my overcoat that hangs up stairs I would lik to have kept if it can be without too much trouble if not then let warren wear it. The Bugle has just sounded and I must close

Hervey Johnson.

Hervey Johnson
Ft. Leavenworth Kansas
Care Cap't Rinehart
Company G. 11th O.V.C.
To follow the Reg't.

Our letter is changed from B to G.

Hervey

---

[20] Earlham College, a Friends' institution of higher learning, was established at Richmond, Indiana, in 1847.

[21] Private George Sebastian, a native of Green County, Missouri, was mustered in the Eleventh OVC on August 14, 1863, at Leavenworth, Kansas. Following detached service as a woodcutter and quartermaster escort at Three Crossings, Platte Bridge, and Sweetwater Station, he was honorably discharged at Fort Leavenworth on July 14, 1866. Private George Sebastian, CMF.

[22] Sergeant Hervey D. Merwin, a native of Morton County, Ohio, was mustered in the Eleventh OVC on August 12, 1863, at Leavenworth, Kansas. Following detached service as Acting Provost Sergeant at Platte Bridge and Fort Laramie, he was honorably discharged at Fort Leavenworth on July 14, 1866. Sergeant Hervey D. Merwin, CMF.

Camp Collins, Kansas
Aug 29th/63

Folks at home.

I thought when I wrote my last letter, that the next time I wrote, we would be on our march across the plains. B[ut] things have turned out different. We were to have started the next day after I wrote. We got everything ready our tents struck, horses saddled, wagons loaded, when there came an order for fifty men from each company armed and mounted. None of us privates knew it though. We were all ready to start, and orders were given to forward. We started, but not toward the west. We went out south through Leavenworth City. When we got there we thought we were going across the river into Missouri but we kept on south, we soon discovered that we were on a forced march, we knew not whither.

I never saw such a time before the roads were dusty, and we run our horses so that we could not see three feet before us; we marched on in this way till ten at night, when we came to the kansas river. We were near three hours crossing the river and while the forward companies were crossing, the others were down in the dirt asleep. I got off and tied the halter strap round my wrist, and laid down in the road and slept till it came our turn to cross we got on the ferry boat and went over. we stopped and got something to eat, and fed our horses at De Soto,[23] a small town on the southern bank of the kansas. The Officers told us that we would not go on till morning; so we unstrapped our blankets and laid down to sleep, we had nomore than got to sleep when we were ordered to saddle up and hold ourselves ready to march at a moments notice; we started about three in the morning, riding like maniacs, several horses stumbled and threw thier riders and dragged them in the dust but no one was hurt much

At De Soto we learned why we were called out The citizens told us that a rebel leader by the name of Quantrel,[24] with five hundred men was

---

[23] DeSoto is located in present northwestern Johnson County, Kansas.

[24] William Clarke Quantrill (alias "Charley Hart") made a daring raid on Lawrence, Kansas, the early morning of August 21, 1863, that resulted in the brutal slaying of about 150 people. Ostensibly the raid was a reaction to depredations committed in western Missouri by the abolitionists, but it is by no means certain that plunder was not a major priority in this tragedy. See Albert Castel, *William Clarke Quantrill: His Life and Times*, pp. 122–43.

committing depradations in Kansas, that he had sacked and burned the town of Lawrence[25] and butchered three hundred of its citizens. That Jim Lane[26] had him cornered and they were preparing for a fight. We soon found this news to be too true. Men women and children were murdered without discrimination; he seemed particularly spiteful against the black inhabitants, they were hunted and shot like dogs. The town was fired and the citizens were not even allowed to escape out of thier dwellings, so that many of those who escaped the slaughter met a more fearful and cruel death by being burned with their own homes. This massacre is without a parallel since the war began, the inhabitants say it was scarcely equaled by the indian massacres in the early settlement of the western country. And it was the perpetrator of this highhanded deed that we were in pursuit of, but not likely to overtake, for instead of Jim Lane having him cornered, he could not get near enough to corner him, in fact Jim came very near being cornered himself for when Quantrel came to town he went right to Lanes house intending to take him but he got out at the back door just as Quantrel came in at the front. The whole thing was done in the night. He left the Missouri border, marched to Lawrence, plundered, butchered and burned, and just as day was dawning he started back, in the mean time Jim Lane, who had fled to a cornfield with nothing on but his night clothes, had gathered together about one hundred and fifty men and started in pursuit. Two hundred men were sent from Kansas City. Two hundred from some other place and our two hundred and fifty made in all about eight hundred men after him on different roads. Our Battalion did not get in sight of him at all some of the others did; several of Quantrel's pickets were killed; none of ours that we heard of were injured. He did not come into the state to

---

[25] One of the most important free-state towns in Territorial Kansas, Lawrence was officially chartered in 1858 following the selection of the townsite in northern Douglas County by Charles Robinson and Charles Branscomb. The town was named after Amos Lawrence, one of the principal organizers of the Massachusetts Emigrant Aid Society (later reorganized as the New England Emigrant Aid Company). William F. Zornow, *Kansas: A History of the Jayhawk State*, pp. 67–68.

[26] James Henry Lane was the flamboyant leader of the "Lane Faction" Republicans in Kansas and served as senator from Kansas from April 4, 1861, until his death by suicide on July 11, 1866. For a perceptive sketch of this "utterly unscrupulous" politico, see Albert Castel, *A Frontier State at War: Kansas, 1861–1865*, pp. 19–21.

fight and they could get no fight out of him. I must give the particulars of the remainder of the march

After leaving De Soto we reached a small town[27] about sunrise where we stopped and got something to eat and fed again. We soon started again on a fast run and ran for several miles, every moment expecting to come on the enemy. This was on seventh day and there being no breeze on the prairie the heat was most oppressive. We reached a small river a branch of the Osage about noon, and stopped to water. Here the first Lieutanant of company E. was killed by sun stroke;[28] his body was sent back to Ft Leavenworth to be interred. We then marched on, and soon struck the trail where Quantrel had passed along. We followed it for two or three miles. I never saw as hot a day in my life Men and horses were completely wearied out We came to a small stream with thinly wooded banks about three in the afternoon. Here our Lieutenant told us to halt and rest for half an hour, though it was directly contrary to the General's orders, which were, to follow on the trail as fast as possible, at this place several more of the men were sunstruck though none fatally, several horses fell down apparently unable to move further The men appeared to care for nothing, some tied their horses, some let them loose, and all nearly, laid down in the dirt and went to sleep. half an hour passed but no order came to move, and nobody moved. we finally concluded to stay all night. The Officer[29] told us to take care of ourselves and horses We had nothing to eat ourselves nor to give our horses.

---

[27] The town was Lanesfield (or Uniontown) in southwestern Johnson County. Report of Brigadier General Thomas Ewing, Jr., U.S. Army, Commanding District of the Border, August 31, 1863, *The War of the Rebellion: A Compilation of the Official Records of the Union and Confederate Armies*, series I, vol. 32, pt. 1, p. 581. See also O. B. Gunn and D. T. Mitchell, "Gunn and Mitchell's New Map of Kansas and the Gold Mines," Archives Division, Kansas State Historical Society, Topeka.

[28] This was Lieutenant David S. Dick. Report of Ewing, *War of Rebellion*, p. 583.

[29] Second Lieutenant Caspar W. Collins was the son of Colonel William O. Collins (see letter of October 18, 1863, n. 3). Lieutenant Collins was mustered in the Eleventh OVC at Columbus, Ohio, on July 20, 1863, two months before his nineteenth birthday. His death at the Battle of Platte Bridge on July 26, 1865, precipitated a great deal of controversy between the administrative leadership of the Eleventh OVC and Eleventh Kansas Volunteer Cavalry. See Second Lieutenant Caspar W. Collins, Company G, Eleventh OVC, CMF; J. W. Vaughn, *The Battle of Platte*

Some of the boys went to the fields and got corn. I had half a dozen ears in my feed bag, that I bought at the Fort before we left, I coked them on some coals and eat them. I then thought of my mare, I saddled up and took another boy with me, and went to a farm horse about a mile off, and asked for our supper and horses fed; they said they reconed we could have it if we would wait till they cooked something, we told them we wer soldiers and often eat cold victuals they said they had nothing cold, they appeared to go about cooking rather reluctantly, we waited however and in half an hour we were invited to supper which consisted of warm cornbread, butter, coffee, sliced onions, fat bacon, buttermilk, &c. I then asked the woman what I must pay for our horse feed and supper. She said to speak to the old man about it. He told me to pay the old woman for our supper, and we might have our horse feed for nothing. I paid her twenty five cents for both of us, and went back to our men, they had all laid down to sleep we unstrapped our blankets, and laid down and had slept an hour or two, when we were ordered to saddle up, and move back about a mile to a hill near a farm house, and picket our horses out on the prairie to graze. When we got up there I tied my mare to the fence, threw my saddle over into the yard, and laid down and went to sleep on it. My mare made so much noise pawing the fence, that I did not sleep much till I got up and pulled an arm full of grass for her.

Morning came at last and we found ourselves in the vicinity of St. Marysvill,[30] a town of twenty or thirty houses. I bridled my mare and rode over to town to get something to eat. I called at a private house. The people seemed very hospitable, they were very willing to cook for the soldiers, of whom there were several there besides myself. as I went back to where the

Bridge, chaps. 9, 10; Spring, *Caspar Collins*; "THE DEATH OF LIEUT. CASPAR W. COLLINS, 11TH O.V.C. CAUSED BY THE COWARDICE OR INCOMPETENCY OF THE COMMANDING OFFICER AT THE BATTLE OF PLATTE BRIDGE — THE TRUE HISTORY OF THE MATTER — OFFICIAL INQUIRY DEMANDED BY COL. COLLINS," *Highland Weekly News*, Hillsboro, Ohio, January 25, 1866; Jake Pennock, "Diary," *Annals of Wyoming*, vol. 23 (July 1951), pp. 18–21; and Alfred James Mokler, *Fort Caspar (Platte Bridge Station)*.

[30] St. Marysville, in northern Miami County, was just north of present Hillsdale. This town was founded by H. L. Lyons and James Beets in 1856 and later was re-named Lyons. Dead Town Lists, vols. Lu-Ma and Sab-Sar, Manuscript Division, Kansas State Historical Society, Topeka.

horses were, I met the men coming towards town. they stopped near a spring and picketed the horses. We remained there during the day putting up tents to keep the sun off us, by sticking our guns and sabres in the ground and spreading our blankets over them. Just at night we were ordered to move again, we started off in a north eastern direction. We did not think we were going after the rebels again, for we were told at that town that Quantrel had got back to Missouri and disbanded his men. Any how we went on and about ten in the [evening] we encountered a storm. I think it exceeded any storm I was ever out in before. the wind blew a perfect hurricane, the thunder and lightning was terrific, and the rain and hail fell in torrents. About one o'clock we reached Olatha the county seat of Johnson County. We stoped there. Tom Cooper[31] and I left the company as soon as we stopped and went to hunt a place to dry ourselves and warm, for it seemed almost like winter after the storm, we found the house of a printer, he welcomed us in and made a fire for us and after we were warm and dry we laid down Tom on the lounge, and I on the carpet, in the morning we went some place else to get our breakfast for the printer's wife was not at home; we got a very good breakfast, and felt much refreshed; we found a wagonload of corn in a yard and every man went for it and fed his horse. Tis getting dark and I must quit for the night.

[Hervey]

Camp Collins, Kansas
Sept 1st/'63

Sister Sibyl,

I recieved thy letter this morning, which was mailed on the twentyeighth, and has been about five days on the road. Thee talked of receiving my letter, but said nothing about which one. I have written seven or eight letters, and have recieved but two, and to which of mine they were answers, I am unable

---

[31] Private Thomas W. Cooper, a native of Highland County, Ohio, and close friend of Hervey Johnson, was mustered in the Eleventh OVC on July 14, 1863. Following detached service at Horse Shoe Station, Mud Springs, and Three Crossings, he was honorably discharged at Fort Leavenworth on July 14, 1866. Private Thomas W. Cooper, CMF.

to tell. When thee writes of recieving my letters, pleas name the date of such letters. I was very glad to hear from home and to hear that you were all well. I am in good health and have been for some time, there are but three or four sick boys in the company. I began to [write] a letter three or four days ago, describing a scouting expedition that we had. I filled two sheets with it, and will finish in this letter.

I believe we were at Olatha when I left off. We went from there to Kansas City arrived there in the afternoon, camped in the woods below the city for the night. next morning Tom Cooper and I took our guns and went to the woods to look after game, saw two squirrels shot at them about a dozen times with no effect, got tired of hunting and went back to camp got there about two o'clock, found several of the horses saddled ready to go somewhere. The boys told me that they had an inspection of horses, and those which were disabled were to be sent back to the fort I saw my mare amonge the discarded ones so I saddled her at once, we were soon off from camp and took the boat for the fort, arrived there after night found nobody there, didn't know what to do, Lieutenant told us to tie to the fence and be ready to start by five in the morning. another Lieutenant told us to go on, that our men and teams were camped about eight miles out on the prairie. some of the boys went with one some staid with the other, myself included. we left by eight in the morning, stopped at the groceries along and got something to eat and arrived in camp about one, it being fifteen miles instead of eight it is getting late or I would describe the camp, I will however say that it is near a splendid spring which bursts out on the prairie, it is about eight or nine times as strong as the spring at Grandfathers old place. day before yesterday the rest of the boys who were left at Kansas city came into camp from the Quantrell scout the results of which were, when all summed up, as follows The loss of one of the best men of the Battalion. the loss of several horses a ride of onehundred and forty or fifty miles over Kansas and Missouri the loss of two or three weeks of time that we ought to have been on our road across the plains and gained not one thing. there is great bustle in camp this evening preparing to move tomorrow it is getting so dark that I can scarcely see the mark[?].

Direct thy letters as before   Farewell

Hervey Johnson
Co. G. 11th O.V.C.

44

Camp Near Ft. Kearny
Nebraska [Territory].
Sept 20th/63

Dear Sister,

After two weeks march I have again taken the pen. We arrived here three or four days ago, and have been resting ourselves and horses since our arrival. We have had fine weather for traveling so far, the roads are very dry and hard. Water and wood are pretty scarce. We are camped on the south bank of the Platte river three miles below fort Kearney.[32] You may be surprised at water being scarce so near as large a river as the platte, but such is the fact, the platte is as dry as the big road, and the way we get water is by digging in the bed of the river which is composed of fine sand. At the depth of eighteen inches in the sand, water may be found almost any where in the bed of the river we dig out a hole and set in a box or barrel and the water rises immediately. I don't like this country here much on account of the sand, which has been plenty for the last one or two hundred miles, and getting worse the farther we go west.

We were paid off yesterday, I received thirteen dollars. the captain gave eighteen of us permission to go to the fort to get such articles as we wanted. I went among the rest. we have to pay very high for goods here buck gloves are from two to three dollars. boots eight dollars, and every thing in proportion I am on guard to day at the commissary wagons. my duty is to allow no soldier to get in any of the wagons, or take any thing out of them, we have three reliefs of guards, each relief standing two hours and resting four, I am off duty now, but go on again at one o'clock, We got two recruits yesterday for our company you will be surprised to know who they are. I was surprised when I saw them in this part of the country they are Kiah

---

[32] Fort Kearny, established in 1848 and located on the right side of the Platte about eight miles southeast of present Kearney, Nebraska, was first called "Post at Grand Island" and then "Fort Childs." It was officially designated Fort Kearny on December 30, 1848. Although the commonly accepted version has it that this installation was named after General Stephen Watts Kearny, one theory suggests that it was named after Lieutenant Colonel James Kearney, an army engineer who drew up the plans for the fort. Almost from the start its name was alternatively spelled Kearny and Kearney. See Frazer, *Forts of the West*, p. 87, and Robert G. Athearn, *William Tecumseh Sherman and the Settlement of the West*, p. 20, n.

Sanders[33] and Joseph Denny.[34] They were driving ox teams from Omaha to Denver city.[35] They drove up here day before yesterday not expecting to see so many Ohio boys. they heard that Sam and Al and I were here, and came into camp to see us, they soon concluded to give up bull whacking and go a soldiering. Kiah is well and hearty he says he don't intend to write home till we get to Laramie, so if you see his folks you may tell them where he is.

my health has been good since we left f't Leavenworth. The health of the boys [is] good generally. The next letter that I write to you, may contain sad news to some one, I hope it may be otherwise, but time alone will develope things unknown to us at the present. for the present good of those concerned I will not disclose what might bring suspense upon the inmates of a happy home.[36] farewell. write soon as before

Hervey

---

[33] Sergeant Hezekiah Sanders, a native of Leesburgh, Ohio, enlisted in the Forty-eighth Regiment Ohio Infantry on September 9, 1861. At Moscow, Tennessee, from June 30 to August 25, 1862, he was officially designated a deserter from his original Company A, but three months later, on November 18, 1862, was discharged on a surgeon's certificate for medical disability. He enlisted in the Eleventh OVC at Fort Kearny on September 20, 1863, and, following detached service at Fort Laramie and absence with leave as a government mail carrier, he was honorably discharged at Fort Leavenworth on July 14, 1866. Sergeant Hezekiah Sanders, CMF.

[34] Sergeant Joseph Denney, a native of Highland County, Ohio, enlisted in the Eleventh OVC at Fort Kearny on September 20, 1863, but was not officially mustered in until March 5, 1864. Principally assigned to the stable police at Fort Laramie, he deserted at Fort Halleck on August 12, 1864. He returned to Company D of the Eleventh OVC in late November 1864 and was honorably discharged at Fort Leavenworth on July 14, 1866. Sergeant Joseph Denney, CMF.

[35] Present Denver, Colorado.

[36] See letter of November 15, 1863, for a clarification of this cryptic note.

Fort Laramie

October 12, 1863 — March 8, 1864

Hervey Johnson's initial experiences at Fort Laramie came at a time best designated as the lull before the storm. While the young, homesick recruit spent the bulk of his off-duty time keeping his family in Ohio informed about the monotony of garrison duty, the harsh character of military justice, his desire to be assigned to a more exciting place such as Denver City, and what he considered to be the degraded nature of the Indians, relationships between the various Sioux tribes and the white emigrants were deteriorating at an alarming rate.

The Fort Laramie Treaty of 1851 provided for the disbursement of $10,000 a year for a period of fifty years to those tribes whose leaders had certified this momentous document. Large numbers of Sioux were thus encouraged to camp near Fort Laramie, the principal distribution point for the annuities, especially during the hard winter months when natural forage for their horses and the life-sustaining buffalo were in short supply. Also attracted by the federal largess, private traders, unconcerned with the cultural implications of their economic ethics, soon established themselves in the vicinity and in a short time had conditioned the Indians to purchase on a regular basis the more fashionable paraphernalia of the white man's culture — trinkets, whiskey, guns, powder, and lead. Here also the various bands had a common meeting place where they could discuss the problem of increasing white emigration to their hunting grounds, the consequences of too many "powder-and-lead men" among their ranks, and especially the awesome implications of future attacks — possibly fashioned after General William Harney's vicious campaign against the Brulés at Ash Hollow in 1855.

But the Indians had other good reasons to be disturbed about the future. The discovery of gold on Cherry Creek in 1858 prompted the rush of at least a hundred thousand would-be miners to the western edge of Kansas Territory (after 1861 Colorado Territory). Relocation treaties providing for more concentrated reservations were demanded by the invaders — as, for example, the abortive Fort Wise land cession treaty of 1861 that led the Southern Cheyennes and Arapahoes along the tortuous trail culminating in the Sand Creek Massacre of November 1864. Meanwhile, troop demands of the Civil War caused the evacuation of

49

many regular soldiers stationed on the frontier and the deployment of less experienced and often less patient volunteers.

However, from the widest perspective of deteriorating Indian–white relationships around Fort Laramie in the early 1860's, no one event was more significant than the completion of the transcontinental telegraph. At one o'clock on the afternoon of October 1, 1861, the much-heralded magnetic wire reached Salt Lake City from the east. That evening the first message was transmitted to Cleveland and printed in the Salt Lake City *Deseret News*. It was from Brigham Young to J. H. Wade, president of the Pacific Telegraph Company, and in part read, "Utah has not seceded, but is firm for the Constitution and laws of our once happy country, and is warmly interested in such successful enterprises as the one so far completed." One week later the wire from Sacramento was completed and, amid celebrations in honor of the momentous event, was connected to its eastern counterpart on Main Street of the strategically located Mormon settlement.

From the start the "talking (or singing) wire," as the wondering and increasingly distressed Indians designated this remakable technical achievement, was a success. Wiring to Frank Fuller, Acting Governor of Utah, on October 20, 1861, President Lincoln stated that "the completion of the Telegraph to Great Salt Lake City is auspicious of the stability and union of the Republic." Nine days later Wade announced that "over 200 private messages passed over the line the first day it opened, and that messages continue to come in at both ends as fast as the operators are able to transmit them, thus indicating that it will soon be necessary to put up one or two more wires to meet the urgent wants of the commercial public and the Press." With East and West connected by a vital link of virtually instantaneous communication, and the dream of unfettered access to the wonders of the Orient becoming a clear possibility, the *New York Times* on October 26, 1861, took the occasion to emphasize the poetic grandeur of the moment.

> It is easy for one to overlook the poetic element in this great achievement, so accustomed have we become to the telegraphic marvel. But what genuine grandeur is there in that wondrous line! From the Hudson it stretches across seven great and populous Free

Telegraph Office on Main Street, Salt Lake City, Utah, where the lines
from the East and West were joined on October 24, 1861.
Courtesy of the Western Union Corporation, Mahawah, New Jersey.

States to the Missouri River, a thousand miles — then across the Great Western Plains amid solitude and savages to the Rocky Mountains, as many leagues again—then leaping across the mighty chain of the Cordilleras — thence Westward still to the waters of the Pacific and the City of the Golden Gate — till the extremes of the Continent are united by the magnetic wire, and the dwellers by Hudson hail the settlers of Sacramento.

Less than a year later, on July 1, 1862, Congress passed the Pacific Railroad Bill authorizing massive federal subsidies for the construction of a trunk line through the heart of Sioux country. Two months later came the shocking news that nearly 800 Santee Sioux and white settlers had been killed in the New Ulm Indian war in southern Minnesota. Armageddon seemed at hand.

Finally, additional gold strikes on the Beaverhead branch of the Jefferson (1862), on Alder Creek (1863), and especially at a celebrated place called Last Chance Gulch near the future site of Helena, Montana, in the spring of 1864 dictated that relations between Indians and whites would not improve. By the spring of 1864 the Indians of the north-central Plains were sullen, angry, and freely advocating a plan of armed resistance. While dignitaries on both sides discussed what proved to be unrealistic means of preventing a bloody conflagration, it was up to inexperienced young men such as Private Hervey Johnson to keep the overland route peaceful and the telegraph operational. Under the circumstances it was a Herculean and not very enviable assignment.

Fort Laramie [Idaho Territory]
Oct 12th/63

Dear Sister Sibil.

I have at last seated myself for the purpose of answering thy last letter which I recieved on the first of this month I was glad to hear from home, but it did not do me much good for I was very sick that day, so sick that I could scarcely sit on my horse, indeed I had to get off and lay down on the grass several times. I had, by doing this, got some distance behind the command, perhaps two miles. the battallion halted about ten to graze the horses and just as I rode up to the rear I saw a croud of men around the ambulances I rode up between the ambulances and heard the Captain say: here's one for Hervey, give it to him. I saw that they were distributing letters I got off my horse and laid down on my over coat to read my letter We were on the open plain two hundred miles from either Kearney or Laramie. The letters were brought up by a Lieutenant from Kearney. I got one the same day from Cousin Matilda written on the eighth of last month. Sibils was dated the 6th. Uncle John's folks were well

We arrived here last seventh day after a toilsome and weary march of seventy days including our whole journey from Camp Dennison having left there on the first of August and arrived here the tenth of october. No person can immagine how wearisome it is to travel across these plains till he has experienced it. we have traveled for days together with out seeing a familiar object without it was now and then a solitary pricklypear, which plant is a native of these desert plains. The plains are nearly bare of live grass there having been no rain of any account for sixteen months there was no water in the south platte as far as we followed it, and but little in the north platte, which we followed for near three hundred miles, while I was sick I ate nothing for nearly a week I had the yellow jaundice and had no appetite for any kind of food with out it was fresh fish and these we had plenty some times and some times we didn't. Where there were fish the boys could catch them very easily by wading in and spearing them with their sabres, they would catch some nearly two feet long in this way I tried fishing last sixth day with another boy. I let another boy who had no horse have mine and I concluded to follow up the river in quest of fish I started very early with my sabre looking all along the river for fish but had the luck to

53

find none till in the afternoon we killed six the largest was two feet long the smallest one foot, it was the dearest mess of fish I thought that I ever had for we got so far behind that it was after night when we got into camp I think we wa[l]ked nearly twenty five miles that day, I will be content after this to ride my horse and let fishing alone. the health of the boys is good at present I am as well as common Sam Engle is at fort Karney he was unwell when we left there but getting better That massacre that semira spoke of occurred at Lawrence[1] I thought I gave full particulars of it in one of my letters I must close for the present.

Hervey

Fort Laramie [Idaho Territory]
Oct 18th/'63.

Dear Mother

Thy letter of the sixteenth of last month came to hand last sixth day and was read with pleasure as all letters are from home The reason I did not answer Sibils last letter sooner is because we were on the march, & there is but little chance for writing while marching, but now as we have arrived at our destination I hope it will be so I can write at least once a week if not oftener. We are now quartered in a large two story building on the ground floor; we occupy five rooms, capable of accomodating sixteen to twenty one persons each. The upper story is unoccupied with the exception [of] one room which is occupied by the post tailor. Our quarters are very comfortable. The building is a frame, weatherboarded and plastered and filled in with unburnt brick. There are two fireplaces in the room we (that is mess No 2) now occupy, but it is probable that we will now remove to a room heated by a stove.

I might here say that our company is divided into squads or messes, each squad being in charge of a sergeant. The sergeant of the mess to which I belong is John Maberly.[2] He is the son of an old schoolmate of Mothers her name was Hussey. She used to live where Joseph Wright now lives.

---

[1] This is a reference to Quantrill's raid. See letter of August 29, 1863, n. 24.

[2] Efforts to locate the official military and/or pension files of John Maberly were unsuccessful. Military Service Records Division, NA, to the editor, February 22, 1973.

The most of the houses in this country are built of mud or unburnt bricks, they are called dobeys. We first came in the region of dobeys as we entered the platte valley, there they are built of sods cut square and laid up like bricks The most of the buildings in fort Kearney are built this way, so are most of [the] houses along [the] route between here and there

Kiah Sanders and Joseph Denny are getting transferred into the old battallion There has been several desertions from this batallion since it left S't Louis, one company has lost nearly half by desertion Our company has lost by desertion, one at Dennison, one at cincinnati, one at St Louis two at Leavenworth and two on the march two discharged at Leavenworth making nine in all.

I might here relate a few incidents of our march across the plains. I will first relate w[hat] happened to myself one night while on Camp guard. I was on post No 8 and had recieved my instructions concerning persons coming in and going out of camp. Some teamsters presently came towards me wishing to go out of camp, and as I had instructions to let noperson out, I called for the Corporal of the guard. My post was just in the rear of the Adjutants tent and the Colonel and several officers were round the tent. The Corporal not appearing at the first call I called him again, and again, and the fourth time he came when I began to reprimand him in rather an angry tone for his tardiness. I meant nothing by what I said, but he being a frenchman and on duty his first time, I thought I would tease him a little. Well the officers heard me, and called the corporal to them at once, he soon came back and told me to report to the guard tent under arrest by order of Col. Collins.[3] I laid in the guard tent that night then walked twenty two

---

[3] William Oliver Collins was born in Somers, Connecticut, and graduated from Amherst College in 1833. The untimely death of his young wife and his failing health encouraged him to migrate to Hillsboro, Ohio, where he became a law student of David Starkweather, Aaron Manelno, and Dwight Zaron. Collins was admitted to the bar in 1835, served as prosecuting attorney of Highland County from 1837 to 1840, secretary of the Milford-Chillicothe Turnpike Company, president of the Hillsboro and Cincinnati Railroad Company, and collector of internal revenue for the Sixth Congressional District of Ohio. In 1843 he married Catherine Willis Wever, future mother of Caspar Collins. In 1861, while serving as a member of the state senate representing Ron and Highland counties, his appointment as colonel of volunteer cavalry was authorized by the War Department. His first command was over the First Independent Battalion, Ohio Volunteer Cavalry; subsequently he commanded the Eleventh OVC until he was mustered out in April 1865. See Agnes W. Spring,

Fort Laramie, Idaho Territory, from a painting on linen signed by Charles Frederick
Moellmann, who enlisted in Company G, Eleventh Ohio Volunteer Cavalry,
less than a week after Hervey Johnson joined the company.
Courtesy of the American Heritage Research Center, University of Wyoming.

miles the next day, in the guard house another night then walked to fort Kearney the next day against noon another night in the guard house, and next morning I was released by the officer of the day. I thought it was a very cool way of doing, to put a man under arrest for three nights and two days, without any charges against him or without letting him know what he was under arrest for, and then release him without an order from the commanding officer, but that is the way they did up things on the march and that was the reason there were so many deserters. If I ever felt like deserting twas when I had to walk all that time.

There are numbers of boys in this battallion who would gladly be out of it, if they could get out honorably, they dont want to get out of the mountain department, but they do want to get where they will be treated like soldiers and not like dogs it may be better here in the fort, than it was on the march, at least, I hope it will. There are several boys here in irons for desertion, some of them are among the best boys of the command They are waiting the issues of a court-martial, which comes off in a few days, then we may be called onto witness the execution of the sentence of death upon comrades, yes I may be one of those to whose lot it shall fall to execute the requirings of military law on those against whom I have not the least ill will. I hope it may be ordered otherwise, but this is a place where military law is carried out to the letter.

As an instance of the strictness exercized here, I will relate what this letter came near bringing upon me this evening. I had been to meeting, which was at two o clock got back at three took up my pen to write, and continued writing till the bugle sounded the stable call, which is at half past four It is then the duty of every man to fall out and water and curry his horse. Well when the company fell out in regular military style, I thought I would not go till I had changed my clothes, as I did not want to wear my best to the stable. so I came straggling up to the stables after the company had arrived there, the Lieutenant asked me why I was so far behind. I gave him my reasons. Well, says he, you will sleep in the guard house tonight

Caspar Collins, The Life and Exploits of an Indian Fighter of the Sixties, pp. 35–36, 53–56; Brief History of Each Company, Muster Roll File, Eleventh OVC, Archives Division, Ohio Historical Society, Columbus.

The sergeant then reported several others. Lieut[4] said put them all in the guard house. I was beginning naturally to feel very bad about my lodging place. I stood round a while, got someone else to take my horse to water. The Lieut came to me after [a] while and asked me if I would come out next time at stable call. I told him I wanted to do what was right. I talked and apologized to him for a while, and he concluded to let me off for the present.

Well back again to the incidents of the march At Ft Kearney the first sergeant of our company with several men started back after deserters. all the men but two came into camp three or four days ago Our first sergeant and a corporal were left behind. the men who came up did not know where they were. But a dispatch came here, that the corporal had deserted and the sergeant was under arrest for horse stealing at Karney.

One night while we were lying quietly in our tents near the north platte, not dreaming of anything going to happen, we were suddenly waked up by a most terrific wind storm, which leveled every tent in camp, the sand filled everything, some of the men got up and tried to put up thier tents, but to no purpose, for my part, I laid still (twas while I had the jaundice) with my blankets over my head to keep the sand out of my ears and eyes, the wind blew with unabated fury till daylight when we arose, it looked odd to see not a tent standing, there were near fifty tents belonging to the command. I must close here. direct your letters to Fort Laramie, Idahoe Ter.

Hervey

Fort Laramie [Idaho Territory]
Oct 24th/63

Sister Sibil,

Without waiting for an answer to my last three or four letters, I again resume my pen. It is not my intention to wait for letters but I intend to

---

[4] Jacob L. Humfreville, a native of Piqua, Ohio, was mustered in at Fort Laramie in October 1861. In March 1863 he was appointed Second Lieutenant, Company G, Eleventh OVC, by the governor of Ohio to replace William H. Brown, who had been promoted. In November 1864 he was promoted to captain of Company K, Eleventh OVC, a post he held until he was mustered out at Fort Leavenworth on July 14, 1866. Captain Jacob L. Humfreville, CMF.

write every week, and you may write as often as you please We had quite a snow this morning but It has nearly all gone off. We also had a snow on the eighteenth. I am well at present. have had no reason to complain since I came here. I have gone into an artilery company, called the Mountain Battery, it is composed of forty eight men from the different companies. Our guns are called Mountain Howitzers.[5] We have but four guns. Have been drilling some with the artillery. not made much progress yet. I wrote a letter yesterday to Sam Kinzer.[6] He is in the 7th Iowa Cavalry. His company is stationed at a government post called Cotton wood Springs,[7] on the road from Kearney to Laramie. I saw him as we passed that place on our march, but did not get to speak to him; he is a sergeant I think from the stripes he wore. There are also two companies of the same regiment stationed at Fort Kearney. I met with two of my Iowa acquaintances there in Company C. They are both quaker boys. I must quit writing for the present an clean up my arms preparatory to inspection tomorrow.

Morning. 25th I got up this morning and made a fire before the rest of the boys did, but as soon as the room got warm the other boys piled out, so that I expect I won't write much, they make so much noise. The sky is very clear, and weather quite cold this morning, but not so cold as it has been since we came here, one morning we got up and went down to the river

---

[5] See letter of August 13, 1863, n. 17.

[6] A native of Hendrix County, Indiana, Sergeant Samuel O. Kinzer was mustered in the Seventh Iowa Volunteer Cavalry at Davenport on June 30, 1863. Following detached service as a recruiter for the Seventh IVC and as post provost at Camp (Fort) Dodge, Kansas, he was honorably discharged at Fort Leavenworth May 17, 1866. Sergeant Samuel O. Kinzer, CMF.

[7] First called Cantonment McKean (after Major Thomas McKean, Thirty-eighth Pennsylvania Militia), the military installation at Cottonwood Springs was officially designated Post of Cottonwood in February 1864, Fort Cottonwood on May 18, 1864, and Fort McPherson on January 20, 1866, after Brigadier General James B. McPherson who was killed near Atlanta on July 22, 1864. It was located on the right bank of the South Platte about eight miles above the forks of the Platte. The actual site Johnson made reference to was two miles east. According to Captain Eugene Ware, Cottonwood Springs "was the only spring as far as then known along the Platte for two hundred miles." Here was located a stage station and telegraph office, while "on the other side of the road [was] a place where canned goods and liquors were sold, kept by a man named Boyer. . . ." Fort McPherson was abandoned on June 20, 1880, excluding the post burial ground which is still maintained by the federal government. See Robert W. Frazer, *Forts of the West*, p. 88; Captain Eugene F. Ware, *The Indian War of 1864*, pp. 44–46.

to wash and it was frozen over, it was pretty cold washing that morning. This post is situated in the fork of the Platte and Laramie, near the north-bank of the latter, it is surrounded by low hills sparsely covered with pines, a few cottonwoods grow along the banks of the river, and the grim peaks of the Rocky Mountains, rising above the adjacent hills, are distinctly seen, looking like distant thunder clouds. This morning the snow is plainly visible at the distance of seventy miles, capping some of the highest peaks. We could distinctly see Laramie peak, sixty-five miles above here, three days before we got here.

While on our [way] here we saw a great many Buffoloes, Antelopes, wolves and other beasts some of the boys killed several buffaloes and antelopes, one boy took it on foot one day with his rifle and killed three antelopes and two wolves, But the funniest little thing that inhabits the prairies is the prairie dog. We camped once for three days near a prairie dog village, and twas amusing to see them sitting around their holes in little groups of three or four, and on the approach of any one, the first thing he sees is the end of their tails just getting out of sight, and the next thing is their heads poping up to see if any one is near. We might wake anytime at night and hear their clatter, which sounds like so many young puppies learn-ing to bark. The wolves too would occasionally give us a specimen of their vocal attainments. I never saw a magpie till after we started up the north platte. they are a much larger bird than I had supposed them to be. They are nearly as large as a wild pigeon

The wolverine is another animal that inhabits the wilderness. I saw a dead one laying in the bed of the platte river once, as we took our horses across to graze them. I did not get to see a living one. They are about as large as Uncle John's prince The wolf is not so large. But the most curious living thing that I saw was a fish. I went fishing one day with another boy we had caught three or four, I believe they were pickerel, I was walking along on the bank carrying the fish and the other boy's overcoat, while he waded in and killed the fish with his sabre. I saw something laying on the bottom that I took to be a fish I showed it to him, he waded in and struck it a blow across the back of the head, then run his sabre through it and carried it to the bank, he was afraid to take hold of it with his hands, he uttered several exclamations of surprise and told me to take it off I got the thing off his sabre and looked at it, we did not know what it was, so we called it a shovel-head Their heads are more like one of these round pointed shovels than any thing else. their mouth is a round hole in the middle of the under side of the head, there were hundreds of these fish in places along the river; we killed three and might have killed fifty more but we did not know that they were fit to eat. The largest one of these fish that we killed was two feet long, its head was four inches long and three inches wide. The body of the fish was nearly round and about two inches through so that if the fins were taken off, the fish would look like a spade.[8] Another curios animal that I saw was the beaver, I saw a boy shoot one under water, but the greatest curiosity is the trees they cut down, I have seen whole scores of cotton woods cut down by them. I have seen trees as large as my body gnawed off by them.

But the Indians I have hitherto neglected saying any thing about them I do believe that of all specimens of humanity that I ever saw, the Indians around here are the most low-lived, dirty, sneaking, and impudent. I have read a good deal about the Indians, I have heard them eulogized, poetized, and all manner of things I have seen and heard, written and spoken, complimentary to them, but I have seen enough of them, and those who like the stock may handle it. There are however, some Indians in Kansas who dress like white people, act like white people, speak inteligible english, and are in fact citizens. There were a great many young indians at Ft Leavenworth dressed in soldiers clothes, some of them with corporal stripes. But here I believe I hate them worse and worse every day, they run all over the fort picking up every thing they get their eyes on, just imagine what you would think on sitting down to dinner, to see six or eight squaws poking their heads in at the windows and door, and it does no good to give them any thing, for they are ten times worse to hang round the kitchen after you have given them a scrap than they were before. I believe I will let the Indian subject drop for the present and take it up some other time. No, there is one thing that I forgot, it is the way the Indians travel. They take a pony and strap a pad on h[is] back, then they fasten a pole on each side of the pad, so that one end of each pole rests on the ground, the poles reach back behind the pony several feet, so he looks like he was in shafts, they then pile their

---

[8] Apparently these were shovel-nosed sturgeon (*Scaphirhynchus platorhynchus*).

luggage on these poles behind the pony and go stringing along like a gang of gypsies.

Sibil, I backed[9] a letter to day, to one of the Maberley girls, not for my self but for a young fellow from Rainsboro. He saw some of my penmanship and thought it looked better on the back of a letter than his would, but after it was done he did'nt like the way her name was spelled. I spelled it like I have here. I did not know whether it was right or not. Another boy from Rainsboro said that she would think the fellow that backed that was a good speller or else not. I just thought that if the spelling inside was no worse than that on the outside he ought to be well satisfied, I saw some of his spelling I did, myself, I did.

Write soon Thy Brother

Hervey.

Hervey Johnson
Fort Laramie, Idahoe Ter.
Care Lieut. Humfreville
Mountain Battery.

Fort Laramie [Idaho Territory]
Nov. 1ˢᵗ/63

Sister Sybil,

I have arisen this cool november morning, built on a blazing fire of pine knots and cedar, lighted a candle, and seated myself to write while the other boys are asleep. We are all in good health, with the common exception of colds. We live very comfortably here; as much so, almost as we do at home, we don't have to get up of a morning till day light, and then we have a good warm room, good beds. we have ticks filled with hay to sleep on plenty of blankets, some of the boys have quilts, and some buffalo robes. I would like to put in every winter of my three years at this place, but the summer I would like to spend in the mountians. The talk is now that we will go next spring upon the yellowstone or head waters of the Missouri There is a new gold

---

9 I.e., addressed.

mine in that region and the Colonel intends to see it,[10] and the boys have no objection to going there. One thing certain, it won't do very well to undertak to bring us back to the states before our time is out.

It is evening now and I must finish by candle light. I had to quit this morning to go on inspection and muster, It was the monthly inspection, and we had to put on a good deal of style, as they call it here. It has been drizzling snow all day, and the ground is white again. The snow that fell last week had nearly all gone off. I believe I will give a description of our regular days work here. The first thing in the morning, the bugle sounds revielee; that is at daylight, then twenty minutes after roll call is sounded, at this every man must be ready and fall out in ranks, those who are not there to answer to their names, are sent to the guard house. As soon as roll is called, the men are all marched off to the stable, which is nearly a quarter of a mile. there every man has to begin on the right side of his horse and curry till the sergeant says, change   Then they curry the other side till he calls them to attention, then they every man stands by his horse, while the sergeant and Lieutenant walks along and inspects them   after they are inspected, the men fall in and march back to quarters, then at half past six the bugle sounds the breakfast call, The boys are generally all present at this call. At nine the guards are mounted and placed at their posts   At half past ten we are marched to the stables again to water the horses, as soon as the horses are watered, we march back again to quarters. At twelve the dinner call is sounded, nobody absent. at half past one drill call, at half past two recall from drill. at five water call again, we then water and curry our horses again, then inspection and march back to quaters. at six supper call, at sundown roll call, at nine o'clock roll call again, at fifteen minutes after nine the bugle sounds "lights out," then every man must be in bed and the lights and fire out.

Well, as it is getting late I must begin to close. I want thee to get thy likeness and send it to me if thee can   I would like to have all your pictures I think all you girls might get yours on one plate and send it. Cousin Matilda

---

[10] Johnson is apparently referring to the Alder Creek mines, which were discovered in the spring of 1863. They were located east of Bannack City in present southwestern Montana. The unidentified Colonel probably was Colonel William O. Collins, commander of the Eleventh OVC.

promised me hers. Kiah Sanders told me to tell you, if you saw any of his folks, to tell them that he is well, he is trying to get transferred from company G. to D. of the old battalion. In thy next letter please tell me if thee can send thy likeness. Pleas write and tell me all about everybody.

I remain thy Brother,

Hervey.

Fort Laramie [Idaho Territory]
Nov 8th 1863.

Sister Sibil

This fine sabbath morning I have seated myself to address another letter to thee. The weather is very pleasant here at this time. It is more like spring weather than any thing else, with the exception of the grass. there is not a living blade of grass to be seen nor has been for three or four hundred miles back along the road except close along the river. The last green grass I saw was sixty miles below here on the platte river. You may wonder what we do for hay for our horses, when grass is so scarce. They haul hay from Scotts Bluffs sixty miles from here. some years they haul from Ash Hollow one hundred and eighty miles below here. Teams are constantly coming in with hay. Scotts Bluffs is a ridge of bold precipitous rocks across which the old California road passes, through a narrow, winding passage. the rocks on either side are almost perpendicular three or four hundred feet high and cut full of names as high as a man can reach   we did not stop as we marched through or I might have found some familiar names.

Ash Hollow is a deep rock bounded gulley leading from the hills on the south into the river, it is noted as the place where General Harney with eight hundred Regulars engaged fifteen hundred indians and defeated them.[11]

---

[11] Johnson has reference here to General William S. Harney's defeat of the Brulé Sioux in September 1855. Located about thirty miles due north of Julesburg, Ash Hollow was described by Ware as "a wide gulch with a dry arroyo running from the south nearly north, into the North Platte River. . . ." A deep canyon led from the plateau to the bed of the North Platte; ash trees in the adjacent ravines prompted John C. Frémont, in 1842, to give the location its name. Ware, *The Indian War of 1864*, pp. 230–31.

We camped in this hollow one day and night on account of the wind. It was on the second of september. We started from our camp and marched three miles, but the wind was so high and cold that we stoped when we came into this hollow where we found a good shield from the wind. Some of the boys found several indian relics, such as beads and other trinkets, the graves of the soldiers who were killed were also seen there. I left my name and the date, inscribed under the shelf of a high rock at this place.

The greatest natural curiosity that I saw on the march was the Chimney Rock.[12] This rock at a distance looks like a church spire or monument, on approaching it, it appears not so well defined but still retains its monumental shape; it rises out of a broad mound, several hundred feet in diameter, and deeply indented with rough gullies; the rock is at least three hundred feet high. we first saw it soon after we started one morning, but did not pass it till next day, afternoon. Another curiosity is the Court House rock[13] it is in the vicinity of the chimney rock we did not pass near it, but at the distance we were from it, it appeared very much like the pictures we have seen, of some Chinese temple, or other ancient edifice.

We passed, one day through a prairie dog village that must have contained a thousand or fifteen hundred acres, the little inhabitants were frisking about in every direction, now and then we could see an owl sitting out on the little mounds sometimes a badger too might be seen lolling lazily about. They all live together Owls, badgers, and dogs, in one happy com-

---

[12] Located 575 miles west of Independence on the Oregon Trail, "No one going to the West in the early days over this trail," according to Grace Hebard, "failed to make mention of this famous landmark." The rock was nearly 500-feet high, and although many travelers predicted it would become a low mound in a few years, this slim spire of sandy clay and soft sandstone withstood the elements with remarkable endurance. However, Captain Howard Stansbury, who observed the rock on two occasions in 1852, contended that its height had been substantially reduced by lightning "or some other sudden catastrophe. . . ." See Grace Raymond Hebard and E. A. Brininstool, *The Bozeman Trail*, vol. 1, pp. 78, 89; Captain Howard Stansbury, *An Expedition to the Valley of the Great Salt Lake of Utah*, p. 51; Paul C. Henderson, *Landmarks on the Oregon Trail*, pp. 13–14.

[13] Located near present Bridgeport, Nebraska, Courthouse Rock, according to Ware, "supposedly [was] named by early travelers who thought it resembled the county building in St. Louis. Another story suggests that the rock was named after a dozen outlaws who were shot at the top of the formation, following a hasty trial." Ware, *The Indian War of 1864*, p. 442.

munity. I had intended when I got to this place to send home some native flower seeds. I saw so many beautiful flowers in Kansas and Nebrask as we came through those states; but when I got here the flowers and every thing else were dead. I must close; dont forget to write soon and send thy miniature.

Thy Brother Hervey.

Fort Laramie [Idaho Territory]
November 15th/63

Sister Sibil.

'Tis Sabbath morning, and as the boys are all in bed, I thought I would write another letter as I could do it without being molested. The weather here is now and has been very fine, with the exception of now and then a windy day, windy weather is the worst we have here on account of the dust and sand that it stirs up. The whole Battallion of us has been at work the last two or three days sweeping out the Fort and parade ground. We have swept over six or seven acres. The Colonel has been expecting his wife from the states, and I suppose he wanted her to see things in nice order, when she made her appearance. She arrived last night in the ambulance from Julesburg[14] Twas nine o clock when she came, so I have not seen her yet.

---

[14] Catherine Willis Wever Collins, wife of Colonel William O. Collins and mother of Caspar Collins, remained with her husband in Indian country for approximately a year. Spring, *Caspar Collins*, pp. 53–56. According to Clyde C. Walton's notes, there have been four "Julesburgs," all located near the Lodgepole Creek confluence of the South Platte in present northeastern Colorado. The first was the Jules Beni ranch, which served as a Pony Express stop and stage station. This "Old Julesburg" was virtually destroyed by Indians on January 7, 1865. The second existed until 1867, when the town site was "moved to the other side of the river." The third "Julesburg" was a Union Pacific construction camp, while the fourth was founded in 1881, apparently to accommodate the Union Pacific cutoff to Denver. One mile west was Fort Sedgwick, the traditional starting point on the Bozeman Trail. Established on May 17, 1864, as Camp Rankin, this post was designated Fort Sedgwick on September 27, 1865, in honor of Major General John Sedgwick, who was killed at Spotsylvania on May 9, 1864. This military installation was abandoned on May 31, 1871, and transferred to the Interior Department on July 22, 1884. Ware, *The Indian War of 1864*, p. 459; Hebard and Brininstool, *The Bozeman Trail*, vol. 1, pp. 72, 89; Frazer, *Forts of the West*, p. 41.

The mail came in last night also. I dont know whether it brought anything for me or not I think it ought to, I have got but one letter since I have been here, and I have written at least a dozen to different persons. The mail arrives and leaves here but once each week. Arrives on sixth day and leaves third day; it is two days behind time this time on account of the driver losing two of his mules.

There is some sickness among the men here, but I am well. I never enjoyed better health than I have since I came here. I am as big and fat almost as Johnathan Carey I have not seen Sam Engle for more than two months, we left him very sick with the brain fever at Fort Karney. Albert got a letter from him the other day, he is getting pretty well again I was glad to hear from him, there was not a boy in the company more respected than he was, we were all sorry to leave him there, but he was not able to go further. I hope it will not be long till he comes up here.

I intend to go up the platte to day five or six miles to see if I can get my jacket altered to fit me There is'nt half the boys that get clothes to fit them from the goverment so we have to get the tailors to alter them for us. We have to pay very high for our tailoring here nine dollars for altering and trimming a jacket, five for pants. I bought a calico shirt yesterday for two and a half, a dollar for pair suspenders. I am going to get a pair of Indian moccasins made to send to thee I spoke for them yesterday I cannot get them for two or three weeks They will cost three or four dollars. I can get moccasins for fifty cents but if I make a present I intend it shall be a nice one all I ask is for thee to pay the postage on them as I shall send them by mail I believe I will not finish my letter till I see if the mail brought me one.

Evening The letter that Warren wrote on the fourth of tenth mo. I got this morning It seems like it takes three times as long for your letters to reach me as it does mine to reach you, or else you don't tell when you get mine, or don't answer them as soon as you do get them. I am very glad to hear from you any time. On the second page of this will be found an explanation of what I said in my Fort Karney letter.[15] I knew that I could'nt say anything about Sam without telling that he was sick and I knew what

---

[15] Since the second page of this letter was not found, the "sad news" mentioned in the letter of September 20, 1863, remains unexplained but may have been related to Sam Kinzer's illness.

would be the effect if I did he was crazy for a week before he went to the hospital, shortly after he had a gathering in the side of his head, I felt alarmed for him a while; but I am glad to tell you that he is nearly well. Tell Harmon that I would be glad to reply to a letter from him if it would suit his convenience to favor me with one. Dont forget about that picture of thine that thee was going to send me. I understand from a letter that Tom Cooper got that Sam has gone back to Earlham. No more at present.

Thy brother,

Hervey Johnson.

Fort Laramie [Idaho Territory]
Nov 23rd 1863

Dear Sister.

Though I scarcely get a letter from home once a month, it does not discorage me from writing one each week. I have recieved but three since I came here, two from home, and one from Sam Kinzer at Cotton wood springs; the latter last mail. I have mailed from one to four each week since I came here, to different places, home, Iowa, Camp Dennison, Jamestown, Ft McKean &c and I must confess that I have as yet recieved very little encouragement to continue. I look for a handful of letters each mail, and I sometimes get one, but oftener none.

I am still enjoying good health. Albert[16] got badly hurt one day last week. He with several others have been out in the hills chopping wood, and, I believe it was last second day, on returning from work to the tent, that he was walking along with his jacket under his arm and his ax in his hand, down a tolerably steep hill. Making a misstep, it started him to running, and the hill being covered with coarse gravel, he could not recover himself, but rather run faster than ever; he finally threw his ax forward, at the same time dropping his jacket, which becoming entangled with his feet, threw him a distance of several feet against the end of his axhandle, breaking his breast bone, and two ribs. Tom Cooper and Kiah and I, went to see him next morning. He was brought to the fort that night in the ambulance.

---

[16] Albert Johnson. See letter of July 18, 1863, n. 4.

He was lying on his back very comfortably. He said he had no pain except when he moved about, and it was very irksome lying in one position all the time. He will recover in a few days and be about again I think.

I went over on platte river last first day to take my jacket to the tailor to have it altered, one of the boys went with me with the intention of finding game along the river, but not seeing any along the platte, we went across to the southward toward laramie river; on going down from the hills to the river, we passed where an indian had been laid up to dry, twas in the forks of a scrubby cedar ten or twelve feet from the ground[17] His buffaloe robe, blankets, bow and quiver were all there, and the whitened bones protruding at different places tended to produce anything but pleasant sensations We did not suffer our curiosity to extend so far as to disturb the remains of the dead, for nothing would create a war sooner, between the whites and indians, than for the former to interrupt the remains of thier dead. We passed on down towards the river, and on coming into a level spot, at the foot of a hill we had descended, we saw a "koyote", the indian name for wolf, but he was too far off, for us to give him a chase, so we let him go his way in peace. Passing on down a ravine, we soon came upon the broad bottom of the Laramie. At some distance before us we espied another koyote, and gave him chase, he was too far off however, and running almost as fast as a horse, he gained some willow brush on the bank of the river, before we came up to him; the brush being very thick it was impossible to find him without going into it, on doing which, he ran out, and had got out of reach before we knew it; as it was getting late we did not attempt to follow him, but made our way back down the river to the fort. One of the men started out yesterday to look for deer, he came back in two or three hours almost froze to death The weather was very rough yesterday, cold, windy, and snowy, the snow is perhaps two inches deep but it is more mild to day, and the sun is shining out very brightly. We had an oyster supper in our room last fifth day night, there are twelve of us, and the supper cost us sixteen dollars and seventy five cents.

---

[17] Here Johnson had occasion to observe the Sioux custom of placing the remains of deceased persons on racks some eight to ten feet above ground. The principal purpose of this custom was to prevent the corpses from being molested by animals of prey.

I am writing in a room, called the "Soldiers Reading Room". It was fitted up and furnished at the Colonel's expense, there are four large tables with benches around them, on the tables are found all the principal newspapers, and magazines published in the United States, besides telegraph despatches, which are coming in every day. The walls are also decorated with maps. Here those who are fond of literary pastime, may sit and amuse themselves without being molested. I find it very convenient to me as a place to write in. There is also a libray of three or four hundred volumes here, to which the boys have access. As I have not much more space I will bring my letter to a close, hoping that I may hear from home as often as practicable. Tell Moll and Vine to write. Please write and tell everything that is going on in the neighborhood

Hervey

Fort Laramie. [Idaho Territory]
Dec. 1st 1863

Dear Sister.

Again, I have seated myself to address a few lines back to my distant home. I hope they may find you in the enjoyment of happiness and prosperity. I cant immagine why you dont write and let me know something about home. This is the eleventh or twelfth letter, that I have sent home since I came here, and not a reply to one have I got. I at first thought that there had not been time enough for to get a letter from home; but I am almost persuaded that something else is the matter. We have been here nearly three months, and if that is not time to send a letter to the States and get an answer, I don't know how long would be sufficient. Several trains of ox teams have started, and arrived here from the states since we came here. Six yoke of cattle with a heavy load make the trip in thirty days, why is it then that if a letter had been started, that it has not reached me yet. Some of the boys have got letters in sixteen days from the day they were mailed. And that from Ohio too; and from Highland County too; but not one have I recieved that was dated within the last three months.

From letters that the boys get from Ohio, it seems that there is a good deal of sickness there. A boy in our company recieved inteligence yesterday, of the death of an only sister and nine in another company, recieved letters containing bad news from home. now if there is any thing the matter I want you to let me know, for I will have to know it sometime and what is the difference when. I am sure that these are not pleasant anticipations, and I hope that I may be disappointed in them. I am still enjoying good health. there is but little sickness in the garrison. The weather has been very cold for the last four or five days, the mercury as low as thirteen below zero; but it is moderating now, and the snow is going off. I was on guard one of the cold nights; it was no amusement at all to walk for two hours at atime and carry a heavy gun, but it was cold enough to keep me awake, and the wolves kept up such a continual howling as made [the] night hideous the moon shone very brightly, and I could see them running along the river on the ice. One of them ran along within two or three rods of me. they were thick around the butcher pen, which was not far off. We are not allowed to fire our peices except in case of alarm, or I might, in a night or two, get enough wolf skins to make a nice robe I have seen them running about the parade ground inside the fort. they are often seen about the cookhouse after night picking up scraps that have been thrown out. On the night of the twenty fifth Nov. I had occasion to be out and I saw an eclipse of the moon; it was almost total; only a small portion of the moon's face being visible. I do not know whether the same was seen in the states or not. . . .

Well I must bring this to a close hoping that I will soon hear from home.

Hervey Johnson

P.S. Albert Johnson has got up and returned to duty.[18]

Hervey Johnson

Fort Laramie Idahoe Ter.
Dec. 9th. 1863.

Dear Mother.

Although contrary to my first intention, I had almost made up my mind to quit writing letters home. I had written so many and recieved no reply.

---

[18] See letter of July 18, 1863, n. 4.

But last night after dark one of the boys brought one in to me, which as soon as I saw I knew it was from thee. I therefore concluded that I *would* write again. Every letter that I have got yet, I have answered the same or the next day after receiving it. This letter, which dated the twelfth of 11th mo., was read with pleasure I was very glad to hear that you were all well and enjoying your selves. The Three letters that thee speaks of as having been sent me, and having had no account of, are just the same to me; I have no account of them either I am sorry to say. It may be that they will come straggling in some of these days. the mail has got to be very irregular on account of the weather, and there is a letter laying in the office now, that I put in last week. There was a very full mail last night, some of the boys got as high as seven, and some ten letters.

I heard from Sam Engle[19] again last night. He is at fort Karney four hundred miles below here. He is expected to join the company pretty soon No person will be more glad to see him than I will, he was my bunk mate till sickness compelled him to be taken to the hospital. Tell Harmon that I would like to get a letter from him. Those prisoners that mother wished to know about have not all recieved their sentence yet. Those who have are wearing what the boys call government watches, that is a twelve pound cannonball chained to thier left leg. The other cases had to be sent to Washington, and returns have not yet been recieved, so that what thier sentences will be, no one knows yet. One who wore the ball and chain has been released, and two who walked all the way from Leavenworth have also been turned out. Those who have not recieved their sentences yet, wear hand cuffs. Those who wear the ball and chain are kept constantly at hard labor. It is a pittiful sight to see them at their work, either chopping, or hauling wood, or carrying water dragging thier ball after them as they go.

I went up the River last first day to see if my jacket was finished, it was not, nor would be for some time It did not make much difference to me for I have not money to pay for it with. I am in debt about twentyfour dollars, but as soon as the paymaster comes round, I expect to lift about seventy five or eighty dollars which will square me up and leave a little beside Tell the

---

[19] *Ibid.*

Old aunts that Albert is well or was a few days ago he is out in the mountains now cutting wood. . . .

Preparations have been going on for two or thre days for a funeral which comes off to day at two o'clock. Tis of a sergent of the ninth Kansas who was killed last first day by the falling of a part of a mud wall near the stables. He had been tending a saw mill up in the mountains and came down to the fort to get provisions, had got every thing ready, and was on the point of starting back, when the accident happened which terminated his life. He leaves a wife and five children Two of the boys went up last first day to inform her of his death, and bring her down to the fort. She took it very hard, but she said she derived some consolation, from what he often told her as he would come in from his work. She said she had forebodings that something would happen [to] him while he was gone, before he went away; but he told her that he was the happiest man in the mountains and she need not fear for him, the same that he often told her as he would come in from the mill. The flag is flying at half mast and the garrison is out in line awaiting the sound of the bugle to march off to [the] cemetery. The bugle sounds, six young officers are seen to come out of a room bearing the coffin on three muskets, the coffin wrapped in the american flag. The band falls in in front, and strikes up a mournful air, the corpse follows, and the files of soldiers close in behind, and they all march round the parade ground keeping step to the mournful music. having left the parade they march off to the graveyard which is situated on a little eminence, two or three hundred yards north of the fort, the soldiers form around the grave the coffin is lowered, fourteen guns — the number allowed according to the rank of the deceased — are fired over his grave, the Soldiers march off at a quick pace and the funeral is ended. I should have said before the guns are fired, the Chaplain makes a few remarks appropriate to the occasion.

The health here is pretty good. I am well as usual; we have nothing to complain of, without it is the quantity of rations which we draw; we do not get enough, that is, not as much as we would like, in fact we dont get as much as the government allows us, but some how or other we all fatten on it. I have got to be as great a hand for coffee as orpah is, I don't believe I could do without it. I believe I have written about all I can think of so I will close, not however till I have said something to mother in a confidential way.

73

Thee wanted to know if I ever thought of E,[20] saying that she did of me, and that she would be happy to know that she occupied a place in my thoughts. I was at her fathers the day that I left home, we walked out together and talked the matter over, and came to the conclusion that we had better dissolve partnership I told her what I thought of, and my reasons for so thinking, I told her that I was going away that it was not probable that I would be back for three years, that we had been keeping company for nearly four years, and were no nearer what we wished to be, than we were four years ago. that the state of Governmental affairs had wrought a change in individual affairs that no human could possibly have anticipated or avoided. Under these circumstances I made bold to lay the proposition before her, to which we both aggreed, she told me she had been thinking of the same, I told her to have her own mind about it and not be afraid to say what she thought, that it was not because of any thing that I had against her, or because there was someone else who engrossed my attention, but that she might be free. I knew that in the time of my absence she might meet with opportunities that would be better for her, and I wanted not to be the cause of her losing such opportunity I told her this, she seemed in good spirits, did not make any objections to what I proposed, we parted friends, and I told her that if we ever met again that we would meet as friends and not as l - - ers, she aggreed to this, I asked for my miniature which she had, she said she must keep it, she made me promise to write to her, which I have not done. I have often thought the thing over since I came here, and wished, almost that I had left things as they were. I do not want to be counted faithless, for there is no one on earth for whom I have greater regards than E. I thought it was to our best interest to do so, *especially* for hers.

No more at present

Hervey,

---

[20] Possibly Hervey's future wife, Elizabeth Engle.

Fort Laramie Idahoe Ter.
Dec. 23rd 1863.

Sister Sibyl.

I seat myself this morning for the purpose of replying to thy letters, of which two came to hand yesterday. One dated the second of Nov the other the twenty eighth of same month. The first has no doubt been straggling along the road somewhere, and perhaps there are several others in the same fix I got one last mail before this, that was dated between those two dates. I am always very glad to hear from home, and to know that you are all well, you have no idea how glad I am when I get a letter from home, it makes me feel almost like I am at home, to read a letter from there The whole garrison was out at work sweeping, when the mail came in. We worked till the mail was opened, which was about noon, and nary lick would we do after we got our letters till we had read them,

we are cleaning up preparatory to having a big time, day after tomorrow there are going to be several hundred indians here during the hollidays, to have a big war dance. It will be a novelty to the most of us. if it goes off I will write and tell you all about it. They are getting alarmed at the presence of so many "powder and lead men" in their country, and are anxious to form treaties with them, although they do not know what we are here for. There are now at this post, five companies of Ohio boys and three companies up the road further; all of the eleventh O.V.C. besides Colorado and California troops further up in the mountains, a Wisconsin Battery, and a regiment from Missouri is on the road here. The object I think of so many troops here is to open a military road to Bannock City[21] up on the headwaters of the Misouri or Yellowstone. perhaps you can see the place, by looking on that

---

[21] Bannack City was the end of the Bozeman Trail, which was blazed by John W. Bozeman in the winter of 1862–1863. The discovery of gold in southwestern Montana (then Idaho Territory) in late 1862 precipitated a significant migration to the Beaverhead and Ruby river valleys, and by January 1863, Bannack "City" had a population in excess of two thousand persons. The trail, which began at Fort Sedgwick and headed northwest by way of Fort Laramie, the Powder River country, and Bozeman Pass, was closed in 1868 following angry objections voiced by Red Cloud and other Sioux notables the previous year. Hebard and Brininstool, *The Bozeman Trail*, vol. 1, pp. 120–23, 205, 214; James C. Olson, *Red Cloud and the Sioux Problem*, pp. 10, 67, 70–71, 76.

map that Warren bought before I went away; look for fort Benton[22] in the northwestern corner of Dacotah Ter. somewhere south of that is the place. it is said to be the richest Gold country in the west. A city has sprung up there within the last two or three years, and there is an immense tide of emigration to that part, but owing to the hostility of the indians, who swear that there shall never be a road through thier country, emigrants have to go by way of denver and Salt lake, a route which is six or seven hundred miles out of the way. The road that we propose to open, will be nearly direct from this place to its termination. I may be mistaken in my suppositions as to the object of the troops here, but I formed my opinions from what I see.

the late quartermasters trains that arrived here, or rather what they were loaded with, seemed to tell a good deal, if shovels, spades, axes, and picks, have any meaning in them. It may be an expedition against the Mormans but I hardly think that probable, unless more troops than we know be sent out. There was a train of four hundred emigrant wagons, started for Bannock last summer, and were stopped by the indians and turned back, and had to go the old road. The indians told them that if they would go back, and not attempt to cross thier hunting ground, that they would not molest them, but if they insisted on going through their horses and wagons would be captured and themselves murdered. Well the train halted outside the indian country and sent to this post for an escort of soldier to take them through. About sixty men were armed and equipped, went up there, but the train had taken another road before they arrived. It is my opinion that what the Indians told the emigrants, was intended more for a scare than any thing else. I believe had they put on a bold face and went on through, they would have made it without molestation, for the indians very well know, that had they attempted such a thing, as the destruction of a train, that enough soldiers would be sent out from the states to kill every one of them. They have a pretty good idea how many soldiers there are, from what their chiefs tell them, some of whom go to Washington every year.

---

[22] This post, originally an American Fur Company establishment built in 1845, was leased to the United States in the fall of 1869. Its permanent location was on the left bank of the Missouri River at the present town of Fort Benton, Montana. Named in honor of Senator Thomas Hart Benton of Missouri, the military reservation of this installation was transferred to the Interior Department on January 5, 1883. Frazer, *Forts of the West*, p. 79.

Anoth[er] thing, it is my opinion, had the train consisted of 8 or ten wagons, instead of four hundred, they would have waited till they got into their country and then captured the horses and wagons, they know that it will not cause much disturbance to take a few wagons as it would to take a great many, so they feel perfectly safe in committing small depradations for the sake of getting wagons and horses. as events transpire I will write and tell you about them.

I am as well as comon. In fact I never enjoyed better health than I have since I came here. today we have the first rain that we have had since we came here, and it is a mere mist not worthy to be called a rain. It has been nearly two years since there had been any rain of account here. The soil is loose and gravelly and when the snow melts it runs away so that it never gets mudy here, we have had some very cold weather here the forepart of last week, the mercury was as low as fourteen deg below zero, but the last few days have been very fine. . . . Please write often.

Thy Brother
Hervey Johnson

Fort Laramie, Idahoe Teritory,
New Years Day 1864.

Sister Sybil

It is just six months to day since I enlisted; but time has flown so rapidly that it seems as but a few days. As it is New years day, and every body is wild with excitement, I thought I would seek the quiet of the Soldier's Reading Room for the purpose of writing to my friends at home. I don't know how I would pass this day if I was there, but however that might be, as I cannot talk face to face, I will through the medium of the pen. Though many hundred miles separate us, this is a privilege of which we are not yet denied. And how I prize it. Were it not for this, and the access to books and papers, with which we are favored, I scarcely know what I would do; it is all the respite a soldier has, from the dull monotony of garrison life.

A great portion of the garrison are now almost wholly absorbed in a grand dinner given by Co. A. of the old battallion. As I was not invited of

77

course I did not get excited so much about it as I might have been. Those who know, say that every thing that could be brought on a table any where was there. meats of all kinds, eggs, chickens, Oysters sardines, lobsters, green corn, berries of all kinds, nuts, raisins, candies, in fact every eatable that could be named. All the wines, catawba, sherry, champagne, bourbon, old rye, stews, toddies, gin slings, punch &c. I didn't see any of it, but I'd like to have the money it cost. it would be of considerable assistence to me in a financial way. It may surprise you a little but it is nevertheless true that the dinner cost Co. A. somewhere in the vicinity of six hundred and fifty dollars!!!!!!. All the officers of the fort were there with thier wives, that is those who have them here; and the most of them came away drunk, from the Colonel[23] down.

I went on guard yesterday morning, the weather was tolerably cool, only fifteen deg. below zero; I froze my ears while mouting guard, till they were as hard and white as a turnep. There were thirteen of us guards, and all but three or four froze thier ears some froze thier feet and some thier hands. I got some snow and held [it] to my ears till the frost was out, they pained me considerably, but I went on duty. To day they are swelled up, and feel like they had been beaten with a shingle for half an hour, I guess they wont come off, but then I would rather not have quite so much in mine any more. The Col. came into the guard house about noon, and he said the mercury was at eighteen, and the sun was Shining at the same time, the cold kept on increasing, I went on post at seven in the night, and when I came off at nine the mercury was about twenty four, but still I hadnt suffered like I did in the morning. About eleven in the night the Colonel came in with a hot "stew" and gave us all a drink around. He said the mercury stood at twenty seven when he left his quarters, it fell to twenty nine by twelve o'clock, and from that time it began to moderate, though it was not warm as it was yesterday morning. It was curious to me why my ears froze in the morning with the mercury at fourteen when I was out only fifteen minutes, and I walked post two hours with the mercury at twenty four, and did'nt suffer scarcely at all though I had on no more clothing, than I had in the morning.

[23] Colonel William O. Collins, regimental commander of the Eleventh OVC. See letter of October 18, 1863, n. 3.

Jan 2nd/64 I have been down to the woodyard chopping and nearly froze my ears again, two of the boys that were with me froze their ears, it is snowing now and is about three inches deep. While we were chopping it snowed about as fast as I ever saw it. There has been no mail in for two weeks, and no one knows when it will come. The last account we had of it, it was at Mud Springs,[24] a telegraph station about one hundred and twenty miles from here. The conveyance had broken down near the station, the snow was so deep that the mules pulled the ambulanc in two trying to get it through The mail will not leave here till the one from below arrives and as there is not much prospect of that even if they get the conveyance repaired, this letter will remain in the office sometime before it goes out, there are some half a dozen letters laying there now that I have put in. unless there is a great change in the weather it will be impossible for the ambulance to get through Scotts Bluffs, on account of the snow which fills in the hollows through which the wagons have to pass. I am afraid we will have to suffer here yet this winter for the want of wood, there have been from fifteen to twenty six horse teams hauling constant since we came here, and the wood-pile grows daily less. we had to come in this morning before we got enough cut because there was nothing there to cut but big green pine logs that wouldnt split, nor burn if they would split. The teams have just now got in, but it is too late in the evening to go out to work, and those who didn't get their wood today will have to go without tonight.

Sibil I intended to send thee a new years present before this time but I have not got it yet, and dont know when I will. I gave the work to an interpreter some time ago, and he gave it to some squaw to put together. I think I will get it by the time we are paid off, and nobody knows when that will be. there is fifty two dollars coming to me, besides some that the boys owe me, about thirty dollars must come out of that to pay my debts and then I will be square again. please write soon

Thy Brothe

Hervey Johnson

---

[24] Located approximately seven miles north of present Dalton, Nebraska, Mud Springs got its name because of a buffalo wallow nearby. Ware, *The Indian War of 1864*, p. 460; Paul Henderson, "The Story of Mud Springs," *Nebraska History*, vol. 32, no. 2 (June 1951), pp. 108–19.

Fort Laramie Idahoe Ter.
Jan. 16th 1864.

Sister Sibyl.

Again after two or three weeks since writing — I have taken up my pen.
I have not received a letter from home since New Year, and it will probably
be two weeks yet till I get one. I received a letter from a correspondent in
Iowa about ten days ago. . . . There are seven or eight letters of mine in the
office here now awaiting the departure of the mail, so I think when this
comes to hand, there will be two or three others with it, I have forgotten
how many were directed home.

Well Sibyl we have had some of the coldest weather here that any one
could form an idea of. In an other letter I spoke of having my ears frozen,
but the weather was'nt a patching to what it has been since For six or eight
days the mercury averaged about thirty below zero, and part of the time it
was as low as forty, and even fifty below. I never saw so many boys with
ears, fingers and feet frozen in my life. I have heard of none yet being frozen
to death, but several were taken to the hospital. A great many cattle and
other stock, the property of Mountaineers perished from cold, several belonging about the post here were almost frozen to death, my ears have all
peeled off from the freeze they got sometime ago. I mean the skin has peeled
off they are very tender and can bear but very little cold. The Mountaineers
say that they never knew it to be so cold before. The mail that went out the
next day after christmas has not returned this is why I said it would be some
time before I would get a letter from home. During the cold weather that
I spoke of there were about thirty of us engaged in cutting and packing ice,
we finished day before yesterday. I think we got up something near three
hundred four horse loads. The ice was about six inches thick, with ten
inches of snow on it when we commenced, we scraped the snow off so that
it would freeze thicker, and when we quit it was twenty inches thick.

From telegraphic dispatches I learn that the draft has been postponed in
Ohio, and from the same source we have interesting information that leads
us to hope that the war will soon come to a close. I care not how soon such
a thing is brought about, I am willing to quit at any time, not that I am sick
or tired of my situation, but that I would be glad to see our country once
more enjoying the blessings of peace and prosperity.

The whole garrison was thrown into a state of excitement this morning by the announcement of the sudden departure, for parts unknown — of one of the prisoners, who had been confined for desertion, he had been in irons three months, and was awaiting the arrival of his sentence from washington, which he believed would be the sentence of death. He made his escape sometime in the forepart of the night by cutting through the wall of the room in which he was confined with his pocket knife. I was astonished when I saw the hole through which he made his escape, it looks like it is not large enough for a boy as small as daney Cowgill to go through, though the man is as large as Harmon Engle When the companies went to the stables this morning they found two horses missing, and further disclosures showed that another man was missing, he was a member of Co. E. and had served a short term in the guard house. A few days before they escaped, there had been several petty roberies committed The post barber had thirty dollars, and a colts repeater taken from him. the gunsmith shop was also entered and relieved of some six shooters and a small breechloading rifle. The theft was charged against some teamsters that were discharged a short time ago, and they were ordered to leave the post. After they had left a small party was sent out to retake the missing articles, but they could not be found. since the escape of these two men no person doubts where the missing arms are. Two or three scouting parties were sent out this morning in pursuit of the fugitives. one party went southward intending to go as far as Denver City, should it be necessary, the other party went up the Platte river with four or five days rations A third party also went out, but I could not learn where they were going to. I will write and tell all about it as things transpire.

Please write soon.

Hervey Johnson

P.S. Here are some seeds that I got one day when I was out. they are the seeds of the soap weed, an evergreen that grows among the hills. I dont know whether it bears flowers or not but I judge it does from the pods that are left on the dry stalks plant them in a course gravely soil, limestone prefered. I do not know whether they will grow or not but there is no harm in trying them.

Hervey

81

Fort Laramie Idahoe Ter.
January 21st 1864

Sister Sibyl

Although tis scarcely a week since I wrote last, I thought perhaps I might think of enough to fill another sheet. The mail has not arrived or departed yet, but we heard today that it was within sixty five miles, and would be in in a few days. no mail will go out till that arrives. I am well, and there is but little sickness in the garrison. The weather has turned warm and pleasant, and seems almost like spring.

The scouts that I spoke of in my last as having gone out after runaways returned last evening with both the fugitives. They were a sorry looking spectacle, the one who cut out through his room in particular, he was affected to tears at his situation. Almost as soon as they arrived, they were marched to the smith shop, each between two armed guards, for the purpose of having irons put on them. They soon came back, one with handcuffs and the other with ball and chain. They were put into the guard house, and strict orders concerning them were given to the guards. There were very few of the boys who were not sorry to see them brought back, for my part I wished that they might escape, especially the one who supposed that his sentence would be death, for I was satisfied that he was innocent of that with which he was charged, and had already suffered enough for being absent from the command about ten hours; having been in irons for three months besides walking nearly three hundred miles. I was on guard when he was first arrested. He was brought into camp about nine in the evening; four picket pins were driven into the ground in the form of a square six or eight feet apart each way, he was then made to lie down on his back in the center, while his hands and feet were securely tied to the pins, and in this manner he remained till morning. We guards were compelled to stand by, and see it all done, and then hear his groans and cries, with out speaking a word.

Perhaps I may as well tell how they were caught this time. The party that went towards Denver City, having been out two days, and still keeping up the pursuit after night, had arrived at the Cheyenne Pass[25] about nine on

---

[25] Cheyenne Pass is in the Laramie Mountains approximately fifteen miles southeast of present Laramie, Wyoming, on the "Lodgepole Creek Emigrant Route."

the evening of the second day. One of the party observed alight in an old building — a part of the remains of an old fort that stood at the pass — and on riding up to the spot they found their game asleep!! They were awakened by a shout from one of the party, to find themselves once more prisoners. They saw that resistance was useless and gave themselves up at once, they gave up their arms, were mounted on the horses they had taken and brought back to the fort.

There was another man put in irons to day, on the charge of having assisted them in getting the horses from the stable. He had been in the service, but was drummed out of it some time ago for some misconduct, and was at the time of his arrest, in the Quartermaster's employ, driving team. He had some grudge against somebody no-doubt. I have not heard positively from Sam Engle for a month; but some of the boys told me that he was on his way up here, in company with one of our boys, who was discharged from the Fort Karney prison, where he had been confined for stealing horses, while in pursuit of deserters. There is a man in prison here now for losing or selling a horse while he was drunk. His sentence was — hard labor with ball and chain for the remainder of his term of service — two years and five months — and all his pay and allowances stopped except one dollar per month; he is subject to fits of hydrophobia and just now as I write one of the guards came in, and said he had one of his fits, and had run all the prisoners and guards out of the prison; the Officer of the day commanded the Sergeant in charge to have him put in the cell but no person was found with sufficient courage to go in and take hold of him. So they left him alone to let the fit wear off. He has been discharged from the service once onaccount of his malady. Since his arrest and confinement he has sent to the states for his discharge and when it arrives he will be released again and become a citizen.

Now to a subject of a less melancholy nature. I have often thought of sending home my picture since I came here, thinking that you no doubt would like to see how I look since I came here, and see what a change of appearance, the change of climate, and mode of living have made in me; you will all no doubt be surprised, and perhaps you will hardly recognize

Hebard and Brininstool, *The Bozeman Trail*, vol. 1, pp. 89–90; Frazer, *Forts of the West*, p. 186.

me. Well you are not to blame, you may lay it all to the climate and mode of living I want you to preserve it, that "when this cruel war is over" and I shall have returned to my home, I may have the pleasure of seeing the picture I had taken at Fort Laramie. You may now break the seal and look "behind the scenes."

Hervey.

Sibil this is not to be opened till the letter is read because in it will be found an explanation of the contents of this. it can be opened by cutting off the ends with a pair of scissors.

This is the likeness of one of the most noted warriors of the Sioux-pro's nation, I should have said the most noted of chiefs and warriors, for he is the Chief of the Ogillallah Sioux. He is known by the name of the Great Bear and has had a hand in all the mail and emigrant robberies that have been committed in the last number of years. He was at the Wakpominah or distribution of presents at the indian agency near this post, some three or four months ago and had his picture taken and this is from the original taken at that time[26]

Fort Laramie Idaho Ter.

Jan. 31st 1864.

Dear Sister.

It is now one month since I have received a letter from home, and as we have had but two mails since I got the last from home, I know not whether to lay it to the irregularity of the mails or to your own irregularities in writing. Perhaps it is the former, if so I will not complain, if the latter I have some reason to grumble; for my own part I never wait till I get a letter frome home before I write one. I always have one ready for every mail, and sometimes three or four as it was with the last mail that went out. I wish my friends at home would do the same way. you certainly could, and with less expense than it costs me to write so often, and I have no idea that

---

[26] These paragraphs appear on a separate sheet of paper enclosed with the letter. The first paragraph was written on one side, the second on the other. The picture or "miniature" was not found with Johnson's letter of January 21, 1864.

you would wish me to write less often. The paper on which I write costs me at the rate of ten cents for three sheets, and envelopes about the same each, so that each letter costs about ten cents and four or five letters each week at that rate will amount up to considerable in cost, at the end of a year. I will not dwell on this subject longer, but hope you will give it some consideration.

I believe I never gave you a description of the way we managed things on our march across the plains, I have often thought of doing so, but as often had some thing else to write about. In the first place then, the first thing in the morning, the camp was aroused by the sound of the bugle, this was generally about four o'clock, we were allowed fifteen minutes to get up and dress ourselves, at the expiration of which time, roll call was announced by the bugle, every man must be present or have an excuse for his absence, the cooks were excused and any one whom they may have to assist them in carrying wood or water, after roll call breakfast call was sounded but it was scarcely ever ready at the call, sometimes because we could get no wood, at other times because we were so far from water that it could not be got in a minute, at the next thing was guard mounting, those who were detailed must go whether they had their breakfast or not, guards were divided in three reliefs each relief standing two hours at a time while in camp, but all guarding together while on the march, the first relief were posted immediately if they had had their breakfast well and good if not, they got nothing to eat till we stopped to camp in the evening unless some of the boys would give them something out of their haversacks. those on the second and third reliefs could go and get their breakfast after guard mounting. Every man must have his horse fed, cleaned, and watered if water is handy, tents must be struck and rolled up, cooking vessels cleaned and loaded in the company wagons, of which there are two to each company, horses saddled, every man puts a cracker or two, along with a piece of sow belly (bacon) in his haversack, straps on his accoutrements, and we are ready at the command, to lead into line; the horses are led up side by side in a line, the riders holding them by their bits The command is given, "count off by fours from right to left" each man counts and remembers his number, whether it be one, two, three, or four. The command then is — "prepare to mount", when numbers one, and three, lead out the length of a horse in advance of the numbers two, and four each man then steps back to the side of his horse, puts his foot in the stirrup, and at the command to "mount"; every man raises to his saddle at once, number two and four then ride up between one and three, and they are all in a line close beside each other again. Everything ready, the bugle sounds "forward", when the commander of each company gives the command, "twos right", "march", when they turn square to right, by two abreast, and march off, and fall in — each company in its proper place in the battalion.

The first day of our march each company fell in in the order of their letters as E. first, F. second, G. third, &c. The second day, F. company was in advance and, E. in the rear The third day, G. in advance, and F. in the rear, and so on every company in advance and rear in turn, Twenty men were detailed out of the advance company each day, as rear guards. Their business was to ride behind the train of wagons which was in the rear of the command, and keep up all stragglers, and pick up any thing which the men might have dropped. many a time have I had them to hurry me up, when I had occasion to fall behind, The rear guard were independent of the camp guard, whose business it was on the march to guard the prisoners, and in camp, to guard every thing belonging to the command. Before starting in the morning every man was made to fill his canteen with water, for it was not often that we got a chance to stop to get water; during some of the long, hot days of september we suffered very much for water, we would often drink all we had before going but a few miles, and then it was just as the officers took a notion, whether we could get off and fill our canteens again. sometimes the captain would tell half a dozen boys to take all the canteens in the company, and go ahead to the nearest well, spring, or creek, and fill them against the rest would come up. Sometimes they would get the water, and the men would get a drink, sometimes they would get the canteens filled, and the Major would ride up and make them pour it all out.

Well we would worry along and do as well as we could without. We would walk and lead our horses three or four miles each day, some times we would stop and let our horses graze for half an hour. We would stop to camp, at from one to five o'clock in the afternoon, being obliged to stop, sometimes earlier and sometimes later, on account of fuel and water. When the Col. though it was getting time to stop, he would take a dozen men and go to hunt a camping place, they would go clear out of our sight but we would follow their trail through the grass, and when we came in sight of them, some of the boys would give their horses to others to lead, while they themselves would take a cornsack or blanket, and go for something to cook our suppers with; they always found plenty of good fuel, where the buffaloes had run a year before; and often after we had been in camp an hour, the boys would come in under a load of "buffalo chips"; they would have better luck sometimes though and get in as soon as we would. This was our principal fuel for a good part of our way. Sometimes we would get tired of this kind of a fire, and would carry wood a mile and sometimes two miles; sometimes we could get neither within a mile or two miles. I have known the boys to go four or five miles to get a sack full of buffalo chips. I have carried brush myself on my horse for six or eight miles before coming to camp, and then as apt as not, the camp would be near the river where there was plenty of wood; but I would hold to it. I would not throw it down, after carrying it so far, if I did see plenty of wood near the camp. After getting into camp, the two company wagons would drive up oposite each other about fifty yards apart. A large rope was then stretched across between the two wagons, the ends being fastened to the top of the hind wheel of each; this was to fasten our horses to at night, our camp generally fronted the west, and every company had its wagons and rope, parallel to each other, and far enough apart for a row of tents and cooking place between I believe I will tell the rest about it in my next letter.

I am well and I believe the health generally is good. We had another deserter the forepart of last week, he was a half witted fellow belonging to Co. E. he stole a pony belonging to the son of one of the officers, he put right down the telegraph line, he had neither arms, ammunition money, or provisions he passed a telegraph station about sixty miles below here. The operator telegraphed here, and got word back to keep him there, some of the boys went down after him and brought him back. He is now wearing a government watch that is, an eighteen pound cannon ball chained to his leg. no more at present write soon.

Hervey Johnson

Fort Laramie. Idaho Ter.
Feb 4th 1864.

Dear Sister and folks at home,

The mail arrived today and I had the good fortune to find myself the recipient of five letters. . . . I don't know how it happened that they all came at once. I was so glad that I did not know what to do. I have not paper or stamps now to write and answer to all three from home, so I must just put it all in one. I was so glad to hear that you were all well and enjoying your selves, I was glad to hear that the ditch I commenced was getting on to completion. It was my intention that I or my means should finish it, but as we have not been paid off for six months, the prospect of me doing any-thing towards it, seems not very flattering .

The miniature Sibil sent me, came safe. I was very glad to have them. they look very natural, I am afraid that I cant keep them from getting scratched. I showed the picture to some of the boys, They were all very much taken with it, the girls in particular took their attention. . . .

In my last letter I was telling something about our manner of living on the march, and intended to tell the remainder in this, but I will forego it for the present. Mother wishes to know how the people who were not soldiers here lived   It is this way, They are mostly traders, and live by trad-ing with the Indians. Every man has what we call a "ranch", that is a kind of store, there are but four any where near this place, Ferotes ranch[27] six miles off, (he is the tailor) Bovey's,[28] four miles off. Bordeaux[29] ten miles, and the

---

[27] Johnson may have been referring to Gilman's ranch where in May 1864 "a professional tailor" named Farley "had quite a patronage" in spite of the fact that for one suit of clothes he charged "three prices." Ware, *The Indian War of 1864*, p. 129.

[28] Here Johnson was referring to the ranch operated by G. P. Beauvais, whose name was variously spelled "Bovery," "Bouvery," and "Boverie." Charles H. Springer, *Soldiering in Sioux Country: 1865*, p. 82, n. 69. One observer in 1864 reported that "Mr. Beauvais, like many of the trappers and ranchers here, had wan-dered down from the neighborhood of Montreal." Ware, *The Indian War of 1864*, p. 465.

[29] Also called Horse Creek Ranch because it was located on a small stream of that name, the ranch was purchased by Bordeaux from a man named Reynolds sometime prior to July 1861. In 1864 the facility was described as "a large rambling log build-ing, with sod end[s] to it, and additions and outbuildings attached to it, so that it was a sort of wandering, straggling caravansary and store combined." Ware also described

Farm House[30] one mile, the latter is the boarding place of the Officers. Each man has several large wagons, "ships of the American desert", and thirty or forty yoke of cattle, they start to the states in the spring loaded with venison buffalo robes and furs, which they exchange for corn, oats, flour, tea coffee, sugar, and everything else in a mercantile line. These they again trade to emigrants for money, and to the indians for furs and skins. They live as well as anybody, and though their dwellings are comfortable, they are miserable looking structures, built sometimes of mud, sometimes of cottonwood poles, daubed with mud, and covered first with a layer of poles, then a layer of skins, then one of dirt, the floor is also dirt, I might add.

Morning Feb 5th The man that I spoke of as getting killed belonged to the ninth Kansas regiment, did'nt I say so in my letter?[31] The mill he was running was put up by the Government for the purpose of furnishing lumber for building quarters for the soldiers, and of course it was tended by the soldiers. One of the prisoners who escaped and were caught at Cheyenne Pass some time ago, took leg bail last night about six o'clock and this morning about thirty men started in pursuit. fifty dollars is offered for his capture. The men have orders not to take him alive, so I suppose they will shoot him whereever they find him. It is a little strange how he got a way for there is a guard constantly pacing back and forth in front of the guard house door It must have been this way — There is a water closet near one end of the guard house, for the prisoners, they go into it when ever they have occasion, for the guard paces in front of it. but there was a board

---

Bordeaux as a "French trader and bourgeois for the American Fur Company" who had been spared at the Grattan Massacre "because of [his] Indian wife." Ware, *The Indian War of 1864*, pp. 197, 461; Charles H. Brown, Telegraph Trail of the Transcontinental Telegraph, 1861, Hebard Collection, Western History Research Center, University of Wyoming Library, Laramie.

[30] The "Farm House" probably was one of the several "hog ranches" located in the immediate vicinity of Fort Laramie, which, in addition to boarding and other retail facilities, offered distinctive feminine attractions to lonely military personnel. Springer, in 1865, reported that "Messers. Adolph Cuny and Jules Ecoffey ran [a] 'Hog' ranch located on the boundaries of [the] Fort Laramie [military reservation] near Beauvais' [Bordeaux'] in the 1870's." In 1865 Cuny and Ecoffey were engaged in the Indian trade around Fort Laramie. Springer, *Soldiering in Sioux Country*, p. 82, n. 69.

[31] See letter of December 9, 1863.

89

off behind and this fellow in stead [of] coming back in to the guard house went out the back way I suppose. I could fill another sheet or two, but as this will take my last stamp I think I had better quit.

Hervey Johnson.

Fort Laramie [Idaho Territory].
Feb 12th 1864.

Dear Sister.

This morning I again seat myself for the purpose of writing. . . . The weather here is very fine now and has been for two weeks. There is no snow scarcely to be seen except on the distant tops of Laramie Peak and the snowy range. The Platte and Laramie rivers have neither raised nor fallen since we came here, but I judge we will see high water in the spring, from the immense amount of snow that has fallen in the mountains, it is fifty feet deep in some places and so solid that loaded teams drive over it. The health here is very good at this time, two of the boys who got their feet frozen during the cold weather will have to have them taken off. Some of the Officers have commenced the erection of a gymnasium, for the developement of our muscular powers. At the same time the Col. is putting the cemetery in repair. It looks rather suggestive I think. The man who broke guard and got away a short time ago, has not been caught yet that we have heard of. A party of six or eight men with three pack mules have been gone five or six days. We have heard nothing of them since they left. They went toward Denver City.

Three or four days ago considerable excitement was raised in camp by the report of some horses being stolen from the wood chopper. Every body thought that the deserter had been laying round near the post, waiting till the excitement caused by his escape should lull, that he might have a better opportunity to get away; and when they heard of the horses being stolen, they felt certain that the deserter had a hand in the mischief. A small party was immediately equipped and mounted, and sent in pursuit; but they were disagreeably disappointed, when, after having ridden twelve miles after night, they found the horses loose near a place called the "stone ranch",

90

(the habitation of some hunters and trappers) but nothing could they hear of the thief. There are so many mexicans, spaniards, creoles, and half-breeds, about here that it is almost useless to attempt to catch a deserter They know every "nook and corner" of the mountains, and if a runaway gets in with them, they can keep him hid till a suitable opportunity of getting away presents itself.

I will try to say something about the Indian dance that went off last week. The dance was performed by about thirty or forty squaws, and seven bucks. The squaws were dressed in their best "sunday clothes", which consisted of a dress of antelope skin with long fringes around the bottom, the body ornamented with gaily wrought beadwork, the moccasins the same Several of them had mexican blankets wrapped around their waists in a way, so as not to interfere with the display of beads and fringes. It was difficult to tell who was the leader of the dance; whether it was an old squaw with a war club, or the chief musician. The dance was conducted entirely according to the rules of indian society. I suppose they could see a good deal of sense and regularity in what they were doing, but I could'nt. The signal to commence, was given by the leader of the band giving his instrument certain raps which they all understood, when they would form themselves in a circle, with their faces inward towards the centre, and move round to the left by short steps or jumps sidewise, keeping time to the music with their voices, which more resembled the quaking of ducks than any thing else. Perhaps you could judge better of the effect of the music, if I would give a description of the instruments. Those played by the bucks, were six or seven cheese hoops, with antelope skin stretched over them; on these they beat, and managed to get all the music out that there was in them — with sticks wrapped with rags. The squaws had different kinds of machines for the manufacture of music. They were old oyster cans, pepper boxes, powder flasks, and sardine boxes, filled half full of pebbles to these were fastened sticks for handles, and while the dance was going on, they shook or rattled them to their own delight and satisfaction. None of the bucks had any of their implements of war, one old squaw held a war club, two others held sabres without scabbards, and another had a lance made of a Lieutenants sword, most of the other squaws had sticks and green willow brush, which was essential in some way to the right conducting of the dance. They under-

91

stood it themselves I suppose, but then I couldn't see it   They all had their faces painted more or less, some perfectly black, some half black and half red, and — well it is useless to describe how they were painted, for no two were alike. From what I have written you can get but a very faint idea of the real, and yet it is the best I can do by way of describing it.

I will finish now with something else. I have been attached to the "drum corps" at this post, so it is my duty after this, to learn to play on a fife. I will therefore quit carrying a Spencer rifle for an instrument that is not so heavy. perahps I never told you what kind of arms we had. They are an entirely new and different pattern from any arm yet introduced into the United States service   Tis called the Spencer Repeating Rifle.[32] Metalic cartridges are used for loading it, seven cartridges are fired from it one after another with great rapidity, and it is loaded with seven more much quicker than the old peices are with one. It is my intention to bring one of them home with me when I come home. it is getting late. My pen is so bad that I must quit.

Write soon and tell every thing.

Hervey Johnson

Hervey Johnson.
Fort Laramie
Idaho Ter.
Care Capt Rinehart
Co G. 11th O.V.C.

Fort Laramie [Idaho Territory]
Feb 23rd 1864

Sister Sibyl

I feel very little like writing this morning, but perhaps I will meet with no better opportunity than the present. So I will proceed. I was on guard

---

[32] Patented in 1860 by Christopher N. Spencer, this famous rifle could be fired seven times in ten seconds, or, with reloading, fourteen times in one minute. Despite the fact that the cartridges often exploded in the magazine and the danger that a jar of the rifle butt might set them off, this weapon was mass-produced for Civil War use. James Monaghan, ed., *Book of the American West*, pp. 387–88.

yesterday and last night and this is why I feel so little like writing. I am very well, and the boys generally are the same. The weather is fine to day, but yesterday morning the wind blew a perfect storm, it was not cold, but it raised so much dust and gravel, that it was almost impossible to stand in it, gravel as large as peas would strike me in the face and sting like bullets. The wind fell by night so that it was very pleasant during the remainder of the time I was on guard.

Yesterday was the anniversary of Washington's birthday, it was commemorated here by ceremonies appropriate to the occasion. Thirteen guns were fired in the afternoon, and twentysix at night. The fifes, drums and brass band keeping up the noise at intervals. It is a pretty sight after night, to see the discharge of artilery, the lightning flash, the echoing roar, reverberating along the hills, the fearful velocity with which the ball or shell speeds onward — these are calculated to inspire one, with emotions, such as none but a soldier can appreciate or feel. It is not often in the daytime that we can see a shell after it leaves the gun, but last night their course was marked by a streak of fire At the distance of a mile and a half or more, the shells would explode in mid air, scattering balls and fragments of shell in every direction. One of the boys got hurt yesterday when they were firing the salute, he was number one, or the one who loaded the gun, and had to stand nearly opposite the muzzle of the peice, when it was discharged, he had neglected the precaution of standing on his toes, and closing his lips, with his teeth apart and when the peice was fired, the blood gushed from his eyes, ears, mouth, and nose. Often when we have been drilling with the guns, and it has been my place to load or fire the peice, I have felt like my eardrums were bursted at the time of the discharge, and even for a day or two afterward, there would be a continual roaring in my ears.

The party that went out after a deserter some time ago, has not returned yet nor I believe has any thing been heard from them. In about six days from this we will be mustered again for pay, we understand that the pay master will be here on the second or third of next month, six months pay will be due us by that time There is so little to do here, that the boys just lay around and do nothing but wear fine clothes. We nearly all have two suits of clothes one for every day and one for sunday. We have our jackets and pants cut to fit us without a wrinkle, and striped with buff cloth, instead of the coarse

93

lace that the Government has put on. We have our clothes washed and done up nice once a week, for which we pay one dollar per month, we wear white shirts and collars. Almost every company has its barber, so we all get shaved once a week and sometimes twice if we want to We wear fine shoes and boots, or moccasins. Our boots and shoes blacked up like we were going to meeting. In fact we dress just like we were in a big city where there were plenty of the fair sex looking at us all the time. If I were going to get married, I would just as soon take my suit of soldiers clothes for a wedding suit as any other, they are just as nice, and nicer, too, than any citizen's suit.

There has been a battle lately, between the Sioux and Crows,[33] in which the former were defeated. The Sioux Chief is here at the fort now,[34] he is a very inteligent looking fellow, tall, and straight. He wears a string of beads around his neck, to which is suspended in front a large medal of solid silver. On one side is the head of Andrew Jackson with his name and the date, (1829.) On the other, is the hand of a white man grasping that of an indian, a tommahawk and pipe, and the words, "friendship and peace"; it is the token of a treaty of peace between the whites and indians in Jackson's time. I have seen several such medals since we have been in this country. I remember of seeing one while on the march. it was in the possession of an old Cheif of the Cheyenne tribe. It had the head and name of Martin Van Buren on it. It is now night and I will quit for the present.

Morning 24th I have just been out with the drum corps practising, and will now finish my letter. Some excitement was raised in camp last night by the report that the Chief of the Crows had sent us word that he was coming down to clean out all the Govern't Posts along the road. He had heard that we were going to open a military road through his teritory in the spring, and he is determined that we shall not. Well the report receives but little credit among the knowing ones here, but even if it should prove true, the boys would like something of that kind, for a change. We have an idea, if they undertake to clean us out, that they will find us the nastiest thing they ever

---

[33] The Sioux and Crows were hereditary enemies, and during this period incursions of the former into the Crow country generally north of the Big Horn River often resulted in hostilities. See Olson, *Red Cloud*, p. 44.

[34] Here Johnson doubtlessly was referring to Red Cloud, one of the most powerful and influential Sioux leaders of that time. For a balanced biographical summary of Red Cloud, see *ibid.*, ch. 2.

undertook to clean yet. There is also a report in camp that we will leave this post and go to Denver City. The Officer in command there — we understand — has been ordered to Washington to answer the charge of incapability of holding office.[35] It has been reported that his men are undiciplined that he can do nothing with them at all, that he allows them to go about the City dressed in citizens clothes, and "many other things prejudicial to good order and military discipline." If the report is true, Col. Collins will go there and take command, and company G. will go with him. Nothing would suit us better. We would like to go there and stay six months, and then go somewhere else. to Utah for instance, or New Mexico. any thing but staying at once place all the time.

I will bring this to a close here. The mail leaves tomorrow I believe. . . . Write soon and tell about every thing around home.

Hervey Johnson

Fort Laramie, [Idaho Territory]
Mar. 8th 1864.

Dear Mother and Sister.

Your letters, of 1st mo. 27th and 2nd mo. 8th have come to hand. It had been nearly four weeks since I had got a letter from home and you may imagine that I was glad when I got these. I also got one from cousin Jared, and one from Sam Kinzer. Sam says he is detailed on the recruiting service and is going to Iowa for that purpose. I am well at present, though a part of last week, I thought I had something like the chills, but it is all over now.

---

[35] At this time the commander of the Military District of Colorado was Colonel John M. Chivington. The post commander at Camp Weld, also headquartered at Denver, was Major Edward W. Wynkoop. Wynkoop was critical of Chivington's handling of Indian affairs in Colorado Territory and made little effort to disguise his views. The result was that Wynkoop was transferred to Fort Lyon where he was stationed in late November 1864 when Chivington and a Colorado militia attacked the Southern Cheyennes and Arapahoes at Sand Creek. In 1865 Wynkoop was appointed United States Indian Agent for the Upper Arkansas Agency. Troops in the Department of Kansas, Major General Samuel R. Curtis, U.S. Army, Commanding, *The War of the Rebellion: A Compilation of the Official Records of the Union and Confederate Armies*, series I, vol. 34, pt. 2, p. 206. See also letter of December 8, 1864, n. 9.

A member of our company died last week. He was the oldest man in the company, had been sick in the hospital ever since we came here. He leaves a wife and family some where, to mourn his loss. The troops here have been all payed off. I received seventy-eight dollars, fifteen of which I had to pay the Sutler twenty two or three I had to pay to boys I owed. Several of the boys owed me some too, so that after my debts were all paid, and I got all that was coming to me, I have about fifty six dollars left. I gave fifty to the Paymaster and received a check which I enclose in this letter. The money can be received for it, on presenting it at the bank in Hillsboro. . . .

The Paymaster Mustering Officer, and Chief of Cavalry, started this morning for Denver City. They have been here about a week mustering in, inspecting, and paying off troops. The party I spoke of as going after a deserter, returned a few days ago but their bird had flown. they went to Denver City, but could find nothing of him They heard while there that he had been there, but the people not knowing that he was a Soldier, paid no attention to him.

A train of wagons passed up the platte some days ago. After they had been gone two or three days, a party of about forty men were armed and sent after them. The authorities here, suspected that they were conveying supplies of ammunition to the Indians. This is why the men were sent after them They returned a few days ago with about thirty kegs of powder, several hundred pounds of balls, shot, and lead, and about a bushel of percussion caps. It all was brought and put in the Magazine at this post, It appears that the owner of the train, had license to trade with the indians and sell them ammunition. The Government is bound either to allow them to buy ammunition or to furnish them something to subsist upon. I suppose Col. Collins thought that if the indians got this that they might turn it against us, or the emigrants, instead of using it killing game. The owner of the train, had a day set, and place appointed, to meet the natives and trade with them. No doubt they would feel more like attacking us now, after being disappointed in getting their ammunition, than they would if they had got it. Well, the owner lost nothing by being robbed, for the Gov't paid him for it all

Sibyl wanted to know when I am coming home. When I enlisted, it was with the understanding that we would be mustered out of service at the expiration of the term of the old Battalion.[36] But since we came here, we have been told that we have to remain three years in the service. If this is the case, I will be at home about two years from next fall. I only hope that the remaining two years and four months will pass away as fast in proportion as the first eight months have. It seems but a short time to me, that I have been in the service. Things may turn up, so that we may get discharged before our time is out. a great many think the war cannot last another summer, in case it does not of course we will all come home. If we, who, were mustered in, with the understanding that we were to serve the unexpired term of the old battalion — are not mustered out at that time, we are going to know the reason why. I understand that there is recruiting going on in Ohio for this service. If it is so please let me know who of my acquaintance have enlisted. Sibil asked me to write something for the literary. I shall do so when opportunity offers for something else than what will interest you at home. If you can get any thing out of any of my letters that would be fit for the purpose, you are at liberty to take it. I think you might afford to send me some specimens of your poetry, or literature, or, I should be happy to receive a copy of the paper edited by Moll and Semira. There was another big Indian dance here yesterday, but such things are getting old, they dont interest me now as much as they did at first

write soon, and write often.

Hervey Johnson.

---

[36] The "Old Battalion" was an informal designation for the First Battalion of the Sixth Ohio Regiment, which initially included Companies A, B, C, and D. Enrolled in the late summer and fall of 1861, this battalion was later designated the "First Independent Battalion of Ohio Volunteer Cavalry" and in the summer of 1863 was permanently attached to the Eleventh OVC. See Compiled Records Showing Service of Military Units in Volunteer Union Organizations, Ohio Cavalry, Records of the Office of the Adjutant General, RG 94, M 594, R 141, NA; *Official Roster of the Soldiers of the State of Ohio*, pp. 547–48; *History of Ross and Highland Counties, Ohio*, pp. 138–39.

Deer Creek Station

March 25, 1864 — October 23, 1864

In March 1864, when Hervey Johnson assumed his first "combat" assignment at Deer Creek Station, located approximately 100 miles northwest of Fort Laramie, relations between the Indians and the military were reasonably stable. This was largely due to the inclement weather and consequent paucity of emigration to the Bannock mines in Montana Territory and Mormon settlements in Utah Territory. It was, however, only a temporary respite, and with the inevitable melting of the winter snows and the sprouting of spring grass the situation changed rapidly. The Indians' reasonable concern about accelerating penetration of their hunting grounds was matched by violent confrontations to the south — confrontations involving the Southern Cheyennes and Arapahoes and the vociferous ranchers and miners of Colorado Territory that climaxed on November 29, 1864, when Colonel John M. Chivington attacked an undefended Cheyenne–Arapaho village at Sand Creek. Within a few short weeks Johnson and Company G of the Eleventh Ohio Volunteers were involved in a frustrating, guerrilla-like campaign against the Sioux of the north-central Plains.

An April 22, 1864, a detachment of the First Colorado Volunteer Cavalry under the command of Lieutenant Clark Dunn engaged the Cheyennes at Fremont's Orchard on the South Platte, some sixty miles northeast of Denver City. Generally recognized as the formal beginning of the Indian War of 1864, this bloody encounter aggravated the long-standing fear that a concerted uprising of Indians inhabiting the area from the central Colorado Territory to the southern watershed of the Powder River in Dakota Territory would disrupt vital telegraphic communications at a critical juncture of the Civil War and terminate overland transportation to the Pacific coast. In fact on occasion this did happen, confirming that this concern was not misguided.

Responding to the situation, Brigadier General Robert B. Mitchell, commander of the District of Nebraska (which included all military personnel stationed between Omaha and South Pass) held a parley at Fort Laramie in mid-April with such Sioux notables as Spotted Tail, Two Strikes, Two Crows, Big Mandan, Prickly Pear, and Eagle Twice of the Brulé and Oglala bands. Mitchell warned the Indians to stay away from the Platte valley, the overland routes, and the telegraph. It was up to the assembled tribal leadership to control the "bad men" among their ranks, and as an incentive toward this objective, Mitchell promised more bacon, blankets, and corn. The Indians, largely through the articulate words of Big Mandan, retorted that they had no intention of relinquishing the disputed area without reasonable compensation, and that they were tired of bad white men distributing "drunk-water" and cheating their people. The debate continued, but nothing very certain was agreed on, except that the contending parties should meet again at the same place in about fifty days.

Meanwhile, Johnson learned a great deal about the realities of frontier military life. He adjusted reasonably well to a simple diet and crude living quarters. He met Brigham Young, Jr., mistaking him for church President Brigham Young, Sr., and he responded uncritically to the attitude most gentiles (i.e., non-Mormons) entertained about the allegedly unwholesome character of the Mormons. He spent long hours cutting timber and hay, watching for white men (mostly Copperheads, in his opinion) who stole horses, mules, saddles, blankets, and clothing from the government with unrestrained abandon, and he displayed more than a casual interest in some of his more enterprising comrades who fleeced the emigrants in trade arrangements bringing them profits amounting to 200 percent.

Johnson also became more confident of his ability to fight the Indians, and in an important letter to his sister Sibyl, dated July 18, 1864, he admitted what could happen to a Quaker in Indian country: "I have often thought before I became a soldier that I would never try to kill or take the life of any one, but I have got over that notion now. I could shoot an indian with as much coolness as I would a dog, and I will do it if [I] can."

Deer Creek. Idah Ter.
[Dakota Territory]
Mar 25th 1864

Dear Sister.

Again after so long a time I have taken my seat for the purpose of writing home. When I wrote last we were on the point of leaving Fort Laramie. We left next morning after I wrote, the most of us had to walk, as our horses were out at the herd, and could not be got up in time   We went only twelve miles the first day, stopping at the Stone ranch an old building, built by the overland stage company, but unoccupied now except by two or three bull drivers who are making it their present residence while getting things in readiness to start for Banac City. Company E left the fort the same day that we did, but two or three hours after. They had a terible time before they got away. they were nearly all drunk. One of them was so drunk that he could not get on his horse. He was told to get on by a Sergeant, but being inclined to argue with the Serg't about it, the latter drew a revolver and shot him, the ball tore out one of his eyes but did not kill him; the Serg't was put under arrest and is now in the guard house awaiting his trial by court martial. The wounded man is getting along well. Another man was riding about over the fort with his revolver in his hand, menacing every one he met, (there was no load in it)   The officer of the day attempted to arrest him, but could do nothing with him. He drew his sword to strike the man, when he was knocked down by a blow on the head with the revolver. This brought things to a crisis. The Commander ordered Companies A. B. D. & G. under arms, expecting a battle with Co. E. The men were ordered to fire on Sulivan (the man who knocked down the Officer)   Something near a thousand shots were fired at him, but he being mounted, and his horse running at a full gallop only received one shot which took effect in his thigh   (He has since died from the wound)   Several balls passed through his clothes, and one wounded his horse very badly. You may wonder how two or three hundred men, could fire a thousand shots at a man, before he could get out of reach, on horseback, at full run. It was all done on the parade, a lot not larger than our orchard, and that befor he got half way across it. Two hundred men with the arms we have, can fire fourteen hundred shots in almost less than no time.

103

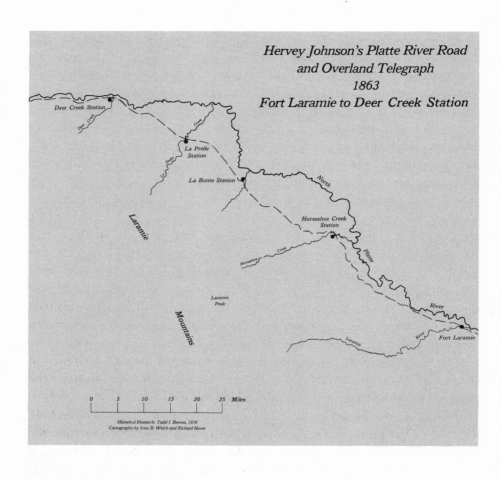

Hervey Johnson's Platte River Road
and Overland Telegraph
1863
Fort Laramie to Deer Creek Station

Deer Creek Station

Deer Creek

La Prelle Creek

La Prelle Station

La Prelle Creek

La Bonte Station

North

Horseshoe Creek Station

Horseshoe Creek

Platte

Laramie

Laramie Peak

Mountains

River

Laramie River

Fort Laramie

0   5   10   15   20   25   Miles

Historical Research: Todd I. Berens, 1978
Cartography by Ivan B. Welch and Richard Howe

Well things began to quiet down and Co. E. got started and got to the ranch about dark, there were half of them drunk then, but no further difficulty occurred. we made our beds down after supper, on the floor, a dirt floor it was, and about three inches deep in dust, which flew about in clouds when we would step about. We slept soundly, awoke next morning by three o'clock, got our "grub" and were off by daylight. We traveled twenty six miles that day, and stopped at a telegraph office called "horseshoe," on horseshoe creek Tom Cooper[1] and Joseph Ambrose,[2] a Hillsboro chap, constitute the garrison at this place. The road from Stone ranch to horseshoe is over a rough rocky country. A range of mountains lay off to our left at a distance of from eight to fifteen miles Our route lay along parallel to the platte river, but on account of the mountaneousness of the country, we lost sight of the river and did not come to it again till we were within eight miles of this post. The third night we camped on a creek called La Bonte (from a frenchman of that name) Dick Johnson[3] is my partner, we spread our blankets down under a tree, built up a big fire at our feet and went to bed, arose next morning, got our breakfast, and those who were on foot started off by daylight; we had thirty miles to go that day. We walked about ten miles against half past nine, and concluded that we were so tired that we would wait till the wagons came up and see if we could get to ride, as we knew that some of them started with corn, which must by this time be nearly used up, as there were something near a hundred horses and mules along with the outfit. The teams were hauling for Co. E. They came up in an hour, and we piled on to several wagons we rode ten miles and reached a creek called La parelle Here Co. E. concluded to camp for the rest of the

---

[1] See letter of August 29, 1863, n. 31.

[2] Private (Corporal) Joseph W. Ambrose, a native of Hillsboro, Ohio, served with the Sixtieth Regiment, Ohio Infantry, from September 13, 1861, until July 3, 1863, at which time he was enrolled in Company G, Eleventh OVC. Among other places, he served at Horseshoe Station and Fickland Telegraph Station. On March 30, 1865, he was charged with desertion, but the charge was removed and he was "furloughed" to enable him to enter the United States Military Telegraph Service. From January 7 until June 11, 1866, he was listed as "absent without leave." He was mustered out at Fort Leavenworth on July 14, 1866, and honorably discharged on February 8, 1867. Corporal Joseph W. Ambrose, CMF.

[3] Efforts to obtain the official military and/or pension files of Dick Johnson were unsuccessful. Military Service, Records Division, NA, to editor, February 27, 1973.

105

day. Our team and those of our Co who were mounted had gone on ahead to a creek called Box Alder, so we had ten miles yet to walk. We began to be the tiredest set of men you ever saw before we had gone far, we fooled along shooting at the telegraph poles and any thing else we could see. about an hour before sunset we came in sight of a smoke curling up from among the bushes, upon further examination we discovered the wagon. The boys had supper ready for us by the time we got there. We ate with a good relish. Some of the boys went a fishing, but I was so tired and sore that I laid down by some brush to sun myself. Night came on and we made our bed on the ground under a willow tree; we slept well, considering the wind which kept blowing all night.

next morning we got up, built a fire, cooked the fish the boys caught, and some "sowbelly" besides, for our breakfast, ate it and put out. The wind was very sharp, I had to tie my ears up with a handkerchief to keep them from freezing. After walking two or three miles, we came to the platte. The road here struck off up the platte bottom. Looking across, over the hills to the left of the river, we thought we saw a herd of deer or elk or something of the kind. We saw that the river made a turn to the left about four miles from where we were, and we concluded to go over and see what it was we saw. We had a very tiresome walk over hills and ravines, and all for nothing but to find out what a herd of ponies was. We kept on in the same direction and came to the river again, and soon came in sight of this place. It is a very pleasant place situated at the mouth of a small stream called Deer Creek. We all staid here, both Co E. and our own detachment. They all left in the morning but six of our company including a sergeant. we six constitute the garrison at Deer Creek Station. The Sioux Cheyennes and Arappahoes are the principal tribes that inhabit the country around us. They are all peaceable, a little too much so to suit me

Though I have finished one sheet, I do not feel that my stock is exhausted yet, quite. The other nine men of our Co, who came up with us, went on twentyeight miles further, to a post called platte Bridge. Co. E. go on and garrison Sweet Water Bridge, South Pass, Three Crossings and Upper Crossing. A detachment of Co E was here when we came, but they went away with the rest of the Co. A detachment of Co E. was at Platte Bridge also. The posts that Co E now garrison have been occupied by Co H. which has

106

been ordered to the Fort on account of there being so many desertions from it. We count on having a good time here this summer unless the Utes and Crows come down on us, which is hardly probable. We have nothing to do but hunt, fish and get firewood. One of the boys and I went the next day after we got here, about two miles up the river to get some wood. Cottonwood is all that [you] get to burn here. Pine and cedar are too far of in the mountains to be handy to haul. The third day I went fishing. I caught several good fish, from ten to fifteen inches long, the next morning I went hunting. didn't see anything but four sage hens and they flew too quick for me. The sage hen is a kind of grouse that stays among the sagebrush it is about the size of our common domestic hens. sage brush is a kind of shrub that grows almost everywhere along the rivers, on the hills, in the ravines and mountains it is from one to three feet high. It takes its name from its strong resemblance, both in looks and smell of our garden herb of that name. Day before yesterday I went fishing in the afternoon, caught several nice ones they were mostly pickerel, some of them were twenty inches long. They are equally as good a fish as the bass, or pike

When we were at Horseshoe on our road up here, we got news by telegrap that five of Co. H. had deserted. Three or four nights ago, one of our boys had occasion to be out rather late and he saw a man that he took to be one of them. We supposed that they were about here for no good purpose, and put a guard over the horses. In about an hour and a half we got a despatch from platte bridge, stating that Capt Shumans[4] deserters, were supposed to pass Deer Creek that night, for the Serg't to post his men in the right place and take the runaways. But the dispatch was two hours too late, "the birds had flown". Had we got word two hours sooner we might have caught them or "caught a tartar". The next night about ten o'clock word came to the serg't, to send three men down the road to Laparelle to stay with Jules Coffee,[5] a mountaineer, who was coming from the fort with

---

[4] Efforts to obtain the official military and/or pension files of Jacob S. Shuman were unsuccessful. Military Service, Records Division, NA, to the editor, May 9, 1977. Also see letter of March 9, 1865, n. 32.

[5] Jules Ecoffey, whose name was variously spelled "Coffey," "Ecoffe," and "Acoffay," was a Swiss trader and graduate of the University of Freiburg who, in association with Adolph Cooney, had been trading with the Sioux near Fort Laramie since 1854. He was a close friend of the Sioux Indians and enjoyed particular stature

the mail, and who it was supposed would be at that place, and might have information of the deserters. We sent word back that our horses were out with a pony herd. word came back that we must get the horses. There were two or three horses here that belonged to other companies. I asked the Serg't who must go to Laparelle. He said that Page, Kelley, and Johnson must go. I told him to see that the horses were got up and fed, and we would go to bed a while. We told him to wake us up at two o clock, for we would not go down there and stay all night in the cold where there was no house or any thing to shelter us. We went to bed and were called up at one o'clock.

By half past one, we were off, and a twenty mile ride before us. The night was cool, and I had the toothache bad enough to kill a horse, the sky was clear when we started, but when we got ten miles it began to snow. We got to the Laparelle an hour and a half before day light, we could not see anything of the wagon or anything else, it was snowing a perfect storm. We tied our horses to some brush, and laid down in the snow and went to sleep. We awoke by daylight, feeling pretty stiff and cold got our horses and left the road and went up the creek in search of a trappers cabin, which, we were informed, we would find up there somewhere, we thought it might afford us shelter from the storm if we could find it, and it might be that the mountaineer had camped there. After considerable search, we found the cabin, it was deserted, we tied our horses up, took off the saddles, put them in the cabin to keep them dry. with some matches we soon started a fire, took off our overcoats and gloves and dried them. One of the boys laid down his saddle blanket and we piled down on it and went to sleep. It was half after nine when we woke up, or thereabout, judging by the sun which, by this time was shining dimly through the clouds The storm was not yet over though somewhat abated. we waited awhile till we could see a streak of sky around to the northwest, when we saddled up and started back to the road, the snow ceased shortly after we left the cabin but the wind made it

among the followers of Red Cloud. Eventually at loggerheads with a number of Indian Bureau officials, Ecoffey was dismissed as an official agency trader by Red Cloud agent J. J. Saville in 1874. See James C. Olson, *Red Cloud and the Sioux Problem*, p. 160; Captain Eugene F. Ware, *The Indian War of 1864*, p. 201; and George E. Hyde, *Spotted Tail's Folk*, pp. 195–96.

disagreeably cold. We thought that by this time the mountaineer would pass the Laparelle and we would see his tracks in the snow; but when we got to the road no person had gone along, We waited round there a while, talked with an old indian who had his wigwam on the creek. He made us understand that three white men passed there two days ago, going towards the fort, but he had seen nothing of Jule the Mountaineer.

With this information, we thought it prudent to go somewhere where we could get something to eat and feed our horses with. Deer Creek being the nearest place we bent our heads in that direction. I recon it was ten o clock when we started home, we reached here about two. We had got about five miles on our way back, when we came on to a trail of five horses in the snow, as they were going the same direction that we were, we concluded to follow them, they left the road and went across the country we followed about four miles when the trail struck the road again; here we came in sight of them; there were two men or indians, with five ponies. We overtook them in sight of Deer creek and found them to be two hunters who lived at the post. They were returning hom with the results of the chase, which was five elk. They had it cut up and packed on ponies. We traded twelve pounds of bacon for sixteen of elk. We had some cooked for dinner to day. It tasted well. My sheet is full and I must quit write as often as you can.

Hervey

Direct your letters to Fort Laramie in the usual way

Deer Creek [Idaho Territory][6]
April 9th 1864.

Sister Abi

I have just finished washing the "dishes", and have seated myself to reply to thy long and interesting letter, which I received yesterday just one

---

[6] Located just east of present Glenrock, Wyoming, Deer Creek Station, on the route of the Oregon Trail, served as a Pony Express station prior to its designation as a telegraph station in 1861. According to one early telegraph operator, "Deer Creek was one hundred miles west of Fort Laramie, and twenty-eight miles east of where Casper was later situated. The Station had been in existence two years when I arrived

month from the day it was written; had I been at the Fort I would have got it a week sooner. I was very glad to hear from home. It had been three weeks since I had got a letter from any where. . . . The boys here are all well, with the exception of what the mountaineers call snow blindness, two of the boys have it. It is caused by looking continually at the snow. you may think that we need not look at the snow but if a man is out there is nothing but snow for him to look at.

About two weeks ago a man by the name of David Cotter went to the Fort from here with our mail, and to bring back what ther was there for us He got there, and back to within thirty miles of home when he was met by one [of] the Rocky Mountain snowstorms. The day set in warm and fine, but before noon there was appearance of rain, it rained but very little just a mere sprinkle, but by three o'clock it began to snow and blow. I never saw such a snowstorm before. we could not see two rods from the door. It continued this way that evening, all night and next day, and ceased sometime in the night. We thought no person could live in such a storm. There was Cotter twentysix miles from any house with a squaw and her children, (the family of an old trapper here.) I expected we would never see him again alive, but he managed to get through safe after being out through the whole of the storm. I have not heard yet whether any person perished or not. Two men went out into the mountains from here several days ago to hunt. They have not come in yet. I guess they have a shanty out there somewhere that they go into for shelter

The Operator went out day before yesterday to see what was the matter with the line. There had been no electric current, for two or three days, from the east. He tried all through the storm to get a current but could not except to the west. He was "called" by the Salt Lake Operator, and told to go out on the line and see what was the matter, for "business" was three or four

there as telegraph operator, and was used by the pony express and Holliday Stages. Bisonette had established the trading post there some time before my advent, but when I landed [there] in 1861 it bore evidence of having been inhabited, perhaps several years before." Three miles up Deer Creek from the telegraph station was the Upper Platte Indian Agency operated by Major Thomas S. Twiss. "Life of Oscar Collister, Wyoming Pioneer, as Told by Himself to Mrs. Chas. Ellis of Difficulty, Wyo.," *Annals of Wyoming*, vol. 7, no. 1 (July 1930), pp. 345–47. See also Paul C. Henderson, *Landmarks on the Oregon Trail*, p. 26.

days behind. Our operator told him that we were in the midst of a storm that no man could live in if he went out, and he told *us* he wouldn't go out to save the Pacific Telegraph Company[7] from breaking and he didn't, till the storm was over. But he found enough the matter with the line. The poles were down, the line broke and on the ground in several places.

The shanty that we live in here is an old concern built by the Overland Stage Company. It is built of cottonwood logs hewed, the cracks daubed with mud, a big fireplace fourfeet wide in one end, a door and window in the other, a box with shelves in it in one corner serves for a cupboard, one side of the room is occupied by our dinner table, this is used however for various purposes. We sit on it, lay on it, eat on it wash dishes on it write on it, put our pots and kettles on it &c. Its a very handy institution. The other side is occupied by our sleeping arrangements, they are made of pine and cottonwood poles, nailed and tied together so as to make a platform to lay our blankets on The floor of our house is made of hewed logs, the cracks filled in with mud to make it all level. When we want to clean up the floor we take a shovel. The roof is built or commenced after the style of a log cabin roof except that the rib poles are farther apart, then comes the rafters, these are round poles of pine with the bark shaved off smooth, there is philosophy in this, for when the poles are smooth there are fewer places for the bed bugs to harbor in. Well, the rafters instead of being two feet apart, are as close together as they can be placed. The whole thing is then shingled with a coat of mud and it is complete. The weather has moderated considerably, the snow is going off very fast, but still there is a bank in front of our door three feet deep. I would like to know how that ground is where the ditch was dug, is the ground dry or still wet? Did the ditch hold all the water that ran in it. Does it cave in and fill up. tell me all about it. What peice of ground are you clearing up. was that dirt that we hauled around the barn of any advantage, Has Dan Miller fixed up the fence all the way yet. How does the young orchard look. And the colt is it going to be of any account Have any of the "Old Ones" said anything in meeting yet about me going into the army. I would like to write more, that is some-

[7] For a summary of the construction phase of the Pacific Telegraph through present Wyoming, see Robert Luther Thompson, *Wiring a Continent*, ch. 25; James D. Reid, *The Telegraph in America*, pp. 490–97; J. Ross Browne, *Resources of the Pacific Slope*, pp. 434–37.

Drawing of Deer Creek Station in the 1860's. Note the telegraph repeater station in the lower right-hand corner. Artist unknown.
Courtesy of the Wyoming State Archives and Historical Department.

thing for your literary, but paper and envelopes are scarce and postage are "wanecha," and no person knows when there will be any there has been none at the fort for the last two months. what I got I bought of the boys. I think some of you might afford to send me some specimens of your poetry or dialogues or composition, or even a copy of your paper. If there is any thing that I have not asked about just write and tell me.

write soon.

Hervey

Deer Creek Idaho Ter
April 18th 1864.

Folks at home.

Having nothing to do this evening I thought I would write to you again. I am well with the exception of [a] toothache which is at times very troublesome The rest of the boys here are well. There are about a dozen men of Companies B. and D. here at this time. They are escorting some deserters to the fort. They are the same deserters that I spoke of in one of my letters[8] from this post. Two of them came in and gave themselves up at Sweetwater.[9] They did it they said to save their lives for they were on the point of starving to death They had got separated from the other three in some way and left with nothing to eat. I believe the other three were reported by some indians who had seen them. They were found near Rocky Ridge telegraph station.[10] Their feet were frozen and they were snow blind besides They

---

[8] See letter of March 25, 1864.

[9] Sweetwater was about forty-five miles due southwest of Casper on the Pony Express route near the Sweetwater Crossing of the Oregon Trail. A "long mile" east of famous Independence Rock, this remote frontier post was named after the Sweetwater River, which empties into the North Platte nearby. Henderson, *Landmarks on the Oregon Trail*, p. 38; Sweetwater Bridge Station File, Western History Research Center, University of Wyoming Library, Laramie.

[10] Also called St. Mary's Station, Rocky Ridge was located approximately 10 miles south of the Oregon Trail, about 300 miles west of Fort Laramie, and about 20 miles east of present South Pass City, Wyoming. It was burned by Indians on June 1, 1865. Grace Raymond Hebard and E. A. Brininstool, *The Bozeman Trail*, vol. 1, pp. 85–86; J. W. Vaughn, *The Battle of Platte Bridge Station*, p. 15.

114

offered no resistance to their captors. They were put in irons afew minutes ago by a Lieut of C. B. two of them have hand cuffs, the others ball and chain It is probable that one or two of them will be shot As the subject is not pleasant to dwell upon I will try to talk about something else.

We are well satisfied with our new place of residence. It has one drawback though and that is the irregularity of the mail. We however manage to be satisfied with it; we will perhaps on an average get a mail once in three weeks, but this needn't deter you from writing once a week. We have almost any thing here in the shape of fresh meat. Mountain sheep, Elk, and Bear. One of the boys killed a bear a few days ago in the mountains There are two or three more at the same place and I am going out to try my luck some of these days. a good fat peice of bear broiled or fried is as good as fresh pork some of the boys dont like it though. I have been learning the Sioux language a little, got so I can say (no—ea) (yes, tuh) (what—dah-coo) (come in, tel-mah-he-u) (sit down eah-tah-cah) &c. when I want to know an indians name, I ask him Da coo a escha ap so. If I wish to know what an indian wants I say, Da coo yat chee. If I want to know if he is married, I say, Gow-ee-chu yat too so. When I ask a squaw if she will marry me I say, Heegk ah nam ah zee. When I tell her I'll marry her, I say, Chee yu zink a tah. When I tell her I'll kiss her, I say, E che pu tah kah. If I want to know where an indian lives I ask him, Too-k-tae-yat-te-so. When I tell one I am going to his house, I say, Yah-te-kah-men-neck-tah, and when I tell him, I'm going home, I say, Wah zho nie tah ze. perhaps this will do for the present.

There is a store just across the road from us, but nothing much in it. It is owned by one Bisonnette[11] a frenchman, who has been in the mountains forty years. It is a little singular, but it is a fact that nearly all the mountaineers are natives of France They all have squaws for wives and [are] raising up families of halfbreeds. some of as pretty children as I ever saw are halfbreeds; they are of a brunette complexion, with black eyes, as sparkling as chrystal and hair, and eyebrows of the same color. And they

---

[11] The more common spelling of this French trader's name was Bisonette. In addition to his extensive trade with the Sioux of the Powder River and Pole Creek areas, Joseph Bisonette operated a scow ferry on the North Platte, using the force of the current to propel his vessel. "Life of Oscar Collister," pp. 345–47.

are smart too and would make respectable citizens if taken to the States and educated I have a notion to bring one home with me when I come, if I can get one. Here they grow up in ignorance and degradation. I do not know of but one or two halfbreeds who seem to care any thing about white men or learning the English language. One is Joe Bisonette, the son of our neighbor across the road; he dresses like white men and wants to be a white man, speak english, wears fine white shirts and fine boots like a real dandy, but he is not very talkative. Mitch Buazer is another, but he can talk and make himself as free among whites as if he was one himself. Pete Bisonette, Joes brother wont speak a word of English he runs with the indians and dont care for anything.[12]

There is a missionary station about four miles up deer creek. they are Germans and poory calculated to teach the natives. Old Major Twiss,[13] a retired officer of the regular army lives up the creek above the missionaries. he has an indian wife and several children but he is bringing them up right, he won't allow them to speak a word in their own language, dresses them like white children, teaches them white manners, and is going to take them to the states to give them an education. There is some what of a curiosity just across the creek half a mile from our house, in the shape of the burning hill. It is close on the creek. I went over to see it one day. It is a coal bank on fire[14] it is about fifty feet above the bed of the creek; it has been burning

---

[12] Pete Bisonette's apparent preference for the life-style of the Oglala Sioux doubtlessly contributed to Red Cloud's confidence in Joe Bisonette as an interpreter at important parleys with the federal government. See Olson, *Red Cloud and the Sioux Problem*, p. 136.

[13] Major Thomas S. Twiss replaced John W. Whitfield as Upper Platte Indian Agent in 1855. Following his replacement by Joseph A. Cody in 1861, Twiss, a West Point graduate and former officer in the regular army, took his Indian wife and children to live with the Sioux of the Powder River country. Edward E. Hill, "Upper Platte Agency, 1846–1870," in *Historical Sketches for Jurisdictional and Subject Headings Used for the Letters Received by the Office of Indian Affairs, 1824–1880*, pp. 2–3; Ware, *The Indian War of 1864*, p. 463; Alban W. Hoopes, "Thomas S. Twiss, Indian Agent of the Upper Platte, 1855–1861," *Mississippi Valley Historical Review*, vol. 20, no. 3 (December 1933), pp. 353–64.

[14] The apparent mineral resources of the upper Platte country were of considerable interest to travelers. Stansbury, in 1849, commented about an important coal "cropping" near Deer Creek, and in 1860 Sir Richard Burton reported, "The banks of the [North] Platte were stained with coal; it has been known to exist for some years, but has only lately been worked. Should the supply prove sufficient for the wants of

since eighteen hundred fifty. The coal lays on a bed of solid sand stone. It has burnt back from the bank of the creek and the earth and stones that lay on the coal fall in as the coal burns under it. The ground over the bank is full of large cracks through which hot steam and smoke issues constantly. There is one coal bank in the bottom of the creek, it is full of huge knots and forks of trees petrified. Some of them only half petrified. I might fill another sheet but I will leave it till next time   Now dont forget to write three or four times a week.

Hervey Johnson

Deer Creek. [Idaho Territory]
April 22nd 1864.

Sister Sybil

Assistant Surgeon Ziegler arrived here this morning, on his way from the fort to Sweet Water. He brought me *one letter!!!!* It was written just one month ago. I was very glad to hear from home again. I get, on an average one letter in three weeks   I dont know where the letters that you write *one a week*, go to, I "cant see 'em from where I stand". perhaps they were not written to *me.* That's the reason perhaps that I dont get them   Any how I have no reason to doubt that you write one each week, and perhaps half a dozen, I don't know. By the way, did you ever get a letter from me, written on board the Steamer Sioux City? or one I wrote last winter with some flower seeds in it? I have no account in any letter yet from home, of either of these two letters.

I am well as common. I understand that the scurvy is very bad at the fort. none of us have it yet and I think there is no danger from it here   It is caused by the salt provisions that the Gov't furnishes. Here we have fresh meat, dessicated vegetables; and wild onions all we want. yes, and dried pumpkin too, I forgot. I got it of a Spaniard at the Cheyenne village, day before yesterday. He brought it from Mexico to trade to the indians for robes. There were three of us went up to the village   It is on the Platte

---

the settlers, it will do more towards the civilisation of these regions than the discovery of gold." Howard Stansbury, *An Expedition to the Valley of the Great Salt Lake of Utah*, p. 49; Sir Richard Burton, *The Look of the West, 1860*, pp. 173–74.

about 17 miles above here. we started about eight in the morning. As we came near the village, the hills and ravines were literally covered with ponies. we soon reached town hitched our horses in some brush near the river and took a walk to see the town. The natives manifested much curiosity at our guns. They thought they were big medicine. Every thing that they cant comprehend they call medicine (pah-zu-tah.) I never saw the like of little dirty, ragged, half clothed, and naked pappooses before, they were all sizes ages and sexes. There are about two hundred and eighty teepee's and I recon about a thousand indians, including old and young, bucks and squaws. The bucks were sitting around in little groups talking trade, while the squaws were occupied dressing robes, cooking, putting up their wigwams, and other *household duties.* One squaw got one of the boys to help her put up her teepe while her old man sat by and laughed at him. it made me mad enough to knock the old fool over but it is just the way with the brutes, there an't one of them that will get a stick of wood, make a fire, put up a wigwam, pack or unpack the ponies, or any thing else like work, the squaws do every thing. I have seen a squaw carry a sled load of wood on her back for two miles, while her buck was loafing about the store. (ig) Noble sons of the forest indeed but I believe I was saying something [about] the village.

Well an Indian village is not like a human village The latter is stationary, always seen in the same place. The former is wherever it suits the inhabitants to put it The one I spoke of has only been there three or four days I dont know where it came from. It will stay where it is perhaps a month then go some where else. They brought it there for the more convenience of trading with the whites, there are seven different traders there. The principal commodities of the indians are robes and moccasins, deer, beaver, antelope, and elk skins, ponies, and squaws. in exchange for these they receive coffee (pahzutah sappah) (sugar, chehumpah) (corn, wah a maiza) (all kinds of cotton goods, minnie cooah) (blankets, she-nah ho tah) and other articles of traffic. We got tired of staying there and started home.

on our way back one of the boys shot a prarie dog but it managed to flounder about till it got to its hole, then *how are you dog.* They allways manage to get into their holes if they are killed a rod from them. as we came on further we met about a dozen wagons and fifty men on their way to Banac. They said they wer from Wisconsin, Illinois, Iowa, Ohio &c *It was'nt visible to us.* The men were all walking except the teamsters. We thought they would make splendid infantry, they stood walking well, had only walked a thousand miles, and five hundred more to walk. I expect they thought like we did, but not fancying the name or the calling of *infantry* changed it to that of *emigrant* by making tracks for Bannac in order to avoid the draft. I think they were from Missour and other copperhead localities, for they are nearly all copperheads. I look for the biggest kind of a *stink* to be stirred up this summer along here, if they spit out much of their treason in our presence. there are only six of us but we consider ourselves a *big thing*, whether copperheads can *see it* or not.

Emigration has commenced a month earlier this year than common seventy-five strong able bodied men have already gone by here. I am going to keep count of how many pass through the summer they have made a fair beginning. Three of the boys have gone up to the indian village to day. They went to deliver a message to the traders concerning the expedition fitting out at the fort for opening an emigrant road to Banac. The message instructs them to say nothing about it to the indians. I suppose Collins[15] dont want them to know he's coming. I dont know whether I will have to go or not. It is probable that I will though because I belong to the battery. I would like to go, but not under Col. Collins. I may be deceived but I dont think he is the man to command an expedition of that kind. I would prefer being under an Officer of the regular army one who has been out here and who understands indian *tactics.* There are a great many emigrants waiting now at the fort for Collins to start with his outfit [There was][16] a small battle between the first Colorado [Cavalry and the] Cheyennes near a place called Fremonts Orchard [on the] South Platte between Julesburg and Denver somewhere,[17] two Colorado boys were killed and several wounded.

---

[15] Colonel William O. Collins. See letter of October 18, 1863, n. 3.

[16] The bracketed words have been added because there is a corner missing on the original letter.

[17] The engagement took place on April 22 about three miles above Fremont's Orchard, which was located on the banks of the South Platte approximately eighteen miles west of present Fort Morgan, Colorado. It involved fifteen mounted troops under the command of Lieutenant Clark Dunn of the First Colorado Cavalry and a

the indians left nine killed and a good many more wounded. They had been stealing cattle and committing depradations on the ranches along the river and the soldiers went out to punish them the indians managed to get away with fifteen cattle. But the soldiers are still after them. one hundred men and two peices of artilery were sent out from the fort to cut off their retreat and capture them if possible. The news didn't cause any excitement here. I am writing in the telegraph office. The bell has rung and I must go to supper.

23rd. I now resume to finish my letter. More emigrants passed to day, and there will be more tomorrow or the next day. I dont know hardly what to write, I guess I'll tell what we had for dinner to day. Three of us went out and got a pan full of onions. these we had sliced, and salted, and pepered, and vinegared, they were splendid. then we had cold bread, and hot Coffee (Our cows havent got to coming up yet or we would have milk.) but the best thing we had was *baked bear*, and the next was a good appetite. Bear meat, I think is hard to beat, that is, the way we cook it. I'll just tell you how to cook it, so if you catch a bear this summer you need be at no loss how to manage it. In the first place [boil it until it is] about done, then pour off the water, and [have some] more water ready hot, to put in again, then if [it] has not been salted, put in some salt, and let it [boil] a few minutes. When you think it boiled enough, take it out and put it in a dutch oven, put a little bacon fat over it and some peper and bake it till brown over the top, it is then fit for use. This is supposed to *be* very *interesting to you.*

Sybil, I promised to send thee a pair of moccasins a good while ago, and I am almost ashamed to say any thing about it now. I still intend to send them yet, as soon as I can get them. I have been disappointed about them two or three different times. I got a pair of Sioux moccasins the other day that I intend sending to Warren. I think they will just fit him. he may get

---

small band of Southern Cheyennes and is generally recognized as the beginning of the Colorado-Kansas Indian War of the 1860's. The two "Colorado boys" killed here were J. G. Brandly and A. F. Baird. Contrary to Lieutenant Dunn's assertion that "some eight or ten of the Indians" were killed, the Indians insisted that only three braves were wounded. See Report of Captain George L. Sanborn, April 12, 1864, *The War of the Rebellion: A Compilation of the Official Records of the Union and Confederate Armies,* series I, vol. 34, pt. 1, pp. 883; Stan Hoig, *The Sand Creek Massacre,* pp. 37–42.

them the next mail after this. I will try to get a pair of Snake moccasins for thee. There is a squaw living near us that makes nice ones. I shant promise when I can get them. I would like very much if you would step in some of these days and take dinner with us. I think when I get home I will go to keeping house by myself   I believe I can cook good enough now, anyhow I will against my time is out. I will dispense with that Indispensable article called a wife if I do. This is supposed to be put in merely to fill up the sheet. I want you to continue to write once a week.

Hervey.

Deer Creek [Idaho Territory]
May 2nd 1864.

Sister Sybil

Bob the Sutler's clerk arrived here yesterday from the Fort with the mail. He brought me one letter from Lydia J Moon. It was in reply to one I wrote to her on last Christmas day. Those letters that you write "every week" there at home are still invisible to me. Perhaps I'll get them all at once some of these days, but for my part I'd rather take them one at a time, then they'll last longer, but any way to suit the mail carriers, as I said before I'm content, or might as well be.

Well, since I wrote last I have been over the country some   Last first day John Page[18] and I went up to Platte Bridge thirty miles above here with Doc Ziegler. Doc rode Page's horse and Page rode in the ambulance. We stopped at the Cheyenne village about an hour, looking around. Then Doc and I rode on ahead to the Arappaho village six miles further   We found the village up a ravine at the foot of the mountain about four miles from the road on the left as we go up. There were about a hundred tepees. there were two or three traders there. Doc an I walked about to see how the natives employed themselves, we passed near a little group of squaws very attentively engaged at something. I stopped to see what they were doing.

---

[18] A native of Highland County, Ohio, Private John W. Page was employed as a schoolteacher prior to his enlistment in Company G, Eleventh OVC, in June 1863. Most of his service was at Deer Creek as a telegraph operator for the Pacific Telegraph. On July 14, 1866, he was honorably discharged at Fort Leavenworth. Private John W. Page, CMF.

I found they were gambling. They had a shallow willow basket with a raw hide bottom in it, in the basket were several little dice or triangular stones with spots and marks on them, by striking the bottom of the basket on the flesh side of a buffalo hide, which was spread on the ground for the purpose, the stones would bounce and fall, then by the number of spots up, or by some laws of the game which they understood themselves, they would decide who was winner; in this way they kept beads, spoons, sticks, knives and forks, and other articles constantly changing hands. Another object took my attention, it was a group of young squaws, apparently from twelve to fifteen years old. I watched them a moment, and what do you think they were doing. Nothing much but picking the lice off of each other and eating them, a simple innocent amusement I thought — neah seeche, wapalooski otah (you are mean and lousy) in the Sioux language. I couldn't think in Arappaho. I dont know what Doc thought, in several tents they were playing cards, and carrying on various kinds of amusements. In some we found squaws that were real good looking, and men the same way We saw some great strapping big luxurious fellows lolling about the lodges with out a particle of clothing except a strap around the waist and a rag six or eight inches wide tucked under it behind and before. I soon got tired of staying there and wanted to go on but Dock wanted to stay all night with the traders. I finally concluded to go and he concluded to stay.

Instead of going back to the road I put off across the country in the direction of the [Platte] bridge.[19] In going over the hills I could see far to the north west like a huge sun tipped thunder cloud piled up against the sky, and stretching as far to the north as the eye could reach, the snowy tops of

---

[19] Platte Bridge Station was erected in May 1858 on the south side of the North Platte at the present town of Casper, Wyoming. From 1840 until the Mormons established a ferry at this point in June 1847, the crossing was known as Camp Platte. Platte Bridge Station became a permanent post in 1865, and on November 21 of that same year was renamed Fort Caspar in honor of First Lieutenant Caspar W. Collins who, on July 26, 1865, was killed by Indians in the Battle of Platte Bridge. It should be noted that the present spelling of Casper, Wyoming, was a consequence of the erroneous spelling of Caspar in early government reports. After Fort Caspar was abandoned in the fall of 1867, the 1,000-foot bridge built by Louis Guinard in 1859, as well as the post buildings, were burned by Indians. Robert W. Frazer, *Forts of the West*, pp. 179–80; Vaughn, *The Battle of Platte Bridge*; Agnes W. Spring, *Caspar Collins, The Life and Exploits of an Indian Fighter of the Sixties.*

the Wind River Mountains. I traveled several miles and came back to the road in sight of the bridge, got to the bridge two hours before sundown. There are twelve men of Co G. garrisoning the bridge, the bridge is a strong structure built wholly of pine from the mountains. it rests on about thirty or forty piers built up square of pine logs and filled in with stone. The owner of the bridge is a frenchman living in New York All emigrants who pass over the brige have to pay from three to five dollars per team, Goverment teams fifty cents each. soldiers passing and repassing, go over free.

The next morning after we got to the brige several of us concluded to take a hunt. we rigged up a wagon, put in robes and blankets and provisions for two or three days. We set out across the river, took across the country to the northward, and at the distance of six or seven miles we came in sight of antelope, elk and deer, but the country was so level that it was impossible to get near them, after fooling away half the day and getting but two or three shots at the game, we started in a southwest direction for the platte river. After some time we reached the river at a place called the Red Butes.[20] These are two huge mountains with thinly scattered pines over them. The bases of them are of red rock or earth, the red earth reaches for several hundred yards up the sides of the mountain. The river flows through a narrow passage between them. The scenery is beautiful. To stand off at a little distance, it is impossible to see where the river comes from; the place appears to be walled in by high mountains through which it looks like there was no opening at all. One would think that the river flowed through a tunnel if he didnt know better. Well we soon began to think a bout getting something to eat. We had a grouse that one of the boys shot, but could find no wood to cook it without going several miles up the mountain. we finally pulled up some sage brush and started a fire made our coffee broiled our grouse, then eat our dinner. we laid around there some time resting ourselves and grazing the horses. One of the boys went off up the river to look

---

[20] Red Buttes was located on the south side of the North Platte, approximately twenty miles southwest of present Casper, Wyoming. The numerous terraces and headlands surmounted what appear to be simulated, turreted castles and were apparently named by early fur trappers. Robert Stuart and his returning Astorians camped near Red Buttes in October 1812. According to Jim Bridger's survey of 1866, the Bozeman Trail left the Oregon Trail at this point. See Henderson, *Landmarks on the Oregon Trail*, p. 36 Hebard and Brininstool, *The Bozeman Trail*, vol. 2, p. 121.

for ducks, he came on a grizly bears track in the brush, he followed it for some distance till it turned off to the north, when he came back to us. We were consulting whether to stay out there that night or not, when it began to blacken up in the west and soon huge masses of cloud began to roll up from behind the mountains threatening a storm. This in connexion with the knowledge that grizly bears were in close proximity induced us to think of starting for the bridge, from which we were about ten miles distant. we were soon on our way   the road lay along down the river for some distance, it was very rough on account of having to cross so many ravines that broke down from the mountains. The road finally left the river and crossed over a spur of the mountain that ran down near to the river side. There was some of the awfulest roads I ever saw. I don't see how so many emigrants go over them with as much safety as they do. We got back to the bridge with out getting much wet and thus ended our hunt. We staid at the bridge till ten next day and started home. got home two hours before sundown. I must close. Please write soon. Persevere and *continue to write every week.*

Hervey

Deer Creek. Idaho [Territory].
May 7th 1864

Sybil.

As it is always my style to sit down and answer a letter when I get one, I have acted on that principle to day, first answering a letter that I received from near home, then writing one home. The letter I received was in reply to one I wrote on the thirteenth of March, the letter was written on the fifteenth of April, was two weeks coming to the Fort, it generally takes a week to come from the fort. It seems to me that you are very neglectful there at home or you dont direct your letters right, something must be wrong or I certainly would get a letter once in a while. Well as I have said I must be satisfied. When the mail comes and brings no letter from home for me I just have to get one of my old letters and read it. It aint as good as a new letter of course but it is the best I can do

I am well at present. There is no news of importance. Emigration continues to pour along in a continual stream. copperheads are plenty. They

124

cant see a soldier, aint interested in anything that concerns the soldiers. We thought awhile back that we were going to have some trouble and we may have yet from the south platte Cheyennes. We understand that they are being pursued by colorado soldiers and are trying to get on the north side of the north Platte. It is supposed that they are now laying behind the mountains waiting an opportunity to come out and get across the river We do not know at what point they will cross the river, it is thought by some that here is the place others think at a creek ten miles above here, or ten below at another creek. it is hardly probable that they will cross near a military post. They may and I think it most probable that they will go up along the mountain chain to the Red Bute Canon (pronounced — canyon) forty miles above here and there they can come out from behind the mountain. It is impossible now and will be for some time for them to get over the mountain on account of the passes being snowed up. all the trouble we anticipate is from their depradations on stock, for they will be very apt to steal horses or cattle, or if they should catch a man out alone and off his guard, they would be apt to go for his hair We are not afraid of them attacking us, but if they attempt doing any mischief in our neighborhood, somebody will be apt to get hurt.

The remainder of Co. G. will soon leave the fort for this place and Platte Bridge something near two hundred soldiers are coming in to the fort from the states. nineteen I hear are for Co. G. Several boys are coming also who were left sick along the road, some at St Louis some at Ft Leavenworth, some at Ft. Kearney &c. For my part I think there is all the men at this post that is necessary. at least I wish there would no more come, things will go harder a great deal where there is more men than where there is few. I feel like I am about played out at letter writing. I know that you would not have me quit. Indeed I sometimes feel discouraged about it. Well its impossible to feel any other way when a fellow writes a letter every week and only gets one in three weeks. you may think I have an awful sight to say about not getting letters. The fact of it is when a man gets played out — and nothing will play him out quicker than what I've mentioned above here — it is not supposed that he has a very large stock of ideas on hand and such as he thinks he is aptest to write. I hope this will account for the very frequent repetition of the old song that I have been sounding in your ears.

125

I feel more like I was played out than ever. It must be near ten o clock and I must quit. there are some boys going to the fort in the morning they will take my letter This is the first time I believe that I ever left a blank page. I am too sleepy to write any more. Now don't forget to be sure and write to me every week it may be some satisfaction to your selves if to no one else.

Hervey.

Direct to Deer Creek
via Fort Laramie.

Deer Creek [Idaho Territory]
May 15th, 1864

Folks at home.

I have no grumbling to do this time, for yesterday the remainder of Co G. came up and brought me four letters. One from mother acknowledging the reception of a government check from me, (the letter bears no date.) One from Sibil of April 18th, one from Warren of April 24th, and one from [————] april 20th. In regard to the check — if something has not already been done with it — I will leave it with uncle John to draw the money or retain the check, according to his own judgment. I could have used the money shortly after I sent it home, if I could have had it again, and with good advantage too.

I am well, tho' I am considerably fatigued with waiting on a sick man. I have been for five days and nights in the sick room. The man is a telegraph operator from Salt Lake City he is a Mormon, He came here to take this office two weeks ago, he was unable to walk or help himself then. he had a black man to wait on him when he came but drove him off because he wanted pay for his services and because he was too independent to take all his abuse He told him that he was nt going to pay him any thing, that the soldiers would wait on him for nothing that they were paid by the Gov'nt for waiting on telegraph operators &c. well when the nigger left I guess he waited on himsef for about a day, when the Serg't concluded that it was too bad to let the man lay there alone and suffer so he went in and talked with him, and agreed to wait on him for a dollar a day. He attended him for two days and nights and got sick himself; then another waited on him three days and nights and he got sick, then he went two days without any attendance of any account when we concluded we would take it day about waiting on him. I took it the first day, then another boy took it, and the boy whose turn came on the third day would'nt go so I went myself and staid with him till this morning when he was taken to the hospital at the fort by some Mormons who were going east from Salt Lake. O! he was the awfulest looking specimen of humanity I ever saw. five dollars per day would be no compensation for waiting on him. he was swelled all over as tight as his skin would stretch we could scarcely touch him without hurting him, but still we had to lift him and turn him over twenty times a day. Some times he would lay for hours and groan and swear and curse and call on his Maker. for the last night and day he had no control over himself so that I had to stand by and clean him with chips and rags, he nastied the bed and himself up so and to make it like the mormons, the pup went off with out paying us a cent for our trouble.

Mother talked of it being very wet in Ohio this spring. we have had but very few showers this spring yet of any account, it had been nearly twenty four months since rain had fallen in some parts about here. Emigration continues to pour along, sometimes as high as one hundred twenty wagons pass in one day. You seem to feel sad at the report that the recruits for the west are to take our places and hold these posts while we who have been drilled are to be sent to Texas.[21] Well now we would like to have a little texas or mexico or salt Lake in ours, but there is no prospect of getting it, I dont know who would start and circulate such reports. . . .

Warren wishes to know how the fish get up here in these parts when the Platte river is dry in the fall; there is nothing curious at all about this though the river is dry for hundreds of miles during the summer and fall. The fish ascend in the spring during high water and those found here in the winter

---

[21] Here Johnson is referring to the abortive Union effort to invade the Red River country, March 12–May 20, 1864. While most of the fighting in this campaign took place in northwest Louisiana, the ultimate objective was the Union seizure of Texas. Because the Union suffered high casualties (a total of 8,162), it is understandable that volunteers such as Johnson and his Ohio comrades feared a speedy transfer to a more dangerous theater of war. See Ludwell H. Johnson, *Red River Campaign: Politics and Cotton in the Civil War*, pp. 5, 277–88.

and spring are some that stay here during the summer and fall. Because the Platte river is dry at a certain time, it does not follow that all its tributaries are dry at the same time. The traveler will notice as he ascends the Platte river, that the first water he sees is in little pools about over the bed of the stream further up it is like a sluggish little stream which widens and deepens as he advances towards its head and finally assumes the appearance of a small river. Up in this country the water runs all the year and there are plenty of holes for the fish. . . .

[Hervey]

Deer Creek Idaho Ter.
May 26th [18]64

Sister Sybil

As is usual with me after the *mail* comes in I have taken up the pen to write. The arrival of the mail happened to day just before noon. some of the boys got letters, but I did n't. I didn't look for any, shant look for any for three or four weeks, then I intend to look for three or four. I dont expect I can see 'em from where I stand though, as Deer Creek has been heretofore, an unfavorable place to look from. As this is not supposed to be interesting I will not enlarge on it.

I am well and have been. I dont believe I can write any thing that will be of interest. We have had some very wet weather since I wrote last. Our mud shingled shanties leak like a brush roof, the muddy water just pours in, it has been sprinkling some to day but cant make out to rain much. the weather is cool for the time of year, vegetation has begun to look green, it's early aint it? Emigration still continues to pour along, from both east and west, large trains of Mormons are passing continually, going to the states to bring back goods and also those "Saints" who are so unfortunate as not to be cumbered with an extra amount of this world's goods. There are thousands of these poor Saints brought across the plains every year, by teams that are sent for them from Salt Lake. A large train of them has just passed, going to the east for that purpose. Those Mormons who passed here and took our operator away were missionaries going to Europe to promulgate the "gospel" among the "gentiles" A man by the name of *Brigham Young*[22] *was* along with them, I talked with him without the least timidity, didn't feel at all like I was in the presence of holy men, in fact I didn't think he was any better man than I was The reason they go to Europe to preach I suppose is because it is too unhealthy a place in the United States for the spread of "religion". The people of the U.S. cant see it in the same light that Brigham does. Well, it verifys the scripture where it says "A prophet is not without honor except in his own country". A great many are leaving Salt Lake for "keeps", they are refugees from Mormon tyranny, a train of these passed a few days ago, they had been in Utah twelve years and could not get away till now. General Conner,[23] who has command of the troops west of the rocky mountains told Brigham if he didn't let people leave salt lake that wanted too, that he would blow the city to atoms. Brigham believes it I

---

[22] Johnson erroneously believed he had met Brigham Young, Sr., second president of the Church of Jesus Christ of Latter-day Saints, but in fact the person was Brigham Young, Jr., born December 18, 1836, in Kirtland, Ohio, to Mary Ann Angell and Brigham Young, Sr. The elder Young could not have been in the vicinity of Deer Creek in late May 1864 since in the spring of that year he journeyed to Cache Valley, up Bear River to Paris, and then back to Fish Haven in present northeastern Utah and southeastern Idaho. The dates for this journey were May 16–26, 1864. By June 1 he had returned to his farm home near the Great Salt Lake to celebrate his sixty-third birthday. On the other hand, Brigham Young, Jr., had returned to Salt Lake from his first English mission in the early months of 1863, and less than a year later was called back to England with Daniel H. Wells to preside over the European mission. The two men and their wives left Salt Lake City on April 30, 1864, and sailed from New York on July 11. The chronology of their eastward journey across the Overland Trail corroborates Johnson's account of the meeting at Deer Creek Station. See Preston Nibley, *Brigham Young: The Man and His Work*, pp. 390–39; Dean C. Jessee, ed., *Letters of Brigham Young to His Sons*, pp. 19–20, 46–47.

[23] Brigadier General Patrick E. Connor was born in County Kerry, Ireland, and came with his parents to New York City at an early age. He enlisted in the army at the age of nineteen, distinguished himself as a captain during the Mexican War, and then joined the gold rush to California. On July 6, 1862, he assumed command of the Military District of Utah. Always active in various mining enterprises, this activity dominated his interest in Utah after he was mustered out on April 30, 1866. He came to be recognized as "the father of mining in Utah," where he died on December 17, 1891. See LeRoy R. and Ann W. Hafen, eds., *Powder River Campaigns and Sawyer's Expedition of 1865*, p. 23, n. 10. A general biography of Connor is Fred B. Rogers's, *Soldiers of the Overland, Being Some Account of the Services of General Patrick Edward Connor and His Volunteers in the Old West.*

guess, anyhow Conners camp[24] is on a bench of the mountains overlooking the city and that has a very good moral effect, though they did stop a train of refugees this spring but troops were sent out from fort bridger who sent them on their way rejoycing and sent the Mormons back to salt lake with their tail feathers drooping. Uncle Sam is going to have a little job of cleaning up to do over there when he gets through with the south. I know of more than one man who would like to have a hand in the job.

The operator who was taken away from here may claim aline, all that can be [said] of him is that a solitary grave fifteen miles from here marks the final resting place of his mortal remains. As nothing good can be said of him, I will "no further seek his merits to disclose, or drag his frailties from their dread abode."

Twentyseven of our Company are here now, we see a good deal harder times now since they came than we did before. The Bannock expedition has blown up, emigrants are going through on their own hook. I want to know if you have to pay for my letters when you take them out. I got twenty five envelopes stamped at the fort like the one is that this letter is in, paid 75 cts for it. A great many of the boys did the same, and thier friends write back their letters are marked paid, but they have to pay for them before they can get them. no postage stamps to be had at the fort nor has been for five months. there is a swindle some where paying postage twice on a letter is more than is fair. write soon.

Hervey.
(write every week.)

Deer Creek. [Dakota Territory]
June 1st 1864

Sybil.

I have just been out fishing, and as I had a little time this evening, and as a man is going to start to the fort tomorrow, I thought I would write a letter for him to take down. . . .

---

[24] Here Johnson was referring to Camp Douglas, which was established October 26, 1862, on a bench just north of Red Butte Creek, overlooking Salt Lake City. Originally designed to protect the Overland Mail and Telegraph and to watch over the Mormons, the post was named after Senator Stephen A. Douglas. It was designated a fort on December 30, 1878. Frazer, *Forts of the West*, p. 166.

It has begun to rain since I sat down to write. We have had fine warm weather for several days past till this evening; we were up the creek fishing and the appearance of rain drove us in. We did not have much luck fishing, our seine was too short and the water too rapid to do much. We caught enough for one good mess for thirty men. We have been living on venison and antelope for several days. Some of the boys were out hunting two different times lately, the first time they brought in a deer and antelope. the second time they brought a deer a bear and twelve mountain grouse. There is a party going out tomorrow again. I am going to try to be one of them. I want to get a shot at a bear, they are thick in the mountains. I dont think I'll do like some of the boys when they see one, that is, let the bear take off in one direction and they take the other.

Albert[25] came up a few days ago from the fort, he had gone out with the escort of a surveying expedition, and they having run short of rations, he with three more men were sent back to the fort for more. When they got there the Col. thought he would send someone else back with the provisions; so they came up to the company   Al showed me his duck's *ghost*. It looks quite natural I think, all the boys that saw it think it is splendid; none of them know who it is but me. They all declared they had seen her somewhere. I told them no doubt they had, for she had often been there   Mat in her letter told Al that Sis Millner sent her "respects to Hervey and would like to hear from him". I'm up a stump, I'll eat molasses if I ain't. I don't know what her post office address is. I wish I did; what must I do. something may turn up yet. This is leap year, and I know what I'd do if I was a woman. If I could only see Kiah Sanders, he could tell me what I want to know, I wrote a letter or two for Kiah but I have forgotten where I directed them to. I have meant no harm by what I've written here, and I hope it will go no further than our own family. I must commence to come to a close if I can find anything to close with. It is said that an old lady by the name of Grant is going to the new gold region. Her name is Emma I'm told, Emma Grant. I'd like to see Emma once more. The fact of it is, about two thousand Emma Grants have already gone to the gold country this spring. I will now

---

[25] Albert Johnson. See letter of July 18, 1863, n. 4.

subside. Id like to hear from home occasionally, anyhow let nothing deter
you from writing once a week   Hervey Johnson

                                        Deer Creek. Idaho Ter.
                                        [Dakota Territory]
                                        June 6th. 64
Sister Sybil.

The mail came in yesterday and brought me two letters; one from thee
written May 8th, the other from Iowa, May sixth. Thee said it had been
three weeks since you had got a letter from me. I thought there must be
something the matter for it was three weeks since I got a letter from home.
Thee says that you know I am so far from the Fort that I cant send letters
as often as I did before. I will just remark that, if I cant *send* as often I can
write as often as I ever did and I believe if I did as you do, you would not
get letters from me as often as you do. That is wait till you get one from me
before you can write. It is certainly not necessary to say more on this subject,
as I have made frequent allusions to it heretofore. I was very glad to hear
from home again. Thee spoke of thy letters being so uninteresting, that is
a mistake. nothing is more interesting to me than thy letters. I have several
correspondents in different parts of the country, but none of them send me
as interesting letters as those I get from home. . . .

I dont know hardly what to write that would be interesting   I went out
to the mountains to hunt with three other boys a few days ago, it was a bad
day, it raind nearly all the time the first day and night. We made our camp
about two miles up in the mountains close to a little grassy spot where our
horses could graze, and on the verge of a deep rocky canon that runs clear
through the range. I might as well tell at once that we didnt get any game.
After we got our camp fixed we all started out in different directions, one of
the boys got about two hundred yards from camp and concluded it was no
use tiring oneself to death climbing about over the rocks   (We had to take
it on foot up there), so he went back to the fire and made down his bed. It
was Bill Boardman[26] a brother of the Editor [of] the Highland news. I

_____

[26] William Boardman was a native of Highland County, Ohio, and a brother of
J. L. Boardman, editor of the *Highland Weekly News* in Hillsboro. Letters from

went over the top of the mountain. it was very disagreeable raining all the time   I didn't see a thing but some grizzly bear tracks   While up there I had a splendid view of the country.   To the east west and south nothing could be seen but a continual succession of mountains as far as the eye could reach. To the northwest north and north east a vast succession of hills and prairies, through which the Platte and its numerous small tributaries may be seen winding along thier courses.   I went down on to the low prarie lands behind the range and walked out a mile or two from the mountain, then went back to the mouth of the canyon on which we camped.   This canon is formed by a small stream that runs from the prairies and mountains on the south. it is a narrow rocky gorge with almost perpendicular sides.   I climbed up its rocky sides and walked along the edge, it made my head dizzy to look down   such awful rocks and precipices I never saw.   I wish you could see them.   The cliffs on rocky fork are nothing in comparison.   I wound my way down the edge of the canon back to camp, found all the boys there in bed. I dried my feet alittle and one of them got up and we two started westward to find a canon that we knew crossed the range some where in that direction, after a tiresome tramp of two miles over crags and ravines we knew we were near the place by the rush of the torrent that runs through it.   It would be useless to attempt to describe the scene.   The thick pine forest through which the rain and wind was whistling, the huge masses of rock laying in piles upon each other, in utter confusion, as if placed there by some awful convulsion of nature, the rapid mountain torrent roaring as it rushes onward through its narrow rock bound channel, all tend to give an awful yet pleasing sublimity to the scene.   I always enjoy such scenery, and I have but half my satisfaction, when I know that I am incapable of describing or of con-

---

William, as well as from Caspar Collins and William Mooney, kept the people of Highland County informed regarding the highlight experiences of the men of the Eleventh OVC.   See *Highland Weekly News*, November 12, 1863; January 28, October 20, 1864; July 6, 1865; January 25, April 5, June 21, July 26, August 2, August 9, 1866.   Writing to his sister Sibil on October 19, 1865, Johnson reported "William Boardman has gone to Salt Lake, went with the 2nd California from here [Fort Laramie].   General [Patrick] Conner had him detailed to go there and 'shove his quill' against the Mormons.   He is to carry on the Local department of the Camp Douglas Union Vedette. . . ."   For a sample of Boardman's pro-Connor journalism, see *The Daily Union Vedette*, Camp Douglas, Utah Territory, October 26, October 30, November 8, November 13, 1865.

veying any adequate idea of what I wish to describe, and when I know too that those to whom I would describe, in all probability can never enjoy as I am permitted to, the privileges of seeing the works of nature in her wildest freaks. I wish you all could see what I have seen. You would say it would make a poet of the veriest blockhead. I am going to the mountains again soon, perhaps tomorrow, to cut timber for building quarters. I may say something more of mountain scenery at a future time.

I might add that we got back to camp before night, eat some supper and laid down, but didn't sleep much. our bed was on a bare rock under a pine tree. It rained all night and our robes and blankets got soaked. Next morning got up and moved down the range about five miles to another canon. here the boys left me and I went in alone   They went back to Deer Creek. I hunted round till after noon saw three deer shot three times at them but they were two far off. Sam Engle will be here tomorrow with three or four other boys that were left sick at Ft Leavenworth. I will close Write again. get a sheet of foolscap and fill it

Hervey Johnson

Deer Creek Idaho [Dakota] Ter
June 16th/. 64

Folks at home.

I just came in from the mountains last evening, and I now embrace this as the first opportunity to answer the long and interesting letter from Warren and Sybil, dated 17th of last month (May) which I received some days ago. I would have written sooner but the letter was brought to me while I was out at work and there was no chance out there to write. I have been out in the mountains ten days cutting timber for building, it is as hard work as I ever done. We had to cut the timber on the mountain side and drag it down with oxen to some level place where it could [be] loaded on a wagon   It is killing work on men and oxen. It is so steep that cattle can scarcely climb up to the timber and so rocky that it cut the oxens feet till they could scarcely walk. We cut and dragged down something over two hundred logs and poles. Some of them we had to drag a mile. there were five of us. Sam Engle was one. we had our camp in a deep canon or ravine

134

close by a little brook of the purest water. The sun never rose where we were till along towards ten o clock it generally set sometime along in the afternoon but daylight always lasted till dark.

wild animals were plenty all around us but we didnt get to see any but a few deer and wolves, tracks of the bear were thick all around us but they never came to our camp. The next day after we went out I captured an eagle a young one we were on the track of a bear when I saw the nest in a tall pine, I climbed up the hill side till I got on a level with the nest and threw a stone at it and the bird raised up one of the boys shot at it then with his revolver, knocked some of the feathers out of it. He thought it was an old bird or he would not have shot at it. I helped chop the tree down and got the bird, it was slightly wounded on the breast and one leg by the pistol shot, I brought it down to camp and kept it there till I came in to the post. It is some larger than a goose, its toes are as large almost as my little finger, it is so young that it cant fly yet. I turned it loose last evening it runs around eats fish and any kind of fresh meat. we are going to keep it for a company pet. I cant find out what species of eagle it is. I thought at first it was a bald eagle but black feathers are growing out on top of its head. We have a little wolf here a kind of company pet. it runs and plays with the dogs just like it was one of them.

The Indians are getting very mischievous and troublesome, they have killed several emigrants and stolen a great deal of emigrant stock. two men traveling alone were pounced upon one night by eight indians, who shot both of them killing one instantly and only wounding the other who crawled in to the brush and hid. their horses took fright and ran off the indians after them. The indians soon returned and sacked the wagons taking away blankets, clothing, three gallons of whiskey, and several hundred dollars in gold and greenbacks but they couldnt find the other man, if some person could have followed them he could have taken every thing from them in two hours, for they would have been drunk enough to know nothing in that time. The tailor that I spoke of in some of my letters last winter was shot too the indians had stolen his ponies and he had gone out with an other man to take them back, they came upon the indians, when one of them the son of the chief who had been living with foote the tailor, said: "Mr Foote I've got you now where I want you." Foote made preparations to resist them but

135

was shot down being struck by six balls, he will recover. the other man was killed on the spot. Several indians have been killed, but none of them by white men. They are fighting among themselves The Missouri Sioux say they are going to kill all the Laramie Sioux that stay among white men. I dont know what will be done with them, let alone I recon, that has been Col Collin's plan so far.

Emigration still continues as brisk as ever. There is a train now on the opposite side of the river that looks like it was near a mile long. The expedition to the gold region has fallen through emigrants are going that way without an escort. Col. Collins thought there wasnt men to spare to go, at least that is what he said, but my idea is that he was afraid of the natives. If we were to get into skirmish with them he would run and hide tell us to let them alone they are too strong for us, or give them some bacon and flour. The Col might make a good farmer but he aint fit to command a regiment He might make a good private if awkwardness was any help. The boys have to laugh at him often at "dress parade" he draws his sabre so gracefully, handles it with such skill, gives the commands with such accuracy, then returns his sword to the scabbard, the wrong side foremost and works half an hour to get it out to put it in right. I don't want any more Col Collins in mine if I can help it.

concluded next volume

Morning 16th

I concluded I would finish my letter this morning. Sybil in her letter speaks of having received my *last* letter over a week ago but because she had just put one in the office for me she thought she would wait till some thing transpired that would be worth writing. The one she put in when she got mine out I have never seen. I know this by comparing dates. It is my style to answer a letter at once when I get it if I have time, at least I have done so, so far, and sometimes when I dont get one I answer it, as has been the case for the last three or four weeks. Sybil would like to know who I am going to send that *other* picture to; as though one picture besides the one I sent home was all I had. I have had eight or nine taken since I came to Laramie. wouldn't you like to know who has got them? Sybil heard that Em Mackerly

136

A Mormon emigrant ox train fording the Platte River at sunrise near Chimney Rock in 1847. Alfred Lambourne, who traveled the emigrant road as a child, recreated this scene in a painting in 1874. *Photograph of the painting, which apparently has been lost, courtesy of the Union Pacific Museum.*

had got *one* letter from me. Did she hear whether she answered it or not? I want all the information I can get. I wouldnt be surprised if a good many girls in the neighborhood had got letters from me (with other boys' names to them). I am a great hand to *study up something bewitchin'* to put in a letter. I can suit a certain class of boys exactly. I am no sardine you bet by the way did any of you hear of any one else in the vicinity getting a letter from me? it might be if you would put yourselves to a little trouble, that you could find every body I am writing to. inquire around about two weeks before you get this letter and perhaps you will hear of one. Go to Boston to meeting, there is a good place to find out news. Sis Milliner would like for me to write to her, so Sybil says, well perhaps she would, for I know she has read one of my letters, but I dont believe she knew it, the first letter she got from fort Laramie for instance. I have forgotten what her given name is. I dident pay much attention to it. I do love to write to the women. I'd write to *her* for a cent if I knew her name. I wish I could remember it. Tell Mat to tell her — I am in earnest now — that *she* might write, it's leap year anyhow, and what is the difference. I'll answer letters from any of the girls who may want to write. tell me what Sis milliners given name is please, I am interested.

I have not seen Albert for two months, tell Mat Parker that he has gone on a Surveying expedition with Lieut Collins[27] of Co. G. Will be gone some time. Sybil winds up her letter by saying that it is the dryest letter that I ever got. I beg leave to differ with her and wind up mine by requesting you to continue to write once a week though I wish you would contrive some way to prevent all the letters from coming in a pile. paper is only 75 cts per quire or I'd write another sheet.

Hervey.

Deer Creek Idaho [Dakota Territory]
June 23rd/. 64

Sister Abi.

I now attempt to answer thy long and interesting letter which was dated May 25th. I feel very little like writing. I am so lazy, I feel more like going

---

[27] Lieutenant Caspar Collins. See letter of August 29, 1863, n. 29.

to sleep than doing any thing else. I am on guard to day, have been the most of the day watching emigrants horses and mules to see if any of them belonged to the Gov't. three or four hundred horses and mules went along this morning We found only two with the U.S. brand on them. We take them right out of the team where we find them. The men are nearly all [illegible] anyhow, and the Capt[28] goes for every thing they have that is contraband. he took a cavalry saddle from a man this morning. none of them have any business with Government property and all property found in their possession which belongs to the Gov't, such as horses mules, saddles, blankets, clothing &c. is taken from them, unless they can show papers to the effect that they have a right to them.

I am well, the rest of the boys are the same Sam Engle and Albert Johnson have been sent to Platte Bridge to stay. The weather is very warm and mixed up a good deal with storms. I went across the river yesterday with another boy in the canoe to bring some men over. We got back in to the mouth of Deer Creek with our cargo when it began to rain, and such a rain and wind storm I hardly ever saw before, we hauled our boat up under some willows that stood on the bank and tied it, and concluded we would stay there till the men came back from the store, as we had to take them back across the river again. We got as wet as we could be, we made the men pay us three dollars for bringing them over and taking them back. they growled at it, but we thought we had earned the money, it cost us four trips across the river and it being high and swift made it very hard work. The emigrants leave a great many letters for us to take to the fort to be mailed, we make them pay ten cents for each letter they leave one of the boys took down about four hundred the other day. quite a business place our town is when forty or fifty wagons stop here, the boys trade horses and ponies with them, steal their dogs and anything else they can lay hands on This is the greatest place in the world to make money. I have wished forty times that I had kept that money I sent home. I could have made two hundred per cent on it here this summer. We can buy wornout cattle of emigrants for little or nothing and let them run on the prarie two or three weeks they will be ready to travel again, then they can be traded again for other cattle that are worn out, and

---

[28] Captain Levi M. Rinehart. See letter of July 18, 1863, n. 5.

almost the price of an ox received to boot. that is the way they trade out here. a great many stop here to get their horses and oxen shod and if they dont pay for it I dont want a cent, only five dollars for shoeing a horse, only eight for shoeing an ox only four, for finding nails and nailing on four shoes, &c. We are tearing up jack generally here, we have built a new stable and corral large enough to hold two hundred horses and are now building another house to live in ourselves. The telegraph office the capt'n quarters and kitchen, and our shanty are in a row and we have built a nice arbor along in front, covered it with pine boughs, it makes such a nice shade that the emigrants like to come and sit under it.

24th I thought I would finish my letter to day. I will have a chance to send it down tomorrow. The mail came in to day, it brought me two letters, one from mother dated 4th of this month and one from Lyd Moon. The postage stamps and paper and envelopes came through safe. The stamps will come in good place sometime. I had several stamps already and a good many stamped envelopes like the one this is in. have stamps at the fort now, I had also something over a quire of paper   I guess I can make use of it if I can keep it where it wont get soiled. I have to go to morrow to the mountains for timber again. I have been up ther two or three times since I wrote. We are so busy now building and getting ready to pass the winter comfortably that I cant write as interesting letters as I could other wise. When we get done building we will go to hauling wood and then as soon as it will do we will go to making hay. We can get eight dollars per ton for cutting and curing hay. The weather is so warm that we sleep out doors in wagons We spread our gum blankets and bed ticks over the bows for a cover and it is as dry and cool in there as any where. It is getting dark and I will have to close   I may write again tomorrow if I get back in time or day after tomorrow   Tom Cooper[29] starts soon to take charge of a telegraph office, he has learned to telegraph this last spring, nearly all the offices in this country are run by soldiers   they get 65 dollars per month besides their soldiers wages. write soon

Hervey

---

[29] Private Thomas W. Cooper. See letter of August 29, 1863, n. 31.

Deer Creek, [Dakota Territory]
July 5th 1864.

Sister Sybil

I again seat myself to write. I dont know when I will have a chance to send it out. We dont send out or get the mail near as regular as we did when we first came here. The Capt. has appointed one of the boys to carry the mail to and from the fort, and he goes only once in two or three weeks. Since I wrote my last I have been out with a scouting party for five days. Some emigrants had some fortytwo horses stolen about eighteen miles below here on the north side of the river. They pursued the indians overtook them, had a fight with them, killed four and wounded several, got back twenty seven horses and one pony that they had shot an indian off of. One of their own horses was shot dead in the fight by an indian and the man wounded that was riding him. The men brought back the horses they had retaken and sent up here for reenforcements to pursue the indians further. the two men who came up left their buggy and mules on the other side of the river and came over in the boat. They staid all night here, and next morning found their two mules had been taken.

The Capt ordered fifteen men to get ready and go over the river We took our saddles and arms over in the boat and swam our horses over, the river was as wide as across the lot back of our barn and very swift but no accident occurred. I swam my mare and led a pony for one of the men that took the boat over. All safely across we started out in a northeast direction and soon struck a lodge trail along which several horses and mules had been taken very recently, we followed it for several miles and soon found that the mules had been taken along it. in about fifteen miles we came across a small stream we stopped to drink and rest a little and soon started on, we crossed several creeks with no water in them, one of them was fifty yards wide the weather was hot, and the country so sandy that it was difficult getting over it, we suffered much for water too. A person of observation must be struck with the vastness of these plains while traveling over them, among all the sketches and descriptions of them that I have ever read, I have never yet found the author who has told the half. I acknowledge my own utter incapability of doing the subject justice. I had often heard of the

American Desert, but I never expected to see such a desert as does really exist between the Missouri and Great Salt Lake.

Well as I was telling about our trip I will go on. We followed the trail we were on for thirty five miles, when the owner of the mules, who was going with us told us we had gone far enough. we didnt like this for we could see by the trail that we were gaining on the indians but perhaps it was the best for us, for none of us knew the country, and besides we had no provisions and were out of water. We turned back to the small stream and got water and rested awhile and then struck off down the stream intending to reach the platte river. followed the stream some distance and left it turning off to the right, although we had the whole afternoon before us   I thought we would never reach the river, it was up and down hills and across ravines continually. The only guide we had was laramie peak, we knew that by going towards it, we would find the river. At last we came on top of the bluffs that overlook the river, it looked as though it was only a mile to the river but I think we traveled at least six or seven before we got to the platte. The country between the bluffs and river is one succession of sand hills and ravines with scarcely a particle of vegetation. We finally reached the river and found the train from which the stock had been stolen, after a ride of I think at least seventy miles, they made us a supper of which we partook with a relish, we then spread our blankets and laid down to rest after first putting out a strong guard. no disturbance occurred through the night   in the morning, we got ready, filled our canteens with coffee and water, our haversacks with bread and our saddle bags with meat and started out again   We were intending to be gone three or four days. Several of the emigrants armed themselves and went with us   We went down the river several miles to a place where the road ran over the bluffs, when we reached the top of the bluffs we turned off to the left towards the north   after riding several miles we stopped in a deep ravine to graze our horses on a patch of grass we found there. we soon started on and found the trail where the men had returned from pursuing the indians a day or two before. we saw a good many deer I shot at a big [one] that I saw laying down in a ravine, I only scared him I guess for he ran off out of sight. We followed the trail on the back track till we came to the place where the men had the fight   we saw the horse the indians had shot and found one arrow they had not picked up, we soon

142

found the trail where the indians had gone on after the fight. we followed it for several miles and picked up a pair of Cheyenne moccasins that were pretty well spattered with blood   we supposed they had dropped off the feet of one of the dead savages that the others were carrying off. There is a wagon Just about to start to the fort so I must close up, I could fill two more sheets but perhaps it would not be interesting to you. I might say this much that no person got much hurt. I will tell some more about it when I write again. be sure to write often, if Sybil has got a photo I want her to send me one.

Hervey

Deer Creek. Idaho [Dakota] Ter
July 10th/. 64

Sister Abi

I have seated myself to answer thy letter of June 6th, which I received night before last. I was very glad to hear from you again, it had been almost two weeks since I had got a letter from home. I had been getting one every mail for some time back. you could tell that by the tone of my letters I recon. I got a letter at the same time from Oskaloosa, from G. T. Carpenter Proffessor of Oskaloosa College.[30] He told me of several things that were interesting to me, and some things that were very painful. The most if not all of the boys with whom I associated while there at College had gone to the war, and many of them are now no more, while many are lingering out a painful existence in some military hospital. . . .

I believe I will tell the rest about our indian hunt and I might as well say in the first place that we didnt see a red skin while we were out. After picking up the pair of moccassins we kept on and the trail soon struck in to a ravine or dry branch which ran off towards the north east. we followed down this for several miles when we were overtaken by a hail storm, the most of us had nothing on our heads but forage caps and you'd better beleive

---

[30] See letter of August 5, 1863, n. 12. Reverend George T. Carpenter and his brother W. J. Carpenter were the first two instructors employed by Oskaloosa College. Leonard F. Parker, "Higher Education in Iowa," in Hebert B. Adams, ed., *Contributions to American Educational History, No. 17*, p. 136.

our ears and noses suffered   I never saw such a hailstorm before   our horses thought somebody was pelting them with stones and they wanted to run to get out of the way. The storm ceased, and we found that the hail had almost beaten out the trail we were following, so that we lost it about a quarter of a mile from where we were overtaken by the storm, at a place where the indians had stopped to water the horses, it was a little puddle about ten feet long full of grass and dead weeds, it was the first water we had seen since we left the platte river, our horses were very dry, I rode my mare down to the edge and she plunged in and stuck fast in the mud, she floundered about, threw me off in the mud and threw herself down. I got out covered with black mud, my mare got out too and I mounted her, she dident drink any. I guess she thought It wasnt healthy. I didn't feel quite as dry or warm either, especially on the outside, after my immersion as I did before, the air which had been hot and dry all day, was now cool and damp so that I shivered as I rode along.

After we had lost the trail we kept on down the same branch thinking we would find it again somewhere along. we began to think about stopping for the night. We went on till we found a patch of cottonwood in the ravine. we found it to be a very good place to stop at, though there was no water near. I pulled off my saddle, tied up my mare and went to look for a place to make my bed where I would be dry for another storm was threatening us, when I came back to my saddle I found all the water I had in my canteen had been drunk up, some of the boys got thirsty and went for it there are always some along who are too lazy or careless to furnish themselves with anything. We rested very well that night, as it happened it didn't rain so we didn't get wet. Next morning we started out, after eating a piece of raw sowbelly and a handful of dry crackers, to hunt some water, we found some nasty slimy stuff, a piece up the ravine from where we staid all night. When we started on we spread out as wide apart as possible, to look for the trail we had lost   I was on the extreme right and when we got opposite to the place where we lost it, I found it going in a due north course, there was one man with me when I found it. the boys were scattered out so far that only ten of us got together, we fired guns, but they were so far off that they didnt hear us, a man was sent after them but he went on with them, then the sergeant went but he could n't find them. there were thirteen of

144

them eleven soldiers and two emigrants, there were only four soldiers of us, the sergeant two corporals and one private and six emigrants. we went on folowing the trail towards the north till we came in sight of the mountains what range it was I didnt know but we concluded with the force we had that it was useless to pursue any further though for my part I should liked to have gone on. I never wanted to see indians before as bad as I did then, I was beginning to get spunky to think that we had rode so far for nothing and another thing while the emigrants can get sight of them and have brushes with them they always keep out of our sight. they never interrupt a train when there are any soldiers with it, they know as well as we do where we are. I would have liked nothing better than to have overtaken about fifty of the rascals with a hundred horses, It would have been as good a thing as I'd want, (horses are very high out here now.)

Well after we left the trail, we started off towards the west concluding we would try to kill an antelope, of which there were a great many on the plains. we got several shots at them I shot at one not more than two hundred yards off resting my gun on my mare's back but never touched it. we dident get *any one*. we turned our course in towards the river again. one horse gave out, Tim Foreacre's,[31] and we had to leave him about twelve miles from the river. We got into camp that night about dark found all the boys that had left us there. I am getting tired and think I will quit for the present as it is perhaps not interesting to you to read such rigmaroles as this. write soon. No. I guess I will have to get another piece of paper. I'll wait till after dinner though I guess and maybe I'll feel better. dinner is about ready now, so I'll quit.

I'll try to finish in a small sheet. Next morning Tim and I went back to try to get his horse as we went down the river I saw a large bird standing on a sandbar it was of a grayish color, had very long legs, and its head was about a foot long. I shot at it and wounded it so that it could not fly, but it started towards the other side of the river so I could not get it. I shot at it eight or nine times but it was moving down on the water so that the shot struck behind it all the time. I don't know what the name of the bird is,

---

[31] Efforts to locate the official military and/or pension files of Tim Foreacre were unsuccessful. Military Service Records Division, NA, to the editor, February 22, 1973.

it is larger than any bird I ever saw before. I described it to some men and they said it was a pelican.

We went on to the place where we came down from the bluffs the day before and went back on the same tracks, the route lay up a ridge between two ravines. it seemed twice as long as it did the day before when we came down it. It was eight or nine miles from the river up this ridge to the divide where the hills sloped the other way when we got up we started in the wrong direction to go to where we left the horse and wandered about for two hours till I happened to see a pile of stone that I had piled up the day before for a guide, we went to the place and could see where we had left the horse, but no horse was there. we looked round for some distance but could not find him, so we started home. Tim lost his canteen of water so mine had to do us both. we were dry by the time we got back to the river when we got there I saw the same bird that I shot in the morning floating down. it had been all day coming down about ten miles. we went on towards camp my mare gave out so that it was about ten o'clock when we got to the place. I had to walk and pull her along. when we got there nobody was there they had moved further up the river. we concluded we would wait till morning for our dinner and supper, so we tied our horses to some rose brush and lay down and went to sleep. next morning we found the train about three miles up the river went there and got our breakfast and then went home.

The Captain has gone to the fort to get our money. there is four months pay due us. he will not be here for some time yet. I hope that the answer to this letter will come by coach, I learned today that in three weeks we would have a mail line through here by this place The mail agent passed by today going east I must quit

Please write soon
Hervey Johnson

Deer Creek [Dakota Territory]
July 18th 1864

Sister Sybil.

I have seated myself again to write. Thy letter of 20th June came to hand two or three days ago. I received at the same time two other letters from

Highland County. I would have written sooner but have been two busy to do anything not connected with a soldiers calling, have been out scouting after the indians almost every day since I wrote last, sometimes twice and three times a day. Emigrants are collecting in large trains for the better protection of themselves and property. A great many have been killed, their wagons plundered and property burned, dead and wounded men are picked up every day and buried by the soldiers and emigrants. The emigrants are firing now in sight of us across the river, several boys have just started across to see if they are attacked. The Captain is looking through his field glass, he says he can see no indians. I would go over myself, but I was up half the night on guard last night. A man has just been brought up from a train and tied to a telegraph pole for saying the soldiers were all d - - d rascals how long he will be permitted to remain with us I am not able to say, perhaps all day.

Two hundred men and two peices of artilery arrived here yesterday from the fort. they are awaiting orders this morning. They want to be sent to hunt up and attack the indian village, dont know yet whether the Col. will send them or not. Three of our boys started down the road last week with ammunition for some recruits that were on their way to this place. They were driven back by the indians, they were eighteen miles from here, when they were attacked. They said the road was strewn for miles with arrows clothing beds flour bacon salt and other plunder, six dead men, one of them a negro were seen by them scattered along the road, all of them had been killed by arrows, The indians were piling the plunder together and burning it; The wagons were not destroyed, the harness was all cut to peices by the indians to get the mules out. Three men, two of them badly wounded, one by three arrows in the back the other shot through the thigh, are the only men survivors of the train. there were only two women and two children boy & girl, in the train, they were all captured and carried off by the savages The two women made their escape a few nights ago with the little boy, one of them and the boy is here now, the other has not come in yet, perhaps she has been recaptured by the indians. a party of our company were out yesterday and found the body of the little girl with several arrows sticking in it A large gray wolf was eating the child when they found it, some tools were procured of a train and the body was buried, the body of a man was also

147

found yesterday and buried, The bodies found had all been stripped of the clothing except pants and boots and hats. Those three boys that went down the road said the first thing they saw when they come to where the indians were was the little girl. they started off the road to go to her (she was some distance off in the bluffs), one of the boys thought she had been placed there to draw them into ambush, so they took a circuit off some distance around, the girl walked up and got out of sight behind the hill and presently four indians dashed up towards them from behind the hill and were surrounding them, the boys dismounted leveled their pieces and fired, they were at a distance of two hundred yards and running at full speed. one old fellow the boys took to be the chief, threw up his arms dropped his spear and reeled on his horse, but was carried out of sight before he fell, the rest ran behind the hill but soon reappeared, they saw the boys were ready for them however, so they did not come so near but kept off and finally disappeared alltogether. The boys then started on and came in sight of smoke, they soon discovered it was caused by indians burning the property of a train. The boys thought there were two many for them so they turned and came back to the station. twelve men then mounted and started down.

The Captain and another man were on the road some where coming up from the fort with our money and we were afraid they might be attacked. The men went on down met the captain all safe   all turned and came back with the Capt except two who were sent on with the ammunition to meet the recruits. these two fell in with a squad of indians and fought them for some time firing as many as eighty balls at them. the rapid firing was what saved the boys for they did not give an indian time to get within bowshot of them after firing before they were ready to fire again. They fought their way through them and arrived safe with the supplies. They all got in day before yesterday, five or six of the recruits are from about Jutersburg.[32] Suptin, Patton, Roads, Sincler, Baldwin and Grim, are all from that neighborhood.

The boys that went over the river have returned. they said the emigrants were shooting sage hens. several times   we have been fooled that way and had a ride for nothing. A few evenings ago an emigrant came up to the station almost out of breath, we asked him what the matter was   he said the

---

[32] Jutersburg was near Leesburg in northern Highland County, Ohio.

men in the train that had camped below his were fighting with the indians. Our boys heard firing in that direction and thought something was up, so when this man came up they mounted and went down and found the emigrants were shooting jack rabbits. One day last week two indians made their appearance behind our quarters they passed along four or five hundred yards off and got about a quarter of a mile above us then turned and crossed the road and made for the river. I was out in front of the quarters and saw them as they crossed the road and ran for my gun, there was a herd of horses just crossing the river as I came in sight of it. I thought I could reach the river by the time the indians got across and got down to the herd which was half a mile right north of our quarters. I ran with all my might, saw the indians just as they had got across the river. The captain and several of the boys were by this time close behind me on horses, they dashed on past and plunged into the river which they had to swim, by this time I had reached the river and the indians had got opposite me on the other side. They were riding as fast as their ponies could travel. I fired at them but without effect, the ball cut the dust in the bank beyond them just in the rear of their horses, They then set to yelling which scared the herd I prepared for another shot but they got out of sight behind some brush. by this time they were about a hundred yards below where I first shot at them and the Capt and one of the boys had got across, the indians pushed on after the herd but the capt was two close behind them. The herd ran into a ravine but instead of running across it they ran down it towards the river. The indians concluded the herd was of no account to them so they left it and took out north over the bluffs. Several other boys had now crossed the river and joined in the chase. On they went over hill and ravine till they reached the top of the bluffs firing every opportunity they got. They lost time on the indians till they got to the top of the bluffs but afterwards they gained on them but did not get in shooting distance They rode perhaps ten miles when our horses began to fag. the men all stoped but the Capt and another man they pushed on and the captain had to stop for something, the other man kept on alone. the indians saw that they had but one pursuer and stoped and set their bows, he fired at them and they, thinking they could catch him before he could load again, started for him, he never turned but kept right on towards them with his gun to his shoulder. They saw he was

149

not afraid of them so they wheeled about and went on again. They got out of sight in a ravine and he lost them. He turned and came back thinking it was useless to pursue them further, and I have no doubt it was.

The woman that escaped from the indians said that two indians came into camp while she was with them and said they got a herd but the soldiers got after them and they had to leave it. She said they would laugh it seemed to tickle them to think that they could outrun the soldiers day before yesterday some emigrants were up on the bluffs about half a mile from here watching their stock, one of them saw something and came down nearly out of breath told us he saw eighteen indians we were on our horses in an instant and out to hunt them we took a ride of about ten miles but nary indian did we see nor any sign of one. We keep horses saddled and bridled ready to mount at a moments notice, and it is always the first man that gets a horse that gets to go on a scout. The men who came up yesterday have received orders, about one hundred and sixty of us start to night or tomorrow morning to hunt the indian village. There are about three hundred wagons camped near here and a good many of the emigrants are going with us, we want to get one hundred of them if they will volunteer, if they wont then we will "press them into the service".

I have often thought before I became a soldier that I would never try to kill or take the life of any one, but I have got over that notion now. I could shoot an indian with as much coolness as I would a dog, and I will do it if [I] can I never want to see an indian come about where I am They have been fed and clothed a great many of them by the whites, they live among the whites, are the best friends of the whites, but as soon as the white mans eyes are off of him he is watching an opportunity to kill him I never want to be a friend to the indian any more. He will come up to the white man and shake hands with him, then step off a few steps and shoot him. This was done when that train was plundered and burned The indians rode up behind the train and followed for some distance, then they came round and shook hands with a man asked him for bread, he gave them all they wanted they then wanted meat they got it, they then wanted to trade horses the indians were riding american horses they had stolen, the man did'nt want to trade, but the indian was so urgent that an exchange was made, it was all done on the most friendly of terms. The indians were satisfied, rode off

150

and began shooting at the men with whom they had been but a minute before. I would experience a thrill of pleasure in shooting such brutes, and I would not hesitate to take a scalp if opportunity offers. As perhaps this is not interesting to some of you at home I will say no more about it except that when a man takes up an occupation it is his duty to follow the business of that occupation.

I have had two pictures drawn, one of Fort Laramie the other of Deer creek. I thought you would like to see how the places where I have been staying look.[33] The view of the fort is taken from the south east. The water that can be seen in the foreground is the laramie river. The large building in the back is the Head Quarters of Commanding Officer. Large building to right of flag staff is where Co. G. staid last winter. Small buildings in lower right hand corner are laundress quarters, quartermaster stores and stables & telegraph office, mound like pile of hay is pile of corn something near one hundred thousand bushels. building with stones piled around it is the guard house small buildings around upper left hand corner Officers quarters. Square building with flat roof arsenal and magazine. long building with square front saddler, shoe, tailor, gunsmith shops and post office, nex[t] to right suttler store next to the right sutlers residence. back of it the hospital. High mountain in the distance Laramie peak. Deer Creek Station was taken from the north so that the platte river is not seen. The building under the flag is the one in which we at present reside. the one that joins up to the left hand end of it is the stable. Our quarters the stable and the posts you see set around form the corral in which we keep our horses at night. The long building by the wigwam is Bisonettes house and store it looks better in front, we are looking in the back yard now. The brush seen in the left is along the stream called deer creek. I thought I would send you this picture that you might see what a dreary looking place it is where I am playing soldier.

I would like for Sybil to send me her photo and Semira too. . . . I dont know of any *purty boy* here that would do to send thy photo to except *me*. I would send home some flowers but there are none now except in the moun-

---

[33] Johnson's drawings were not found with his correspondence of July 18, 1864.

Sketch of Deer Creek Station attributed to Charles Frederick Moellmann.
Courtesy of the Western Heritage Research Center, University of Wyoming.

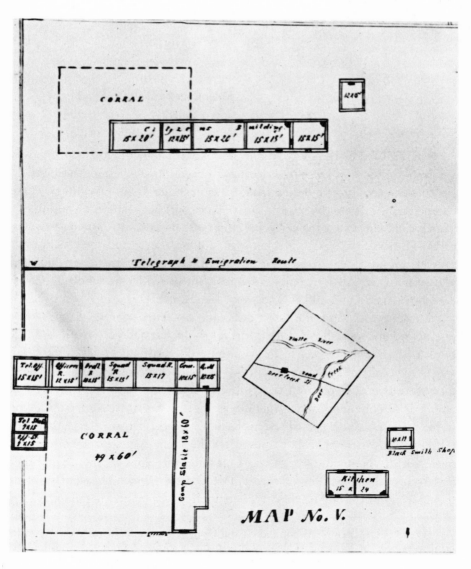

Map and floor plan of Deer Creek Station in the 1860's, with the telegraph and emigrant routes indicated. Draftsman unknown.
Courtesy of the Wyoming State Archives and Historical Department.

tains and I have no time to go for them. I understand we start to night at one o'clock towards Powder River. I must quit write often.

Hervey.

Deer Creek [Dakota Territory]
July 25th 1864

Sister Sybil

We returned yesterday from our indian excursion, and as I may go away again soon I thought I would write now. I dont know when the mail will go out so I can send it, the indian troubles have made it very irregular. There was no trouble along the road while we were out; but yesterday evening two of our Company horses and several emigrants horses were stolen at a place called Horse Shoe Station,[34] where four of our boys are staying sixty five miles from here. We were gone five days there were about one hundred and sixty of us, thirty of co G. a detachment of Co E. the whole of Co H, detachments of Cos I and K, and two peices of artilery.

We started out in a northeast direction, the remainder went north. We saw no indians though we crossed several trails that had been made by large herds of horses that they had been running off. A small squad of Co E ran into a band of indians forty or fifty, in the afternoon and attacked them, they were overpowered and compelled to retreat. The second Lieutenant who was in command of the squad was shot off his horse the arrow going in near the spine at the small of his back. I saw the arrow after it had been taken out, it was shot in six inches, after the Lieut. was shot the other boys made for this command which was four miles off, They reported what they had seen and the whole command started after them. They got sight of them but night coming on they were compelled to give up the pursuit. They

---

[34] Horseshoe Station was located on the Oregon Trail approximately forty miles northwest of Fort Laramie (or about fifteen miles south of present Glendo, Wyoming). Horseshoe (or Horseshoe Creek) Station was a mail station built in 1857 for a Mormon named Hiram Kimball who had a federal mail contract. Burned during the Utah War of 1857–1858, the post was rebuilt and successively used as a Pony Express station, telegraph station, and garrison for volunteer troops in the mid-1860's. Charles H. Springer, *Soldiering in Sioux Country: 1865*, p. 81; Hebard and Brininstool, *The Bozeman Trail*, vol. 1, pp. 80–81.

154

did not get into camp till next morning. The Lieut was left out all night supposed to be killed.

Our camp was on a creek about thirty miles from here. Next morning an ambulance was sent, to bring in his body, when they got to the place he was still alive his clothing all taken off except shirt and boots, two arrows in his body, one through the next and one in the back. The feather was cut off the one through his neck and it was drawn through, They gave him some water to drink and it ran out at the wound in his neck. They tried to pull the arrow out of his back but the barb pulled off and was left in his body but was afterwards taken out with an instrument. He was brought into camp and died next morning, His entrails were taken out and the place filled with salt [for embalming] he was buried in a shallow sandy grave.

We left the place and went on camped again then next day reached Wind river. No indians there Scouts were sent out in three different directions but found nothing, camped on wind river for the night, left at half past two in the morning to come home came back by the place where the Lieutenant was left staid all night, took up his body and started for Deer Creek before daylight, arrived here and buried the Lieutenant with military honors five days after his death.

Night before last two of the boys from Platte Bridge came down and told us that the indians were coming in there and wanted to go down to the fort to get something to eat. They said they saw a heap of bad indians with a heap of ponies but would not go with them because they were bad indians. Co E was just starting to the fort. The captain turned them back with the artilery. Several of our boys went from here too. The Captains plan was to take the chief and some of his best men prisoners and keep them so till they would tell who it was that was committing depradations along the road, and where the stock was they had taken, and if they would not tell, to kill them and their squaws and papooses burn their lodges and take their ponies. Our first Lieutenant[35] who was with us on our wind river expedition

---

[35] Lieutenant (Captain) Henry Clay Bretney was mustered in at Camp Dennison, Ohio, on July 20, 1863. On October 28, 1864, he was appointed commander of Company G, Eleventh OVC, and following his controversial performance at the Battle of Platte Bridge, he was arrested, court-martialed, and, on November 1, 1865, cashiered from the service on the charges of "drunkeness on duty" and "conduct unbecoming an officer." Captain Henry Clay Bretney, CMF, and General Orders No.

and who also has commanded of the troops at the bridge was here at the time the news came that the indians were there. He was very angry at it, because he gave the Sergt. whom he left in charge imperative orders to shoot any indians who came about. He hastened up there to the bridge mounted his men and went out and pitched into the indians. We have not yet learned whether any body was hurt or not. The Indians ran away with the boys after them. they got a citizens hat that the chief wore. It was a perfect blunder on the part of the Lieutenant and I hope he will be courtmartialed because he acted contrary to express orders, if he had gone according to orders they might have got all the indians there was there and their ponies, besides perhaps finding agreat many horses that had been stolen and bringing the theives to justice, but as it is I doubt if they have got a single indian or retaken a single horse. I have some notion of going tomorrow to cut hay for the Capt. there are five or six of us going at it   he gives us five dollars per ton, for cutting curing and putting it up in small stacks.

26th. A portion of the troops who went to the bridge yesterday have returned. They had a fight with the indians, captured several horses sixteen or seventeen squaws, who are held as hostages for that woman that was taken by the indians some time ago, an old indian chief has been sent out to bring her in, he says he knows where she is. If he does not bring her in those squaws will *go up.* Several of our horses were killed in the fight and one man wounded. His name is St Clair,[36] he lives in or near marshal, he was shot through both legs below the knees with slug. Our boys destroyed all the lodges and every thing the indians had and they are making their way towards the fort back of the mountains. You may think that they are receiving rough treatment from us, but it is nothing compared with what is their due. The very next morning after they came there they tried to run off the

40, Headquarters, Department of Missouri, Company Order Books, Company G, Eleventh OVC, Fort Laramie National Historic Site Library, Fort Laramie. Also see Hebard and Brininstool, *The Bozeman Trail*, vol. 1, pp. 182–83; Vaughn, *The Battle of Platte Bridge*, passim; Spring, *Caspar Collins*, pp. 84–88; Dee Alexander Brown, *The Galvanized Yankees*, pp. 35–50.

[36] Efforts to locate the official military and/or pension files of Private Chavil St. Clair were unsuccessful. Military Records Division, NA, to the editor, February 26, 1973. It is known that St. Clair was a member of Company G and was reported to have died of natural causes on January 14, 1866. *History of Ross and Highland Counties, Ohio*, p. 139.

Government horses at the bridge, and at the same time were making friends with the boys there. The boys couldnt see it in the same light that the red skins did so they went to peppering them. I must come to a close. I wish you could send me a pair of suspenders and small necktie. . . . write often

Hervey Johnson

Deer Creek Station
[Dakota Territory]
Aug 6th 1864

Folks at home.

. . . Well we have been having some pretty stiff times though I believe I have told most every thing in my former letters. The indians have not been so bad since I wrote before as they were, emigration has about played out. large trains get this far and turn back, both on account of indians and discouraging accounts of the gold countries. A few days ago one of our boys who was cooking for some hay makers started down from the hay ground to get some horses; he had gone a mile and a half and was attacked by three indians on foot, they were armed with rifles, they shot several times at him doing him no injury but making several bullet holes in his clothes. He unloaded his spencer at them in such a style that they dident feel like coming nearer than two hundred yards. he wounded one of them in the arm so he could not hold his gun. The boy came on down to where Major Twiss lives about four miles from the hay ground. The indians went back into the bluffs. While the boy was there an indian came down from the bluffs and the boy told the major to tell him to not come near or he would shoot him. The major told him not to shoot for he was a friendly indian. he came up and talked with the Major & told him they were going to the fort. The Major told him to go back and tell the indians to go around back of the mountains and not come near deer creek for the soldiers were all mad. There were seventy indians. the boy said he could see them stringing along over the bluffs.

We had got word that indians were about and several of the boys were soon on the scout. I was ordered to hitch to a small spring wagon and take

157

three men and go up to the majors and bring down a wounded indian that had been there aday or two. I got up there just in time to learn that he had escaped while the major was talking with the indian that came down from the bluffs. The boys scoured the country all around but could not find him. they found his tracks in the sand along a little creek that put into deer creek near where the Major lives. they followed the tracks up the stream to the mountains. they found where he had left the stream and got on a pony. There were five or six pony tracks there. The wounded indian was a chief, he went by the name of Bill Grass,[37] could speak English tolerably well. he was wounded in the fight at Platte Bridge.

Two of our boys were sent to the fort for the mail a few days ago, they took down about thirty ponies that had been captured at the bridge. The Colonel we understand is giving them back to the indians again, it is just what we expected. The boys here declare they wont go twenty steps to fight the indians again. If they do they will kill horses ponies and every thing else. not another captured pony shall go to the fort. We cant exactly see the interesting part of it, after riding for a week after indians, fighting them, taking their ponies and lodges, saying nothing of the fatigues and privations that must always be undergone on every scouting expedition. *We* think that if the indians can kill white people, take their horses, burn their property &c, we have a right to retaliate, to play them the same game if it is a dirty one. We cant see the military part of giving back captured property to the enemy, nor do I think we will see it again.

Enough of this. I was up Deer Creek yesterday cutting some hay. wild fruit is found there in the greatest abundance. Goose berries, Choke Cherries, Bull Berries Dill Berries Three different kinds of currants red, black, and yellow. I send home the seeds of the three varieties. I also send some grains of wheat for Warren to plant. The wheat was growing among the grass. It was scarcely ripe 5th of Aug. It was a curiosity to us, the grains were so thick on the head as many as sixty were counted on one head an

---

[37] Grass, sometimes called "Brave" Grass, was known to his Oglala people as Pah-gee. He was one of the signators to the Oglala Treaty of May 25, 1868, and played a substantial role in the deliberations leading to the closing of the Bozeman Trail. Charles J. Kappler, *Indian Affairs. Laws and Treaties*, vol. 2, p. 1004; Olson, *Red Cloud*, pp. 85, 106, 123, 126, 136, n. 70.

inch and a half long. I dont know whether it is spring or fall wheat. Warren can plant some of it this fall and some next spring. Mother was telling the prices of some articles. Coffee here is $1.00, sugar 75 cts tea $4.00 soap $1.00 per bar ink .35 cts bottle molasses $3.00 per gallon bacon .25 cts hams .40 cts dried fruit 25 cts per pound segars ten cents each tobacco 1.75 per pound &c. But the place to buy goods is in Virginia City where Coffee is 40 cents, calico 18 cts good shirts $1.25 pants $3.00 bacon 15 cts &c. The country up there is perfectly overstocked with goods, and nobody wanting to buy but every body wanting to sell. About twenty thousand persons have passed this place this summer for the west, this added to the emigration of other routes on some of which it has been greater than here will make something near eighty thousand persons that have left the states and Canadas and emigrated westward. I must close. Write soon.

Hervey

Deer Creek Idaho [Dakota] Ter.
Aug 11th/64

Sister Sybil.

    Though it has been but a few days since I wrote, I thought I would write again this morning, I scarcely know what to write as nothing has transpired since I wrote last. The weather is hot and sultry in the day time and cool at night. There has been no rain of consequence for some time and every thing is parched up except along the water courses, and even there there is no grass except near the foot of the mountains or so far from the road that emigrant stock has not grazed it.

    I went out a few days ago in charge of four or five men to cut some hay. We went down the road to Box Alder creek about ten miles, we then went up the creek toward the mountains. The grass had all been eaten off for some distance up the stream but as we got further up it began to get better, up near the foot of the range we found good mowing. It would seem like a delightful country, and it would be if it were all like it is on these streams where they issue from the hills; we are down in a valley, and the bluffs on either side the mountains above and the thick brush below hem us in an[d]

159

make it appear like a little paradise. We unpacked layed around, picked some wild fruit, mowed a little; eat our supper and then went to bed, or to grass rather, for my bed that night was a pile of fresh grass. I expect I will hardly know how to sleep in a house if it should ever be my lot to get where there are houses again, I am so accustomed to sleeping on the ground, under a log, on the soft side of a board or any where that might happens to catch me, you may think it strange that I talk this way, as you no doubt think that we have houses out here, We have old shacks, but we dont call them houses, we call them dobeys, shubangs, a kicheta teepe &c.

But I was saying something about hay was'nt I? Yes — well, next morning we got up before the sun worked a while, eat our breakfast, then worked again awhile, then rested some and picked berries, then worked some more, and then concluded we would quit and go home. We packed up our traps and started, came across a flock of sage hens, killed four of them and shoved on, we stopped when we got back to the road to look at and read the inscriptions on some graves that were near. There were four headboards and but one broad grave. The names of the men were given and the inscription was "Killed by indians on the 12th of July". There is a grave of a little girl somewhere there but we couldnt find it. She was taken from the same train to which the men belonged, but was not killed till a day or two afterward. I believe I mentioned something about this in a former letter.[38] The woman who was captured and made her escape, has gone to the fort with her boy and husband who has recovered from his wounds. The other wounded man is still here not likely to recover. The other woman that was taken has not yet been brought in. An old indian chief was sent out after her but has not yet returned. Her husband is here waiting on the wounded man. There is a man here with his family going to stay all winter. he lost all his stock so he could not get on further. Emigration has pretty much ceased. scarcely a train a week passes. Day before yesterday, a train passed with about sixty mounted men. They called themselves the Emigrant Escort. They were sent out by the Government to escort emigrants across the plains, but they waited till emigration was over it seems before they started.

---

[38] See letter of July 18, 1864.

Well I commenced to tell about going after hay and quit two or three times. I believe I will finish now. We started on after looking at the graves and saw another grave some distance from the road. it had been torn open by the wolves and covered up again but a day or two befor we saw it. There were no boards or stones about the grave. I think the body was not found till some days after he was killed and then it smelt so bad that it could not be moved, but was covered up just as it lay on the ground. we went on and got here about supper time.

It sounds foolish I think, but it is just like a woman, to talk about being careless, and going away into the mountains, and climbing about *by myself*. Sybil seems to think I ought not to do so. I have often wished you could come out here and go with me about through the mountains, but it would be little satisfaction to me to go around with women that were afraid of bears and indians or of falling off some precipice. I have the first time yet to feel anything like fear when I have been out. It may sound like boasting, but I would not be afraid [of going] anywhere by myself. Some how or other I dont feel at all like I thought I would. I cant tell why it is, but if the indians had been as bad when we came to the fort last fall as they have been this summer I would have been scared half to death. I had seen rebels, scouted after them, been shot at by them, helped take them prisoners, but it never scared me half so bad as the *thoughts* of coming right in among savage indians did last fall. I was glad they were quiet when we came here, but one years life among them has taught me to care little whether they were quiet or troublesome. There is more excitement, and time passes faster I find when they are troublesome but it is little difference to me how they are.

This is after dinner. The boys killed a beef this morning and we had some heart and liver fried for dinner. they are articles that I never would touch at home, but I aint near so nice now as I was then, last evening we had a mess of frogs for supper. they were splendid, real "proper good" as grand father used to say. We have had several messes of them this summer. I told you once how to cook bear, now I might as well tell how to cook frogs, and I think you will go right off to the branch or blinco or some good pond and get a mess. The first thing to do is the same as you do when you go to cook anything — that is to get the frogs, which is very easily done after they are killed. I generally take a club and hit them a rap over the "mug". Some hit them two raps, and some three, every one has his own way; either of the three ways I have mentioned is very effective. You can take your choice, or use all three. After the frog is dead take something sharp and cut off both hind legs about three quarters of an inch above where they grow together. I would reccommend a knife for that purpose. I always put the legs in a bucket or something brought along for the purpose — and the other part I throw away, *it's* not much account, though that's my opinion. I dont know how others may do. I'll leave it to your judgment. I'm just telling how to cook them. The next thing is to take the peeling off, which is done by a simple twist of the wrist and sleight of muscle. this being done they are ready for use after being washed and fried. The frying of them is a very simple process. it is done like you would do any other squirrel or chicken. I dont think it necessary to give my direction about eating them nature is the best guide, though it might be necessary to say that the bones are unhealthy, we dont eat them here.

We have a gray wolf here that is a nice pet, it runs about with the dogs and seems as much at home as it would if it was wild. We thought we had two wolves or one wolf and a coyote but the coyote has turned out to be a fox, a red fox I believe it is as playful as a kitten. The Eagle that I caught has died It staid around here a good while and was the wonder of all emigrants, a great many of whom did not know what it was. They would always ask a great many foolish questions about it and other curious things they saw, and always got as foolish answers. One day I was sitting out under the shade of the arbor, not interrupting any body, and an emigrant came staring up and looking at the bird awhile said "Mister what kind of a bird do you call that there" I told him that was the bird of liberty, that roosted on the liberty pole, and crowed, and sung yankee doodle and hail columbia. He went off satisfied with the information. We have been bothered to vexation almost by importunate questions of the emigrants. A hundred men will pass in a day all ask the same questions such as how far is it to grass? any wood there? is the road sandy? how far is it to the crossing how far is it to the bridge? What is the toll. how far is it to Bannac how far to fort Bridger, how far to Salt Lake, is there a post office here? What do you know about the new route? is Bosemans route a good one? how is Bridgers cutoff. How far is it by Lande's cutoff.[39] We generally tell them any thing we think of at the time — such as — you can cross *there* if you want to there is grass down in the Platte. or — do you mean Bill Grass? he's dead. yes we heard some thing about the new route, all the emigrants along the road are talking about it. there's wood up along the Platte. It is amusing as well as vexatious, because it is the source of much amusement among ourselves to be asked the same questions a hundred times a day.

We get a crowd of them around us and have our own fun telling marvelous tales about the gold country, some one will ask how far is it to grass, then ask half a dozen questions about the road and other things, then ask how far it is to feed, then a dozen more questions, then ask if there is any grass up there. more questions, then is the feed good up there, and so on. Some times we ask them some questions. Some soldier asked one where he was going. he said he was going to Idaho. Well, your'e here, said the soldier. One fellow came by driving some mules horses and cattle, some of us got at him and was asking him what he would take for that ox, did he want to sell that mule, wouldn't he sell us a calf, and all such questions as that, finding he would not sell any of his stock, I asked him what he did want to sell. he said nothing but himself. I told him he was sold and that cheap too, and turned round and came away. A great many have big letters painted on their wagons such as "Bound for Bannick or bust." We told them they would all "bust". Some would have painted up "Bound for Big—— and then a horn painted instead of the word. We told them when they come back they would have themselves painted coming out at the little end of it. Several of the boys have been up in the mountains several days cutting timber, some how either on purpose or by accident they have let fire get out and the mountains are all smoking now. One of our boys Jim

---

[39] The Bridger and Lander cutoffs were variations of the Oregon-California-Utah Trail west of South Pass. For a short time following construction of Fort Bridger on Black's Fork of the Green River by mountain men Jim Bridger and Louis Vásquez in 1843–1844, the Bridger Cutoff served as a popular emigrant trail to the Great Salt Lake region, California, and Oregon by way of Soda Springs and Fort Hall in present southeastern Idaho. In late 1844, however, the Greenwood (later known as the Sublette) Cutoff provided a shorter route to the Northwest, and in 1859 Frederick W. Lander established an even more direct route from South Pass to the upper Snake River country and Oregon. See Taft A. Larson, *History of Wyoming*, pp. 9–10.

163

"The Course of Empire," an early lithograph depicting the effects of emigration on the inhabitants and landscape of the West. *From A. W. Hoyt's "Over the Plains to Colorado,"* Harper's New Monthly Magazine, *vol. 35, no. 205 (June 1867), p. 1.*

Patton[40] was accidentally shot some time ago, he is recovering slowly. one of the boys was showing him how nice his pistol worked, when he accidentally let it fall, the hammer striking the floor discharged the pistol, the ball striking him in the abdomen and coming out at his side. I believe I will quit. I thought I would not have much to write but I have written more than I thought I would.

Please write soon and tell every thing I dont want to see any more letters sent here on notepaper   if you havent foolscap I will try to send you some.

Now don't forget to write.

Hervey Johnson

Deer Creek [Dakota Territory]
Aug 19th 1864

Sister Sybil

I have seated myself again to write though nothing of importance has transpired since I wrote last. we have had no mail for some time. We have no difficulty in getting it from the fort, but the Indians on the south Platte are so troublesome that I suppose the stages have difficulty in getting through. Last night two horses were taken from a mormon train by some Arrappahoes who had been here two or three days. They have a village fifteen miles from Platte Bridge. They have been hitherto, or pretended to be friendly to the whites, and have been allowed to come about the post, or go where ever they want to. There had been no indians about here for some time, three months perhaps I mean friendly indians, and we were thrown into some excitement three or four days ago by the alarm of Indians!!.

One of the boys was across the road for something, and happened to look up the road, where he saw indians coming down, riding at full speed, he ran over and told us what he saw, and in less than half a minute every

---

[40] James F. Patton, a native of Highland County, Ohio, enlisted in the Eleventh OVC on February 23, 1864. A private in Company G, his tour of duty included Horseshoe Station, South Pass, Deer Creek, and Fort Laramie, mainly with stable police. Following his recovery from his gunshot wound, he was sick in the hospitals at Fort Laramie and Leavenworth from July 1865 to January 1866. He was honorably discharged at Fort Leavenworth on April 17, 1866. Private James F. Patton, CMF.

man was ready with his gun for work. The indians came on without retarding their speed, The Capt. told us to stay back while he went out towards them. By this time we could see that there were but four of them, as soon as they saw so many of us, two of them stopped and the others came on. The foremost one, before he got in pistol shot of the Capt, began flourishing a paper which he held in his hand, which, when the Capt saw, he allowed them to come up to him. We were disappointed, we expected to have a little *mix*, but soon learned that they were friendly indians on their way down to the Agency thirty miles below the Fort. They had papers with them from Lieut Bretney[41] commanding at the bridge showing who they were and where they were going. They were allowed to stop here for two or three days. Yesterday evening they left for Platte Bridge again fearing they could not get below on account of the emigrants who would be very apt to stop any indians they should meet travelling along the road.

It was but a short time after they left here that the event occurred which I have mentioned in the forepart of this letter. Three men came down from the train to let us know about it and get some help, they acted like they were the only men that had ever lost any stock, and made as much fuss as if they had lost a hundred horses. We couldent see where the amusement was, so we didnt go. Any set of men that will let four indians, and two of *them squaws* with *heavily laden pack ponies*, drive off two horses and not go or try to help them selves a'nt fit to own horses indians can do better with them than they can, and they may have them for what we care. But we dont believe the indians took the horses, they were passing along the road just as the men were driving the stock down from the hills to water. After they had passed, the men noticed that two of their horses were gone, they supposed of course that the[y] had driven them off, so one of them went to see. he rode pretty fast, made a good deal of dust. the Indians though a good ways ahead of him, saw the dust, and I supposed imagining there was some soldiers after them, started in a run. This was enough for him, he came back to camp and instead of getting together the men and going after them, sent *three* men down here to tell us!!! I have no doubt but the horses strayed off from the herd and had got out of sight in some ravine and they had not

[41] See letter of July 25, 1864, n. 35.

even looked from them. Word came in this morning that about twenty indians attacked the haymaker again, the same boy that was shot at before, had to run the gauntlet again I did not learn the particulars. The Capt and a squad of men have gone up there. I am on guard today and could not go. I believe I will not finish my letter till they come back, or perhaps till tomorrow, We are looking for the mail every day, it may come this evening.

Morning 20*th*.

No mail yet, so I guess I'll finish my letter. The boys came in yesterday evening from the scout, not having found what they went after. They ascertained though that there were about 40 indians about there somewhere. The boy who first saw them was coming down from the hay ground to where our horses are herded and passing near a thicket several arrows were thrown at him from the brush. He looked in the direction from which they came, saw the indians, fired one shot at them, whereupon they began to make their appearance in such numbers that he thought it prudent to light out of there. Their object was, I think to take our herd, but their attack on this boy was what baffled them and saved our horses for he ran straight to the herd and told [the] herders and they ran the stock into the corral which was some two miles further down the creek. Three or four indians tried to get the herd out of the corral one night about eleven o'clock, but the boys were too sharp for them. Those horses that were taken from the emigrants night before last, wer found next morning up in the bluffs where they had strayed from the herd.

We are very busy now preparing our winter quarters, we might have had them completed a month ago but for the indian troubles. There is stirring news from the northwestern frontier. Military men prophesy a protracted indian campaign on the northern border. Fort Pierre[42] on the upper Missouri was attacked by a band of Sioux during the absence of a

---

[42] It is probable that Johnson is referring to Fort Randall since Fort Pierre, named after Pierre Chouteau, Jr., located three miles above the mouth of the Bad (Teton) River, was officially abandoned on May 16, 1857. Established August 4, 1856, on a plateau just north of the point where the Missouri River crosses the present northern Nebraska line, Fort Randall was named after Lieutenant Colonel Daniel D. Randall, deputy paymaster general, and was abandoned on December 6, 1889. Frazer, *Forts of the West*, pp. 136–37.

portion of the garrison under command of Gen. Sully[43] on a scouting expedition. The indians were repulsed with loss. After his return, Sully started after them, attacked them and cleaned them out. On the 17th we understand by telegraph that Sully with three thousand men on their way from Fort Rice[44] to Ft Alexander[45] on the Yellowstone received inteligence that there were seventeen hundred lodges camped near the latter place prepared to give battle. Dispatch did not say whether he attacked them or not. rather seemed to think he would change his course and avoid them so that should the fort be attacked they would better be able to make a resistance. Three Coaches loaded with passengers were attacked seven miles east of Fort Cottonwood[46] on the Platte a few days ago. Simultaneous attacks on Fts Cottonwood and Karney are shortly expected by combined bands of Cheyennes Kiwas Utes Snakes Comanches and Arrappahoes. Major Gen. Curtis,[47] Com'd'g department left Omaha for the west to devise measures for the protection of the overland mail and emigration. The settlers along the platte below Ft Karney are moving themselves and stock in to more thickly settled parts for better protection. New posts are being established for soldiers at different points along the road. Everything indicates indian war, and stern preparations are being made to meet it. You may feel scared when you hear

---

[43] A graduate of West Point and veteran of the Mexican and Civil Wars, Brigadier General Alfred Sully distinguished himself in various Indian campaigns in the Military District of Dakota. He died at Fort Vancouver on April 27, 1879. *The National Cyclopaedia of American Biography*, vol. 12 (New York: James T. White & Co., 1904), pp. 285–86.

[44] Fort Rice, established July 11, 1864, by Brigadier General Alfred Sully, was located opposite the mouth of Long Lake Creek near the present town of Fort Rice, North Dakota. It was named after Brigadier General James Clay Rice and was officially abandoned on November 25, 1878. Frazer, *Forts of the West*, p. 113.

[45] Located twenty miles below the confluence of the Rosebud and Missouri rivers, Fort Alexander was an old trading post built in 1842 for the American Fur Company by Charles Larpenteur. Springer, *Soldiering in Sioux Country*, pp. 77–78.

[46] See letter of October 24, 1863, n. 7.

[47] Major General Samuel Ryan Curtis, a graduate of West Point, was long identified with Iowa politics and during the Civil War distinguished himself for his leadership abilities at the Battle of Pea Ridge, Arkansas. Heavily involved in railroad and military activities in the lower Missouri River valley, his important role in Indian affairs along the Kansas, Colorado, and Wyoming borders in the mid-1860's earned for him a prominent position in frontier history. See Allen Johnson and Dumas Malone, eds., *Dictionary of American Biography*, vol. 4, pp. 619–20.

these things, and perhaps you have heard them long before this. I would have been frightened I know, but somehow or other such reports cause but little or no excitement among us here now.

Some time ago two or three old Arrappahoes came down and told some halfbreeds near this place that three or four hundred Sioux were coming to take these posts along the Platte in a short time, it was a few days after the fight at Platte Bridge and they were coming to take their revenge for the death of those who were killed in the fight. But they didn't come. Two more military posts have been established between here and the Fort, one at La prelle[48] twenty miles below here and the other at La Bonte[49] twenty miles further down. Two companies of the seventh Iowa Cavalry have arrived at the fort, and some more are expected soon from Colorado. The talk has been that we are to be relieved by Iowa troops and sent to the Missouri border, or perhaps to the posts along the upper Missouri. Not much credit however is to be given such reports. One thing though looks a little as though some of them might be true. Those Iowa troops at the Fort, the probability that more of the same will be sent there, the fact that Col Collins has been appointed Inspector General, and that Major Wood of the 7th Iowa is in command at the Fort might be taken by some as confirmation enough of the report. But I think these troops are being sent here because they are needed.

I believe that Capt Rinehart is preparing to resign. He has been rather neglectful of his duties since he came up the road has been trading a good deal, buying and selling stock, he laid out seven or eight hundred dollars a few days ago for cattle, has been buying merchandise of emigrants such as canned fruits oysters tobacco segars &c which the man that he boards

---

[48] La Prelle Station was located on La Prelle (or La Prele) Creek, roughly eighty miles northwest of Fort Laramie. According to one account, the message announcing the assassination of President Lincoln was first received in Dakota Territory at the La Prelle telegraph station on April 15, 1865. Hebard and Brininstool, *The Bozeman Trail*, p. 81.

[49] Located approximately ten miles south of present Douglas, Wyoming, on La Bonte Creek, La Bonte Station was a mail, stage, and telegraph station on the Oregon Trail. Camp Marshall was established in the immediate vicinity in 1864 and served as a garrison for various volunteer military units. It was named after Captain Levi G. Marshall, Company E, Eleventh OVC. Springer, *Soldiering in Sioux Country*, p. 81; Brown, *The Galvanized Yankees*, p. 171; Henderson, *Landmarks on the Oregon Trail*, p. 26.

169

with, keeps to sell for him. He has been heard to express a wish that he was out of the service. I think he will resign and set up a trading post some where in this country. It would be the most profitable busines that a man could engage in.

Well I must begin to quit. It may be two months befor you get this letter, but I will still write and want you to continue to do the same. Write and tell me every thing, some of you seem to think that you write so often that you tell the same thing over and over again. I have never found it so yet in any of your letters. I think you could certainly find subject enough there where people are stirring around you all the time if I can out here where there is nothing but the same old thing every day. Now dont forget to write.

Hervey.

Deer Creek. [Dakota Territory]
Aug 23rd. 1864.

Sister Sybil,

Although I just started a letter home yesterday I thought I would write again today, as I am on guard and dont have to work. Day before yesterday evening the mail came up, bringing me six letters. One from Abi July 12th One from Sybil July 18th, with Semira's miniature. One from Mother and Sybil dated 27th July. One from Cousin Alex at Jamestown. One from Lyd Moon, and one from J—— at Lynchburg. So you may suppose that I have some writing to do if I keep up the correspondence. I shall not endeavor to reply to the letters from home singly but all at once. It had been a good while since I had got a letter from home and you'd better believe I was glad when the mail came.

Abi would like for me to come over and get a mess of roasting ears. I would like to come, but cant today. We have green corn out here put up in cans that we can get by paying only $1.50 cts per can, we hardly ever want it that bad though. I expect we have as good dinners as you have, we have Coffee sometimes and sometimes we have bread with it. We have a cow, have milk for our coffee and to cook rice with, make *gravy*, bake buiscuits (I dont know whether it is spelled right or not) buy pickels, peper sauce, mustard molasses canned fruits, have bought seven or eight bushels of dried apples, have applesauce apple pies, &c. cant complain in the least. When our neighbors come along we have a little for them. I would like to have [a] peice of raspberry pie if you please. We have trot lines set in the river, catch a good many fine catfish and pickerel, the boys found one this morning a cat fish of about 15 lbs weight. wouldn't some of you like to have a mess of fresh fish?

You had a baptising did you? we had one here too, one of the boys got a little too much "how come you so" and the capt thought it necessary that he should be baptized, the ceremony was accordingly performed, I dont think he felt any chang, he couldn't lay on the ground any better afterward than he did before. You needent say anything to me about people having bedbugs, maybe you think we havent any here, didnt you ever see any in my letters? if you didn't its a wonder, they are in everything here, we are used to them, dont mind them a bit, that is dont mind the bugs if we only had the blood to spare, house flies though!! Why thick is no name for them. they are absolutely — well its no use to enlarge on the subject, I can scarcely write for them

I now take up Sybils big sheet, that is the right kind of a letter, you must excuse me for not writing on fools cap, that note paper mother sent me must be used, and if I can get all I have to say, in two or three sheets you ought to be satisfied, besides foolscap aint to be had every day in this country. It is some little trouble to go a hundred miles to town, and then maybe not get what we want when we get there.

I am glad to know that my letters are so interesting to you. I try to make them as interesting as I can, but it seems to me that I write so much that they cant be interesting all the time. You must have nearly a bushel of letters by this time. I had so many that I had to burn some because I had no place to keep them where the other boys would not get them. I was sorry to have it to do. I suppose you keep all of mine dont you? Do you ever let the neighbors or our relations see them? I would have no objections to it if any of them want to. Apples are getting ripe are they? I would like to have one, but we generally get all we *want* at $1.50 cts per dozen. we dont want many.

Hurrah for Orpah!! People will think the Engles and Johnsons are "perty thick" wont they? What do you know about Herzey, he aint married yet is he? I know John Evans. He has a sister Sue. He "kinder hankers arter" Sybil dont he? Sybil wanted to know how Jennie was the last time I heard from her. Jennie who? Which one do you mean, there are so many Jennies. Ill never tell you how she found out I was at Fort Laramie. Say something more about it the next time you write. Semira's picture I am of the same opinion that Sybil is about it — that it dont look much like her, or like she did when I left home. She looks old and care worn. I expect there is something heavy resting on her mind. No doubt it is the anxiety one naturally feels in her situation. I mean as school teacher. I think it will all wear off when school is out, and cool weather comes so that blankets may be used with comfort. I have not yet received a letter from Cousin Josephine.

The potatoe bugs there in Ohio are like the grasshoppers here, I do think I never saw a snow storm where the flakes were thicker than the grasshoppers have been here. All over the country, they are as thick as a swarm of bees striking us in the faces when we walk out like gravel in a wind storm. . . .

Well I don't know that I can think of any thing more to write. Two teams left here yesterday morning for the saw mill they are going for lumber to finish our quarters. The Saw mill is some where in the thick pine region about the foot of Laramie Peak. Mons de Wattwyl,[50] a captain of the Swiss army was here for a few days. He is on a tour through this country, he expects to go through the south the coming winter. Jim Patton[51] who was accidentally shot at Horse Shoe Station has nearly recovered he came up here when the mail did, The wounded man that has been laying here for some time is expected to recover now. A doctor came up in the ambulance that brought the mail, and he examined the wounded man and took out the barb of an arrow from the wound in his side. If it had been taken out a month ago he would have been well before this time but the doctor who first examined him said there was no arrow in him. A band of indians made

---

[50] Captain Alfred de Wattewyl (sometimes spelled Watteville) secured permission through John Hitz, Jr., Acting Consul-General of Switzerland, to join the Eleventh OVC so that he might gain topographical knowledge of and collect natural specimens from the American West. Permission was granted by Colonel William O. Collins, regimental commander. Spring, *Caspar Collins*, p. 58.

[51] See letter of August 11, 1864, n. 40.

their appearance here day before yesterday, we were called out into line, the Orderly and an interpreter went out to meet them. They found them to be Arrapahoes, they were going to join some of their tribe at or near Platte Bridge. Every thing here is nearly parched up except close to the creek, there has been no rain for two months here. there is plenty of rain some-where, black clouds are seen around every day. The office here and the one at the bridge were both tore up by a charge of electricity some time ago there was no cloud in sight it was supposed to have been struck some where above Platte bridge.

I must close.

Please write soon

Hervey

Deer Creek, [Dakota Territory]
Sept 4th 1864

Sister Sybil

I scarcely know how to begin a letter, it has been so long since I have written one, almost four weeks, but as the mail has got to running again I must try to get my hand in again. I have had no letter from home or any where else for about six weeks. I understand the mail will be at the Fort to day, when we will get it here is more than I can tell. When it comes I expect I will get about sixteen letters. I will tell you how many I get when they come.

Indian hostilities ceased in this part of the country about six weeks ago, but were kept up later on the road between Denver and Karney. There has nothing of importance happened in this part lately. I have been to the fort twice in the last month. The first time I went down with the team for rations. The next time I was sent there under arrest with thirteen others, on suspicion of taking some boots that belonged to an emigrant. The circum-stances were these. In August some time an old pilgrim came by on his way to the states from Bannac. He had with him about fifty pairs of boots that he had taken out there from Michigan. The man that had been hauling them for him wouldnt haul them any further, so he stopped here to try to get

173

some body else to haul them further. He wanted the captain to take charge of his boots for a few days. The capt. told him he didnt like to do it, he told him that boots were a thing that would walk off, and that soldiers would steal and he couldnt help it. The man finally prevailed on him to take them but Capt informed him that he would not be responsible for them. he told him he might put them in his room but at his own risk. The room in which they were placed was between the Captains Office and the room of which I was in charge and the only entrance was through my room or the Office, the weather was very warm and bedbugs were so bad that no body slept in the house. the door from my room was fastened on the inside, there was a window in the back end of the room and it was nailed up on the inside. The night after the boots were put in the window was broken open and the door too between our room and the one where the boots were. The boots were taken out not even the sacks they were in were left. For a month the Capt tried to find out who took them. There were two guards on at the time, one in front of the door and one in the rear, but neither of them could tell any thing about it. Things went on for some time the Capt received orders several times to find them boots and punish the theif. finally a pair of boots were found in the blacksmith shop, some pairs were found in the brush scattered about. The blacksmith was arrested and the Provost guard sent up from the fort after him. While they were here, [Captain] Rinehart concluded he would send some more to the fort with them, he arrested me and several others who belonged to my room, thirteen in all took our arms from us kept us under guard that night and next day sent us to the fort, we had five men of our own company four provost guards over us. they let us do as we pleased going down, we could have run off from the guards at any time had we been disposed to but we dident care about it. When we got to the fort we were placed in a room to ourselves under guard, next day we had our examination preliminary to a court martial. We were examined one by one and sent to the guardhouse, not being allowed to speak to each other. That evening at retreat the prisoners were formed in line as usual to answer roll call. thirteen new prisoners answered roll call that evening. After roll call the Officer of the day called out the names of seven of us telling us to step to the front as we were called, when we were all out, he told us we were released and to report immediately to head quarters for duty. Six men were detained in the guard house, one of them is one of the guards that was on the night the boots were taken. There is no positive evidence against any of them and the circumstantial evidence is such as would not warrant an Officer in preferring charges against any soldier.

The next day after our release we started back to Deer Creek. I was sent up the Laramie river about seventeen miles with two men to get some beef cattle for Deer creek. We staid all night at the beef herd, and next morning started out in a northwest direction with our cattle. There was no road and we had to guide our course by the mountain peaks, after travelling about twenty five miles across plains and mountains we reached the road and soon joined our comrades whom we found camped some miles further up the road than where we struck it. We had a good time that night. The boys had brought up some potatoes turneps, carrots, parsneps beets &c these were cooked alltogether and soup made over them I never eat any turneps before but these were good. There are several things a man learns to eat in the army that he wouldent at home. but the good time we had was after we went to bed. We had not lain down long before it began to rain, we couldent help it so we just let it rain. it rained all night, we laid and took it all never "keerin a cent" because it was all in the three years, next morning we got up and built a big fire and dried ourselves and clothes and blankets and robes, eat our breakfast and started on. we got here all safe ourselves but had to leave several horses at different places along the road, mine was left fifty five miles from here, she was brought up yesterday by one of the boys coming up from the fort. I have been for the last few days on Box-Elder[52] in charge of the company herd. I had a good time there nothing to do but see that the boys did their duty. we had a good corral to put the horses in at night and little dog tepees to sleep in. These were made by driving two forks in the ground six or eight feet apart, then laying a pole in the forks and leaning up stricks on the pole from each side, then covering the whole thing with dirt. The weather is beginning to be wintry. The first snow fell the middle of September. Since that snow showers have been frequent. a portion of our company left here a few days ago to take charge

---

[52] Box Elder Creek empties into the North Platte approximately ten miles east of present Glenrock, Wyoming.

of the posts up the road, they go as far as south pass.[53] they relieve Re. A. whose term of service expires shortly   The remainder of our Company may go up before spring.

I will close.

Please write

Hervey Johnson

Deer Creek. [Dakota Territory]
Oct 9th/64

Sister Sibyl.

The mail arrived yesterday so I seat myself to write again. It brought me six letters three from home dated as follows Aug 8th, Aug 16th, and August 29th. It had been a long time since I had a letter from home and I scarcely knew what to do I was so glad. I was not uneasy as I suppose you must be when you dont get a letter every week, because I have learned to take things cool, and not imagine the worst when I cant hear all the truth. I have enjoyed good health the past summer very few of the boys have anything to complain of. I said I have enjoyed good health, I forgot that I had been troubled with the toothache a good deal during the past three weeks. I had a front tooth drawn last spring, and I expect I will have seven or eight more pulled before spring, by the way I feel. . . .

Companies A. B. C. & D. of our regiment have been ordered in from the outposts to the fort, preparatory to going to the States to be discharged. The first Sergeant of our company is going with them. He was transferred to our company from Co A. and is going home on furlough, having reenlisted as a veteran. He talks some of staying at Hillsboro the coming winter. If he does he will come out to see you. I asked him to, and gave him mothers name and P.O. address, he said he wanted to go and see all the boy's folks.

---

[53] Located approximately ten miles east of South Pass on the right bank of the Sweetwater River, South Pass Station was established in 1859 by Russell, Majors & Waddell, a major overland freighting firm. Because it was twice burned by Indians, this station was also known as "Burnt Ranch." Writers' Program of the Work Projects Administration in the State of Wyoming, comp., *Wyoming, A Guide to its History, Highways, and People*, p. 322.

His name is S. B. White,[54] his wife and family live in Piqua, I believe it is the County Seat of Piqua County. Now because he is a soldier and a sergeant, dont look to see a ruffian when you see him, because if you do you will be disappointed. There are some soldiers that I would not ask to go to our house, but I am not ashamed for you to see him nor for him to see you, he had won the respect of the company, and we are sorry to lose him; he may come back to us next spring but it is not probable. I hope he will.

Gold and silver have been discovered at South Pass and almost every soldier who was stationed there the past summer has a claim. They intend coming out next spring to work their claims. The Diggings are principly quartz and are said to be very rich. Lieut Brown[55] of Co. A. will bring out a quartz crusher in the spring I think. Emigration will soon be directed thither and times will be as lively as they were in Bannac and Virginia cities on the discovery of gold at those places. The boys caught a wolf in two traps yesterday morning. They were beaver traps and were fastened to stakes driven in the ground by the carcass of an ox. the traps were set for wolves, but one wolf got caught in both. he pulled up the stakes and "shoved out." the boys tracked him by the trail he made dragging the traps in the sand and found him setting in the edge of the river about a mile from the carcass. he had got over the river but the traps caught on some brush and held him there. one of our tame wolves went with the boys, when he saw the wolf caught in the trap, he set to barking at him and cutting various shines apparently making sport of his brother wolf in his predicament. I

---

[54] A native of Gettysburg, Pennsylvania, Samuel B. White enlisted in the Sixth Regiment OVC in November 1861. During his five years of service he served successively as private, sergeant, and second lieutenant, mainly on detached service at Fort Laramie. From November 3, 1864, to March 10, 1865, he was under arrest at Fort Laramie by order of Colonel William O. Collins. In May 1865 he was commissioned second lieutenant by the governor of Ohio following Captain Levi Rinehart's death (February 13, 1865). White served as commander of Company G until his second arrest (again for reasons unknown) in May 1866, and on the following June 13 he was relieved from duty and ordered to Fort Leavenworth to be mustered out. Second Lieutenant Samuel B. White, CMF.

[55] Lieutenant (Captain) James A. Brown, a native of Darke County, Ohio, enlisted as a private in the Eleventh OVC on October 22, 1864. Following detached service at Fort Laramie, he served at Omaha and Fort Kearny prior to his honorable discharge at Fort Leavenworth on July 14, 1866. Captain James A. Brown, CMF.

went fishing yesterday up deer creek, caught three fine pickerel. They were nearly two feet long, they were as much as I wanted to carry any how.

We thought awhile here that we would not have to build a stockade but with the mail we got a printed order from Gen Curtis Commanding Department — that all forts or military Stations west of the Kansas and Nebraska settlements must be surrounded by stockades. This will give us plenty of work to do all winter. we will have about 4 acres to enclose, it will be no small job, if we build it of timber we will have it to haul from eight to twelve miles. stone would be easier come at, plenty of good building stone within half a mile of the post. We dont like to work much, but it is all in the three years, and time passes faster when we are at work than when we are idle. One of the boys has just now come in with three big catfish that he caught on a trot-line. They are catching them every night and morning If we had a seine we might catch bushels of them every day.

We have a store opened here now, where we can get almost any thing we want that is by paying nine or ten prices for it. Boots are worth from ten to fifteen dollars per pair, shoes from four to ten, mens coats common like I have bought for six dollars at Hillsboro, are worth eighteen and twenty here. I paid twenty five cents for a skein of black patent thread, thirty five for bottle of ink, pair of suspenders for dollar and half, common hats are six dollars, candies nuts raisins &c are worth one dollar per pound. flour is worth from fifteen to twenty dollars per hundred, bacon thirty and thirty five. Beef cattle are worth about sixty dollars a piece, work cattle about three hundred and fifty per yoke.

There came very near being a murder committed two or three evenings ago in the store across the road. An old mountaineer attacked a telegraph operator with a hatchet intending to kill him, striking at him several times, but the man managed to evade his blows and get out of the room. The cause of the fracas was this. the Operator had taken the old mans child a half-breed to keep last winter. Somehow or other the child ran off and froze to death and was eaten by the wolves; the man making no efforts to find her. Her carcass was found by her mother some time afterward, the old man her father, vowed vengeance then on what he called the murderer of his child. I was in the store when he attacked the man. He began with a mouthfull of oaths, saying "You've killed my child that you promised to take care of for me, you let her go off and the wolves eat her, for eight days you never went to hunt her", at the same time letting into him with his hatchet. The man was not hurt; he went out and went down to the camp of Co. A. who had stopped near here while on their way to the fort, The old fellow put up his hatchet and got a revolver intending to go down there and finish the work but was prevented by some men who were about the store.

I would like to be at home this fall, so would the most of the boys, then if the copperheads wanted to raise any disturbance they would be welcome. I am not so scrupulous now as I once was, I believe if I was where they were making a disturbance I would as leif shoot as not and if any body happened to be before me he might get hurt. I would be like the Quaker I read of when he got into a battle and was drawing a bead on a rebel, he says — "I am sorry for thee but thee is right where I am going to shoot" Sibyl said in her letter that she could not see anything like a fort about Laramie, that is just what I thought when I first saw it. It is just like all the frontier posts, Leavenworth, Karney, Cottonwood, Larned, and all of them, but I guess after this they will look like forts if the orders of Gen. Curtis are carried out.

Why was it that Elias Overman had to pay for a substitute? He wasnt drafted was he?

I have just returned from the Bean Hotel as we call our cook house where I refreshed myself with a plate of beans, we have beans about thirty four times a week; coffee twice a day, the coffee tastes like it had got wet, that is it tastes very strong of water. It is suspected that the cooks let it fall in the water barrel, that is the way it is accounted for any how. Sybil wanted to know whether we have any vegetables or whether any body tries to raise any thing or not. There is very little of any thing raised here, at the Fort there were three or four gardens planted. They raised almost all the garden vegetables but they have to irrigate the land. about four miles up deer Creek there is a garden planted by some missionaries. I saw corn, wheat, beans, potatoes, cabbage, onions, radishes, turneps, and so forth growing in it. we could get vegetables when we would buy them, Some of the boys paid one dollar per dozen for onions as large as hulled walnuts. Green apples last winter were worth $1.50 cts per dozen at Fort Laramie. I didn't take any in mine. The garden up deer Creek is made to produce by irrigation, the water is led to it through a ditch nearly a mile long; as a general thing

179

this country will never be fit for agricultural pursuits. Along the water courses small farms may be opened, but then the streams generally go dry in summer so that when water is most needed it cant be had. The only wealth of the country is in its mineral resources and its adaptability to raising stock — cattle horses and sheep. Inhabitants here could raise their own meat but would have to depend on the country farther east for their bread. We are now having our winters hay brought in, about two tons came in to day. there is to be one hundred tons furnished this post, the price is from forty to fifty dollars per ton.

When I was at Box Alder with the herd I went up to see the canon or the gap in which the creek flows through the mountains. I went up the mountain on the west side of the canon. It made my head swim to look down in places, the rocks were perpendicular, and far down in the gorge ran the creek looking like a silver thread winding among the huge rocks which lay at the bottom of the ravine. I would stop and amuse myself by throwing stones down. It looked from where I was that I might throw a stone across the gorge but to do my utmost I could not make a stone reach the water at the bottom. I would stand for half an hour at a time looking down on the wild confusion below. I amused myself by climbing about on the rocks and overhanging precipices till I was tired and concluded to go back to camp. Instead of going back the way I came I thought I would go down into the canon if I could get there. I started down cautiously winding my way first in one direction then in an other along the side of the canon stopping occasionally to gaze on the solitude, now rolling down huge rocks which would go crashing among the pines seeming to jar the very mountains — I could hear them long after they had gone out of sight and after one would think they had reached the bottom — bounding from rock to rock, loosing others as they went, with noise resembling the discharge of artilery. As I passed down I went near some places where I didnt care about staying long, these were holes in the rocks that looked as if they might be the habitations of something bigger than a wolf, any how I didnt want to meet a grizzly there by myself though I had my spencer with seven cartridges in it. I finally reached the bottom, on looking up it seemed to me that no one would ever attempt or think of attempting to go up such a place, in fact I dont believe it could be done because some places I had to jump down, others I had to let myself down by brush, some places I had to walk along a narrow place scarcely wide enough to allow me to keep my ballance, (some places that I jumped down would be very difficult for me to jump up again) When I got to the bottom things looked very different from what they first did from the top of the mountain, the trees which first looked like small willow brush were now large cottonwoods and willows, the stones which appeared insignificant, were large rocks. It looked from the top as though a horse might be led through without difficulty, but no horse could ever get through there. At the bottom I found grapes in abundance, the vines instead of running up the trees run about on the ground and over the rocks, in a good many places where they were accessible the grapes had been eaten by the bears. Bruin is said to be very fond of grapes and other wild fruit. I worked my way out of there by following the stream down, finding something to admire at almost every step. When I got back to camp it was after noon. I started out early in the morning. The canon is not more than half a mile from camp, so you can see how much time one who admires the works of nature, can spend in going but a short distance. I hope this will excuse me. Write soon

Hervey Johnson

Deer Creek. Idaho [Dakota] Ter.
Oct 23rd/64

Sister Sybil.

This fine Autumn morning I have seated myself to pen a few lines for the perusal of my friends at home. I hardly know what to write. I sometimes doubt whether it is worth while to write at all. The indians are still so troublesome in Kansas that there is no certainty in the mails. We did hear that coaches had got to running throug again but I guess it was nothing but rumor. I do not know whether you have got half of my letters during the past summer. I have had no account yet of any that I have written since the twelfth of July. We have had no account yet of the election that went off in this month in Ohio and other States. the draft also that was to come off on the 5th of Sept. is still in the shade to us. we have not heard a word about it. The last mail we got, was brought up from Fort Karney in the ambulance which was sent after it with an escort of soldiers from here. We do not know when the next will come, it may be in a few days, and it may [be] two months.

Captain Rinehart is at the Fort now, we suppose under arrest. He was ordered there four or five days ago. Several of the boys were ordered down at the same time. I am expecting to have to go again before long. Ever since that squad of us was sent to the fort under arrest, we determined to see a few things straightened up, Our Orderly Sergeant went to the fort to get his furlough to go home, while there he inquired into matters and things, got some of the boys released that were confined in the guard house, got charges preferred against the Capt and boys to appear as witnesses against him. If I go to the fort I shall go as a witness. It would be useless for me to attempt to explain the whys and wherefores of these proceedings. It will suffice to say that when a Captain gets to paying attention to emigrants and *squaws* to the neglect of his duty to his men, it is time that the men should take matters in hand. We are going to see things through if we lay in the guard house the remainder of our term of service for it. The word here is that Bill Grass The indian chief who was wounded in the fight at Platte Bridge — has gone north to raise a band of Sioux to whip out company G. He was at the fort a good while till he got well of his wounds, and when he left he told them there that that was what he was going to do. He said Company G. fought him and he was going to have revenge.

We have not yet got to work on our fortifications nor do we know when we will, we have no teams, nor men enough if we had teams. Our company is scattered along at six different posts and it is probable that we will have to take charge of two more. The length of road that we are on is two hundred miles, and if we take two other posts it will be about forty miles longer, this will take us into Utah.

We are about to lose our two laundresses, (if it would be considered any loss). They are the wives of two soldiers who belong to our Co. They are such a babbling telltale set, that the boys got tired of them and got up a petition to the capt to have them removed, and to have no further connexion with the Company. They are both here now, waiting an opportunity to go to the fort. They will probably go to the states when the old Battalion goes. In one of my letters I said something about our Orderly going home on

182

furlough and that he would probably go to our house.[56] It is not now certain that he will go, as it seems that they are going to keep the old battalion till next spring, it was his intention to go with them this fall, but if they dont go till next spring I dont think he will go at all. But if he does go and you get to see him, I want you to treat him as you would like to have me treated if I should go among strangers.

I hardly know what to finish my letter with. I have been filling it up with uninteresting stuff, everything here is so dull, nothing going on to write about The boys are catching wolves almost every night. They bait dead horses with Strychnine, the wolves go and eat as much as they want and then make for the river, as soon [as] they drink they drop dead. They caught our two pet wolves and some of our dogs.

Well I must quit. It seems to me that there is a dull prospect of you getting any interesting letters from me the coming winter

Write soon and tell every thing.

Hervey Johnson

---

[56] See letter of October 9, 1864.

Sweetwater Station & Platte Bridge

November 6, 1864 — September 1, 1865

The brutal massacre of no less than 130 (and perhaps as many as 175) Cheyenne men, women, and children at Sand Creek, Colorado Territory, on the early morning of November 29, 1864, is commonly recognized as the cataclysmic event in Indian–white relations during the Civil War decade. Although others were involved, the principal engineer was Colonel John M. Chivington, commander of the District of Colorado, bull-chested minister of the Methodist Episcopal Church, political opportunist, and erstwhile leader of the infamous "One Hundred Days Men." The repercussions of this tragedy extended to distant Sweetwater Station on the headwaters of the North Platte where Private Hervey Johnson was then stationed.

Appropriately, Johnson learned about the Sand Creek Massacre via the telegraph, and, in a manner indicative of his growing contempt for the Indians, he wrote to his sister: "That is the style I would like." This obviously was a swaggering statement for one who had never been in a pitched Indian battle as gruesome as the one at Sand Creek. Yet Sand Creek was fairly typical of the military approach to the Indian problem of the sixties. As the War Department in the West saw it, the Indians had too long been coddled, supplied, and even armed by civilian Indian agents whose nefarious alliances with shoddy government contractors and corrupt politicians had clouded their perceptions of the Indian as he really was. Rather than fight expensive and indecisive skirmishes in remote places, it was far better to confront the enemy in pitched battle and let the chips fall where they may. In this context Colonel Chivington's attack at Sand Creek served its grim purpose, for within a short time the Indians of the central and northern Plains determined to take the offensive, regardless of the consequences.

Contrary to their typically docile behavior during the winter months, the angry Indians attacked and virtually annihilated Julesburg and the surrounding ranches in northeastern Colorado Territory in January and early February of 1865. From there they moved north and west, with the certain intention of destroying the telegraph and closing the overland routes. Bloody engagements with the Eleventh Ohio Volunteers at Mud Springs and Rush Creek in present Wyoming in February were further warnings that the spring and summer of 1865 would be anything but monotonous for the military. An additional inducement for the Indians to take the offensive was the relative ease with which well over a thousand "peaceful" Oglalas and Brulés were able to make their escape while being removed from Fort Laramie to Fort Kearny under the incompetent direction of Captain W. D. Fouts.

By late May and early June, lightning-like attacks as far west as South Pass were disrupting telegraph service, discouraging emigration, and providing the beleaguered garrisons at St. Mary's, Three Crossings, Sweetwater, and Deer Creek with no lack of action. Casualties on both sides were almost routinely reported and in the aggregate constituted a grim backdrop for the Indians' brilliant attack on Platte Bridge on July 25–26. It is no exaggeration to state that the military at this point were simply unable to contend with the Indians' strategy of rapid strike and retreat, a generalization that is all the more plausible in the wake of Major General Patrick E. Connor's abortive Powder River expedition later that summer.

Hervey Johnson was advanced to corporal on June 1, 1865, but the promotion left him completely unimpressed. By this time he was a confirmed critic of the officer class, what with their drunken behavior, their inequitable system of justice, their business interests on the side, and their inability to control desertion among the enlisted ranks. Commenting on his obviously unsought promotion, Johnson stated, "I only get two dollars more on the month than the ordinary soldier. Ten dollars more . . . would not pay. It has happened that I have done nothing yet to cause me to be reduced to the ranks, and it is not often that non-coms are reduced at their own request, but I think I shall try it; that is if things don't change." Fortunately for his personal safety, Corporal Johnson did not participate in any of the more spectacular battles of the summer of 1865, although he visited Platte Bridge just a few days before the attack of late July. Perhaps his greatest disappointment was his failure to be assigned to Connor's Powder River force. On the other hand, as will be seen in the following letters, Johnson was not denied the opportunity to engage the enemy in and around Sweetwater Station and to demonstrate his ability to take care of himself under combat circumstances.

Sweet Water [Dakota Territory][1]
Nov 6th 1864

Sister Sybil

As I have now got settled down at a new place I thought I would write again. On the 2nd I was ordered up here from deer creek with four others, we got ready and started, stayed at platte bridge[2] the first night, left there in the morning, went about ten miles and found a horse running loose on the river bottom, we captured him and packed our blankets and robes on him and led him along with us. At noon we stopped and built a fire of some dead sage brush, broiled some beef that we got at the bridge, and eat our dinners, which consisted of a small piece of bread in addition to the beef. Started on and reached a camping place called Willow Spring[3] just at sundown. We turned our horses loose having first stripped them of saddles and equipments. It was very cold, the ground was frozen, all the little mountain streams were covered with ice, and the mountains with snow. We built a fire of sage, broiled some more beef and eat our suppers. We then spread down our blankets and robes and went to bed. Our camp was in a ravine, we chose that place because the bluffs would break the wind from us. we slept very comfortably. about daylight in the morning we all arose, the other boys set about making a fire to cook the remainder of our meat, and I went up to see if our horses, and cattle, (which I forgot to mention we were bringing up to Sweet water) were any where in sight. I could see nothing of them. I went back to camp and was entertaining the refreshing

[1] See letter of April 18, 1864, n. 9.

[2] See letter of May 2, 1864, n. 19.

[3] Willow Spring was on the Oregon Trail and Willow Creek, roughly halfway between Platte Bridge and Sweetwater Station. Although this well-known camping area probably derived its name from a water spring in that vicinity, Sergeant Isaac B. Pennock of the Eleventh Kansas Cavalry reported on May 26, 1865, "South of Willow Springs is an oil spring said to run 50 barrels of petroleum per day 5 or 6 miles." Diary of Isaac B. Pennock, First Sergeant Company I, Eleventh Kansas Cavalry, Manuscript Division, Kansas State Historical Society, Topeka. A Denver paper reported, on June 14, 1865, that on June 2 the "bridge at Willow Creek was burned by Indians," *Weekly Rocky Mountain News*, Denver, June 14, 1865. See also Writers' Program of the Work Projects Administration in the State of Wyoming, comp., *Wyoming, A Guide to its History, Highways, and People*, pp. 383–84; Grace Raymond Hebard and E. A. Brininstool, *The Bozeman Trail*, vol. 1, p. 161.

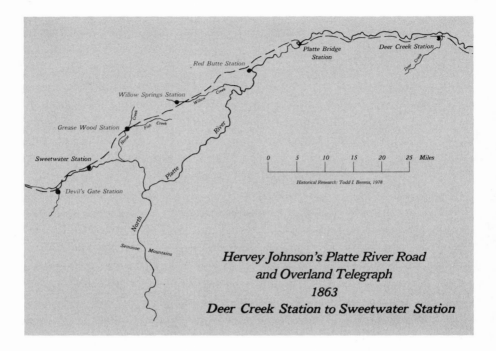

Red Butte Station

Platte Bridge
Station

Deer Creek Station

Deer Creek

Willow Springs Station

Willow Creek

Grease Wood Station

Horse Creek · Fish Creek

Sweetwater Station

Platte River

Devil's Gate Station

North Platte

Seminoe Mountains

0   5   10   15   20   25   Miles

Historical Research: Todd I. Berens, 1978

*Hervey Johnson's Platte River Road
and Overland Telegraph
1863
Deer Creek Station to Sweetwater Station*

thoughts of having to take a perhaps long and fruitless hunt for our stock, and of having to lay out another night or two — when suddenly our horses all came round a bend in the ravine and stopped just where we turned them loose the evening before. we secured them, soon despatched our breakfast and was on our way. We found the cattle about three miles from where we camped, and about a mile from the road.

The country we had been travelling over was a barren waste, a continual succession of mountains hills plains and ravines. Our last days travel the most of it was over tolerably level country, it being in the valley of the Sweet Water River. It would be useless to attempt to describe the scenery that broke upon our view as we passed round the point of a bluff where the road led into the valley of the river. It seemed as if we were going in at one corner of a huge square area that was completely walled in by mountains, on the south and west sides we could see range after range rising above eachother, the nearest appearing like huge piles of rock, and as they reced farther back and higher up everything was lost in snow. We reached our destination some time before night We are now one hundred and eighty miles from Fort Laramie. I am writing in the hospital, the boys are all so engaged at "Solitaire" that there is poor chance to write in the quarters. there is but one patient here, he was wounded by indians some time ago a short distance from here. It is getting late in the evening I must begin to close I expect this to start in the morning. I have not been here long enough yet to tell much about how I like the place &c, there are some curiosities in these parts such as "Independence Rock" [4] and "Devils Gate" [5]

---

[4] Located approximately fifty-five miles southwest of present Casper, Wyoming, on the north bank of the Sweetwater River, this "gray-brown granite monolith" has been described as "one of the most significant erosion remnants in the West." Its dimensions are 1,552 yards in circumference, 1,950 feet long, 850 feet wide; at the south end it is 167 feet high, and at the north, 193 feet. In 1839 Asahel Munger reported that the rock was called Independence from the fact that in 1830 representatives of the American Fur Company spent the Fourth of July there. Father Pierre J. de Smet, in 1840, referred to "that famous rock, Independence . . . that might be called the great registry of the desert, for on it may be read in large characters the names of several travelers who have visited the Rocky Mountains." See Paul C. Henderson, *Landmarks on the Oregon Trail*, pp. 37–38; Hebard and Brininstool, *The Bozeman Trail*, vol. 1, pp. 49–50, 89, 161; WPA, *Wyoming*, pp. 386–87.

[5] Devil's Gate is a passage of the Sweetwater River about five miles above Independence Rock. The walls of the gorge are of gray and black granite and extend 330

but I have not got to see them yet. At a future time I will tell all about them. The remainder of our Co will soon be removed from Deer Creek. Headquarters to be either here or at Platte Bridge I cant tell which.

Direct to Sweet Water Bridge via as heretofore

write soon

Hervey Johnson

Sweet Water [Dakota Territory]
Nov 19th 1864

Sister Sybil

The mail came up yesterday and brought me *one* letter — dated Oct 6th and continued to Oct 13th. I was very glad to hear from home again, it has been two weeks since I got the last. there must be something wrong with the mails or something else. I dont believe you get half of my letters from the way you write; but its no use to grumble.

The general health here of the boys is good, one or two serious accidents have occurred in our company within the last month. I forgot to mention them before. The first was breaking a leg. It was a very cold night, the man was on guard, I had charge of the guard that night and as is the custom in some places I allowed him to take something *warm* to keep up his *sperrits*, (having to stand half of the night) I saw what he took and told the Commissary sergeant to not give him any more, as I was responsible for his conduct. Things went off right for a while till the Lieut[6] got to talking with the guard and *"administered the oath"* a second time. I was out to see him several times, he was still walking his beat, but I saw that he had several *"bricks in his hat."* Things went on till near eleven o'clock, when some of the boys who had been to the Fort came up with some cattle. They went to

---

feet in height. According to Horace Greeley, more than 100 Mormons died of exposure there during an extended snowstorm sometime prior to 1859. Captain Hiram M. Chittenden, in 1902, described Devil's Gate as "one of the most notable features of its kind in the world." See Horace Greeley, *An Overland Journey from New York to San Francisco in the Summer of 1859*, p. 185; Hebard and Brininstool, *The Bozeman Trail*, vol. 1, pp. 49–50; WPA, *Wyoming*, pp. 387–88.

[6] Lieutenant Henry Clay Bretney. See letter of July 25, 1864, n. 35.

the cookhouse to get something to eat, and he seeing a light there went and began to quarrel with them, they got rid of him somehow and shut the door on him, and he went staggering about among some old wagons, and either by accident or on purpose discharged his gun, the ball going through the cookhouse but doing no injury. I heard the report and went out — found him reeling about, several rods from where he had any business. I saw at once that he had "too many sheets to the wind" and I took him in and took his gun from him and made him go to bed, he thought that was as good a thing as he wanted. I took the gun and stood the rest of his time myself. At the proper time I posted the next relief and went to bed and knew of nothing that occurred till morning. It appears that after I went to bed, the old fellow (he says he is seventy years old) imagined he was going to swim some of the boys were awake and saw him, he got up on his hands and knees in his bunk, (a two story one) and pitched out head foremost, he lit among the tables and benches and did not know till morning that he had broken his leg. It is thought that his leg will have to be amputated. I got no censure for what happened, because it was the Lieutenants fault in giving him the tea.

Now I have strung this out over two or three pages and you may think that I might as well have said: he was drunk and fell out of his bunk and broke his leg, — and been done with it. but you see I have to do it in order to fill up my sheet. I will not be so prolix with the next case.

two of the boys were taking a load of corn to the horseherd which is several miles from the post. the mules balked on a little hill. The boy that was not driving being on his own horse rode up by the side of the mules to urge them on, his horse was foolish and got to prancing about, he got mad and having no club siezed his pistol by the barrel and went to beating the animal over the head. The pistol went off the ball entering his right side and lodging in his back. He was brought back to the post where he lingered till next day and died. He was an Irishman a native of Baltimore. He told the boys to write to his parents and tell them that he only regretted having to die that way — meaning that he would rather have been killed in battle with the indians. He was buried with the usual military demonstrations. We have lost a good comrade and a true soldier.

Now I dont know what to finish my letter with. Let me see, Sybil asked me about cutting hay. There were at one time several of us going to cut hay for the Gov't but something turned up to prevent us. two or three times several of us went out and cut a load just to feed what horses we kept up (we only kept up about ten, the rest were kept out at the herd) Two of the boys I believe have been cutting hay all summer for a Government contractor; they got $2.50 per day, or eight dollars per ton. There is something over fifty tons piled up at Deer Creek. Twenty five tons was burnt last summer by an old squaw. I believe this is all that is necessary for me to say about the hay.

You folks needn't make any more apologies about letter paper just write on whatever you have if its a piece of leather, and Ill think I'm fortunate if I get it. It seems that you have been having your share of rain and mud. that is more than we can say out here. I cant remember when we had a shower last. We have been having snow mostly ever since the middle of Sept. . . .

I hope Warren will not sell any more mules at $35. A good mule team cant be bought now for less than from $350 to $500. I found this out by asking emigrants what they paid for their teams. If you have luck to be the possessors of any more mules, manage to keep them till they are two years old, if they are unruly and dont like to stay where they [are] put, tie their heads down to their feet, hobble them, I bet I'd fix 'em if I was there. A man that has been out as far from home as I have, has numerous opportunities of seeing how such diseases are doctored. . . .

I do hope you will have plenty of apples to do you this winter. I dont think about apples once a year. I think I am doing well if I get my beans and sowbelly.

I must close.

Remember to write often

Yours with spec's

Hervey

Sweet Water [Dakota Territory]
Nov 25th 1864

Sister Sybil.

I again seat myself to write. I scarcely know what to say, but I am so lonesome that I must do something to drive away the "blues." I thought when I first came here that I was going to have a nice time, but there was not a stick of wood for winter got up, neither teams to haul it with; we have to hitch up our government horses to haul with which is strictly forbidden by the Army Regulations, this causes a great deal of dissatisfaction among the men who are always ready to murmur at anything.

For several days past I have had to take the men out to the mountains to get down wood, all the wood we burn has to be brought down from the mountain sides, it is the hardest work I ever done. One might think it no labor to get wood down from a hill side, but it has to be lifted over rocks and gullies and ravines for hundred of yards before we can get it where it can be loaded on a wagon.

Our Sergeant has been gone for several days to Platte Bridge, so I have every thing to do, or to see to myself. I will be glad when he comes back, for above all things, I dislike to have the charge of a lot of men. I walked out this morning to the lake which lays about a quarter of a mile from our quarters. It is called the Alkali Lake,[7] there are several of them in this country, they are all small, this one is about as large as our farm. Several wolves were playing on the ice (it was frozen over). None of these lake have any outlet neither have any streams running into them. They are just sinks in the earth some of them have no water in them the bottom being covered with alkali which makes it look like snow many of them have nothing in them but soft mud in which many an ox and buffalo have perished in attempting to cross them. We can see their skeletons laying about in the mud. I came near getting into one myself one night. I was out hunting the horses, and not being able to find them, was returning home it was pretty dark, but I could see that I was coming near one of these ponds, I could tell by the alkali over it, I had got tired of riding and was leading my

---

[7] Alkali Lake should not be confused with Alkali Lake Station, located approximately eighteen miles east of present Ogallala, Nebraska. Captain Eugene F. Ware, *The Indian War of 1864*, p. 468.

pony, and when I got to the edge of the lake I thought I would go across it, it looked dry and solid in the bottom. I stepped off the bank but instead of stopping when my foot touched the ground I found that the bottom was not there, and I did n't stay to see how far down the bottom was, but I certainly would have done so had I not got out of there as soon as I did. If I had been on the pony I would have went in certain. One of our boys did get into one of them, he was driving a bullteam up here from Deer Creek, they camped out, and one morning he went out to bring up the cattle and the first thing he knew he was up to his waist in mud, and he would have staid there too if it had not been for a tuft of grass that was in his reach, and on which he laid hold and drew himself out. He was a pretty looking sight when he got here.

two of the boys went out yesterday and killed an antelope. they said there were thousands of them   I believe I will wind this up for the present or till the Serg't comes home, which maybe to night. perhaps he will bring the mail and with it maybe a letter for me. The Operator informs me that he left Platte Bridge this morning fiftytwo miles from here so he will be here to night.

28th. The mail came as I anticipated and brought me one letter from Sybil dated Oct 18th I was very glad to get it and to hear from you again. I must say I was disappointed though for I was looking for several that were overdue and one was all I got. The Lieutenant and Serg't have gone away to be gone several days, so I have to run the "Shubang" myself. They left with the intention of going to South Pass[8] something over a hundred miles from here. I dont expect they can get through on account of the snow which is very deep in some places along the road. I think some of taking the men out to the mountains tomorrow to get down wood, will either do that or go to tearing down some of the buildings for we must have something to burn.

I am writing on some of that paper that mother sent me, havent got but a few more sheets which wont last me very long   I dont know what I'll do when it gives out. we can't depend on any body to bring anything from the fort. it is so far and camping out at night, things are liable to get lost. agreat many packages and letters that are brought to these outposts by

---

[8] See letter of September 4, 1864, n. 53.

196

irresponsible persons, are almost destroyed when they reach us. The letters look like they have been torn open and read, papers have wrappers torn off and packages of clothing are almost always more or less damaged. In sending a letter to me hereafter, first enclose it in the heaviest envelope you can get, now dont forget this for I have got some letters in fancy envelopes that might as well have been in nothing for all the good the envelope done.

I believe the health of the boys here is pretty good (there are but nineteen of us). I have suffered a good deal since I came here with the toothache, I have several teeth that hurt me   I have tried Creosote but it dont appear to do much good but take all the skin off the inside of my mouth. The best remedy I can find is to take a chew of tobacco and roll it up between my teeth and cheek and let it soak there, I have not bought any yet, neither do I intend to if I can help it, it dont cost much, only one dollar and a quarter for a twenty cent plug; We have not got our money yet, there is seventytwo dollars due me for four months "bleeding for my Country?" We expect to get it in a week or two, the first Lieut has gone to the fort for it. I guess I will get to keep the most of it this time, I dont owe but $8,73 cts and that is for washing. . . . I would like to be at home for a week or two to help make "lasses" but I dont think it would come very natural to me, it seems to me like it wouldent be home — that my natural place is out in the mountain wilds   I have grown so accustomed to this life.

I will here close

Write often.

Hervey Johnson

Sweet Water. [Dakota Territory]
Dec. 8th 1864.

Sister Sibyl.

I concluded I would write some more. I have managed to get some paper by paying a dollar for twenty four sheets. I dont know hardly what to write, but will try to scratch down something. Three or four days ago Sam Engle and another boy started from Platte Bridge to bring us a wagon to haul wood with, they got half way and camped for the night, waked up next morning and found two of their mules gone, they hitched up the other four and started on, the snow was falling very fast, they soon ran into a snowdrift and stuck, they were almost frozen and had no wood to make a fire, so they unhitched and started on here, each riding a mule and leading one without saddles. They got here about the middle of the afternoon almost froze having rode twenty five miles throug a blinding snowstorm. One of the led mules broke loose and they left him with bridle harness and every thing on. The wagon was loaded with provisions for the posts up the road besides clothing and some arms.

Yesterday morning we started out five men with mules and horses to get the wagon. one of them came back in half an hour nearly froze. the other four went on for eight miles and two of them froze out and came back with the mules. The other two thought they would go on and find the mule the boys left the day before and also get a horse that had been left somewhere on the road some time before; they had gone eighteen miles and found the mule picking among the sagebrush, and were looking around for the horse, when they saw — about three hundred yards from them in a ravine — several indians on foot armed with rifles; they were after the horse trying to catch him with a lariat. The boys thought their best hold was to get out of there, as they had no arms or nothing to defend themselves with but a pen knife, so they lit out with the mule; on looking back they saw several more indians, some of them mounted, driving off the horse. the boys came on back here, got in late in the evening.

We think some of sending for the wagon again tomorrow. we have been burning the buildings for several days for fire wood, and if we dont get the wagon soon we must suffer. If the indians have found the wagon, we will hardly see it again and it is very probable that they have, what they cant carry off they either burn up or destroy in some way. By a despatch this morning we learn that three or four men have left the Bridge with the mail or our money, if they get through we will know to night whether the things are safe or not. I shall not finish my letter till after they come.

The operator took off a despatch this morning concerning a fight which took place yesterday on the South Platte somewhere, between the Colorado boys under Col. Chevington[9] and about nine hundred Cheyenne warriors.

[9] Colonel John Milton Chivington, commander of the Third Regiment of Colorado Volunteer Cavalry, was a native of Ohio and a Methodist Episcopal minister

The soldiers surprised and attacked the vilage at daylight, they killed four hundred indians including three or four chiefs, captured four hundred ponies with a loss of only nine men killed and thirty eight wounded.[10] That is the style I would like, this way of following indians night and day like we did last summer has about played out with me. The kind of style is to find their village and let into it about daylight some morning when they dont look for anything in that line, then there is prospect of some fun. There was about thirty ponies stolen about a week ago at Deer Creek, it was supposed to have been done by the Utes. They took a herd about a month before from a mountaineer near the same place.

Morning 9th The boys arrived here last night about dark, got through safe with the mail and greenbacks, they came by the wagon found it all right, going to send down for it this morning. I came near forgetting to say that I got one letter from Mother dated 2nd of last month. I was glad to hear from you again, I was rather disappointed though in getting only one letter, I thought there were several due me. The boys that came up brought some stationery with them. I invested one dollar in the same, purchasing a package of envelopes and three sheets of paper, so you may know something of what it costs to write a letter in this country. My wages came to eighty dollars. I dont know what to do with it I am afraid to send it home the mails are so uncertain and if I keep it here it is probable that I wont have

---

who had served in churches in Ohio, Illinois, Missouri, Kansas, and Nebraska prior to his arrival in Denver on May 19, 1860. Chivington was heavily involved in Colorado military politics before his infamous role in the Sand Creek Massacre of November 29, 1864. Stan Hoig, *The Sand Creek Massacre*, p. 19. See also letter of February 23, 1864.

[10] Chivington reported that his men "killed Chiefs Black Kettle, White Antelope, and Little Robe, and between four and five hundred other Indians," *ibid.*, p. 186. In fact the total was far less, perhaps not more than 130. The most nearly correct list of Cheyenne and Arapaho leaders killed included White Antelope, Standing in the Water, One-Eye, War Bonnet, Spotted Crow, Two Thighs, Bear Man, Yellow Shield, and Yellow Wolf. Thus Chivington's initial report of November 29, 1864, indicating that Black Kettle and Little Robe were dead was incorrect, *ibid.*, p. 154, and Appendix, pp. 177–92. For some of the disagreements surrounding this tragic event, see Raymond G. Carey, "The Puzzle of Sand Creek," *The Colorado Magazine*, vol. 41, no. 4 (Fall 1964), pp. 279–98; William E. Unrau, "A Prelude to War," *The Colorado Magazine*, vol. 41, no. 4 (Fall 1964), pp. 299–313; Michael A. Sievers, "Sands of Sand Creek Historiography," *The Colorado Magazine*, vol. 49, no. 2 (Spring 1972), pp. 116–42.

much of it by next spring, though one good thing in my favor is that we are a good ways from the store.

one of the boys is going to the fort expects to start in a few minutes so I must bring this to a close. I will enclose a drawing of the boys of Sweet Water "bleeding for their country" or doing "frontier service on the Union Pacific Telegraph Line." [11]

Write often

Hervey Johnson

Sweet Water [Dakota Territory]
Dec 19th, 1864.

Sister Sybil

Though I dont know when there will be a chance to send a letter to the office I thought I would write one any how. We are all in good health, the weather is so fine that some of the boys have gone to the mountains for wood to day. I stay here to assist the cooks and unload the wood when it comes. Sam Engle is driving the team. Sam and two or three others went out yesterday and brought in an antelope. We are having it cooked for dinner today. I wish some of you would come over and help us eat it, we are having it roasted. We might have antelope every day if the boys would go out for them, but the snow is drifted so that it is bad getting about any where except in the road.

I was sent last week with two men and a wagon down the road to get some flour that was thrown out of the wagon where it was stuck in a snow-drift, the boys went down before to get the wagon but could not pull it out till they had thrown out ten sacks of flour and left them. The morning we started down was warm and pleasant so that we did not wear our overcoats but had them on our saddles; as we rode along we saw several herds of antelopes grazing about on the plain, and now and then a gray wolf skulking about among the sagebrush. We had gone about ten miles when we could see before us a white cloud laying along on the ground, we expected we would soon come into a snowstorm, and it was not long till we found

---

[11] Johnson's drawing "of the boys of Sweet Water" was not found with his correspondence of December 8, 1864.

Drawing of Sweetwater Station in 1863 attributed to Charles Frederick Moellmann. Note the sentinel boxes in the lower left-hand and upper right-hand corners of the installation. *Courtesy of the Wyoming State Archives and Historical Department.*

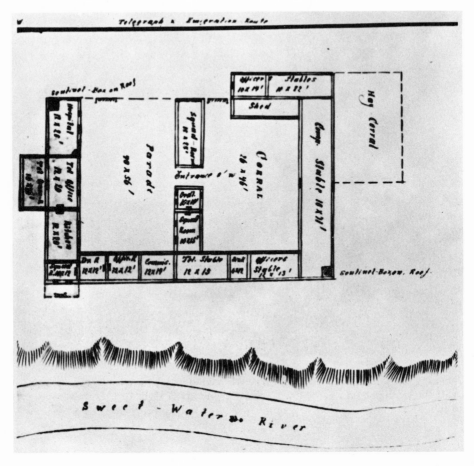

Map and floor plan of Sweetwater Station in the 1860's with the telegraph
and emigrant routes indicated. Draftsman unknown.
Courtesy of the Wyoming State Archives and Historical Department.

that we were not going to be disappointed, we soon found too that we would be more comfortable with our overcoats on our backs than on our saddles. We went on till we came to a small stream called Horse creek,[12] the air was already full of flying frost and the wind blowing so that we could not see but a short distance in any direction; we found the stream frozen over, and we could not force our horses on to the ice till we had carried dirt and thrown over it. We had instructions for me and the other boy who was [on] horseback to leave the team when we got to this creek, and go ahead to look for some horses that had been left somewhere on the road some time before, and to meet the wagon again at Willow Springs where the flour was left. We rode on through the storm having to get off and walk every little ways to keep our feet warm. the boy that was with me came near freezing, he shook like a man with the ague. I thought he had better go no further so I sent him back to the wagon and went on alone, I never had a more disagreeable ride in my life   the wind blew right in my face and the ice was half an inch thick on my beard and around my mouth. I would ride a piece and then get off and stand with my back to the wind awhile then get on and try it again.   Towards evening the storm stilled, the clouds moved away, and the sun shone out pleasant and then I had a view the most beautiful I ever beheld. I was on the summit of Willowspring hill, a high ridge over which the road passes, it looks, to be on it like it is almost as high as the mountains, I was clear above the clouds which had now settled along the valley of the Sweet water and lay rolling and plunging below me like — I had almost said — the waves of the ocean — but I never saw that, so perhaps I am not justified in making the comparison; twenty five miles to the southwest I could see the Independence rock looking more like a big elephant to his sides in the mud than any thing else, and thirty three miles in the same direction I could see that huge gap in the mountains, the Devils gate. I tried to mark the place where Sweet water Station stood, and I believe I did, but it appeared a mere speck on the plain, and was scarcely distinguishable from the piles of rocks that were scattered over the ground and looked like mere black specks. As evening came on instead of following the road further, I struck off along the summit of the ridge and not till after sundown, after

---

[12] Horse Creek drains from the Rattle Snake Range and empties into the Sweetwater a few miles below Sweetwater Station.

winding down a long narrow ridge between two deep ravines — did I again join the boys with the wagon at Willow springs.

The flour was loaded in and twas after dark before we got our camp fixed. It was by the side of a slough at the head of willow spring hollow, it being the only place on the road for twenty five miles either way where there was any wood, and that nothing but willow brush. We kindled a fire and made some coffee, which with two small biscuits each and a handful of corn that we parched on a spade, constituted our supper. It was late in the night when we went to bed, and we would have slept well, had it not been for the mules which were tied to the wagon wheels, and kept up a continual racket jerking and pulling at the chains by which they were tied. We were up in the morning with the sun, fed our mules and made ourselves a break-fast of parched corn, and coffee made of the grounds that were left from supper which was little better than warm water; after breakfast we geared and saddled up, and then left our camp at willow springs, I to go to look for the lost horses, the other two with the team to go to sweet water. That you may form some conjecture of our camp and its surroundings, I enclose a rough drawing of it taken by one of the boys that [was] along, the only thing it lacks is the sage brush which I suppose the artist forgot to sketch.[13] Well nothing of interest marked the trip I made after I left the team, It was after dark when I got home having rode near fifty miles without seeing any-thing of the horses I was hunting. You must excuse my manner of string-ing out my letters like this. I am put to it to find something to write about and have to do it to fill up the sheet so that it may have at least the appear-ance of respectability.

Hoping you will write six or seven times a week I will conclude.

Hervey Johnson

Platte Bridge. [Dakota Territory]
Dec 28th 1864

Brother Warren.

Notwithstanding my aversion at the present to indulging in chirographi-cal exercises, I have nevertheless furnished myself with the material, and

---

[13] The drawing was not found in Johnson's correspondence.

taken upon myself the "onus" of such an undertaking. I have grown so accustomed to circumstances by which I am surrounded that a dearth of news is the consequence and it is with difficulty that I can center my wandering thoughts so as to enable me to pen a decent missive. I might with considerable exertion manage to commit to paper something that could be read with interest, and perhaps profit but the dull monotony of my situation is almost proof against any attempts of mine in that direction.

I am well at present, I had been suffering sometime back with severe toothache accompanied with neuralgic pains, but I have found that all obnoxious weed — tobacco — to be a perfect antidote for that species of human affliction. I this morning invested twenty two dollars in the above named "Soldier's delight," and if it should be the cause of sorrow to my friends to learn that I indulge in such a filthy habit, I will add — that the above purchase was not for myself alone. As I am talking about purchasing, I may as well say what other articles I bought. Two quires of letter cap for four dollars, bottle [of] ink for half dollar, eight skeins thread for two dollars, and a ten cent box of matches for fifty cents. I want to get me a pocket knife and it will cost three dollars.

By the heading of this it will be observed that I am at Platte Bridge having arrived here yesterday from Sweet Water where I have been stationed for the last two months. I left there day before yesterday, camped out at Willow Springs one night and reached here about sundown yesterday. I may perhaps go back tomorrow, I want to take up some beef cattle when I go.

As I am not at home nor in any way connected with the management of affairs there I do not know that it be in my sphere to have any thing to say about it. I have no doubt but the enlargement of your molasses establishment would be attended with profitable results, the plan conceived for evaporating the juice by the same heat that does the boiling must be something novel, at least it is an idea that had not occurred to me. As for my part I can see but little difference in evaporating Juice by heat and boiling it by heat. I acknowledge my inability to comprehend matters in philosophy which are easily understood and explained by others. Should the proposed addition to the establishment, be found, on undertaking it, to be embarrassing in a pecuniary sense, such funds as are at my command will be at your

205

disposal, provided they are acceptable. You will be entirely welcome to what I have, and I would rather have my money expended in that manner than in any other. I have not much at present, but something over two hundred dollars a year is my wages and not being obliged to be at any expense for clothing or board, the whole of it might be invested in some profitable manner, provided I could send it with safety immediately after I receive it. I find it is a possession that is difficult to hold when kept on hand any length of time.

I came near forgetting to mention that I got two letters when I arrived here last evening, one from warren dated 20th of last month, the other from Iowa. I was glad to hear that you were all well, and to hear of the improvements on the farm in course of completion as well as those in prospect. I wish you would revive your Lyceum this winter, such an institution if carried on properly, must be of great advantage to the community in which it exists, in developing the mental as well as moral powers of those into whose hands will eventually fall the future administration of affairs. As to the question "Is war ever right" which was to be discussed by the "Highland Club," and the remark that it was hard to be persuaded that I would affirm the question — I must simply, candidly and sentimentally, state that now is no time to discuss such questions. War has been permitted to come upon us with all its revolting horrors — I believe for the chastizement of the nation, and as for men speculating on the plans of the Allwise Disposer of events away with such monstrosity! it will not stop the war even if you should decide that it is not right, for, as I said before, war is upon us, it must be met, it must must be looked in the face, there is no alternative. It may be urged that the improvement of the mental faculties, and not the stopping of the war, is the object aimed at in such discussions. granted. Could there not be a question chosen more appropriate? one on which there is not such a diversity of opinion? one which would not be so much calculated to produce ill feeling? In time of peace such a question would be very appropriate, but it is worse than useless to discuss it now.

Well I have a page yet that I ought to fill up somehow. Just now a despatch came for five or six more men to go to the fort to appear as witnesses before the Court Martail now in session there. I am looking every day to be summoned there myself as a witness. I hope I wont be sent for. The

Capt[14] is still under arrest and the Sergeant of whom I spoke as coming home and would probably call at our house is detained in arrest so he will not get home this winter, and possibly not at all till time of service is expired. I do not know how the court is progressing, It has been in session nearly two months, and when it will close is farther ahead than any one knows[15]....

Well I must bring this to a close

Write often

Hervey Johnson.

Sweet Water [Dakota Territory]
Jan. 5th 1865.

Folks at home.

As there are some men going to the fort tomorrow, I thought I would write again, as I might not soon have another opportunity of sending a letter there. I intended to have written on the first, but that day I was on my way from Platte Bridge to this post and did not arrive here till after dark, so that I had no opportunity to write. The reason why I wanted to write on that day was because it was just eighteen months from the day I enlisted, making it the expiration of one half of my term of service. I dont know how it seems to you there at home, but it seems to me but a short time that I have been from home, and though we soldiers proudly say among ourselves, that we have but a year and a piece to serve yet, I sometimes think, or feel, that the time yet to expire before the term of our enlistment ceases, is double that already served.

I thought when I commenced writing on this sheet that I could without difficulty find matter sufficient to fill it, but I am afraid I have undertaken a task that I shall fail to accomplish, so you must look over it if I fall into the old string-out style of filling up a page with some little incident that need not occupy but a line or two. I guess I'll have to tell about my trip down to Platte Bridge. There were six of us going down with two loads of

---

[14] Captain Levi M. Rinehart. See letter of July 18, 1863, n. 5.

[15] No verdict was rendered since Captain Rinehart was killed by Indians on February 13, 1865. See letter of July 18, 1863, n. 5.

hay. The morning we started was bright and pleasant, but by the time we got six miles we could see that a storm was brewing. One of the boys started on ahead of us intending to go through the same day. We had not gone far after first seeing the appearance of a storm till it burst upon us in all its fury. The air changed to piercing cold, and so suddenly that we could scarcely get our overcoats on, our fingers were so benumbed.

There is something sublimely grand in the approach of a mountain snowstorm. I could not help but look on it with admiration. We were going in a northeast direction, and the storm approached more from the north. The cloud appeared to roll along on the ground in huge fleecy fragments, I dont think it extended more than a hundred feet high, and appeared to move along with the swiftness of a bird. We expected to be almost lifted from our saddles when the storm struck us, and it was with difficulty that we could urge our animals forward. I was riding with another boy perhaps half a mile ahead of the wagons. The storm blew so furiously that we thought of going back, we thought the teams would go back, not thinking it possible that the mules could draw the wagons against the wind; we kept on though, and shortly saw the boy who went on ahead coming back. He came to us and we stopped and held a parley and concluded to go back to the wagons, we had not gone back far till we could see them coming on through the storm so we turned again and went on towards the bridge. the storm partly abated after we turned, but broke out again as furious as ever and lasted till we had gone several miles, it finally cleared off, but the wind kept blowing bad as ever and the snow drifted like sand. We reached willow-springs sometime before sundown, and after some difficulty got a fire started, warmed ourselves and got quite comfortable. After an hour and a half the teams came up. We got out the coffee pot and three tin cups, made some coffee which with the addition of some bacon which we ate raw, and some biscuit constituted our suppers. We had our fire built about ten feet from a thick cluster of brush, we piled down alot of hay between the brush and fire and made our bed on it, the wind howled around us, but the brush kept it completely off us. we fancied ourselves as comfortable as if we had been in a house, and enjoyed our raw bacon and cold bread with as much relish as we would a supper gotten up in hotel style. It was late in the night when we went to bed.

we arose in the morning before the sun, after as comfortable a nights rest as we would wish to enjoy, after breakfast we saddled up and started on, after going six or seven miles I with one of the other boys left the road and struck off towards the mouth of the Sweet Water, we came on to a herd of about two hundred antelopes which were playing about on the plain. they dident seem to pay much attention to us but waked leisurely along before us as if they were a flock of sheep. I fired at them two or three times without dismounting but my mule was so unsteady that I missed them, had I been near the wagons I think I would have killed two or three, for then I would have been more particular. We kept on our course till we came to the foot of the Red Buttes, we wound around the foot of the mountain, passing over some of the worst looking country I ever saw, till we came back to the road, after striking which we soon made our way to the bridge which was ten miles distant. Ten miles in this country is only about an hours ride. I believe I will bring this to a wind up. I am ashamed of it too but I cant help it.

Enclosed find ten dollars ($10.) perhaps you can find some use for it. I would send a larger sum but the mail is so uncertain that I would rather risk ten dollars every mail than fifty dollars one mail. You will please keep a proper account of it so that should I ever get home and need it, it will be in such a shape that I can get it.

Write soon

Hervey Johnson

Sweet Water. [Dakota Territory]
Jan. 15th 1865.

Sister Sybil.

I recieved two letters from home the last mail, one from Abi dated Nov 14th the other from thee, Dec. 1st. I was glad to hear from you again. It is probable that it will be some time before I again will have the pleasure of reading a letter from home. The indians have been committing deprada-tions along the mail road, robbing coaches, and murdering citizens. Some two or three battles have been fought resulting in the loss of several on both sides. About fifteen hundred indians were concerned in the affair. They attacked the station of Julesberg, took off the stock, and destroyed every thing but the buildings.[16] About thirteen soldiers and citizens were killed, thirty indians were found dead after the fight. During the fight which extended along the road for upwards of four miles a soldier with two or three citizens was sent from one part of the field to another with despatches. on thier way they were attacked by the savages. the soldier made his escape but the others were not so fortunate, one of them was shot but not killed and being unable to get away the indians scalped him, then bored through his skull, filled it with powder, and blew him to pieces. I think there will be more soldiers in this country the coming summer than ever before. The indians have become too bold and saucy, they are already making their threats what they are going to do as soon as grass grows. It appears that they are all combined. No dependence can be placed in any of them, not even those who profess the strongest friendship for the whites. Nothing but a war of extermination will ever rid the country of their depradations, they pay no regard to treaties, and as their disease is severe, the remedy should be in proportion.

We are all well. The toothache from which I suffered a great deal during the fall and forepart of winter troubles me but little now. When I feel any symptoms of it all I have to do is to eat some tobacco and the toothache is no longer remembered. The winter here this far has been mild in comparison to last winter, we do not know how cold it has been, both the thermometers at this post were bursted last winter from freezing.

. . . It is not probable now that the boys of the old Battalion will go home before march on account of the death of Major Fillmore, paymaster of this district.[17]

I will close

Write soon and often

---

[16] The attack took place on January 7, 1865. See letter of November 15, 1863, n. 14.

[17] See letter of March 8, 1864, n. 36. Here Johnson is referring to Major John S. Fillmore, who served as federal paymaster for the volunteer regiments in the West from August 26, 1862, to the time of his death on December 25, 1864. Francis B. Heitman, *Historical Register and Dictionary of the United States Army,* vol. 2, p. 419. See also Ware, *The Indian War of 1864,* p. 238.

I enclose a drawing of our Station that you may see what kind of houses we live in out here[18]

Hervey

Sweet Water. [Dakota Territory]
Feb. 1st 1865.

Sister Sybil

There is a team going from here to the fort tomorrow so I thought I would write and my letter would go directly to the fort, when it will leave there is more than I can tell. The word here is that the mail will be running again in two months, so you will get my letter sometime any how. I suppose there are at this time several of my letters at the fort. I dont think there has any mail left there for four weeks. The portion of our company stationed at Platte Bridge are fortifying that post, preparing for the spring fights. Bill Grass[19] the leader of the band with whom our boys had a fight last summer says he intends to take Lieut. Bretney's[20] scalp. Bretney is in command at the bridge. We at this post dont anticipate much trouble. We are pretty well fortified, there are only about twenty of us here but we think we are about as good as all the indians that will want to attack us.

We have had some very severe weather out here but nothing yet to compare with last winter. Our second Lieutenant froze his ears and nose while on his way from the bridge to this post a few days ago, I guess they wont drop off, they are an awful looking sight and are very painful but I think they will be much better when they get well. The Lieutenant is a young chap not more than nineteen years old,[21] he is the son of Col. Collins. He is a smart scholar, but a perfect boy, and entirely incapable of holding the position of Lieutenant. The Sergeant here has to see to everything, if there is any business to be done over the lines it is always between the Serg't and first Lieut. at the bridge.

---

[18] The drawing was not found in Johnson's correspondence.

[19] See letter of August 6, 1864, n. 37.

[20] See letter of July 25, 1864, n. 35.

[21] Lieutenant Caspar Collins. See letter of August 29, 1863, n. 29.

The boys have been at work the last week getting wood from the mountains. I was out only one day, it is awful work, the snow is three feet deep out there, and the timber all being down is sometimes hard to find. This is "first day" morning before breakfast. Sam Engle is in the cook house grinding coffee, I dont know what he is getting for breakfast. we had bread and coffee and pickles for supper last night, night before last we had bread and coffee and "krout" a dutch mess. Sometimes we have molasses with our bread and coffee, bacon or "sowbelly" as the boys call it is getting scarce here. We have had no beef from the Quartermaster for three months, we have been trying for several weeks to get some here but have failed every time. I brought two beeves to within ten miles of this post, the cattle gave out and it was dark so I left them on a small stream and came on here next morning two men went down to bring them up, they had not been gone long before we got a despatch stating that the cattle were at platte bridge. the things had turned around after being driven forty miles and walked forty miles back again. I dont think cattle will ever fool me again. we could have got here with them that night by one o'clock, but they traveled so slow and the idea of riding till that time of night in mid-winter did not suit me. Somebody has started several times with them since but they would give out and go back or get away and go back some how. we have managed however to have fresh meat a good part of the time. There are a good many stray cattle roaming about over the plain, they are mostly some broken down things that have been left along the road by emigrants. the cold weather brought four or five of them to our hay stack, they were poor, but two of them went into the commissary, one froze to death and we drove the other two away, they were too liberal with our hay. they went off up the river and we have not seen them since.

There was a young woman brought to platte bridge a few days ago from the indian village on Powder river. She was captured last summer at cottonwood springs on the south platte. her father and mother and in fact every person in the train but her were murdered and the train destroyed. She was brought in by a young half—breed the son of Bissonnette an indian trader. The Government paid about fifteen hundred dollars for her, mostly in indian stores, an indian trader was killed a short time ago on Powder river

212

and his goods taken by the indians. The team is about to start and I must close. Write soon

   enclosed find ten dollars.

write soon,

Hervey Johnson

Sweet Water. [Dakota Territory]
Feb. 3rd 1865,

Sister Sibyl.

   As there is a chance to send a letter off tomorrow I thought [I'd] write one to day. There is nothing of importance to write about so I dont know whether I can find matter enough to fill a sheet or not, but I will try. I am well at present, had a severe attack of neuralgia in my face and temple a week or two ago, was laid up a week in consequence of it. We have been hauling wood for the last week, had splendid weather for work, intended to haul again today but stormy weather prevents. An order came this morning for seven or eight of our men to report themselves to the bridge for duty. I suppose they are wanted there to work on [the] stockade. The Commander there is certainly in possession of information in regard to indian movements that others know nothing of, or he would not be making such formidable preparations for defense as he is. You may look for stirring news in the spring but you must not be disappointed if you dont hear it.

   Yesterday we got the news of the attack and burning of the mail station at Julesburg on the south platte by indians,[22] all the soldiers who had been stationed there, with the exception of twenty who had been wounded in the recent battles, were off on an expedition against the indians, so that these had but little or no trouble in accomplishing their purpose. I dont know whether there has been any body sent after them or not. It seems like it is little use to do any thing in that way, for they can hardly ever be found when there are men sent in pursuit of them. They watch their opportunity, and when they think there is nobody about or the garrison is weak they light down on the posts, do all the mischief they can, and are gone before men can

---

[22] See letter of November 15, 1863, n. 14.

get ready to follow them. The only way to "cure them out" will be to send out here about fifteen thousand men, to go into their villages, and plunder burn and kill, without regard to age or sex. *They* make no distinction in their depradations and that is the way to play the game with them. I think very probably there will be something of that kind done in the spring, especially if General Conner[23] takes the management of the concern. Conner is in command of the department west of the rocky mountains, his troops are all old miners perfect indian hunters. Not long ago some of the authorities at Washington asked him if it would be safe for emigrants to cross the plains. He told them if they would give him his way, that it would be perfectly safe in less than sixty days. I dont know whether they will give him the job or not. I hope they will, it will never be done till he, or some man who works on the same plan, gets hold of it. The plan that is carried on at the fort now would soon play out if Conner was allowed to run the machine. Every day there, one may see the old squaws carrying off sacks of flour, bacon, beans, rice, coffee, sugar hominy &c. while their sons are out committing depradations along the road. Such things are not allowed at Fort Bridger, Camp Douglas, and other military posts west of the mountains. There an indian is not allowed any where about. If one is seen skulking about he is immediately despatched. I think if one was to approach this post he would get no nearer than rifle shot, unless we are poor marksmen. Well perhaps I have said enough about this.

It has been nearly a month since I have had a letter from home and I dont know how much longer it will be before I get one. we hear that there is some mail for us at platte bridge and some somewhere else along the road. It will not be under ten days till we can get it here. I dont know that any mail has left Laramie within the last month nor that any will leave before spring. The prospects for it are gloomy at present. Affairs may change though before we know it.

My old mare is dead, the old mare that carried me around through southeastern Ohio, in chase of Morgan and his band of theives, that carried me about through Kansas and western Missouri after the Guerilla Quantrell, then eight hundred miles across the American desert, and on many an indian

---

[23] See letter of May 26, 1864, n. 23.

scout, has at last gave up the ghost. She departed this life on the night of the thirty first of december eighteen hundred and sixtyfour, of internal injuries received while scouting after indians. I am now what the indians call a "walk-a-heap", a cavalryman they call a "pony soldier" or Ah-ke-cha-tah Shun-ka-kah. There is talk of us getting some of the horses that belonged to the Old Battalion. There are at leaste one third of our company dismounted at this time, their horses having died, the most of them last summer

Well I must conclude. I wrote aletter to cousin Sam some time ago. I am looking for half a dozen letters the next time I get any, at least there are that many due me from different correspondents.

Write and tell everything that is going on in the neighborhood about the farm and every where else.

Hervey Johnson

Sweet Water. Montana Ter.
[Dakota Territory]
Feb 11th 1865.

Sister Orpah.

I received Thy letter two or three days ago, also one from mother dated 18th Dec. It had been more than a month since I had got a letter from any where. Thee said that it had been a month since you had got a letter from me. I dont know why it is, but you certainly dont get all my letters. I am well and so are the rest of the boys. The weather is nice. I took a walk yesterday to the mountains, I started with the intention of going to the top and looking over on the other side, two other boys were with me, we had to wade through snow waist deep, it was the hardest days work I ever done, before we got near to the top two of the boys "played out" and would not go any further so they started back down the mountain and I went on up, I was about three hours reaching the top. It is no use to attempt to describe the country as I could see it from the top of the mountain. There was not a cloud or mist to be seen, nothing but snow covered mountains. From twenty to twenty five [miles] to the north east lay a high ridge known as the willow spring hill. Forty miles to the east lay the red Buttes black with pine forests and all around was to be seen at distances of from eight to seventy miles, high barren peaks.

Well perhaps enough about that. The indians are still playing smash out here, about one hundred and fifty men of our regiment and a portion of Co. D. 7th Iowa went out on an expedition in Command of Col. Collins. They returned day before yesterday. The Col. reports that he came on the indians some where on the Platte Just as they had got across. The command halted and made preparations for defense. The indians recrossed the river when a warm engagement ensued which lasted about five hours, night coming on the enemy crossed back again, and the Col spent most of the night in digging rifle pits. In the morning the engagement was renewed but the indians shortly drew off towards the north. There were but two of the soldiers killed. I did not learn the number of wounded but there were several, some of them mortally, forty or fifty indians were killed and wounded. There were about eight hundred indians engaged, there were fifteen hundred in the band it was supposed. They had large quantities of plunder with them, and some white men were seen among them. Woe be to the white man that is ever taken by soldiers in an indian fight, his "hide wouldent hold shucks" I forgot to mention that one of the soldiers that was killed had ninety seven arrows in his body.[24] In one of the charges he got behind and was surrounded and every red skin took a "plug" at him. The men at Platte Bridge are still at work putting the place in condition to resist an attack.

They have got an old indian chief in irons at the Fort. He came in to Deer Creek from Powder river Just at the time that a young woman[25] who had been reclaimed from the indians was passing there on her way to the fort. She at once recognized him as the one who captured her last summer at Cotton Wood Springs. She communicated it to the commander at Deer

---

[24] This unfortunate casualty of the Battle of Rush Creek (February 8, 1865) was Private William H. Hartshorn, a member of Company C, Eleventh OVC. The official details cannot corroborate Hervey's version since the records of Company C were burned. See *History of Ross and Highland Counties, Ohio*, p. 139; Remi Nadeau, *Fort Laramie and the Sioux Indians*, pp. 173–75; Agnes W. Spring, *Caspar Collins: The Life and Exploits of an Indian Fighter of the Sixties*, pp. 65–66.

[25] This should not be confused with the much publicized case of Mrs. Joseph Eubanks (see letter of June 4, 1865, n. 46). The unidentified chief mentioned by Johnson was hanged at Fort Laramie on April 23, 1865. See letter of April 27, 1865. Two months later Johnson reported, "There have been a number of the indians hung at the fort the past spring, and a number more are in confinement awaiting their fate." See letter of June 15, 1865.

Creek who had him immediately arrested and put under guard. He had no arms about him that could be seen, but Bissonnette the trader at that place, told them to search him for he certainly had weapons about his person. They examined all about under his belt and blanket but found nothing. Bissonnett told them he knew he had a knife or something concealed somewhere. They searched again and found in one of his leggins, a knife with a blade a foot long. The old fellow was then manacled and sent to the fort. It was fortunate that they found his knife for he would have killed the guard the moment his eyes were turned if he had been permitted to keep it.

Well from various hints that I get in the letters from [home] I gather that there is to be a *bust up* at Marys. I am sorry that I cant be at home to witness the performance I will be content though to stay where I am as long as I have to and maybe you will have the satisfaction of seeing me go through the "mill."

> Marriage is a curious thing,
>> At least so much I've often heard.
> The "pizen cakes" and wedding ring
>> And other things as much absurd.
> But when the "thing's been gone and did,"
>> And distant friends are getting word,
> If you have any thing for me,
>> Just let it be "a dried up tur–key wing."

I dont think Orpah need make any excuse for her letter It done very well. If she does as well every time it will do. I will close.

Hereafter Direct your letters as follows.

> Hervey Johnson
> Fort Laramie
> Co. G. 11th O.V.C.

Dont neglect to give the letter of the company Orpah failed to do this on her letter.

Write seven or eight times a week

> Hervey Johnson

Sweet Water. [Dakota Territory]
Feb. 19th 1865

Sister Sibyl

As today is "Sunday" and I have nothing to do I thought I would write again. There are two or three other boys around the table writing, (to their "Jewsharp" I suppose) but that dont bother me any, if they wouldent shake the table so. poor fellows, I pity some of the unsophisticated youths, they think it something awful to write to a girl, and still more so to show the answers they get, some of which are rich. More verdant specimens of literature, it would be difficult to produce

We have been engaged the past week in building and repairing. We commenced a week ago to day, and have put up a stable for twenty horses with stalls and mangers, we had no framing tools, so we had to dig and set in posts. the ground was almost as solid as a rock so we had to hew out the holes with an old ax. Our only tools were two old axes, two good axes, two dull hatchets, two hand saws, one gravel pick, and an old chisel. No augers about it. with these we put up our stable in about four days, besides the stable we have put up defences at different places on top of the buildings. One day, I believe it was the thirteenth, while busily engaged on the defences, we were startled by the painful inteligence, that Captain Rinehart[26] was killed that morning by indians. The dispatch stated that he had gone in pursuit of the indians with six mountaineers, that they came upon them at daylight in the morning, and that the capt was killed. We have not yet learned the particulars. I dont know when I was so surprised, it was so unexpected, indeed it seemed to cast a gloom over us all. The Captain was still under arrest awaiting the issues of his trial by Court Martial. His body was taken to fort Laramie and interred in the cemetery there. I have not heard of any indian difficulties except the above for some time. I understand that the mail line is open again, and that the telegraph has been repaired. I dont know that I told you that about thirty miles of telegraph line had been torn down. The Old Battallion is ordered to Omaha to be mustered out of service. I dont know when they will start.

---

[26] See letter of September 4, 1864, and letter of July 18, 1863, n. 5.

It is getting on towards dinner time now, I wish I could be at home a few days to get some pie, or sweet-potatoes, or apples. We occasionally have dried fruit out here and sometimes pies. we have an article called "dessicated potatoes," it looks like corn meal, we mix it up with water and make little cakes and fry them. They taste like irish potatoes mashed up and fried. Another article of food we have, is "mixed vegetables," this is a conglomerated mass of every thing. It looks before cooked like a huge plug of tobacco. There is corn, beans, cabbage, carrots, beets, turneps, "punkins," onions, beet-tops, grass, &c found in it. These articles are all chopped up fine and mixed together and pressed into cakes. I dont wish you could be here and eat some of it, some of the boys like it, but I dont "go much" on it, I would rather take the different things by themselves.

Two of the boys went out this morning to hunt antelopes they said there was a herd about two miles from here. They have just returned, saw plenty of antelope but could not kill any. They brought in two Jack rabbits, I don't know whether you know what a jack rabbit is or not. They are about as large as three common rabbits, and next to the antelope, are the fleetest animal on the plains. There is a little animal out here called the mountain hare, it looks like a rabbit, and is about half as large as the rabbits in the states. I will finish after dinner.

Well, I have finished my dinner and brought up a bucket of water from the river and now I will try to finish my letter. Do you wonder what we had for dinner? I thought we had a good dinner. We had coffee, light bread, boiled beef, and noodle-soup, pepersauce, salt, peper &c. All the water we use is brought from the river. We carry it in a barrel with slats nailed on the sides for handles. We have to cut through the ice two feet to get water.

When is the wedding going off, I would like to know, is it to be "accomplished according to discipline"? It seems like you dont want to tell anything about it, only some vague hints, you say Semira has asked for a turkey to fatten, but you dont tell whether she is going to get married or not, You dont tell what the turkey is for.

Well, perhaps enough about this. It has set in to snowing accompanied with lightning and thunder the first I have heard in this country in the winter time. I believe I cant think of any thing else so I will quit.

219

If there is any thing of the above mentioned going to happen I want you to tell me all about it, who the waiters are, who are invited to dinner, and if you can think of any thing that I havent mentioned tell *it* too.

Write often

Fort Laramie

Co G. 11th O.V.C.

Hervey,

Sweet Water. [Dakota Territory]

Feb 26th 1865

Sister Sibyl

As to day is "sunday" again I thought I would try and write again. The letter that I wrote a week ago to day started down the road this morning. The weather had been very cold here for two or three days, so much so that we kept in doors the most of the time. Four days ago I was sent with another man down to willow springs to dig a wagon out of a snow drift. The team had been three days on the road from platte bridge to Sweet Water and only got twenty five miles, the snow was too deep for them to get any further. Two men left the team and came on here, got here some time in the night, two staid with the wagon. I started down about nine in the morning and got there about three in the afternoon. we had a very disagreeable trip, found a good deal of fresh air stirring on willow spring hill. We found the boys that staid with the team at work trying to get the wagon out of the drift, they had thrown out a good part of the load and dug away the snow so that it looked like any ordinary two horse team ought to pull it out. But four mules would not move it. We then took out one of the mules and hitched in a pony in his place. we then tried again, but they wouldent "budge." We then threw out the remainder of the load, which lightened the wagon so that four of us could start it without the mules, but still they wouldnt pull it out. I did nt know what to do next, I had a notion to load up the wagon, and leave the mules hitched to it till they got ready to come out with it, for I knew they *could* pull it. I concluded however to give them one more trial, two of us got to the hind wheels, the other two got, one on the left with line and whip, the other on the right with a spade. When all was ready the driver gave the

220

word, and with line and whip and mauling with the spade, and lifting at the wheels, and yelling like mad men, we managed to get the wagon to the top of the hill. We loaded up and drove about a quarter of a mile, unhitched, left the wagon in the road and went to camp about half a mile from the road. We took up some corn for the mules, some beef coffee cooking utensils &c for ourselves. It was very cold. the beef was froze so we had to cut it with an ax. we melted ice, made some batter and fried some "slap jacks" made coffee fried some beef and ate our supper, by this time it was nearly dark and we began to think about making our bed. We scraped away the snow, spread down a gum blanket, then two robes on top of it, then about fourteen blankets on top of them. We laid down with two robes and a blanket under us, and the rest over us. I didnt sleep much the storm howled so fiercely above us.

In the morning we awoke and found ourselves under the snow. We got out, started afire, cooked and eat some grub then packed up and went back to the wagon. The wind had layed so that it was not near so unpleasant as the evening before. we hitched up and were soon on our way up the long acclivity called willow spring hill, we got over without trouble and at the foot of the hill on the west side we had to stop completely hemmed in by snow. we got out the spades and went to work. The place was where the road crossed a ravine, we dug down wide enough for the wagon through snow three feet deep for the distance of thirty yards to the bottom of the ravine, then for two rods we had no digging to do, but where the road started up the hill again a perpendicular bank six feet high opposed itself. We let into from the lower side but it was so high and so compact that we worked to very little advantage. We got on the upper side and dug down hill. The snow was so solid that we cut it out in blocks. I never worked much harder in my life than I did there, the cut was so deep and the snow so heavy to throw out. The place looked like a stone quarry, with big blocks of stone piled up around it. Towards noon we began to feel hungry, and I sent one of the boys to get us something to eat. He scratched around in the snow and found some sage brush started a fire, melted some snow and mixed up some slap-jacks and fried them, hewed off some beef and fried it, and called us to dinner.

I have heard it said that we must all eat a peck of dirt in our lifetime, but if a soldier dont eat his peck in three years I dont want a cent. The way the soldier puts it away is encouraging to those who have a life time to eat it in. Dirt or no dirt we eat it with a relish. After dinner we resumed our work and by the time the sun was but two hours high, we had it completed. The next thing was to get the team through. We started the mules, but the driver was so awkward that he couldnt hit the cut but went to one side and stuck fast then some more digging was done, got the wagon straight, started and run out the other side and stuck, then we changed the wheel mules, dug some more, started and pulled out to the bottom of the ravine. The next thing was to get through the deep cut, two of us got the leaders by the bridles, the driver in the wagon with the whip. We started in all right, but ran against the snow on one side and stuck. we changed the mules again, let them rest awhile, two of us got in the wagon one with a whip the other with a spade, and one behind to push. we started them and whipped and hammered them with the spade till we got through. We started on, got about six miles and got fast in another drift. we did not try long to dig out this time. it was getting dark and beginning to snow, we were fifteen miles from home. I told the boys to unhitch and we would go to Sweet Water, the order was executed promptly. we reached here about ten oclock, facing a driving snowstorm yesterday was so stormy that we could not go back for the wagon, to day is not much better. four men went down this morning for it.

27th. The wagon came in last night. To day is very stormy and disagreable. We had some visitors here for three or four days past, they left us yesterday morning. They were three Arappaho indians. What their business was I could not learn, but I know that if Lieutenant Collins has been some where else besides here, they would never have come in to the post. They have a village of forty teepes somewhere a short distance north of here, they say they are going to the bridge to help the soldiers. There is already a large village of the same tribe near platte bridge. I suppose the Gov't is furnishing them ammunition and provisions, so they can assist our boys there. For my part I would not like to trust them, they are all treacherous. The old battalion started home a week ago to day. They take the remains of Captain Rinehart with them, he is to be taken to Springfield

222

Ohio, to be interred instead of Fort Laramie. The particulars of his death as near as I could learn are these. Some Sioux who had been prowling around in the vicinity of Deer Creek Station, Stole some horses of Adolph Cooney, and Jules Ecoffey,[27] two Swiss mountaineers; the captain who had been living with them, went with them to try to recover their stock, some soldiers of Co. E. were with them, and also Dr. Ritchie, the assistant Surgeon. They came on the indian camp on Laprelle creek twenty miles from Deer Creek. The Captain posted the men in convenient places as guards, while he dismounted and went into one of the lodges, He gave the guards orders to "shoot every son of a b - - - h" that run out of the lodges. As soon as the Capt. went in, an indian ran out through a hole which he cut in the lodge and escaped. Next an old squaw ran out at the door she was shot, instantly dead, the Captain ran out after her and he was shot through the heart by the same guard. Then Dr. Ritchie told the rest of the men that there was no place for them, that they had better get out of there. They all ran off then leaving the Captain laying there. I must add that the whole party was *drunk*, from the Captain down. It was whiskey that did the mischeif and nothing else, there were only five indians there, and there were at least twelve men and soldiers. Had they been sober they never would have run from five indians, or committed the sad blunder that deprived us of the commander of our company.[28] I suppose the vacancy will be filled by promoting H. C. Bretney,[29] first Lieutenant, to the captaincy, His position will be filled by C. W. Collins, second Lieut, and one of our sergeants will be promoted to the second Lieutenancy.

I will close. write soon.

Tell me everything that is going on about the farm, and neighborhood Tell Uncle Johns girls that think they might as well write to me as not, and not think because I am a soldier that I am some ruffian or something no better.

Hervey Johnson

---

[27] See letter of March 25, 1864, n. 5.

[28] Here Johnson has reference to Captain Levi M. Rinehart. See letter of July 18, 1863, n. 5. That Rinehart may have had a chronic drinking problem is apparent on the basis of Johnson's earlier letter from Fort Leavenworth. See letter of August 18, 1863.

[29] See letter of July 25, 1864, n. 35.

Morning 29th. Well, I had this letter sealed up once, but I had to tear it open to tell of a little circumstance that happened last evening. We had another fight with the "blood skins." About half past three we were all lounging lazily about the quarters, when the sentinel in the "lookout" shouted "there goes an indian with old bob." (bob is an old lame mule running at large around the station), we were in arms in a second and out of the stockade. A shot or two made the old fellow leave the mule and break for the river a little ways below the Station. we followed him on foot to the river when another indian showed himself. They both swam the river and got out of sight in the bluffs, four of us shooting at them as long as they were in sight. In a few minutes they appeared just entering a ravine at the foot of the mountains. Our attention was now directed to a single indian about a mile to the right of the ravine, on the side of a long ridge that run parallel to the foot of the mountain. He would ride up to the top of the ridge and look over into the ravine beyond, ride along further and look over again then ride round in a circle and make several queer maneuvers. Just at this instant the two indians who had ran into the ravine were seen to dash swiftly out and disappear behind the low ridges at the foot of the mountain and in a few minutes reappear and join their comrade on the side of the ridge. It had been preconcerted here, that should any indians appear, the report of fire arms at the station would be a signal to bring in the horses. It had now been fully half an hour since the firing at the station ceased. We could see the horses plainly, they were beyond the ridge to the right of where the indians were lurking but dident appear to move a step this way.

They the herders had not heard the signal. Six men had already left the station on foot and were half way over there, three of them to watch a gap in a spur of the mountain, the other three to aid the herders. The three indians now sauntered slowly along the ridge in plain view to us, but not to the men with the herd. They soon reached a place where the ridge terminated in a spur of the mountain directly opposite the herd, dashing across here they disappeared. The three men walking anticipated their movement and fired a couple of shots which were luckily heard by the men before the indians got in sight. It was the first intimation they had of any danger, and almost before they had got into their saddles they heard the "indian yell"

224

and saw the indians coming down on them, the horses heard the yell too and the most of them started off down the ravine that ran along the long ridge. The indians not being content with what they had got loitered around to get the remainder of the herd. They fought the boys for half an hour, one of them receiving a "gut winder" which sent him to the "happy hunting ground." He fell forward on his saddle and his pony ran off with him. They are always tied to their saddles to prevent falling into our hands when killed or wounded. Seeing they could not get the other horses, the two remaining indians started off to follow those that had started, when two of the boys put after them, the other starting in with what horses were left. The boys followed till they came opposite the ravine where the two indians first ran. here they were surrounded by about twenty indians who had been laying in ambush there. The boys fought them bravely, keeping them at a respectable distance, we could see it all from the station and thought the boys were "gone up" sure, but they wouldn't scare worth a cent; the indians found it out and went on after the herd. one of the boys was wounded in the hand and the [other] had his horse shot in the back, neither of them seriously hurt. The boys turned back, and the indians turned the horses away from the mountain towards the river. They were just emerging from a little ravine that led out of the bluffs into the bottom when they saw two of our boys on the opposite side of the river waiting for them   They changed their course and the last we saw of them they were going over the top of the mountain in a place where a man would hardly think of crossing on foot. I must get another scrap of paper.

2nd Scrap

I'll try to wind up on this scrap. The boys who started over from the station on foot did not reach there in time to be of any assistance   They met the boy who was bringing the remainder of the herd and came back with him. The three who went to watch the gap I spoke of, discovered another ambuscade that had been planned for the boys, should the herd have been driven through the gap and they attempted to follow, there were about nine or ten indians in it. when the herd disappeared over the top of the mountain these came out of their hiding place and rode off. We lost in this scrape seven horses and three mules. They left us 5 horses and 5 mules.

225

The telegraph line has been out of repair some where for two or three days till last evening, when it was up for about ten minutes. The Sergeant wrote out a dispatch of what had occurred to send to Company Hd. Qrs but did not get to send it   while the line was up a dispatch went over from 3 crossings[30] to some place below stating that St Mary's station[31] sixty five miles from here was burned the night before, (27th) and it was not known what had become of the boys. Lieutenant Collins gave the report. He left three crossings at dark to go to St Mary's twenty five miles. He got in sight of the station, and seeing it on fire he turned back to three crossings. A few minutes ago a dead dog came floating by the station, it was recognized by boys here who had been at St Marys as a dog that belonged to that station, he had been killed by the indians and thrown into the river I suppose, and it is probable that the boys there have met the same if not a worse fate. There were but five there and they could make but a feeble resistance to a large band of indians. We are looking for them to try to burn us out, and are about ready for them to come on. we dont want more than two hundred to come at once though. as there is no prospect of getting to send this down soon I will not seal it up again for a day or two or till I hear from above.

30th. As there is still no communication over the line, The sergeant in command here intends to send two men to the bridge to night to report the state of affairs. I thought I might as well finish my letter and they could take it down. Nothing of importance has occurred since last evening. The evening was quite stormy a good deal of thunder and wind but not much rain. during the evening and night the sentinel saw a good many wolf-skins and buffalo robes and a large box floating down the river. It may be possible that the indians attempted to cross the river somewhere above with their lodges, and what the guard saw might have been lost by them with the exception of the box, it must have come from St Mary's. I hope when the boys return from the Bridge they will bring the mail with them, It is getting so lonesome

---

[30] Located on the Oregon Trail approximately five miles northeast of present Jeffrey City, Wyoming, Three Crossings was a telegraph station and stage station named after the topographical feature that within a mile required travelers to ford the Sweetwater three times. WPA, *Wyoming*, p. 316; Hebard and Brininstool, *The Bozeman Trail*, vol. 1, p. 85.

[31] St. Mary's Station was also the same as Rocky Ridge Station. See letter of April 18, 1864, n. 10.

here since the Kansas boys left that I hardly know how to employ myself. I believe I could write a letter every day in the week if I had that many to answer, but I would soon run out of paper at that rate. I am ashamed of these scraps but I cant help it, if you dont like the looks of them you may copy off the writing on respectable paper. Well, as I do not know what to fill up the rest of this scrap with I will finish right here.

Now dont forget to write often

Hervey.

Sweet Water, [Dakota Territory]
Mar 9ᵗʰ 1865.

Sister Sybil.

As I have nothing to do this morning I thought I would write again. There is mail for us somewhere between here and the Fort. I dont know when it will get here. It is more than a month now since we have had any. Indian troubles are gathering upon us. we dont know what to believe. Rumor says that the Sioux and Cheyennes have separated, and that the former are anxious for peace. One thousand lodges of them have come to camp Mitchell[32] near Scotts Bluffs and are waiting to have a treaty, They are the same that had a fight with the Col. on the north platte some time ago, Two regiments of cavalry are on their way out here, and I suppose the Sioux are afraid of them, having had a taste of the way soldiers fight. The Cheyennes are camped about "three sleeps" from here, so we are told by some friendly Arrappahoes who came in here. There is a small village of Arrappahoes about "one sleep" from here, several of them have been here at different times. A mexican who has been a prisoner among them from a child came in with one of the indians, he speaks english so as to be under-

---

[32] This installation was established in early August 1864 by Captain Jacob S. Shuman of the Eleventh OVC, under orders of Brigadier General Robert B. Mitchell, Commander of the District of Nebraska. It was located approximately twelve miles east of the present eastern Wyoming line on the south bank of the North Platte River. Sometime prior to August 31, 1864, its name was changed from Camp Shuman to Camp Mitchell. The post was never officially designated a fort and was abandoned in 1867. Robert W. Frazer, *Forts of the West*, pp. 88–89. Regarding Captain Shuman, see letter of March 25, 1864, n. 4.

stood. he told us that four Cheyennes were at their village, (they are much afraid of Cheyenns) they wanted some of us to come out to their village and kill the Cheyenns, they did not want to do it themselves because they were not at war with that tribe. At the same time the "medicine man" sent couriers to Platte Bridge to Bear and Shields[33] — chiefs of the Arrappahoes to ask what they must do with the Cheyennes. The soldiers would not believe the report of the couriers, neither would we here believe what they told us. Our visitors went away to the village but came back again yesterday and told us that the Cheyennes had left.

There was a team about starting up here from the Bridge at the time the Arrappaho couriers came there, a telegraph operator who was there and was coming up at the same time with a team of his own saw some of the Arrappahoes talking by signs with some mountaineers. He understood the signs himself. The Arrappahoes were telling the mountaineers that when the team left the bridge the Cheyennes were going to kill the soldiers that were with it and take the mules. No person there would believe any thing of the kind but the operator, he said he believed it. There was one thing that aroused suspicions a little. Our visitors were very inquisitive, wanting to know when the team would start, if there was any rations with it, how many soldiers were with it &c. to these questions of course they received very indefinite answers. Well the teams started (ours and the operators) ours broke down near the Red Buttes, The other with three of our boys who were horseback came on here. The driver and the boy who was with him went back to the Bridge to get another wagon. They got it and started up yesterday morning. They had gone perhaps five miles from where they started when the driver happening to look back saw four indians coming towards them. He told the boy that was with him to get up (he was laying down under a robe) and load the guns (there were three or four in the wagon) for there were some indians coming up behind them. They rode up and begun to talk telling the boys that they wer "good Arappahoes," wanted to trade ponies, wanted the boys to swap their guns for ponies, wanted some

---

[33] Here Johnson has reference to Black Bear, who signed the Fort Laramie Treaty of 1868 and who, two years later, was killed by white miners in the Sweetwater valley, and Little Shield, also a signator of the 1868 treaty, who later became a prominent scout for General George Crook. Virginia Cole Trenholm, *The Arapahoes, Our People*, pp. 221, 227, 231–33, 250.

of the beef they had in the wagon &c, appearing to be very friendly. They rode along for some distance, two on each side of the wagon. The boys were suspicious of them and watched them closely. The driver sat watching the mules and the indians on the left hand side of the wagon, and the other boy sat with his back to the mules watching behind and the other side. The driver saw an indian on the right draw a revolver on the boy, he spoke to him to dodge quick, but it was too late, the revolver was fired and the boy fell over and dropped off the wagon, at the same instant a ball sped past his own ear. He jumped off then and drove near two hundred yards and stopped, unhitched his leaders and turned them around by the side of the wagon and got behind them. The sun was about two hours high when they were first attacked, and it was most miserably cold. He staid behind his defences and fought till dark when he took out one of the team and came on here. He saw the savages go twice to his comrade but could not tell whether they scalped him or not. he could not get back to bring him to the wagon.

I was on guard last night when he got here, it was after twelve o'clock, He had rode about thirty five miles without gloves having lost them in the fight, he was almost froze. Five men immediately got ready and went back I should like to have gone but I had no horse. Fifteen men also went out from the bridge, we have not heard from them yet. They are having an awful time I know the wind is blowing most piercing cold and they are so far from wood or fire. The boy that was killed is Phillip Rhoads[34] he lives near Petersburg, he is some relation of Parkers I think, he enlisted a year ago this winter and came out last spring. I will not finish my letter till the boys come back or I hear something from them.

Morning 10th. Received dispatch last night from the bridge. It stated that the men who left here got to the wagon at seven o'clock in the morning, being five hours riding 35 miles. They found Rhodes body stripped of every particle of clothing, he was shot in the left cheek, the ball lodging some where in the back of his head, his skull was broken in also by some heavy

---

[34] Private Phillip W. Rhoads was born in Hillsboro, Ohio, and enlisted in Company K, Eleventh OVC, on February 13, 1864. In July 1864 he was assigned to Company G, and on March 8, 1865, he was killed in action at Poison Creek (near Platte Bridge). Private Phillip W. Rhoads, CMF.

blow; everything in the wagon was destroyed, except some corn and a box of boots   There was one thousand revolver cartridges, several blankets and robes, guns and sabres, 3 quarters of Beef, clothing belonging to several of the boys, paper envelopes, a bale of smoking tobacco, and about fifty dollars worth of chewing tobacco, in the wagon. My sabre and five dollars worth of tobacco and seventy five cents worth of paper was all I lost. The wagon was uninjured the mules were gone no indians could be seen, it was too cold to follow thier trail.

1st The news of Rhodes death was sent to his parents at Petersburg by telegraph. Some of the boys lost all the clothing they had except what they were wearing at the time, one lost his carpet sack with his fathers, mothers, brothers and sisters pictures in it. It will be joke on the indian though if I ever catch him with my sabre I'll take it right away from him without asking where he got it. Such successful excursions as this one will embolden them to further depradations, and they will keep on till they find them selves soundly whipped yet. It will not allways be so, I dont think Co. G. will be fooled again by "good Arappaho" or "good Sioux" or "good Cheyenne." We have learned a lesson, if there are any friendly they must keep off the road while we are on it, if they do not, they will be politely invited to keep their distance. The Arappahoes I believe are friendly, but it wont do to meet them, or for them to meet us with tokens of friend ship on the road. It has "played out."

2nd This morning the weather is very fine, not a bit of wind stirring, the sun shines out warm and pleasant. I do wish the boys that went down from here night before last had had such weather. There is such a contrast. Yesterday the storm raged at its worst. It was so bad that we would almost freeze going to the river for a bucket of water. Today the boys have all gone out, some hunting, some for a walk, some to take a view of the Independence Rock. Some of our visitors have gone, some are here yet   I suppose they are looking for the village in today.

Well I will quit,

Write often

Thy Brother Hervey

Platte Bridge [Dakota Territory]
Mar 26th 1865

Sister Sybil.

I seat myself this morning to write again. I arrived here yesterday
morning from Sweet Water, found three letters for me from home. . . . You
cant tell how glad I was when I got them, It had been seven weeks since I
had got a letter from any where. Yesterday was one of the awfulest days I
ever saw. We had been two days on the road from Sweet Water to this post.
night before last we camped ten miles from here. our bed was on the ground
as it always is when we are out. In the night there came on a snow storm
which blew at a terrible rate. We were completely covered up with snow,
we could not turn over in bed without rolling in snow, towards morning
the storm increased, we dident know whether to get up or not. We however
concluded to try it so we crawled out and shook the snow out of our breeches
legs and boots and got dressed, built a fire of sage brush, made a pot of
coffee and drank it which was all we had for breakfast. There were four
of us boys, we were escorting some teams down that had been up with
rations. when we got up in the morning we found the cattle had run off in
the storm and the drivers could not find them. It was a decided case of what
we call a "Government soldier out of luck." We couldent see the slightest
prospect of the storm abating or changing its direction. We mounted our
"plugs" and started this way, the snow was blowing like sand right in our
faces, we had our coat capes wrapped around our faces so we could see with
but one eye. We put out at a gallop   I thought we *would* freeze, some one
proposed that we sing something, we then struck up that good old song —
beginning — "O Now I want to go home" &c. We thought we had as well
laugh as cry and consoled ourselves with the refreshing thought that it was
all in the three years and that we ought to be in better luck and learn to take
a joke. Well we have no right to complain, "we would ride" (a remark
generally quoted by the soldiers when they hear anyone growling)

Well about something else. That was a very interesting reply I got from
Warren. I think I wrote him a cap sheet full and all he sent me was 8 inch
on six inches square. I thought by some things I said in my letter to him,
that I would draw him out some, but he dident draw worth a cent. I would
like to see the piece he read on the "War Question", and also the one Sybil

231

wrote in "Hiawatha Style". You seem to fear that I will get so accustomed to this country that I wont want to come back home when my time is out. Dont be alarmed about that. If I take a notion to go into the service again I will try the Gun-Boat service. I have tried the cavalry, infantry and artilery, all mixed up together, and I think I would like to go some place where they had only one thing at a time.

Yes I know Peter Rickman. He is a half blood "nigger," he lives somewhere between Samantha and Vienna, I believe on Old Tom Johnsons farm, *He* never was at Deer Creek, nor any one else of that name. If Mat received a letter from that address, she is sold. Tell her there is no such person out here, and that she has been duped by some rascal under an assumed name. Well I must tell you that the three letters I received from home were not all. I got one from Cousin Joe White, and four from Uncle Sam's neices in different parts of Iowa — the fruits of an advertisement that I sent to a western country paper some time ago, I expect to derive at leaste some amusement from it. The letters I received were all signed by assumed names such as Maud Emberton Kate Clifford Alice Carey, &c. Some of them from their style I judge to be pretty sharp. I may get "picked up" but they will have to be sharper than I am if they make much off of me, at least I am not much alarmed about getting "tuckened up" by them. What makes you feel sorry when you hear what we "poor boys" have to eat out here? Why we have plenty of game and other wild meat such as (I believe I did tell you what it was) bread and coffee and coffee and bread and — and — and coffee without sugar and bread without salt soda or grease. I think we lived about two weeks on the above, got nearly down to our fighting weight in the meantime too, but what is that to us soldiers "we would ride." O yes the wedding, lets see, this is the twenty sixth, few days yet and — well of course some of you will tell me all about it. I expect to start back tomorrow to Sweet Water, when I get there I intend to take a week and answer my correspondents. I believe I have about run out of stuff so I will have to bring this to a close.

Write often and big letters.

Hervey.

232

Sweet Water. [Dakota Territory]
April. 3rd. 1865.

Please read *this letter* at home.

Sister Sybil.

Mail day has come around again, and I find myself in possession of two letters from home, the first of date Feb 6th, the other Feb 11th. I was glad to hear from home, but sorry to hear that you were all sick. When I forget to tell you that I am well, you may take it for granted. You dont often speak of *getting letters from* me, I cant think what is the reason, whether it is getting to be such a *common* occurrence that you *dont* think of it, or whether it is so *uncommon* that you *cant* think of it. I am sure if you dont get letters from me that it is not my fault.

The weather here has been fine for the past week, the ice left the river yesterday; I love to stand on the bank and watch the huge floating piece's of ice as they crowd and grind against each other in their course. It seems like warm weather is near at hand, the snow has all left the plain, and the past few days of warm sun have caused vegetation to begin to appear. . . .

I notice that in some of your recent letters you seem to be terribly alarmed about us freezing to death. I suppose your fears were excited by the extreme cold weather in the states which, I have heard, caused the Mercury to fall to zero. It has not been very cold out here yet, at least I have not made any calculations about freezing. The mercury only got as low as sixty-two degrees below zero and then bursted the tube which was so short that it could get no lower. . . . If you dont see how any one could eat raw bacon, Just go out some day without any thing to eat till night and see if a slice of raw bacon wont be delicious especially if the weather is cold. I would take it raw in prefference to having it cooked. it is better — that is it goes further. one of the boys went out yesterday and shot a wild goose, another brought three deer to camp a few days before, he found them near the foot of the mountains where he was herding horses.

A short time ago about half the horses belonging to Co E of our Reg't were stolen by indians and one of [the] herders was killed. A large train with rations and corn for these upper posts camped about seventy miles this side of Fort Laramie last night, all their stock was stolen including twelve head of beef cattle for Co "G." dont know when they will come on up, but not till they get something to pull the wagons. Six hundred troops arrived at the Fort a short time ago, an expedition is to start out shortly. I understand that thirty of our Co are going . I wish I had a good horse, I think I would be elected as one of the thirty. I am getting tired I will quit till tomorrow.

4ᵗʰ. I have just returned from the mountains, where we have been for a load of wood, and eaten my dinner, and I now propose to finish the letter. For dinner we had bread, coffee, and dessicated potatoes fried. we had wild goose for supper last night. We are entirely out of fresh meat now, we intend to devote the remainder of the week to hunting, as it is not probable that any beef will reach us soon. Some thing was said in one of the letters about you getting some paper to send to me, but hearing that I had got some you thought you would wait till I was about out. I did get four dollars worth. You may think that would be a big lot of it, but it was only forty-eight sheets, and I had to divide it with the other boys, I have bought some two or three times since then. The indians destroyed a lot of paper and envelopes for me too. I have had more trouble keeping myself in such things than any thing else. If you have any that you intend to send to me, dont let the hearing of me getting a dollars worth, discourage you from sending it. Recollect that I am now one hundred and eighty miles from where such things are to be had and the chances for sending there are few. I believe I have a dollars worth of stamps yet, but some of the boys are nearly out and I dont know how long they will last. I understand that soldiers wages have been raised four dollars on the month, if it is the case I will get twenty two dollars a month. General Conner has taken command of the Department of the Plains, Headquarters at Denver City. My sheet is full. Write soon.

Hervey.

Sweet Water Bridge,
[Dakota Territory]
April 11ᵗʰ 1865.

Folks at home.

As I have nothing else to do to day, I thought I would employ myself in writing. I dont know either hardly, what *to* write. Yesterday I thought I would write some today, and I thought too that I would have a good deal to write about; but I fear that my "air castles" have all vanished. It is very lonesome here now, we have nothing to do but eat and sleep and stand guard about once a week. If we all had good horses, time would pass off differently, we would be in the saddle the most of the time scouring the country in pursuit of pleasure and game. Three of the boys are out now hunting. I went out yesterday for a ramble among the mountains, took my gun along thinking I might see something to shoot at. Having no horse I went on foot of course, I would always rather walk when I got into the mountains. I wish some of you could be here to go with me sometime, but then you are all so afraid of "injins" and bears, that I would have to go alone I expect, if you *were* here. I know you would enjoy the scenery though; if you wouldn't, it would be because your tastes are different from mine. I know I spent hours yesterday climbing about, seeing something to interest me almost every step. It seems to me that I would never get tired of such trips. I could sit all day in one place and find amusement and pleasure in gazing on what is around and below me. I dont know how it would seem in a more civilized country to look down from the mountains on a plain dotted with villages, and farm-houses, and marked up with a perfect network of roads, along which pours the busy population, and see every where, the inroads science and art are making upon nature, but here to look upon the unbroken solitude from the dizzy heights, inspires one with emotions such as none but a true lover of nature can appreciate.

The eleventh Kansas cavalry left Fort Laramie yesterday for duty somewhere along the road between this post and the Fort. When it left the fort various were the speculations among the members of Co. G. concerning the object. Some thought it was to strengthen these upper posts while an expedition against the indians on Powder river was set on foot. Others thought it was to releive us, so that we could accompany the expedition, because we are better armed than any other regiment in the frontier service; we hoped the latter might be the case, for we havent as yet burnt enough gun–powder to give all hands a good smell. We will know in a week or ten days what is to be done. Some of the boys from this post went to platte bridge a few days ago. They start back today with the mail. I shall not finish this till after they arrive. The boys have returned from hunting unsuccessful. We are going to have a goose-pot-pie for supper, one of the boys shot one yesterday. I will finish this when the mail comes.

Morning 13th. The mail came last night. . . . Hurrah! for Grant. May glory attend him. We were electrified a few days ago from hearing an order from Gen Dodge to the Governors of Nevada and Colorado, commanding them to fire a national salute of one hundred guns in honor of Grants victory at Richmond and Petersburg. We had not heard that the above named places were captured. The first we knew was the order for firing the national salute. How proud must those veterans feel who have been before Richmond for the last two or three years, to know that their work is accomplished. With what beating hearts, and bosoms swelling with emotion do they tread the streets of the once defiant, now fallen rebel Capital.

Alas! like some of the cities of old, "Her tale of splendor now is told and done, her wine–cup of festivity is split." It is no use to wish I was there but I cant help it. We hope the war will soon be over, and we will all get to go home. What do the people in the states think about it? I recon when they heard the news there was big noises made, and a heap of gunpowder burnt. we could not make any demonstrations here not having the wherewith needful. From the picture I sent you, you seem to judge that there aint much wood on the side of the mountain, well, thats the way it does look, there aint much green timber, and all the dead, is in the hollows and ravines where you *cant* see it unless you would come out here and look.

We dont mind getting wood much   we always feel better after having been out there at work than we would if we lazed around and done nothing all day. Albert Johnson[35] was here last night, he came down from above to take the mail up. He received a letter containing information of the death of his brother Zack. It seems that there must be a good deal of sickness at Camp Chase,[36] but I suppose the boys were like myself when *I* enlisted, *they* knew they were going for a life on the tented field or to die as soldiers. . . .

---

[35] See letter of July 18, 1863, n. 4.

[36] Camp Chase was located at Columbus, Ohio. It was established as a recruiting camp by Governor William Dennison in the spring of 1861. Later it became a Confederate prisoner of war camp. At the time of Johnson's writing about it to his parents, there were 3,200 prisoners incarcerated at Camp Chase. Eugene H. Roseboom, *The Civil War Era, 1850–1873*, pp. 388, 437–40.

I forgot to tell you that I am well. Several of the boys have the scurvy, some pretty badly. Well I must close — excuse this sheet of paper, it is rather dirty, but you must blame "John 'rappaho" for that. I am thankful that he left me any, we thought he had taken it all but we found some of it scattered about in the sage brush, and this is one sheet that he left.

Hervey.

Pay day will be again in two or three weeks. If I have any money to spare I will deposit it in the hands of the telegraph company. They will send it by express from Chicago or Cincinnati to Hillsboro. I will have it directed to Warren. You can use it or let Uncle John have it. There will be expressage on it which you will have to pay. No more

Write soon

Hervey

Sweet Water [Dakota Territory]
April 21st 1865

Sister Sybil.

I thought I would try to write some to day, though I expect it will be dificult for me to find matter enough to fill up a letter.

I am well, the Sergeant who has been in charge of this post has had the Scurvy pretty badly, he has gone to Platte Bridge, so I have every thing to attend to myself. Lieutenant Collins is in command here but he is next as good as a wooden man. The boys are eternally growling about something, and it is impossible to please every one, or to allow every one to have his own choice about every thing. I know I would hate to hear every thing that is said about me behind my back. It is the meanest position in which a man can be placed, that of a non-commissioned officer. I speak only of Co. "G." I dont know how it is in other companies, but in our company, every man is smarter, knows more, and thinks himself a better man, than those under whom he is placed. I am getting tired of it, if our company was at the fort it would be different, or perhaps if we had an officer in command who knew

237

his business and attended to it, it would be better. If things dont take a different turn shortly, I shall ask to be returned to the ranks, and be nothing more than a private soldier.

A private is the most independent soldier there is. He has no responsibility resting on him at all, is not supposed to know anything nor do anything but his simple duty, and obey the commands of his superiors. Sybil wanted to know what kind of an officer I was. On the 26th of last June I was appointed 7th Corporal, I am now third or fourth Corp'l, I dont know which. I only get two dollars more on the month than an ordinary soldier. *Ten dollars* more on the month would not pay. It has happened that I have never done any thing yet to cause me to be reduced to the ranks, and it is not often that non–coms' are reduced at their own request, but I think I shall try it — that is if things dont change

The weather has been stormy here for the last two or three days, snow showers have been frequent. The ground is white. Wild geese and ducks are becoming plentiful on the lake and along the river. numerous other wild fowl are beginning to make their appearance — Magpies, Curlews Sand pipers, and other birds. Vegetation too has begun to show signs of returning life. I was out on the banks of the lake the other day looking at the wild fowl and on returning to the quarters I found the tops of two wild onions sticking up through the snow. You may think there is nothing remarkable in it — and in fact there aint, but *we* think it is something *great* out here when wild onions come, they are the first vegetables of the season of which we can make any use, there are others that come later, there is a kind of sour leafed dock which we relish very much as a salad. I never saw any like it in the States, the leaves are Six inches long and about one inch wide, the weed dont grow more than six or eight inches high, it has flowers and seeds a good deal like buck wheat but not so large. The Cactus, or prickly pear is used by some and the watercress too. The only weed used for salad out here that was familiar to me is the "lambs quarter."

Two men were killed this morning on Laprelle Creek twenty miles below Deer C. by indians one of them belonged to Co. E. 11th Ohio the other to Co I 7th Iowa. They were on the way from D. C. to Fort Marshal[37]

---

[37] See letter of August 19, 1864, n. 49.

on Labonte forty miles from D. C. There were three men together going down with a team, one of the men escaped unhurt to Deer Creek. Six men left Fort marshal this morning to come to Deer Creek — have not been heard from. Tom Cooper is one of them, he is on his way up here to take the telegraph office at Three Crossings forty miles above here. He has not been with the company for more than a year. One company of the 11th Kansas left Platte Bridge this morning for this place, another co. of the same reg't will start up in a few days. There is about twelve hundred men now between here and Fort Laramie at different posts along the road. I do hope we will be ordered to the Fort or be remounted before long, this thing of belonging to the cavalry and having no horses is getting old with me, it is about played out. I am getting tired of it, if there is any scouting to do I want to have a horse and go. But in the situation in which our company is, in regard to horses — I would much prefer to be in garrison.

Yesterday (the 20th) left us fifteen months yet to serve. Do you ever notice the months and count them as they go by and say to yourselves — only sixteen months more — only fifteen months more, till Hervey's time is out? *I* do. You dont feel so sorry *now* do you — because I am in the service — as you used to? I dont believe you do. I believe it is the other way now; I believe you are glad that you have a brother in the army, at least I can infer nothing to the contrary from your letters. It is getting so dark that I cannot see the lines. I will finish at another time.

Morning. 22nd. I have just finished my big washing — which consisted of one shirt, one pair drawers, and an old flour sack to keep clothes in, and I will now try to write some more. Every fellow here is his own laundress. we have been getting our washing done the past winter by an emigrant woman who stopped here last summer with her husband, while on their way to Oregon. They left here some time ago and went to the fort.

Tom Cooper and the men that were with him arrived at Deer Creek last night all safe. Lieutenant Collins left this morning to go and meet the Kansas troops who are expected here today. The pay-rolls of all the troops up the road have been ordered to the fort. I suppose we are to be paid off the last of this month. There will be six months wages due us at that time. It may be that they will not pay us though. . . . This is a piece of Government

239

paper. It is also a part of some that John Rappaho left. I am using it because I am about out myself. I believe I have six sheets of white paper yet.

By candle light evening 9th. The mail came this afternoon and brought me *five letters,* two from home, one from Cousin Sam at Spiceland, one from Sam Kinzer, and one from *Samantha.* You had better believe I was "sat up" with them, it had been a good while since I had got one from any where. . . . The letters from home were very interesting too, but as the mail goes out in the morning I have not time nor space to answer the contents of each as I would wish to. I shall go to work tomorrow however and write another letter. . . . Last night an expedition of 700 men left Platte Bridge against the indians[38] they intend to march altogether in the night time, and lay over in the day time. Their object is to find the indian trail and follow it up till they find the enemy. Major Bridger[39] an old mountaineer is their guide, if there is any man in the west who can find the indians he can. I hope they will be found and punished. There is said to be at this time over one thousand emigrant wagons between fort laramie and the Missouri river without stock to move them, it having been taken by indians. Yesterday was rainy nearly all day, the first rain we have had for about nine months, to–day a snowstorm has been blowing from the north east. It seems odd that where you are the trees were in bloom more than a month ago, while

---

[38] Because Colonel Thomas Moonlight (see letter of June 21, 1865, n. 50) left Platte Bridge the night of May 8, Corporal Johnson apparently did not mail his letter of April 21 until sometime after May 9 (note his statement, "By candlelight evening 9th"). Contrary to Johnson's report of an "expedition of 700 men," Moonlight's official account reported a concentration of "about 500 cavalry" for his Wind River expedition — including men from the Eleventh OVC, the Seventh Iowa Cavalry, and the Eleventh Kansas. In any case, the expedition proved abortive, for while Moonlight's men floundered in a raging snowstorm on the Lake Fork of the Wind River, Oglala warriors from the Tongue River region attacked Deer Creek Station. See Thomas Moonlight to George F. Price, June 6, 1865, *The War of the Rebellion: A Compilation of the Official Records of the Union and Confederate Armies,* series I, vol. 47, pt. 1, pp. 255–56; George E. Hyde, *Red Cloud's Folk: A History of the Oglala Sioux,* p. 118; LeRoy R. Hafen and Francis Marion Young, *Fort Laramie and the Pageant of the West, 1834–1890,* p. 332; Fred B. Rogers, *Soldiers of the Overland, Being Some Account of the Services of General Patrick Edward Connor and His Volunteers in the Old West,* pp. 151–52.

[39] This was the celebrated James (Jim) Bridger (1804–1881), perhaps the most famous "mountain man" in the history of the American West. For biographical information, see Stanley Vestal, *Jim Bridger, Mountain Man.*

where I am, winter has not yet entirely disappeared though the grass has been green two or three weeks. Well, I must bring this to aclose. It is a motley looking letter, some blue and some white paper, and all dirty but you need not excuse it unless you want to   it is the best I can do.

Write often

Hervey

Sweet Water [Dakota Territory]
April 27th 1865

Sister Sybil

As I am alone to-night I thought I would try to write a letter. I have had no letter from home for two weeks. I am sitting up with a wounded man anxiously awaiting the arrival of a Surgeon from Platte Bridge. One of our boys was accidentally shot yesterday while out with a small hunting party. They had gone out to take three or four day's hunt. They made a camping place about twenty miles from here where they expected to stay while they were out. The next day after they left here they returned to their camp about noon to get some dinner. One of the boys, a New Yorker, a kind of self important fellow laid his gun down on the ground and told John Hanniford[40] to make a fire to get dinner for he was hungry. Jonny went to make the fire in what he thought a suitable place (the wind was blowing very hard,) this fellow then told him not to make it there, and showed him where to make it, he had scarcely got it started in the place where he was told to make it before the wind blew it into the grass, when it began to spread with great rapidity. Johnny saw this new yorkers gun was laying where it would get burnt if not moved, so he leaned over to pick it up, he seized it with the muzzle right towards him, it being so near the fire that he

---

[40] John Hannaford was a native of Hillsboro, Ohio, who enlisted in the Eleventh OVC on June 15, 1863. He served as a herder at Platte Bridge and Sweetwater Station and with a Pacific Railroad survey expedition west of Platte Bridge. From March 3, 1865, until his death on September 14, 1865, he was confined to the Fort Laramie Hospital. Contrary to Johnson's letter of September 14, 1865, the official War Department files state that Hannaford "died of wounds," apparently those suffered at Sweetwater. Private John Hannaford, CMF.

could not get hold of it any where else, Just as he raised the gun to draw it towards him from the fire it went off, dont know whether it was the heat, or whether the hammer caught on something that discharged it. The ball struck him in the throat, passing between the wind pipe and artery on the left side and up through his jaw, coming out opposite the left ear. his jaw is broke all to peices and cheek bone fractured. The boys who were with him had hard work to keep him from bleeding to death, they tore up their shirts to make bandages and used a lot of sugar they had with them binding it on the wound. They finally got the blood stopped and got him on a horse, and he rode to the station twenty miles. They would have brought him in the wagon they took out, but while they were busied about him, the fire had burnt the harness up. When they got here with him it was nearly ten oclock in the night, he was an awful sight, his shirt, jacket and pants were covered with blood. we stripped and washed him. I tore up a pair of my drawers for bandages, and then we moved him into a comfortable bed. I have been waiting on him all day, I have to be constantly changing the cloths and keeping them wet with cold water.

It is now after ten o clock at night and the Surgeon has not come yet. I dont see how the boy can get along without medical assistance. We would hate to lose him   he is one of the best boys in the company, always so still, and never meddling with other peoples business, he is the son of the widow Hanniford who used to live on Jim Andersons place. She lives now at hillsboro near where Col Collins lives. John says he dont want his mother to know his situation. His wound still keeps bleeding some once in a while. It makes some of the boys sick to look at it, I have seen several such sights, I would gladly be somewhere else though than here while he is here, but it seems like the other boys don't care whether he lives or dies, and it seems like I have to tend to him. I would rather do it than risk a good many of them and I believe the most of them would as lief I would do it as to do it them selves, they are not remarkable for pushing forward and trying to be the first to render assistance.

Lieutenant Collins has gone to the Bridge to muster the company for pay, so I am here alone, that is as far as seeing to the affairs of the detachment is concerned. I wrote a letter to the commander of the company asking to be put in the ranks, sent it down this morning. Another man of Co E

242

was killed a day or two ago. He was herding the company's horses about two miles from the station on Labonte, when the indians came upon him, drove off the horses, brought him down within a few hundred yards of the station and killed him there where he was found next morning. A detachment of the 11th Kansas went after the indians, they camped on Sage creek[41] fifteen miles from Deer Creek having seen no sign of indians. after they had lain down to sleep they were surprised by a party of about forty indians who came rushing right into camp whooping and yelling running over men, beds, tents, and everything else. None of the soldiers were hurt very bad I guess, they were confused at first, but soon got straight and drove the redskins off, killing several.

Last first day the 23rd the "religious ceremony" of hanging an indian chief was performed at Fort Laramie. He was the one who was taken prisoner at Deer Creek last winter sometime I believe *I* told you something about it. Tom Cooper was here night before last. I asked him if he had heard from the states lately. He said he had. I then asked him what was the word. He said "Dock Cowgill was married." It is probable that we will come home in the fall. Cooper told me that the Major said he was going to get us out if he could. The prospect for peace is fair I believe, and if that is once declared they cant keep us any longer. An expedition of 100 men is going out north from here in a few days. There are two companies of the 11th Kansas here now. I will not finish this till after the doctor comes he may bring the mail.

30th. The Doctor came a few minutes ago. dident bring any mail. He says Hannifords jaw is not broken, but his cheek is fractured, wound not so dangerous as at first supposed.

I send you a picture that I picked up in the Telegraph office it is some of Lieutenant Collin's work.[42] One side is intended to represent some of the

---

[41] Sage Creek should not be confused with Sage Creek Station on the Overland (Cherokee) Trail east of Bridger's Pass or with Sage Hen Creek, which empties into the Sweetwater approximately seven miles northeast of present Jeffrey City, Wyoming. The Sage Creek Johnson refers to was near the starting point on the Bozeman Trail. Hebard and Brininstool, *The Bozeman Trail*, vol. 2, pp. 114–15.

[42] Collins's drawing was not found with Johnson's correspondence of April 27, 1865. For samples of Caspar Collins's drawing, see "Sawmill at the Foot of Laramie Peak," and "Platte Bridge Station," Spring, *Caspar Collins*, opposite pp. 26 and 66, respectively.

horses belonging to Co G. The other is a negro recruiting station. One "culled pussun" is in the act of "presenting arms" to the officer passing, who is in the act of returning the salute. enough for this time

Write soon
Hervey Johnson

Sweet-Water [Dakota Territory]
May 12th 1865

Sister Abi

In my last letter of various dates from 6th to the 9th inclusive, I promised to begin another on the next day after I finished that one, but I had to go down the road to get a wagon out of the mud. Our team was coming up from the Bridge with rations, along with six or seven teams belonging to the 11th Kansas, they were before, and in crossing an alkali bottom, some of them stuck. Our teamster a kind of bull-headed fellow wouldnt wait for them to get out, but thought he would drive around them, which he undertook to do and got himself in a worse fix than they were. He hammered around a while, got his mules down in the mud, and finally came off and left the wagon sticking there. The other wagons got out well enough by hitching eighteen mules to a wagon. I went down next morning with the driver and an other man. We unloaded the wagon, hitched up the mules, but they wouldent budge it, well they couldnt do it in fact. We worked around a good while got covered with alkali mud, got the mules down in the mud, had to loosen the harness to get them up. Had there been a solid footing for them they would have come out with the empty wagon, but for fifty yards all around there was nothing but mud with just enough crust on top to bear the weight of the mules, but as soon as they bore against the chains they would break through. I told the boys to unhitch and we would go and get another wagon and haul up the things and let that wagon stay there. We came back to the station, got our dinners, hitched a couple of mules to an old piece of a wagon, got three or four chains, and six of us went back. we fastened the wagon we took down to the rear end of the other, hitched all six mules to it, plunged round a while, got some of the mules down, got

244

them up again and finally moved the wagon about eight inches and would have got it farther if the chains had not broke. We backed up and hitched on again, and this time we rolled her out. I recon we were the prettiest sights you ever saw, it wasent like it is in the states where a man can get a rail or pole to prize out with, but we had to take hold and lift with our hands like we wernt afraid of getting them dirty. Well we got the wagon round on a dry place about fifty yards from where the things were and loaded up, brought every thing away safe except the mudhole, and we brought as much of that as we could on our boots, clothes, and hands.

You may think that I might have told all this in two or three lines and filled up with something more interesting. The fact is I dont know hardly what to write, so I just fill up the sheet with what comes to hand. I got a pair of boots half-soled the other day, only had to pay $2.50 for the damage, but I would rather pay that to get a pair of pegged boots half soled than to draw a pair of sewed boots and have to pay four dollars and a quarter for them

Well I am glad everything went off so well at the marriage, I only regret that busines in another quarter prevented me from being present. If they had put it off till fall I might have had the pleasure of being there, as I think we will all be home then if nothing happens. We may get fooled though and have to stay till next fall year. If we do come home this fall, I will let you know when we start and then perhaps you wont hear from me till you see me.

Every body up here nearly has been out of tobacco, (this is supposed to be very interesting to you) and the consequence is that I have to lay awake about half of every night with the neuralgia. I have known the boys to pay $2.50 for a plug of tobacco as big as this envelope, and I would give it myself, but I found a plug in the road when I went down after the wagon the other day. I have not made the raise of any paper yet. the sheet I am writing on is one of three or four I had left. I am waiting of Hanniford to day, he is getting along well. I have not seen William Boardman[43] since the 26th of March. He is stationed at Platte Bridge filling the position of company clerk, he is getting along well enough as far as I know. . . .

---

[43] See letter of June 6, 1864, n. 26.

Lieut Collins left yesterday morning with a squad of men to go up the road There was about forty five altogether. They think the expedition that went out will scare the indians across the road above here some where and these went up to intercept them I must close write soon

Hervey.

Sweetwater [Dakota Territory]
May 21st 1865

Sister Sybil

I have seated myself this afternoon to write. The mail came yesterday morning and brought me two letters one from home, the other from cousin Alex at Jamestown. I dont know the date of either as I must have lost them both while out in the mountains yesterday. I went out to take a ramble with one of the other boys after we had read our letters. we walked out and when we had got half way up the mountain, we heard "recall" sounded by the bugle at the station, it was an unusual time of day for that call to be blown. We concluded we would not go back at least. In a short time we saw the herders starting in with the horses. We thought then that there must be something up. we strolled about till we got tired, and came back to the station, about half the men of each of the two Kansas companies had left, started for three crossings forty miles up the river. The commanding officer here got a dispatch from there stating that the place was invested by five hundred indians. The cause of the bugle sounding at that unusual hour was to bring in the horses. They were brought in and the men were of with three days rations in a very short time. About two minutes after the dispatch was received here, the line was out and there has been no communication with them since. It was fortunate that the word was sent at the time it was for had the operator there been five minutes later he could not have got his dispatch here. We are all very anxious to know how they are getting on we cant tell whether the troops that went up from here, arrived or not, so we just have to remain in suspense till they return or till the line is repaired. At the same time that Three Crossings was surrounded the herd at Deer Creek was stolen. After running off the horses the indians came back to fight the

246

herders, a sharp skirmish ensued in which the indians were driven off with a loss of seven killed and twenty four wounded. Not one of the soldiers got a scratch.

Morning 22nd The Telegraph was repaired for about ten minutes last evening about dark but was cut again immediately, we could hear nothing of the state of affairs at Three Crossings, will certainly hear today. Yesterday Lieutenant Col. Plumb[44] 11th Kansas was fighting the indians about seven miles from Deer Creek. The platte river was between the two parties and was so high that Plumb could not cross his command, and so wide that very little execution was done on either side. The latest we heard but two indians were killed and a number wounded. One soldier killed and several wounded. Just now heard from above. The indians attacked the station in the morning before any person knew it, the boys run them off but they kept skirmishing at long range all day till about four o'clock when they suddenly left. Several of the indians were hurt, but the long range of the Spencers kept them at such a distance that none of our boys were hurt. I think their sudden disappearance was caused by the appearance of Capt Greer[45] and his party who must have been somewhere in the vicinity about that time Greer was in command of the troops that went up from here.

The 11th Kansas returned from ten days scout without seeing an indian. They camped near here one night on their way back to regimental head-quarters. It was on the 14th of this month a miserable snowy stormy night and the poor fellows had no tents or any thing to shelter them from the storm nor wood to make a fire. They came up to the station and scratched chips out of the snow. They will leave these parts before long to go to the States to be mustered out of service. Their time is out in October but they will be mustered out sooner by an order from the War department "to discharge all Cavalry Volunteers whose term of service expires by the 21st

---

[44] Lieutenant Preston B. Plumb, a veteran of Kansas military affairs and politics during the early Civil War years, was commander of the Eleventh Regiment, Kansas Cavalry. He later represented Kansas in the United States Senate as a member of the Republican Party, 1877–1891. For an informative yet pedantic biography of Plumb, see William E. Connelley, *The Life of Preston B. Plumb, 1837–1891.*

[45] Captain James E. Greer was commander of Company I, Eleventh OVC. J. W. Vaughn, *The Battle of Platte Bridge,* p. 7.

of Oct." I guess they have got *us* good and tight for another year, though our Major thinks we will be discharged the coming fall. We were all very much elated a few days ago by a report that our company was to be releived up here and removed to Labonte 65 miles from the Fort. but the talk now is that we are to be stationed from Fort Laramie to Green River in Utah Teritory. I understand that there is to be twenty men at each post, sixteen infantry and four cavalry, as there are ten posts it will take all the mounted men in our company, the rest of us will have to be infantry I guess. There are two companies of U.S. Infantry on their way from the Fort to make up the required number at each.

Some of the boys shot two beavers yesterday morning in the river opposite the station, I suppose the high water had run them out of their dams in the mountains. I will quit now and finish this evening or tomorrow morning after the boys get back from above.

23rd. The boys have come back, got here in the night, the five hundred indians dwindled down to a hundred and fifty. They did no further damage than cut the wire in two or three places, and carry off and hide some of it. At about 4 o'clock in the evening of the day the troops left here, the indians left there crossing the river to the north, the soldiers followed them about fifteen miles but not overtaking them they returned. I forgot to say that the indians got Albert Johnsons horse in the skirmish. I just now hear that we are going to the fort in a short time, and in a short time, from there to the States, I dont know how much truth there is in the latter, but I think we *are* going to the Fort. Well I am glad of it. I am getting tired of "up the road" though I would like nothing better than being stationed up here somewhere if we only had something to ride. If we get to the fort I hope I can get some paper, I have but one sheet after this one. I have about a dollars worth of stamps yet, and I came across a boy in Co. "I" 11th Kansas who had some envelopes, I gave him a half dollar for about a dozen. I understand that the 11th Kansas starts in a few days for the states. Co's "I" & "H" leave here tomorrow or next day   I must quit, write soon

Hervey.

248

Sweetwater [Dakota Territory]
May 27th 1865

Sister Sybil.

As I have nothing else to do this afternoon I concluded I would try to write a letter, though it is like it has always been before. I dont know hardly what to write. As I hardly ever tell you that I am well I suppose you will take it for granted when I say nothing about it. The men here are all in good health and spirits. Hanniford — the boy who was wounded is getting along well, he is up and walking about every day. The weather is very warm, too warm to be pleasant yet there is snow on the tops of the mountains north of us where it is exposed to the rays of the midday sun. We have had some few showers of rain in the past week, and some heavy thunderstorms have passed by, but none near us. The Sweetwater river is nearly out of its banks and still rising, I look for it to take the bridge down before long.

Companies "I" & "H" 11th Kas left here yesterday morning to join the Regt. I guess I was disappointed when I thought we were going to the fort. Some of us will leave here for somewhere before long. Four men were ordered to South Pass two or three days ago, and three or four leave here to-night for Three Crossings. Things are awfully mixed up somehow or other, at least thats the way it looks from where I stand. The Commander of the Company says he dont want any more rations sent up the road, that looks a little like we are going down the road. But he is having men sent up the road and that makes it "as clear as mud." I guess the best thing we can do is to come to the conclusion that we dont know any thing about it, or else that the commander, or telegraph, or operator, or something, was drunk when the message was sent that has been the cause of all our speculation.

Day–before–yesterday–morning a detachment of U.S. Infantry camped about six miles below Platte Bridge, were visited by a band of "red-skins" who gave them a token of their particular esteem, by way of showing their decided partiality to mule-flesh. I dont know how many mules the infantry had, but the indians relieved them of forty. Yesterday evening *we* had some fun ourselves. The indians, who have been paying their respects to all the stations both above and below condescended to let us know that although we were in an isolated situation we were not entirely forgotten. They seemed to want us to understand that our horses were regarded with the

249

same considerations, and "hankered arter" with the same avidity that has characterized their visits at other places. I happened to go out to the wood-pile a little before sundown with one of the other boys and on looking across the river we saw three gentlemen fantastically bedaubed with vermilion and chrome yellow emerge from behind a spur of the mountain. They appeared to be in a hurry about something, and were making in the direction of our horses who were quietly grazing near the river a few hundred yards below the station. The boy with me asked — "Who is them?" I said "injins"!!! and we both shot for our guns without saying a word, we met a boy at the gate, he turned back and followed us in, the boys in the room when they saw us going for our arms didnt know what to make of it, they thought we were "on the muss", but they "followed suit" and such a scramble for guns, I got somebody else's and somebody else got mine, and in the hurry I got about four bits worth of hide knocked off my knuckle. We all got arms and were out on the river bank in less time than it takes to tell it notwithstanding all the fuss. There were the horses looking with something like curiosity at what was coming towards them, and the herders waiting to see what was going to turn up. On came the "reds" giving the war-whoop which grad-ually softened down to a soulstirring warsong beginning with the pathetic words — "hitch a-hitch a-hia-hia ha-e-o-hae-hae &c" I would give the rest of the "song", but I went to making music on my spencer and didn't get to hear it all. I think though that their exercises in vocal music were inter-rupted, and the completion of them postponed till another time. Any how they came to the conclusion that they didn't want the horses, and turned out towards the bluffs from us; for a little while it sounded like a young battle was going on, we could see the balls knocking the dust all around them, but the range was so long (it must have been seven or eight hundred yards) and we fired so much at random that we did nothing much more than scare them though as they were going into the bluffs one of them got off his horse with-out any apparent assistance, slapping his hand to his thigh as he left the saddle, and gracefully alighting on the flat of his back. With some assistance from one of the others he remounted and they were soon out of the reach of spencer balls.

As soon as the firing ceased the horses were brought up, the herders couldnt get them to move an inch while we were shooting. As soon as we

250

saw that the horses were safe several of us ran back to the station for more ammunition, when we got to the gate we found it shut and fastened. Some brave public–spirited individual having the safety of things inside in view, including himself no doubt, had determined the indians shouldnt get in there if he could prevent it. I think I know who the fellow is, he is a Missourian who followed our regiment from St Louis and enlisted at Fort Leavenworth. It is all well enough to have the gate closed at the proper time, but if a big party of indians was to run on us when we are all out of the stockade I would rather have the gate open. As soon as the horses were brought in about nine of them were mounted and the boys were off after the still retreating indians. They followed them till sundown, only two or three of them were able to get in anything like shooting distance. They exchanged several shots with the boys while on the gallop. They were armed with rifles and bows. The boys said they could hear the slugs whiz by them when the indians would shoot, with a noise that sounded like corn cobs whizzing through the air, it soon got so dark that further pursuit was useless, nobody was much hurt. one of the indian's ponies was shot in the foot and one of our boys was scratched slightly on the hand by an arrow. I wish something of the kind would turn up every day, it rather breaks the monotony. Well I must begin to quit. I got some paper of one of the Kansas boys paid sixty cents for seven sheets and six envelopes.

Write often

Hervey

Sweetwater [Dakota Territory]
June 4th 1865

Sister Sybil.

I thought I would try to write again this morning. I received Abi's letter of April 30th two or three days ago, was very glad to hear from home. Indians Still as bad as ever. Two or three chiefs were hung at Fort Laramie a few days ago, they came in from the north with two prisoners, (a white woman and her child) for the purpose of giving them up, and in the expectation of receiving a handsome recompense for their ransom. They wanted half a bushel of silver and were equally as extravagant in their demands for provisions. The ire of the "powers that be" at the Fort was aroused, (Col. Collins aint in command now) and "Mr. ingen" was swung up, and it didn't cost a cent to get the woman and child. It is "bad medicine" for an indian to be hung. They think he never goes to the "happy hunting ground" [46]

Lieutenant Bretney and a party of eight men from the bridge went up the road to see what had become of things at St Mary's. Arrived there they found a company of the 1st Nevada from Fort Bridger at work rebuilding the Station. They had repaired the line the day after Bretney passed here and we heard from the boys whom we supposed were either killed or taken prisoners. They had escaped through a rear window when they found the station was on fire and took refuge in an old pit or cellar, The operator attached a wire to his battery and took it in to the cave, with an instrument. while in there he telegraphed to Fort Bridger in Utah what was going on, and also to south pass. The boys had but one horse at the station and the indians got him. While they were in their hole one of them saw an old buck riding about on the horse, he shot at him, shooting him through the knee and killing the horse. St Mary's being a depot of telegraph supplies the indians were very anxious for plunder, but there happened to be four or five hundred metalic cartridges for the Wesson gun stored away in there, and the fire soon getting to them the indians thought it wasn't medicine to stay close around and left. The boys staid in their hole the remainder of the day all that night and next day, and the next night started for South Pass, they walked about six miles and met the boys coming down for them with a wagon. They saved nothing but their arms and the clothes they had on.

The day Bretney passed here the indians came to see us again. I was on "lookout" that day on top of the buildings. When I saw them coming I fired and then jumped off the house to run and help drive in the mules which were about a hundred yards off. The other boys ran out towards the indians

---

[46] Here Johnson had reference to Mrs. Joseph Eubanks (sometimes spelled Ewbanks) and her small daughter whose fourteen-months captivity and suffering at the hands of the Oglala Sioux resulted in the execution of the Oglala leaders, Two Face and Black Foot, in late May of 1865. See Hebard and Brininstool, *The Bozeman Trail*, vol. 1, pp. 149–50; Hafen and Young, *Fort Laramie*, p. 132; George E. Hyde, *Spotted Tail's Folk, A History of the Brulé Sioux*, p. 102; Rogers, *Soldiers of the Overland*, pp. 152–53.

and fired at them, they turned and ran off to a bluff about half a mile and stopped. They stood there expecting we would follow them soon on *our horses*, when they would lead us into ambush, at least that's what we thought. They soon got tired of standing there and concluded to come back to the road, they tried hard to draw us out making all the fun of us they could. but we "couldent see it," finding they were not going to succeed by the means they were trying they went to tearing down the telegraph. We didnt like to see it of course but we had to stand and look at them. we could have driven them off by going out on foot but they would have gone off and cut the line somewhere else. They waited sometime after they were through with their mischief to see if we wouldn't come out, but getting tired they went off taking with them sixty yards of wire. We watched them as they rode away and it was not more than five minutes after they had started till we could see indians dropping out of the bluffs, one and two in a place about two miles from the Station and riding off in the direction these were going, and in a short time a large party made their appearance and rode off in the same direction. They didn't bother us any more that evening. Some were seen prowling about day before yesterday but did n't come near.

Several days ago a supply train was attacked fifty five miles from the fort they had a small mounted escort besides two dismounted men concealed in each wagon. When the indians made the dash on them the men lit out of the wagons. The indians were surprised at seeing so many men make their appearance and ran off. one man belonging to Co "E" was killed, dont know whether any indians were hurt or not Yesterday evening the boys at the Bridge saw six or seven indians riding about across the river from the Station, they sent word to Lieutenant Col. Plumb 11th Kansas who was camped a few miles from the Bridge, he came up with about twenty five men who were joined by eleven or our boys from the Bridge when they all set out after the indians who retreated about twelve miles skirmishing all the way. The boys soon found they had been led into an ambuscade, they were surrounded by a large party one of our boys was killed and one belonging to Co "F" 11th Kas also. Only one indian was known to be killed 4 or 5 wounded, some of their ponies killed and several crippled. Only one of our horses was hurt and that was the one that belonged to the man who was killed. At the time he was killed he was fighting five indians by himself,

253

he fell with four balls in his head a gunshot wound in each arm and arrow wound in his back.[47]

This I expect will be the last letter I write at Sweet water. We will leave here (all but four mounted men) in a short time. I dont know where I will stay. It may be that a horse will be furnished me and I be sent to some of the uproad stations. A Company of the 3rd U.S. infantry arrived here yesterday. fourteen stopped here, the rest go on further up. They tell us boys that we look like we have seen hard times. I expect we do look lank about the jaws, we havent had anything to eat but bread and coffee for a week. Do you ever hear any news from this country through newspapers or other sources than from me? I once in a while get intimations from letters that other boys receive that you people have awful ideas of things out here. I wish you would tell me what the people do think of it.

I forgot to say that the boys went and fixed up the line near the station next morning after it was torn down. I received three other letters besides the one I got from home. If Uncle Ben is at our house when you get this give him fits for me for not answering the letters I sent him. I was out about a mile and a half from the station a few days ago on a large rock watching for indians. I was to fire my gun if I saw any, to let the boys at the station know it. I had not been there long till I saw a big wolf coming towards me. I was laying behind a loose stone so he did not see me at first. He came on and walked by me   I made some motion and he stopped and looked at me I thought he would run when he saw me but instead of that he came right towards me. I threw my whole body from behind the rock but he came right on, I lay down again out of his sight. He came on and reared up on his hind feet and looked over the rock at me. I wanted to shoot, but I knew if I did the boys would think indians were about. I didn't want to raise a false alarm. I just looked at the wolf and he looked at me till we both got a good look at each other   when I arose to my feet, he took that as a signal for him to depart which he did immediately. I staid about for an hour or two and

---

[47] The encounter in which Private Tilman Stahlnecker of Company G was killed took place near Deer Creek Station on June 3, 1865. According to Sergeant Isaac B. Pennock, the Kansas soldier killed was "Barnwell of Co. F." Vaughn lists him as Private William T. Bonwell, same company. *Official Roster of the Soldiers of the State of Ohio in the War of the Rebellion, 1861–1866*, p. 548; Diary of Isaac B. Pennock; Vaughn, *The Battle of Platte Bridge*, pp. 14–15.

then went home without having seen any indians. Well I will close   Please write soon

Hervey.

Platte Bridge [Dakota Territory]
June 15th/65

Sister Sybil

The mail came yesterday morning and with it one letter for me from home. It was written by Abi and dated 19*th* May. I also received one from home about a week ago but we were preparing to leave S. W. at the time and had a good deal to do so that I did not write. I have been here three or four days. The indians have been quiet up in this country for the past ten days, till yesterday and day–before. Last evening a large party made their appearance at Sweet Water, bearing a white flag. The garrison came out under arms and motioned them to keep away, They persisted in hovering about trying to have respect paid to their emblem of peace, but the boys "couldn't see it" in the same light the indians did, and fired on the party, dismounting three of them, They were picked up by their comrades, but instead of returning the fire the whole party moved off to the mountains, where it was supposed they were holding a council. The white rag gave rise to various surmises, one of which was that the party might be a band of Snakes, which tribe, it is well known is at war with the Cheyennes Sioux and Arappahoes. The fact of them not returning the fire of the garrison, more particularly led to this supposition, but then we have been fooled too often. The boys thought they were displaying their flag for the purpose of gaining admittance inside the stockade, after which at a given signal they could pounce upon and butcher the garrison at leisure. We may hear something more from there today,

Sweet Water is garrisoned now by a detachment of Co "I" 3*rd* U.S. Inf. Vols and four of our Co. Yesterday a soldier of Co "A" 11*th* Kansas was killed at Deer Creek, he was fishing, I believe, when the indians ran on him, he defended himself as well as he could with his revolver, the only weapon he had, wounding an indian and killing a pony. as soon as he had fired his revolver around they rushed up and took it away from him, but the men at

255

Drawing of Platte Bridge Station in 1863 by Charles Frederick Moellmann. As can be seen, the telegraph line crossed the Platte River on the west side of the bridge. *Courtesy of the Wyoming State Archives and Historical Department.*

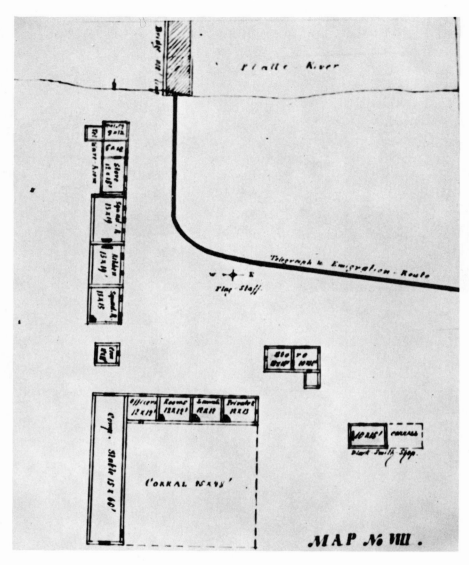

Map and floor plan of Platte Bridge Station in the 1860's, with the telegraph and emigrant routes indicated. Draftsman unknown.
Courtesy of the Wyoming State Archives and Historical Department.

the station hearing the firing got down in time to drive them off before they stripped him. He was shot in three places. Day before yesterday Co "H" 11 Ohio attacked a party of indians who were crossing the platte river north with their squaws and "teepe's", a sharp fight ensued in which five soldiers were killed and seven wounded fifteen indians killed, number wounded not known, large numbers were drowned in crossing the river. among the soldiers killed was Captain Fouts of Co "D" 7th Iowa.[48] He was going to Julesburg with some indian prisoners who had been in confinement at Fort Laramie. After the fight one of the prisoners was found dead in the road with ball and chain still on. The greater number of the horses belonging to the soldiers were either killed or so disabled as to be unfit for service.

There have been a number of the indians hung at the fort the past spring, and a number more are in confinement awaiting their fate. They are kept at hard labor all the time. The Govt has armed about a hundred friendly [treaty] indians and clothed them with condemned clothing and given them half rations, they furnish their own ponies, they are a proud set of fellows, strutting about the Fort with their big leather Dragoon caps and red plumes, and their old infantry coats and cavalry and artilery jackets. They make a good deal of fun of the indian prisoners as they trudge around dragging the heavy cannonball, or hauling water for the garrison, sweeping the parade or chopping wood. It has always been thought that an indian could not be made to work, but the sight of those indians still swinging in sight of the

---

[48] Captain William D. Fouts was commander of Company D, Seventh Regiment, Iowa Cavalry. A native of Main, Indiana, Fouts was mustered in at Davenport, Iowa, on April 18, 1863, and following successive post commands at Forts Kearny and Halleck, was stationed at Fort Laramie. On June 11, 1865, he was ordered to escort 185 lodges of Sioux prisoners to Fort Kearny by way of Julesburg. Fouts had only 135 men under his command, and for reasons that still remain obscure, failed to disarm the warriors. On June 14, near the Horse Creek crossing of the North Platte, some of the more belligerent warriors killed Fouts and four enlisted men. Hyde and Nadeau strongly imply that Fouts was derelict in failing to disarm the Sioux, but on the basis of a letter written one week later by Lieutenant J. H. Triggs of the Seventh Iowa to the Assistant Adjutant General of the District of the Plains, it seems reasonable to conclude that the misguided decision was that of Colonel Thomas Moolight and that Fouts was simply following orders. In any case, Moonlight's subsequent maneuvers were distressing enough to cause General Connor to relieve Moonlight of his command at Fort Laramie. See Hyde, *Red Cloud's Folk*, pp. 120–22; Nadeau, *Fort Laramie and the Sioux Indians*, pp. 179–86; J. H. Triggs to George F. Price, June 21, 1865, in Captain William D. Fouts, CMF.

Fort has a very moral effect on the prisoners. It is a medicine they dont understand because very few of them have got used to it.

17th I concluded to finish my letter today. The weather has been some cold the past few days. this morning we had a real snowstorm. Only think of it — after the middle of June, and snowing like "blixin." It has cleared off now and looks like being pleasant. A train of refugee Mormons passed here yesterday on their way to the states. Gen Conner told all who wished to leave salt lake to go. This party started and Brigham sent some of his officers after them to take them back, but they had an escort of soldiers who prevented Brighams officers from accomplishing their purpose. It is said that Brigham has about nine hundred men in the mountains with the indians to assist in their depradations against the white men. Everything presages a protracted mormon and indian war. There are rumors of our regiment going to Salt Lake. I wish they would do something with us. Gen [Alfred] Sully with five thousand men is somewhere near Fort Laramie coming in from the north.[49]

The most of the officers belonging to the 11th Ohio are going to resign. I dont know what will become of the men when the officers leave us   perhaps officers from the regular army will look after our interests. We did look forward for a while with buoyant hope towards being mustered out of service the coming fall, but all has vanished. The present indian war and the prospect of a war with the Mormons and indians combined have banished hope and fixed us for twelve months more to roam in this wilderness. It is a fate which none but the "gods" and Secretary [of War] Stanton can obviate. There's no use in "bucking" against it. The Overland Mail road from Julesburg to Green river in Utah is completely in possession of the indians. On account of our troubles early in the spring on this road the emigrants all went the mail road; as soon as the north platte and Sweet Water fell, the indians crossed and went over there and the loss of many human lives is the consequence. a portion of the refugee train that passed here yesterday

---

[49] As part of General John Pope's strategy for breaking the military power of the various Sioux tribes in the spring of 1865, General Sully was in the process of marching from the Black Hills to Devil's Lake in northeastern Dakota Territory. Contrary to Johnson's figure, his force was composed of about 1,200 cavalrymen and a detachment of artillery. See Richard N. Ellis, *General Pope and U.S. Indian Policy*, pp. 89–95.

split off from them at green river in Utah and went that road, every one was butchered, not one left to tell the tale. Do tell me what is the popular opinion of this indian war, in the States, no news papers we get ever speak of us, they are all gloating over the close of the war in the south and dont seem to remember the soldiers out here fighting a race, whom it would be flattering to call men.

I must close. Write soon.

Thy Brother

Hervey.

Platte Bridge [Dakota Territory]
June 21st 1865.

Sybil.

The mail came in last night, but brought me no letter from home. I received one letter however from a correspondent in Burlington Iowa which in some *small* degree made up the loss. I say small, because one letter from home is worth more to me than half a dozen from other places. I am enjoying myself here about as well as I can expect taking all things into consideration. Just now is the height of the musketo season, I dont think I ever saw any thing to exceed it. The boys all go about with handkerchiefs tied round their faces and a brush in one hand. of an evening we build smokes all about the parade and in the quarters to drive out the "varmints," I can scarcely write for them.

Yesterday we received inteligence by telegraph of the capture by indians of a great number of horses belonging to the 11th Kansas. Col. Moonlight[50] commanding the regiment had gone on an expedition after indians and I suppose had neglected to take the necessary precaution in regard to his stock. His own horse and those belonging to six or seven under officers were taken

---

[50] Colonel Thomas Moonlight received much of his military-political training under James Blunt and James Lane in eastern Kansas during the early and middle years of the Civil War and eventually became a territorial governor of Wyoming. See Albert Castel, *A Frontier State at War: Kansas, 1861–1865*, pp. 54, 101, 189, 196; Colonel Thomas Moonlight, CMF.

with the others besides those belonging to two California companies. We were glad to hear it. The old Col thought himself so brave and smart that it did us good to hear of him having his "feathers cut". We havent forgotten what he said to Lieutenant Bretney, when he reported nine of our horses stolen by indians. I dont remeber the words but he told him with oaths and curses that it was a disgrace to the regiment to allow our horses to be taken from us and the matter ought to be investigated and the persons or person whose fault it was to be properly punished. I do hope his case will be investigated and he courtmartialed. He went on a scouting expedition with eight or nine hundred men up north of Sweet Water, was gone ten days without seeing an indian, he came in to S.W. and reported to headquarters that he had driven the indians all back into the mountains and that it was not probable that they would trouble the road any more this summer. He had not reached the fort yet on his return till the indians had attacked several stations, stolen horses and burned one station. That is the way he drives indians into the mountains so they wont come back.

Just now a despatch came from Sweet Water stating ten men were sent yesterday to repair telegraph, they were attacked by fifty indians. Edgar M. Gwynn[51] the Operator was killed. He belonged to Co. E. 11th Ohio. Jim Patton[52] of our Co was badly wounded in [the] collar bone by [a] rifle ball. Jim is Newt Pattons son. he lives somewhere near Peters burg. There were three indians killed and a number wounded. There are only four men of our company stationed at S.W. The men who went to repair the line were on their way to South pass escorting a provision train and had camped at S. W. All the posts from Laramie to south pass are garrisoned by infantry (3rd US Volunteers) and four of our Co at each post. There are three regiments of U.S. Vols in this country, the 1st 2nd & 3rd, all infantry. They were recruited out of the military prisons in the north. every one of them except the Officrs have been in the rebel army. The boys are all a quiet civil set of fellows. They enlisted for one year only, their term expires the coming

---

[51] A native of Trigg County, Kentucky, Gwynn worked as a carpenter prior to his enrollment in the Eleventh OVC on June 13, 1863. He served mainly on detached service as a telegraph operator at Rick Ridge, Idaho Territory, and Sweetwater Station, and was killed by Indians on June 22 or 23, 1865, near Horse Creek, Dakota Territory, while repairing the telegraph line. Private Edgar M. Gwynn, CMF.

[52] See letter of August 19, 1864, n. 40.

October. I have conversed very little with any of them yet. I have been thrown in contact with parts of two companies of the 3rd regiment, "I" and "K". Those of "I" company evidently have sympathy with the South, but they keep their places admirably, and speak in terms of contempt of any who would violate their oaths. There have been but three cases of desertion from the reg't and they were from Co "I." The boys of "K" Co are very sociable and good natured, I have heard some of them speak in terms of approbation of the movements some of the southern states are making to come back into the Union. The third regiment was raised entirely at the Rock Island prison, the place where the Gov't is going to build a U.S. Arsenal.

I have a union breast-pin in the shape of Star and crescent, (solid silver) which was made by a prisoner on rock island, one of the Co "I" boys brought it out here, I intend to take it home with me. Yesterday one thousand cavalry disembarked at Omaha, their destination out in this direction somewhere. Troops are arriving daily at Omaha and Leavenworth for the plains. There will certainly be something done shortly. We will either hear of the soldiers being badly cleaned out or the indians badly whipped. If the soldiers succeed, the Gov't will be richer by several thousand horses. From reports of traders who have been prisoners in their hands and escaped they have immense herds of horses. I will close for the present and finish perhaps tomorrow.

Morning 22nd. Heard from S.W. this morning. The fight occurred about nine miles from the station, Gwynn was shot dead, the ball entering his left breast. Doubts are entertained of Patton's recovery, though when the Surgeon arrives there, he may give us some hope. It was a very hard fight, the indians numbering five to one, but the boys compelled them to leave the field. They succeed[ed] in repairing the line, which is working through this morning to Salt Lake. All the horses our boys had in the fight were wounded.

Well Ill finish up my letter with something else. The Platte river is falling very fast, The boys have a seine here, some of them are out every day with it fishing. I have been twice. we have to fish along near the shore, the water is too deep and swift out in the stream There are several kinds of fish in the streams out here, we catch pickerel, catfish, buffalo salmon suckers, shovelheads, hickory-shad, and several small fry. we caught one

263

shovel head two and a half feet in length. I was in the river bathing last evening with a lot of the boys but the musketoes were so bad that it was much pleasanter with our clothes on, we didnt stay in long. I am writing now in a room full of smoke, I have to do it or be eat up with musketos, they raise great lumps and welts on us, that itch and are sore for a week. . . .

24th. The Surgeon and his escort arrived here last night from Sweet Water, Patton is getting along well, he was shot through the upper part of right lung, the ball (a pewter one) was taken out of his back. Gwynn was stripped of his clothing, scalped, his hands cut off, sinews taken out of his legs and arms, and his heart and liver taken out, nineteen arrows were in his body. During the fight the "Indian Medicine man" would ride along in front of his men and try to get them to charge the boys saying, whenever one of the latter would fire — "it never touched" in plain english. The boys waited for a suitable opportunity when one of them drew a bead on him and fired. He said "it never touched" no more. The death of the medicine man was supposed to be the cause of Gwynns body being mutilated so, it was the greatest loss they could have sustained. The indians had some of the horses in the fight that they had stolen from us at Sweet Water. Sam Engles pony was wounded so in the fight that he had to be left, the Indians got him. The four boys of our company stationed at S.W. kept their horses picketed on the river bottom near the Station and would hide themselves to watch. An evening or two befor the day on which the fight occurred, several indians made their appearance there, one of the boys on watch saw one of them skulking up to a pony, leading his own by a lariat, Just as he was in the act of cutting loose the picketed pony, the boy shot him, he clung to the lariat he had in his hand and his pony ran off, dragging him with him. It was too dark for the boys to follow. they went down next morning and saw by the blood that the indian had been dragged about a hundred yards and there were tracks where others had come and put him on a pony and taken him off. The indians got two horses that evening, and one of them a white pony was seen carrying an indian around during the fight a day or two afterwards, the boys tried their best to shoot him but could not. I will close. Write soon

Hervey Johnson

Deer Creek Idaho Ter
[Dakota Territory]
June 28th/65

Sister Sybil

I again seat myself to write. I intended to have written three or four days ago but on account of other duties I was unable to do it I commenced writing to Lydia J Moon and had to quit to go for a load of timber, expecting to finish when I returned, but was ordered with several other boys to equip ourselves and go over the river. We were two or three hours crossing the river. There was a man went over with us who had some cattle stolen at "ash hollow" three hundred miles below here. arrived across the river we laid around in the shade of some cottonwoods watching the trains as they pased. presently the man who came over with us said "there is the train and those are the cattle". The men, as the train drove up, fell out where we were, to inquire about grass, Bridgers route, war news, &c but not once smelling a mice. They began to look like they "felt all over in spots like a wheelbarrow" when the orderly sergt told the boys to take charge of this man, and that man, and that nigger, &c. They drove their teams under guard to a suitable place to camp and the stolen cattle were picked out and the men taken across the river to the Captains head quarters The train was ditained till yesterday afternoon and we had to stay over there as long as the train staid. We had very good living while there for we made the emigrants board us. The only thing that went rough was sleeping or laying awake on the ground without any blanket.

I have had very good luck for the last two or three weeks in getting letters. cant complain at all. Those three letters that Joe Karnes wrote to fort Laramie I have never heard of, perhaps he didnt write to me though if any of the boys had got a letter from him I would have heard of it I think. I should be very glad to have a pair of socks from home, I have drawn but two pair since I have been in the service, have some of those I brought from home yet, have drawn but two shirts, two pair boots, two jackets, three pair pants, one blouse, besides overcoat and blankets. I shall not draw any more clothing unless it is some drawers or pair [of] boots for six months. I think what I have will last me that long. . . . Blankets are a good institution in this country. I know I thought of mine night before last when I was backed up against the side of a log trying to get to sleep some. . . . I have never had but one yet, it is all any of the boys have. but when any of them go in *partner-ship* they put their blankets together, that's the way I done, when I took a *bunkmate* he had to bring his blanket with him, but I suppose the same laws that are recognized in military society would n't pass for etiquette in civil life would they? Tell Semira if she will wait till I come home I will bring her half a dozen blankets with a big U.S. branded in the center of them. U.S. stands for *umbel servant*, very appropriate I think to brand on anything that is given as a present, especially blankets. I think the blankets I speak of are of a superior quality that's why I recommend them, but then it's altogether owing to a persons taste and the way they were *broughten up.* The main point of superiority in these blankets over others is the color. By a simple yet very convenient contrivance in the machinery by which these blankets are manufactured, it is so arranged that no matter how the blanket is used *it wont show dirt.* This is all owing entirely to the color which is a kind of grayish brown. . . .

I asked Semira a good while ago to send me her picture. I dont know whether she sent it or not, any how I havent got it yet perhaps her mind has been engaged with thoughts of an economical nature, and if that is the case why of course she couldn't afford to get a picture taken. A photograph would cost one dollar but then the artist would not take one without taking three or four, and that would cost three or four dollars and that is enough to pay for a blanket. Well I will have to be content with thinking how she looks and imagining the satisfaction she will have when she gets her blankets. . . . This is supposed to be very interesting to you at home especially the part about the blanket, and more especially to Semira, but then you needn't interrupt her about it unless she has a particular desire to see it. With these few remarks I will conclude to stop. Write soon I want to hear from Semira.

Hervey Johnson

Platte Bridge [Dakota Territory]
July 1st 1865

Sister Sybil.

The mail came in three or four days ago and brought me a big bunch of letter paper and a pack or two of envelopes with "nary" scratch of a pen on them. I hardly knew what to think of it, so this morning I concluded to sit right down and send an envelope and sheet of paper right back. I had an idea that some of you folks had something to do with it, and I wanted to send somebody a sheet and didnt know who else to send it to.

I think you might as well have written *some* when you had as much paper to spare as all that. The sheet I send is dirty and torn, but that comes by the wrapper that was around it being partly torn off. Yesterday our company was mustered for pay, we have not been paid for eight months and it is not probable that we will be paid before the first of September. There is one hundred and forty four dollars due me this time. Today is the second anniversary of my enlistment. Two years ago today I signed Uncle Sam's papers and became a soldier. One year hence I think Uncle Sam will sign a paper for me allowing me to go free and wear any kind of clothes I please. Blue is getting old to me. I am getting tired of being among people that wear the same kind of clothes all the time. I would like to go home but I guess I can wait a year yet. I wouldnt think anything about it if it wasnt for the war being over in the States and so many soldiers there going home. But here we are in the midst of a ferocious indian war, and I expect we will have to see it through, that is if it can be put through in a year, and it is probable that will be for troops are thronging into this country very fast. Several thousand of Phil Sheridan's Cavalry are somewhere west of the Missouri river now.[53] If one year wont wind up the business, it will *"let me out"* any how, and after that I dont care who does the fighting, I dont want any more of it "in mine." The boys out here have all come to the conclusion that fighting indians is not what it is cracked up to be, especially when it is fighting on the open prarie against five to one, we always have to fight at such a disadvantage, we always have to shoot at them running, they wont stand and let a fellow shoot at them like a white man.

---

[53] Following distinguished service in the Union Army during the Civil War, General Philip Henry Sheridan was designated Commander of the United States Military Division of the Gulf. In response to difficulties on the Mexican border in the summer of 1865, General Sheridan made a demonstration of power that discouraged French support of the abortive Maximilian regime in Mexico. In this letter Johnson apparently was making reference to Sheridan's Rio Grande campaign. See Philip Henry Sheridan, *Personal Memoirs of P. H. Sheridan*, vol. 2, pp. 210 ff.

Yesterday evening James Williamson[54] arrived here from Hillsboro. He belonged to Co "D" of the old battalion. He had charge of the Telegraph Office here before he was discharged, and has now come back as a citizen operator to take the same office. The line has been cut between here and Sweet water for four or five days, twenty men of Co "I" 11th Kas went up to repair it the next day after it was cut, they were driven back by the indians, who were waiting there, no doubt expecting a small party of soldiers would come to repair it. There were about two hundred indians. One of the Kas boys was shot in the neck with an arrow, not seriously hurt. five of their horses were wounded. In consequence of the line being down we can hear nothing from the west, dont know how Patton is getting along, will probably hear tomorrow as Williamson starts up today to put up the line. It is only ten miles from here to where the line is cut, but our Lieutenant says he shant let a man of his company go out to repair it. He says this way of sending out five or six men to put up telegraph has played out with him. He says if [the] Government cant send men enough to keep up the telegraph, that it may go, he dont want any more of his men butchered up needlessly, he will go to Fort Laramie under arrest first. when he goes there we'll go with him, we are going to stick to him as long as he talks that way.

Morning 3rd yesterday morning as we were all engaged fixing up for inspection, the cry of — Indians!! came ringing upon our ears; we were under arms in short order, and out expecting to have a fight. We could see them thick about on the bluffs. Some were down galloping about over the bottom. We got our horses into the corral as quick as possible, some eight or nine of the boys mounted and put out, we ran out our twelve pounder with plenty of shot and shell, five or six mountaineers and half breeds, mounted their ponies and went out with our boys. The indians ran off three horses belonging to the mountaineers, and twenty five head of cattle, thirteen of which were our beef cattle. The mountaineers and half breeds followed the cattle and retook them about five miles from the station, the indians got away with the three horses. They did not come down to fight us so we had no use for the Howitzer. While the indians were seen around

[54] Efforts to obtain the official military and/or pension files of James Williamson were unsuccessful. Military Service, Records Division, NA, to the editor, May 9, 1973.

so thick, the line was cut some where below. The indians moved off after hovering around an hour or two and we saw nothing more of them. After dinner about twenty five of us went down to repair the line, seventeen of us went in two wagons, the rest including the mountaineers and halfbreeds were mounted. We found the line cut about five miles below the station near where an indian trail crosses the river, there had been about fifty indians there judging from the pony tracks, we crossed a trail of about thirty ponies about a mile from where the line was cut   The mounted men were stationed around on the bluffs while we connected the line, we were not more than ten minutes putting it up, and we didnt stay there long after we got it up. We got back to the station all safe and I for one was very glad that we didnt see an indian. Some of the Kansas boys came down from their camp in the evening. They had been fighting about two hundred indians from eight in the morning till half past one, when the indians retired and camped about five miles from the Kas camp; several white men were with the indians. The Kansas boys killed one white man and several indians, only one soldier hurt, shot in the neck by an arrow wound not dangerous. Train came down yesterday from S. W. Jim Patton is getting along well. I will close Write soon.

Hervey

Fort Laramie [Dakota Territory]
July 11th 1865

Sister Sybil.

I arrived here three days ago. We left Platte Bridge nine days ago with our old "plugs" to turn in to the Q.M. and draw new ones, we will get them tomorrow or this evening. There is an expedition fitting out here for Powder river. Some reports say that only three companies "F." "K" & "G." of our reg't will accompany the expedition. another report is that the whole reg't will go. The expedition will consist of the 16th Kansas, two companies of the 2nd California a portion of our regt, a company of artilery and two companies of pawnee indians from eastern Kansas. It is the general understanding that they are going into the indian country, but I think there is something else in the wind. Gen. Sully[55] has five thousand men somewhere north of here and Phil Sheridan with twelve thousand cavalry is coming this way. there are five or six regiments of infantry out here and more coming. I think the real object of all the soldiers in this country is to wipe out Salt Lake. It is well known that the mormons are leagued with the indians and if we give *them* a sound thrashing and make them sensible of their misery we will have less trouble with the indians.

There are forty of our company here. We expect to take back seventy horses. The 4th of July went off while we were on the road down here. The only incident worth mention that happened [to] us on that day was the reception of the mail. We were camped on Box Alder when the mail escort came along, we got out what letters were for the boys along. There were two for me. . . .

Fort Laramie is visited by three mails a week. I got two letters since I came here one from Sybil June 20th the other from Granville Iowa. the mail is expected in again to day. I am writing in Kiah Sander's room He is Commissary Sergeant of Co "L". He has not heard from his folks for some time, was anxious to know if any letter said any thing about his folks. He sends his best respects to all the people. I showed him some of the scraps Sybil sent me and told him that was some of Semiras "harness", he didnt know what I meant. It was the first he had heard of her marriage.

Fort Laramie reminds me of some of the towns along the Missouri where they are loading and unloading steamboats every day. all around the Quarter Masters Store the big "bull wagons" (ships of the desert) are thronged from morning till night loading and unloading coming in and going out. The Sutler store is crowded all day long with soldiers, citizens, mexicans, halfbreeds, and Spaniards trading. The paymaster is said to be on the way here from Julesburg. I hope he will get here before we leave. The piece of poetry Sybil sent me was real good. I read to Sanders, he came pretty near crying at it. Well I must close. . . . you must excuse the smallness of this letter for I have not time to write a long one   when I get back to the bridge I intend to write a long one.

write soon

Hervey Johnson

---

[55] See letter of June 15, 1865, n. 49.

Sweet Water [Dakota Territory]
Aug 6th 1865.

Sister Sybil

Thy letter of July 6th [I] received day before yesterday. I wrote two letters yeste[rday], one to Frank and Semira and one to a corresponden[t in] Iowa. I wrote such a long letter the last time I wro[te] that I am afraid I cant find enough to fill up [the] sheet. The mail was brought up from the Bridge by a party that went down to repair the line and get some medicine for some sick men here. The line was cut on the 25th of last month, has not been fixed yet. I dont remember whether I told about it in my other letter or not. Lieutenant Bretney and ten men went down, or started to the Fort to get pay for our company   The line was open before they started and we could hear nothing from them after they left. Several of our boys got sick and needed medicine badly and we could get no word to the doctor who was at Deer Creek. The Orderly Sergeant concluded to send twenty men down for medicine   The operator from here went with them taking wire and repair tools, though it was against orders for us to repair line between here and the bridge, our district being from S. W. to South Pass. They left just at dark and next morning about 9 o'clock we supposed they were repairing the line, for somebody was working at it, but it was a mistake. It was the operator from the bridge, he had come out [word missing] to the west end of the break with his instru[ments and] was telling Salt lake of a terrible battle that [had been] fought there.[56] There was a man here who could [phrase missing] and gathered that the place had been invested [with abo]ut three thousand indians, that the battle lasted [number missing] days, that twenty seven men were killed among whom [was] Lieutenant Collins, second Lieutenant of our company. [Abou]t five miles of wire was torn down and most of it carried [away]. He soon stopped working and we could hear nothing [mo]re. We supposed the boys that went from here were "taken in" as he didn't say any thing about them.

---

[56] This was the Battle of Platte Bridge, July 26, 1865. Even though twenty-eight soldiers were killed, including the young and apparently inexperienced Lieutenant Caspar Collins (see letter of August 29, 1863, n. 29), the Indians failed to seize this important installation. This letter from Johnson had one corner missing, accounting for the large number of bracketed inserts. See Vaughn, *The Battle of Platte Bridge, passim.*

The Battle of Platte Bridge, July 25, 1865, probably sketched by an unidentified member of the Eleventh Kansas Regiment Volunteers.
Courtesy of the Kansas State Historical Society.

Day before yesterday morning the sentinel reported that he saw a dust rising from the road about ten miles from here (we can see the road in places for twenty miles.) The dust moved along nearer and nearer as we watched it, till we finally could see men in a body coming. In the course of an hour they got here They were Bretney's party, and the party of twenty that went from here. Bretney and his men got to the Bridge just in time to save themselves, they got there in the night. The line was first cut east of the brige about a mile, a party of Kansas boys went down to fix it, the indians charged them from the brush along the river, one soldier was killed and four indians, one of whom was a noted Cheyenne Chief. the boys scalped him and took his equipments, he had on a buckskin jacket with about seven pounds of beads on it. He had about a dozen white scalps hung to his own scalp-lock, the boys took every thing from him and hacked him up considerably and left him.[57]

Collins was killed while leading a charge. He had charged the indians once lost four men killed and seven wounded, and leading the second charge his horse became unmanageable and took him into the midst of the indians. The last that was seen of him alive, he was riding between two indians who had hold of him, and both of whom he killed with his revolver. His body was found stripped and so horribly mutilated as to scarcely be recognized, near his body was a note written in female hand stating that the writer was a prisoner that the war party consisted of Sioux Cheyennes Arrapahoes Comanches and Blackfeet and numbered fifteen hundred. that one of the Cheyenne Chiefs had been killed and that they were going to stay four days and take the post. (They only staid three days, but didnt take it.)

---

[57] Here Johnson is probably referring to High Wolf, a distinguished Northern Cheyenne leader. In this preliminary but significant encounter to the main battle at Platte Bridge, High Wolf was wounded in the stomach by gunshot, played dead after his mount had bolted into a thicket near the Platte River, and then sustained numerous knife wounds about the heart at the hands of Privates Henry Lord and Jim Porter of Company I, Eleventh OVC. He suffered these wounds with stoic indifference, but when Lord and Porter attempted to scalp him, the Indian leader begged mercy. At this point he was fatally shot through the brain. By "equipments" Johnson makes reference to High Wolf's scalp; as well, he may have been referring to the deceased's scrotum — often a highly prized part of the human anatomy that frontier soldiers used for tobacco pouches. A well-documented account of High Wolf's tragic death is in Vaughn, *The Battle of Platte Bridge*, pp. 42, 48–50.

There was a small train of four Gov't wagons with an escort of twenty six men on their way to the bridge from here, they had got in five miles of the post the morning after Bretny got in in the night. They were attacked and all but three killed, the wagons plundered and burnt and the bodies of the men burnt with them after they had been stripped and scalped. Their charred bodies were found and burried after the fight. This fight was the most obstinate and desperate that has occurred on the plains, the indians showed unusual bravery, often charging our men in the face of a storm of bullets, beating them with lances bows and clubs, in many instances fighting hand to hand with revolvers and knives. One indian was seen trying to scalp a soldier on horse back, the boy had discharged his revolver and had no chance to reload, he was riding alongside the indian who had him by the hair with one hand and was trying to scalp him with the other, and would have done it, had it not been for two of Bretneys men (Tommie Sinclair[58] was one of them) who rode up and shot the indian. There were only one hundred and fifty soldiers engaged. Only two belonging to our regiment were killed, Collins and a man belonging to Co. "I." who was driving one of the teams. The evening of the third day the indians moved off dividing, the larger party going north, the other going south. William Boardman has written an account of the affair, which will appear in the Highland News about the time you get this.[59]

Night before last an indian came up here and untied a horse from the "corral," the guard shot at him before he had got ten steps away, but he missed the indian and badly wounded the horse. The indian was on foot,

---

[58] Private Tommie Sinclair was a member of Company G, Eleventh OVC. *Ibid.*, p. 90.

[59] Boardman's report was delayed until January 25, 1866. Under the heading, "THE DEATH OF LIEUT. CASPAR W. COLLINS, 11TH O.V.C. CAUSED BY THE COWARDICE OR INCOMPETENCY OF THE COMMANDING OFFICER AT THE PLATTE BRIDGE — THE TRUE HISTORY OF THE MATTER — OFFICIAL INQUIRY DEMANDED BY COL. COLLINS," Boardman charged that ". . . we do not see how a Court of Inquiry can fail to find Major [Martin] Anderson [of the Eleventh Kansas Cavalry] guilty, if not of downright cowardice, at least gross incompetence and shameful neglect of duty, deserving the severest punishment," *Highland Weekly News*, Hillsboro, Ohio, January 25, 1866. No official inquiry was held, probably because it was generally assumed that an attempted rescue of Collins on the part of Anderson and his small force would have been suicidal. Nadeau, *Fort Laramie*, pp. 188–97.

had left his pony under the hill, the tracks of several ponies were seen next morning not far off. forty six men leave here this afternoon for the Bridge. I am one of the detail. The line is not repaired yet and no person knows when it will be as there is not wire enough at the stations along to do it. Well I have got my letter nearly finished and when I begun it I thought it would be impossible to find matter enough to fill this sheet but I have done it without saying a word in answer to Sybil's letter for which neglect you must excuse me. I must close up and get ready to start

Write soon

Hervey.

Sweet water. [Dakota Territory]

Aug 13th 1865.

Sister Sybil.

When I wrote last I was on the point of starting for Platte bridge for rations. We brought up only twenty days rations when the company came up, having to leave the most of them at the bridge for want of transportation. We left here about one o'clock, forty six of us in all with two wagons, rather a big escort for two wagons wasnt it, but the boys all say they have quit going about in little squads, so we have to go out with half the company or none at all. We traveled till nearly sundown and stopped on fish-creek eighteen miles from S. W. turned out our horses and fed them and ate a bite ourselves. Didnt see anything that after noon worthy of note but an indian trail crossing the road about ten miles from S. W. Some of the boys followed it for half a mile and found some telegraph wire they had dropped. As it was not our intention to camp on fish-creek, we moved on after resting awhile, the night was cool and the moon shone bright so that it was nice traveling. We went about eight miles and one of the wagon tires came off, had to stop about half an hour to fix it which we did by tieing it on with the wire the boys found, started on struck the platte sometime after midnight soon came to where the line was torn down at the time of the fight at the bridge, it was only off of three poles at this place but following on we came to where it was "tore up" in earnest. Some of the poles were cut off and

275

left laying others were pulled out and dragged into the road and left, some were taken entirely away, the indians having split them up and made "travaux" (I dont know how to spell it) of them to carry away their dead and wounded, a great deal of the wire was pulled into the road and left all tangled up, and a good deal taken entirely away. Just at daylight in the morning we reached Platte Bridge. The first thing we all thought of was to try to get some sleep. I hitched my horse to a wagon wheel and crawled into the wagon, but the horse kept such a jerking that I could not sleep. The sun was about two hours high when I quit trying to sleep. We didnt do any thing that day but lay around. We found two companies of the sixth Michigan cavalry in our old quarters. The two companies number about fifty men alltogether. There are about fourhundred and fifty in the regiment, their time is out in about two months. I dont see what the object is in sending men out here who have such a short time to serve, besides I think they have done enough for one regiment. They belonged to Sheridans command in virginia, were in sixty four battles and were the first into Richmond when it surrendered. There has been one thousand men killed in the regiment since it went into service. Two companies of the second California were camped on the Platte below the Bridge and one company of the Omaha Scouts (Winnebago indians.) They are going on a scout across towards powder river where they expect to fall in with General Sully who is coming in this way with five thousand men.

Gen Conner left Fort Laramie afew days ago with material for building a fort on powder river.[60] He took three hundred loaded wagons, two hundred and fifty soldiers and two hundred head of beef cattle. He sends in messengers to report progress every few days. one messenger brought in news that he had encountered the indians and fought them for five days when the indians drew off. They were expecting a messenger at the Bridge when we were there, but he did not come. We loaded up and started back the next evening after we got to the bridge. It was just about sundown when we started. We came pretty near getting scared that night. Just as we were leaving the platte and coming up a little hill we saw before us what we took

[60] Fort Connor was established August 14, 1865. It was located on the west bank of the Powder River, about twenty-five miles northeast of present Kaycee, Wyoming. The post was garrisoned for approximately a year. Frazer, *Forts of the West*, pp. 180–81.

to be a party of indians. I halted the men. I was in charge of the advance guard and we were some distance ahead of the others. at first I thought of sending some one back to the command to tell them to pick a good place to stand, but seeing something white in the moonlight, I sent a man ahead, he came back and said it was some emigrants, we rode up and found it was a party of men from Salt Lake with a drove of horses. They were taking them to the states to sell. they had a covered wagon along which was the white object I saw. They were like us preferring to travel after night.

We reached Willow springs about daylight, one of our wagons broke down and we had to leave it load and all twenty five miles from here. We came on over Willow spring hill and met a train of Mormon refugees, we passed them and had not gone more than half a mile when we saw indians on the bluffs. one of our party rode up to the top of the bluffs and said he saw eight or nine indians, we went a little ways farther and turned out to feed and eat our breakfast. I posted myself on a high bluff as picket to watch the indians, didnt see but one while I was up there and he was a good ways off. We made certain that emigrant train would be taken in, as well as our wagon that we had left but we didnt care about going back to see. after we had eaten our breakfast and grazed the horses awhile we started on, saw indians just as we were starting but got home safe a little after noon. Next day after we got here Bretney tried to send twenty men back for the wagon, but they wouldnt go so it remains there yet if the indians havent got it, I expect a part of the company will go tomorrow or next day to the Bridge with Bretney, he is Captain now. The telegraph has not been repaired yet and I expect it will be ten days yet before it will. Well I am getting tired and must quit. I dont know when I have felt as little like writing as I have to day, and it seems to me that this is the most uninteresting letter I have written.

Write often

Hervey

Platte Bridge [Dakota Territory]
Aug 22nd 1865

Sister Sybil

As I stated in my last letter from Sweetwater that a portion of the company would soon go to the bridge, you will of course think nothing strange

277

of me being here at this time. But the reason I am here I will tell at length. We started from S. W. (forty of us) with Captain Bretney. There were about thirty of co's "I" and "L" along with us, they had been to South Pass escorting a Telegraph repair train and were on their way back to Laramie, the superintendant [Creighton] came back with them to fix up the line that was tore down here a month ago.[61] Nothing of note happened [to] us on our trip down. We fixed up the line at Willow Springs, and at a place called the "Devil's arm Chair". I will tell you what kind of a place it is sometime. About a mile and a half east of the "chair" the line was down; three poles out. We stopped to put it up but night coming on we moved on a few miles and camped, after night a party went up from camp and fixed it up. Our camp was at the Red Buttes. We moved on in the morning, went a mile and had to go to work to putting up wire and poles. We found it would take too long to put it up as it was before, so we quit and connected the break with insulated wire, a small copper wire wrapped with silk. We attached it to the large wire and let it lay on the sage brush along, moved on two miles further and fixed up another break, then a mile further it was all break. We put up a few poles and some of the large wire, then concluded to lay the insulated wire all the way through so business could go on while we would be putting up the large wire. There were only five or six of us working at the line, the others were guards. We worked on awhile propping the wire up on sticks where the sage was thin. I dont believe I ever saw as hot a day before. We were only five or six miles from the Bridge and the boys were getting tired of waiting for us in the hot sun and beginning to leave, we soon found ourselves alone, the men having all left us, we were nearly dead with thirst and were thinking of going in too, when five or six pawnees with some soldiers from the Bridge and the operator came up to telegraph from the west end of the break. Creighton (the Superintendent) told us to quit, that it was too hot, and we would go to the Bridge. The Pawnees that came up had come in to the bridge the day before with dispatches from

---

[61] Edward Creighton, construction superintendent for the Pacific Telegraph's line between Omaha and Salt Lake City, was a native of Ohio. Creighton's remarkable performance in completing the project in much less time and for much less money than had been anticipated made him a legendary as well as wealthy Western personality. Robert Luther Thompson, *Wiring a Continent*, pp. 291, 361–62, 370. The line was torn down at Platte Bridge.

Gen. Conner on Powder river. He had got over there all safe and was commencing to build a fort. We got here all right staid next day, during which time the greater part of the line was repaired.

Next morning we all started back to S.W. Creighton going back with us to finish up the line. Captain Bretney went to the fort from here so he was not along with us going back. When we got back to where they stopped repairing Creighton asked the sergeant for four or five men to help him put up the wire. I was one that fell out to help him, the rest of the command went on intending to stop at the Buttes to wait for us. we worked on hard and reached the top of a high ridge and saw our boys about five miles ahead of us Just where the last break in [the] line was to be repaired. We went on, got to the place, fixed it up in an hour and started on, got to the Buttes but our boys had not stopped there, we were then in a fix, there were only six of us, Creighton and five of us soldiers. Creighton had a small wagon and three mules. We concluded to go on and try to overtake the boys. We put out as fast as we could, went about three miles and were just turning the point of a hill where the road led along a level plain when we saw the line tore down and poles burning. I was following the wagon along the road, and two of the boys were on the ridge about six hundred yards from the road. They saw the line down the poles burning, and looking ahead saw indians in the road right before us, they ran down to us and told us that it wouldnt be healthy to stop to put up that break, (they saw that we were turning out to it with the wagon) so we wheeled and made tracks for platte bridge, not stopping long enough to see how much mischief was done.

We got back here before night, keeping asharp lookout behind us as we came along. Next day Creighton sent out the operator with thirty men to fix up the wire. He told me he wanted me to go and help the operator, so I went along, we took two or three bunches of wire and a shovel the boys carrying them on their horses. We got to the place and went to work, we found four poles down and the wire off of six, it was in the same place where the men fixed it the night we camped at the Butes as we came from S.W. We soon found we had not brought enough wire. I got on my horse and struck off on the trail of the indians, thinking I might find some wire the indians had dropped. I followed the trail to the top of a ridge found several peices of wire. I gathered them up and went back, put in what I got along

279

the trail and found it was not enough yet. The lieutenant in command of the escort told us we would go back to the bridge. As soon as I got on my horse I rode up to the Lieut. and told him I thought it very probable that we could find enough wire to finish if we would follow the trail further. He called out six or seven men then, and we all put out on the trail, followed it about three miles and found a good deal of the wire what we thought would be enough, and brought it back, went to work and put it up and found it was not enough, by one hundred and fifty yards. There was nothing left us then but to turn and go back. We judged from the trail that there were two hundred indians in the party that done the mischief. Creighton went out the next day himself, took his wagon this time with about a mile of wire in it. He told me to go with him. we got up there and fixed it up, Creighton tried it with his pocket relay when he got it fixed, talked with Sweet Water and found that our boys had got up all right, said that the indians were at work tearing down the line as they passed the place. We came back and I thought I would get to rest a little but Creighton wanted me to help put up some line the wind had blown down close to the station here, so I worked yesterday till nearly noon and got it all fixed up. The machine is running now night and day to catch up with business being twenty eight days behind.

I am to receive two dollars per day for each day worked on the line which will make me ten dollars. Arrangements are being made now to build a telegraph and military post[62] between here and S.W. perhaps at Willow Springs or Red Buttes. Such a post has been needed greatly for some time. Work is to commence at once or as soon as teams can come from the fort. A dispatch from Laramie to S.W. passed here this morning ordering Co "G" to the Fort. this is something we have been wishing for a long time. It is probable that the 11th Ohio will march to Salt Lake in about two months. Brigham is getting a little too sharp on Uncle Sams hands. He ordered Camp Douglas to be moved from the city. Douglas is the military post at Salt Lake.

I came near forgetting to say that when we got here from S.W. I found a letter for me from home dated July 24th. I would like that your wishes

---

[62] This post was not constructed, apparently due to the disruption created by the battle of Platte Bridge on July 25 and 26, 1865. See Vaughn, *Platte Bridge*, pp. 44–89.

concerning us coming home this fall could be realized, but my advice to you is not to place too much dependence in newspaper reports. It is a fact that we have been ordered to be mustered out of service two or three different times, but Gen Conner is keeping us here like tools to put money in his own pocket. Those tribes that have sent ambassadors to washington to sue for peace include all that have been at war out here except the Sioux. I think the best policy for the authorities at washing[ton] to pursue with these chiefs when they get there, would be to imprison them at once till they cease their hostillties, and then treat with them. I cant see any use in making peace with them while they are carrying on as they are out here. I would like for some of our philanthropists to come out here, I mean some of those who sympathise with the indian in his benighted condition, some of those who sit there at Washington and howl and want the authorities to deal leniently with the *poor* indian, I say I would like for these men to try it awhile among the objects of thier misplaced sympathy, and then I think they would find it vastly different and considerably more unhealthy than it is sitting at ease and howling about the condition of the *poor indian.* They would get their minds enlightened in a little less than no time to the fact that the only medicine needed for the indians is plenty of powder and lead and good strong wills to use it.

I dont know what we will do at Salt Lake this winter   it is too far a head yet to speculate on. The sixth U.S. Infantry are under orders and perhaps on their way to Salt Lake now. William Boardman[63] is to take charge of the Telegraph Office that is to be at Willow Springs or Red Buttes. There are six boys of our company that have telegraph offices now and there are five or six more that are pretty good operators. They have all learned out here. They get over sixty dollars per month from the telegraph company, besides their Government pay, rations, and clothing and have no military duty to do. I have often regretted not having learned while our company was at Deer Creek. I could have done so and not interfered in the least with my other duty. The Michigan boys are looking for the mail here to night, I shall not finish this letter till it comes. . . .

---

[63] See letter of June 6, 1864, n. 26.

Aug 23rd. The mail did not come last night as we were looking for, so I concluded to finish my letter today. We learned by Telegraph this morning that the mail would leave the Fort today for up the road. I went out this morning with some of the Michigan boys to get some berries, had to go about three miles, berries are very plenty, the bushes just black with them, and every ravine that runs from the mountains is full of the bushes. They are what are called Bear berries I suppose from the fondness that animal has for them. They are like wild cherries, growing in bunches like them, and the leaves and shrub also resemble those of the wild cherry. The berry when green tastes worse than a green persimmon. What I got I am going to have stewed for supper, then I'll buy a pint of milk and have bread and milk and berries. We had corn bread for dinner, and pie made of apples and split peas stewed up together, and tea to drink. dont you wish you had something good like we have? I must quit write soon

Hervey Johnson

Sweetwater Station
[Dakota Territory]
Sept. 1st 1865

Sister Sybil.

I am back at S. W. again. I did want to manage it so as not to come back, but I had some things here that I wanted brought down to the Fort and I thought I had better see to them myself than trust them to somebody else. The company that is to relieve us will not get here for two or three days yet, so it will be a week yet before we get to the Fort. Some four or five days before I came up here Col. Vinton[64] of the 6th Michigan Cavalry came up to the Bridge from the Fort. He received inteligence shortly after his arrival, of a large band of indians coming northward from the mail road pursued by the 7th Michigan. Vinton thought they might be gobbled by posting troops

---

[64] Lieutenant Colonel Harvey H. Vinton, a native of Grand Rapids who had seen extensive service in various Virginia campaigns during the Civil War, was commander of Company M, Sixth Regiment, Michigan Cavalry. He was mustered out at Fort Leavenworth on November 24, 1865, Lieutenant Colonel Harvey M. Vinton, CMF.

along the north platte to watch for them to cross, so he had Bretney to order thirty five or his company down to the Red Buttes where the indians would be expected to cross the river. They were to come down in the night and meet a company of the Michigan boys there. At the same time he sent ten men up to the crossing place, to post themselves on the mountains where they could see for miles up and down the river to give notice of any approach of the indians. He had all the men at the Bridge to have their horses saddled and three days rations in their haversacks so as to be ready to go up to the Buttes as soon as a company arrived there from below. (He was going to do big things) We went to bed that night expecting to be called up at any moment, but the company from below did not come so we got to sleep all night, next morning the men who had been on the mountains came in. They had seen nothing like indians. They said our men had got down there and were coming on to the Bridge as soon as they got some breakfast. Vinton sent a messenger up to order them to stay there. They had already started and got within three miles of the Bridge when the messenger met them. They turned back and camped in the brush near the Buttes. 40 of the Michigan boys then went up there and Bretney with them. That day a company of Michigan Cavalry arrived at the Bridge from Laramie. They came up I understood to build a post at Willow Springs. They brought up rations for the infantry up here. Five or six or us were ordered up to the Buttes with the rations for the infantry where we expected to get some more men to take them through to S.W. that night. When we got to the Buttes we found that our boys there were nearly out of rations so they could not start up that night but had to wait till next day for our team to come from the Bridge.

I took a tramp out into the mountains next morning with four or five of the boys. we went out to see if we could kill a deer but we didnt see any. Saw plenty of indian trails all about. There is a big pile of pine logs and brush as big as a hay stack up there, it was made by the indians for a signal pile, there are places there where several of them have been burnt, we could see them from Sweetwater burning like a volcano. We saw one burning for two days, before I went down to the Bridge the last time. Our team came up before noon and I concluded to come up here with the boys   there were twenty of us, we started from the Buttes about two in the afternoon and got here about two that night. The teams rested here the next day and yesterday

283

morning started on to Three Crossings, the head quarters of the infantry forty miles above here, they got there before night have started back here this morning, will be here tonight and tomorrow morning I expect some of us will go back to the Bridge with them. Dont that beat any traveling with teams that is done in the states?

Yesterday we were mustered for pay again. We may be paid when we get to the fort but I don't know how it will be. There is ten months pay due us, mine is a hundred and eighty dollars if I get it. The talk about us going to Salt Lake has pretty nearly subsided, I suppose we will know some thing more about it when we get to Laramie. It is reported that the mormons have taken the offensive against the Government, and there will be an army of ten thousand troops wintered there, that may take *us* in. A private dispatch from Col Milo George commanding troops at Salt Lake, to Laramie stated that it had been published in the "Deseret News," the mormon paper, that "polygamy *must* and *shall* be sustained," in defiance of the Government. That thier "Church Government *will* be upheld if by *blood*."

Well, this is the beginning of the first fall month. How quick the summer has passed away, it seems like it has been but a few days or weeks at most since winter broke. I recon the reason the time seems so short to me is because I have been moving on the road the most of the time.

Sept 2*nd*. This morning it seems very much like it is going to snow. We had a hard rainstorm last evening accompanied with thunder wind and hail. I dont believe I ever saw so much dust flying at one time before. The Telegraph line has not been interrupted by indians for a week or ten days. I dont think they will bother it much any more this fall. it is getting time for them to prepare for cold weather. The mail came to the Bridge once while I was there but brought nothing for me. There is another mail there now or will be against we get down there. We did intend to go down this morning but I guess we will not start now till tomorrow morning. If our company is paid off when we get to the Fort I intend to try to send some money home it will reach there in about three days after it is deposited here. I will have it sent to Warren directed to Hillsboro. Our Orderly sergeant has been commissioned second Lieutenant. we have no first Lieutenant, and Bretney is commissioned Captain. I dont believe either of them can get mustered on their commissions. Write soon

Hervey.

Fort Laramie

September 14, 1865 — June 14, 1866

On March 3, 1865, Congress by joint resolution passed a bill authorizing an inquiry into the "Condition of the Indian Tribes." Evidence collected led to the establishment of the Indian Peace Commission and the negotiation of a flurry of new Indian treaties during the next several years. Colonel Henry E. Maynadier, commander at Fort Laramie in 1866, was persuaded that a comprehensive treaty with the Sioux of the Powder River country was the most sensible method of bringing peace to the blood-stained area west of Fort Laramie. The survey of the famous Bozeman Trail in the summer of 1865, coupled with Major General Patrick E. Connor's abortive three-pronged campaign that same season and the government's untimely decision to construct Forts Reno, Philip Kearny, and C. F. Smith in the heartland of the traditional Sioux hunting domain the following summer, undoubtedly contributed to Maynadier's decision.

Peace Commissioners E. B. Taylor, R. N. McLaren, and Thomas Wistar did not arrive at Fort Laramie from Julesburg until May 20, 1866. By that time the momentum for an effective parley was losing its force. Under the leadership of Spotted Tail, Big Ribs, Swift Bear, Standing Elk, Man-Afraid-of-His-Horses, and Big Mouth, the Indians began to arrive at Fort Laramie as early as February and were becoming impatient by late May. Red Cloud was the most perceptive and reluctant of all, particularly when intelligence regarding the construction of military installations on the eastern flank of the Big Horn Mountains came to his attention. Then, with the arrival of Colonel Henry B. Carrington's substantial force from Fort Kearny and the knowledge that he and his men were to garrison the Bozeman forts, the Indians panicked and fled Fort Laramie in droves. The much-discussed treaty came to naught.

Corporal Hervey Johnson left Indian country before the debacle had run its full course. But while he was there he made no effort to disguise his contempt for the proceedings. His comment to the effect that he was neither glad nor sorry that the Indian war was about "wound up" could not disguise the essential fact that he, like so many enlisted men hardened by the rigors of service in the heart of Indian country, viewed the government's emerging peace plan as absolutely absurd. He was, in modern parlance, a converted 'hawk," a not-insignificant accomplishment for a

287

Quaker farmer from southern Ohio whose religious heritage of pacifism dated back to colonial Pennsylvania.

It should also be kept in mind that sitting at a desk at Fort Laramie and processing seemingly meaningless memoranda, as opposed to his rigorous and more invigorating life of securing the telegraph from "savage" Indians at remote settings such as Deer Creek and Sweetwater stations, was clearly anti-climactic. Moreover, the prospect of returning to civilian life, possibly purchasing a homestead in Missouri or Kansas (at $1.25 per acre), and seeing loved ones again would have been a mighty deterrent to viewing the situation at Fort Laramie in the spring of 1866 in a positive manner.

Fort Laramie [Dakota Territory]
Sept 14th 1865

Sister Sybil.

Back at Laramie again where I suppose will be our company Headquarters the coming winter. We have been here three or four days, have not got straightened up yet. The mail came in twice since we came here. I got one letter from home. I found it among the citizens mail, it was the first I had received for a month. I think I know the reason now, why I get no more letters from home than I do. You just direct them to Hervey Johnson. Fort Laramie. neglecting to put on, the letter of the company, and number of the regiment and of course the Post Master thinks it's for some citizen and throws it in the citizens mail where it lays a ceratin length of time and if not called for, is sent to the Dead Letter Office. The letter I got was written twentyeighth of August, there was no name of regiment, or letter of company on it. I dont suppose I would have got it had it not been so long since I had received a letter that I began to suspect something was not right. I have no doubt but that has been the way with a good many of your letters during the last spring and summer. Hereafter if you want me to get the letters you send to me, be sure to write the name and number of regiment and letter of company.

Our company left Sweetwater on the fifth we were seven days on the road, had a pleasant trip with the exception of one night in camp, when the elements were slightly on the muss. I thought it was one of the most disagreeable times I ever saw I was on guard and had to be up from twelve till daylight. It blowed and snowed and rained and hailed and lightined and thundered, and seemed to me as cold as "Greenland". I got up at twelve, put on the third relief, staid up two hours and put on the fourth relief and come to the conclusion that an indian, that would come for mischief such a night as that, was a bigger fool than I was, and that I would go to bed and "let 'em rip". I got off my boots and overcoat, turned down the blankets and stepped into a puddle of water. That felt rather unpleasant so I threw down my overcoat and laid on it, but the blankets were all so wet that it was not much better than outside.

There are about two hundred sick and wounded soldiers here awaiting discharges, some are dying almost every day. Johnny Hanniford[1] died this morning of the fever. The wound he got at Sweetwater had entirely healed up The prospect of us going to Salt Lake has vanished, but you need not believe any of the newspaper lies that you hear about us coming home this fall. If we get home by this time next year we will do well. We are here just like a set of tools in the hands of a schemeing man to put money in his own pocket.

I came almost forgetting to tell you about a hunt I took a day or two before I left S.W. There were five of us out. we started with the intention of taking a short stroll up by the "Devils gate," then a cross the prarie a piece and back home. When we got to the "Gate" we concluded to go south into a range of mountains that lay about twenty-five miles from the station. I have often wished since I have been in this country that I might encounter a bear some time when I was out. I was wishing that day as we neared the mountains that we could see one, little dreaming that any wishes would that day be realized. we saw numbers of antelope as we came near the foot of the mountains. They were very wild and it was almost impossible to get a shot at them. we wounded two or three but did not get them. After we reached the mountains we took an eastern course along the foot of them, it was the most difficult traveling I ever did, there was no road but deer paths and these led into impenetrable pine forests or impassable ravines. The antelope became more plentiful, but it was impossible to follow them on horses. Now and then an elk with his brushheap of horns would rise from the brush and dash over the mountain. After we found there were elk in the vicinity, we wouldnt look at an antelope thinking them to be too small game but we had no better success with the elk than we had with the antelope.

About the middle of the afternoon we began to think of going home, being about thirty five miles from there. we had followed the foot of the range so far that we had run behind another range that lay between the one we were hunting in and the S.W. river. We had to go back around the foot of this or cross it. we thought the latter would be the cheapest. so we struck a deer path that led into a deep ravine that ran in the direction we wished

---

[1] See letter of April 27, 1865, n. 40.

to go. we soon found ourselves at the bottom of the ravine where we found a very good path which we followed about three miles and found ourselves emerging from the mountains on a beautiful plain. there must have been at least ten thousand acres of good meadow grass with a clear mountain stream running through it. we had not come far from the mouth of the ravine till one of the boys saw a bear coming towards us. He was holding up his head and looking around and snuffing the air as though he smelt something. we all dashed after him with our rifles in our hands. we run him about two miles down the stream, when he dashed into the brush one of the boys and myself dashed across, he was making out on the other side and doing his best to get to the mountains It is surprising how they run, it was not till we had run him three miles and wounded him two or three times that he was brought to a stand by a shot from a revolver which dropped him. He then dragged himself across the stream when we all dismounted and one of the men shot him through the head which settled him, and in about fifteen minutes we had him skinned, cut up, and a part of him cooked and eaten He was a grizzly, about a year old. We packed our meat and hide and started for home. Had gone a mile or more when we saw another "bruin," a way we went after him. I cannot give the details of the chase. he was much older and larger than the other and led us a long chase and gave us hard work to keep him from the mountains. You would have thought it was sport if you could have seen us, riding at full speed and firing as fast as we could load, and every now and then halting as some stray shot would take effect causing the bear to stop and show his teeth and growl. He must have had six or seven balls in him and was nearly run down when two of the boys got ahead of him, one was behind. Tom Keelor[2] Ed's brother was close on him and I was about five steps from him and along side of him. Tom was leveling at him when the bear turned and made a spring at his leg. Tom yelled and spurred his horse at the same instant he was right between me and the bear, and I could see the latter on his hind feet under the horses belly I heard something tear and thought certain he was tearing Toms horse in the flank. But tom pulled away from him. I then dismounted and

---

[2] Efforts to obtain the official military and/or pension files of Tom Keelor were unsuccessful. Military Service, Records Division, NA, to the editor, May 9, 1977.

poked a couple of shots in behind his ears at the distance of four or five steps which settled him. He was a Grizzly about three years old.

It was now nearly sundown, and we were twenty five miles from home. We did not take time to skin him but cut off his hams and started for home. The only damage he did was tear the saddle bags off Toms saddle He had stuck his teeth clear through them. I cut off one of his claws which I will send home. We got home all right about twelve oclock, saw an indian signal fire in the mountains as we came along home. I could have written a mu[ch] more interesting letter if [illegible] after the hunt, but we had to go to work to getting ready to leave and I had no time to write. I am writing now by candle light and in the biggest kind of a hurry. A few nights ago five indians who had been in prison here escaped. Scouts were sent in pursuit but they returned unsuccessful. The Telegraph line is tore all to smash again up at platte bridge I guess Ill have to close this up. The next letter I write will be dated from some where in the north west, we leave tomorrow with a train of three hundred wagons for Powder river.

Write often

Hervey Johnson

Hervey Johnson
Fort Laramie
Co "G" 11th O.V.C.

Fort Laramie [Dakota Territory]
Oct. 9th 1865

Sister Sybil.

It has been two or three weeks since you got a letter from me hasn't it? Well I couldn't help it. I took paper and ink with me to Powder river, but our stay there was so short that I had no chance to write while there. We got back here from our trip yesterday afternoon after an absence of twenty–three days. We had a very agreeable time while out, didn't see one indian, that is, wild ones, saw plenty of them with blue clothes on. Our route for nearly a hundred miles lay along the Platte river, and while along it ourselves and stock did well, for we had plenty of wood, grass, and water.

There were many places on the other part of the road, that is from the Platte to Powder river where there is scarcely any of either, and you may imagine there must be a good deal of suffering on account of water. We had about fifteen hundred cattle and as many horses and mules with us.

Oct 10th I was detailed on daily duty yesterday at Head Qrs and did not get to finish my letter. I thought I would write some before breakfast this morning as I have to go to work again after guard mounting What I have to do is assort orders from the war Department, that is get the orders of each year together and every order according to its number. There is another non–com working with me. There are two bushel boxes full of papers and I dont expect we will get through today. While on our way to Powder river we met Gen. Conners expedition, returning to Laramie. There were a good many soldiers to see all at once in this country. The first, second and twelfth missouri 16th Kansas, 6th Michigan 7th Iowa, 25th New York, 14th Pennsylvania 2nd West Virginia and 11th Ohio were all represented in the expedition, and the 2nd California I forgot it. Well breakfast is ready and I must quit.

Evening, it is now dark and I will try to finish by candle light. I have been busy all day with war orders, wont get through before tomorrow night. I was talking with Jim Patton[3] a few minutes ago, he is going to start home in two or three days He will be discharged at Fort Leavenworth. I told him I wanted him to go to see you when he gets back. The Pay master was here while we were gone to Powder river but did not pay our company. we will not be paid now till the first of next month when there will be twelve months pay due us.

There was a soldier put in irons a few days ago for killing his bunkmate for his money. He belongs to the 2nd Virginia Cavalry.[4] His feet are chained about a foot apart, his left hand chained to his feet and a canonball to his left foot, that is the kind of jewelry culprits wear in the Laramie prison. I dont know whether our regiment will stay here this winter or not. There is pretty strong talk now of going to Salt Lake, we will know more about it in two weeks from now. Co "L" of our regt is ordered up the road towards

[3] See letter of August 11, 1864, n. 40.

[4] John Grubbs of the Second West Virginia Cavalry. See letter of May 30, 1866, n. 48.

Deer Creek they leave tomorrow I believe. I understand that Co "I", the company that relieved us, at Sweetwater, is ordered to the Fort. A part of the 6th Michigan has gone to Salt Lake and the rest gone home. The 16th Kansas is building breastworks around Fort Laramie. I received a letter a short time a go from Sam [Kinzer].[5] He was at a place called Cow Creek Station,[6] it is somewhere on the Santa Fe road in Kansas.

When I got back from Powder river I found five letters for me, three from home. One frome Sybil of July 31st One from Mother Aug 14th and the other from Orpah Sept 14th. I cannot write each of you a letter so you will have to be content with one to all of you. Though I address my letters to Sybil they are for you all. I dont know that there was any harm in the least in Ed opening my letters under the circumstances The other two letters I got were from correspondents in Iowa. They are both smart women, one lives near Eddyville, a farmers daughter. The other at Granville a "scool marm". I like the farmers girl the best, though I do not know her name, never saw her, nor ever expect to. She gives her name as "Maud Emberton" and addresses me as "Harry." I told her in one of my letters that with what I have experienced since being in this country, I was perfectly satisfied to go home and stay with Mother and sisters and hunt up my other self. She told me in reply to let that "other self" alone, if I would take the advice of a friend, and also told of several instances of men running off with their neighbors wives in the vicinity of Eddyville. I have an Idea that she is an old maid, and as I never expect to see her I dont care how old she is. Kiah Sanders sends his best respects to all the folks

We have got a new officer in our company now. His name is John Fury.[7] He was mustered as first Lieutenant while we were out on Powder river.

---

[5] See letter of October 24, 1863, n. 6.

[6] Also known as "Beach Valley," after Asahel Beach who received a federal mail contract to operate a post office there on February 10, 1859, Cow Creek Station (and Ranch) was a well-known crossing of Cow Creek on the Santa Fe Trail just southwest of present Lyons, Kansas. Louise Barry, "The Ranch at Cow Creek Crossing (Beach Valley, P.O.)," *Kansas Historical Quarterly*, vol. 38, no. 4 (Winter 1972), pp. 416–17.

[7] A native of Highland County, Ohio, Lieutenant John B. Fury was a former schoolteacher who enlisted in Company B, Sixth Regiment, Ohio Cavalry, on January 5, 1862. Company B subsequently became Company B, Eleventh OVC. His tour of

we all like him very well   He was Orderly Sergeant of Co "C" of the Old Battalion

Have you heard Semira say anything about getting a letter from me? I wrote to her directly after the first big fight at Platte Bridge. I have got several from you since I first wrote an account of the fight but none from her. Joe White and Lyd Moon both have quit writing to me. I am going to send home some procupine quills, they are from a porcupine that some of the boys killed on the Dry Fork of Powder river. I dont expect they will be any curiosity, but I cant help that. They killed two porcupines while on our trip and I dont know how many Antelope. We saw no Buffalo except some that had been killed by the men of Conners command. Well I have written enough. No, I forgot To day is election. I voted for [S. S.] Cox [Democratic congressional candidate of Ohio].

Write soon

Hervey.

Fort Laramie [Dakota Territory]
Oct 19th 1865

Sister Sybil.

I have come to the conclu[sion] that it is not worth while waiting any longer for a letter from home. I do believe that every body that has friends in the 11th Ohio have quit writing to them thinking they are on their road home. For the last three mails there has not been as much mail for the 11th as I could put in my jacket pocket. This morning three letters came for Co. "G." Day before yesterday, one letter comprised the amount of mail for the regiment and two days before that two letters was all there was for Co. G. It is curious that people can't believe anything *we* say about coming home. It seems to me if we were going home that *we* would know something about it as well as the editors of some of those little one-horse papers.

---

duty included detached service at Fort Kearny, South Pass, and Three Crossings. He eventually was promoted to Regimental Adjutant Company Commander and Acting Regimental Adjutant Provost Marshall at Fort Laramie. He was mustered out at Fort Leavenworth on July 14, 1866. Lieutenant John B. Fury, CMF.

I am neither glad nor sorry to say that the Indian war is about to be wound up by a treaty of peace. Several of the principal chiefs came in a few days ago with a white rag, an order was issued from Head Quarters, announcing their arrival, also stating that they were on an important mission and commanding the men of the garrison to pay them due respect and offer them no violence. I thought I would like to be out somewhere in gunshot of where they would pass. I think I know what respect is due them, and they would get it too. The Post Sutler and officers of the garrison are preparing presents to send out to the different chiefs. What kind of presents do you think they were? Nothing much but butcher knives, tobacco clothes, blankets, &c. I have no doubt but the red skunks are laughing in their sleeves at the prospect of a good time this winter, and plenty of fun next summer with the emigrants.

This morning a little after eight o'clock we witnessed an anular eclipse of the sun. The moon passed directly across the face of the sun, making a complete bright ring around the former, when on the center of the suns face. As the eclipse began the atmosphere grew hazy and seemed like twilight approaching, and at the darkest it seemed almost necessary to have lighted candle in the rooms.

The Pay Master arrived here last evening from Denver I understand he is to make his "Headquarters at this fort, dont know whether it will do Co. G. any good or not. I hope he will though; I'd like to pay my debts, dont owe but about fifty dollars. A man came in this morning from Denver with a load of vegetables, such as turneps potatoes, Cabbage, &c. He sells potatoes and turnips at 25cts per pound, cabbage 10 cts per pound or about fifty cents a head I bought a turnep about the size of an ink bottle, paid 15 cents for it. I bought me a store shirt the other day for four dollars so I can put on a little extra style while I am here. I am going to try to buy a gallon of molasses tomorrow can get it at the commissary I guess for a dollar and [a] half

Another train is fitting out here for Powder River, I expect Co. G. will be elected as escort but I hope not, we have turned all our horses over to the Quarter Master, but fifteen or twenty I am on foot again. dont know when we will draw horses again. All our saddles, bridles, lariats, halters, in fact all our horse equipments have been turned in as well as the unserviceable camp and garrison equipage. The object is to get a complete outfit of every-thing as soon as practicable. The non-commissioned officers have all received their warrants of rank and Co. G. is going to take a fresh start. we intend that she shall be second to none in the regiment. Sam Engle[8] just now handed me a segar, I must stop and burn it that's the way I treat such trash — holding one end in my mouth. After I got my segar burnt I didnt feel like writing any more, as I had to go to the stable and when we got back from the stable, supper was ready, and when supper was over dress parade must be attended and when that was over it was nearly night, so you can tell why I didn't feel like finishing my theme.

Today is the twentieth. 27 months ago to day we were mustered into service as a battalion. It dont seem that long ago to me. A large train loaded with ordnance for this post arrived here yesterday from Denver. I expect we will get some new equipments now as I understand there were equipments of all kinds in the train. William Boardman[9] has gone to Salt Lake, went with the 2nd California from here. General Conner had him detailed to go there and "shove his quill" against the Mormons. He is to carry on the Local department of the Camp Douglas Union Vedette, a weekly paper published by the soldiers at Camp Douglas[10] Utah Teritory. If Bill cant carry it on right I dont know who can. I learned today that the Paymaster is going to Fort Conner on Powder river to pay off troops there. From there he will go to sweet water and pay off the 6th Virginia, and by the time he gets here again there will be twelve months pay due us and we will get it all in a pile. The Hospital here is crowded with sick and wounded soldiers and almost every day we hear the solemn tread and mournful music of the band as the remains of some poor soldier are borne to their last resting place.

---

[8] See letter of July 18, 1863, n. 4.

[9] See letter of June 6, 1864, n. 26.

[10] See letter of May 26, 1864, n. 24. The paper Johnson referred to was named *The Union Vedette* from November 20, 1863, to January 14, 1864; *Daily Vedette* from January 14, 1864, to January 26, 1864; and *The Daily Union Vedette* from January 27, 1864, on. For examples of its promilitary and anti-Indian focus, see the issues from September 3, 1864, February 20, 1865, March 3, 1865, August 8, 1865, September 30, 1865, November 8, 1865, and a strong attack on the *Chicago Tribune*, November 13, 1865. Its lead article of May 12, 1866, titled "INDIAN AFFAIRS," may be taken as fairly typical of its editorial policy.

Did I tell you that Jim Patton had started home? I forgot now whether I did or not He has been gone several days. I told him to call at our house when he got home. I am on guard tomorrow I wish you would step over some morning about nine oclock and see us mount guard. We do it up in the right kind of style. Fort Laramie is garrisoned now by Co's F, G and K. 11th Ohio, Co. G. 6th U.S. volunteers, and Co F. 7th Iowa. Well my candle has about played out. I guess I'll have to quit and try to finish in the morning before guard mounting.

Morning 21st Breakfast is over and I will try to finish if I can. I have had the hardest work in the world to find matter for this letter, but I guess maybe I will manage to fill up with some thing. Major Gen Wheaton[11] the commander of this department leaves here in a few days for Omaha. Well I must quit and get ready to mount guard.

Write soon

Hervey

Fort Laramie. Dacotah Teritory
Oct 27th/65

Sister Abi.

It is with considerable good humor that I seat myself this morning to answer thy long and interesting letter, which I received this morning. I think I have a right to be in a good humor about it, because it seemed such a long time since I had got a letter from home, that I had almost come to the conclusion that you thought we were on our way home and it was not worth while to write. This morning I think there were at least twenty letters for Comp. G. besides three or four papers for different boys. It was a big mail for Co. G. considering the amount we usually get. The letter I got this morning was dated Oct 9th, which would make it eighteen days on the road tolerable short time that, but I have known letters to come from Ohio in eleven days. I should like to have been at your house for dinner when you

---

[11] Major General Frank Wheaton was commander of the Military District of Nebraska, which included Fort Laramie. Francis B. Heitman, *Historical Register and Dictionary of the United States Army*, vol. 1, p. 1022.

had roasting ears, but I couldn't come, had business in another quarter, I dont remember now [what] I had for dinner that day, but I expect it was bread and coffee and *ox*. We have plenty now, live pretty well on ox, roasted, boiled or fried according to the whim of the cooks, plenty of bakers bread, coffee, tea, sugar, &c and anything else we want we can get at moderate prices. Butter only two dollars a pound. Pie, six bits (75 cts.) apiece. canned fruits two dollars per can for can of two pounds &c. I dont invest much in these, without it is in a pie occasionally. I bought a twenty five cent bottle of pain killer the other day for only 75 cts. I had the sort throat— have it yet. I thought pain killer would be good for it and perhaps it would if I would apply it oftener. I dont suppose I would have the sort throat, but I wanted to put on style and went and had my beard cut off.

I would like to be lazing around where you are making molasses awhile. I expect Id get in the way of the hands too and get burnt with hot lasses. But as I knew such a thing would not be possible I went and bought a gallon of molasses at the commissary, and so I content myself with eating that, and thinking it would be bully if I only had some warm buttercakes with it. You think it is the superiority of the molasses made there do you? that caused the cane to be brought to the mill from so far. You girls should be very careful while working about the mill and furnace, that you dont get captivated by some *enlisted swain.* I dont think the whole object in bringing it so far, is to get the better molasses, but a curiosity to get a sight of the makers. Well I dont blame them; perhaps thier curiosity is laudable, and moreover perhaps they used to be soldiers once, and if they are like one, a woman is such a curiosity, that I would have even come thirty miles to get to see one at the present time.

I had to quit awhile to go to dinner. We had *calf* for breakfast this morning, and were to have had calf for dinner, but the most of it disappeared at breakfast, so we were short some at dinner, though I didn't get any of the veal, I managed to make out a tolerably respectable dinner on bread and molasses.

I didn't get that "last letter" in which Abi told me about the Show that was going to be, didn't know anything about the show till I read this last letter. I recon the other letter must have been sent somewhere else. I was glad to hear however, that none but the most respectable people attended

the show. the showman must have been highly flattered by the appearance
of his spectators. I recon all the disrespectable people must have felt bad
about it. They must have had a very large and rare collection of animals
if they had all kinds. Did they have any grizzly bears, or horned toads, or
jack rabbits?

Tell Semira and Frank if they dont want to answer that letter I wrote
them that they can let it alone. I find it dont pay to write to people who
dont answer, so Ill not remind them of their duty by writing to them again.
If they take a notion to write though tell them to stick in one of their shadows
they had made when they went to the show. Why is it that you are so
opposed to Semira and Frank moving out west, you don't expect them to
live forever right under the old folks noses do you? That is poor encouragement to me, I am thinking about getting married sometime myself, and in
all probability, before I reach home from this country I will have a spot
picked out to roost on somewhere west of the Mississippi.

If Mat Parker wants to get married and wants to know what Albert
thinks about her, she had better write and ask him. There is one thing
though that I am satisfied of, and that is, that if she marries, he wont consider that he has lost anything by the operation.

I would like to go with you to the hills for chestnuts. Hope you have
a good time and get lots of chestnuts. I'll content myself with going over
to the store and buying a dollars worth of filberts. I can get a pound for a
dollar.

This is morning 28th. I had to quit last evening to go and haul a couple
of loads of hay. It wasnt a very agreeable job to me at all. I never did like
to haul hay, and what made it more particularly disagreeable to me yesterday was the snow and ice with which the hay was covered. In three days we
will be mustered for twelve months pay. The paymaster is on his way to
Fort Conner, he will pay off there and come back by Sweetwater, Platte
Bridge and Deer Creek and by the time he gets back here I think our company affairs will be straightened up, so that we will be remembered favor-
ably. I have just now been detailed to command the funeral escort of Ellis
Luptain[12] a Corporal of our company. He died last evening after an illness

---

[12] Efforts to obtain the official military and/or pension files of Ellis Luptain were
unsuccessful. Military Service, Records Division, NA, to the editor, May 9, 1977.

of two weeks his disease was some internal injury caused by riding a fractious horse. Kiah Sanders is here in our room very sick He had the palpitation of the heart last evening, he is a good deal better this morning. The Indians have been on the road again, the mail escort was attacked a few days ago and two men killed, near Chimney Rock.[13] A company of the 19th Missouri was sent down to reinforce Co. H. of our reg't. There has been some talk of the 11th moving Head quarters to Omaha. I dont know whether it will be done or not. I dont care much about moving [in] this kind of weather. Well I must close

Write soon

Hervey

Fort Laramie [Dakota Territory]
Nov 10th 1865

Sister Sybil.

I dont know when I will have a better time to write than the present, though I dont feel a bit like writing I was "room orderly" day before yesterday and was fixing to write then, as it was my place to stay in the room all day and have nothing else to do, but here came a detail after I had got the room swept and things straightened around, for me to take charge of a fatigue party of twelve men. We had to go to the commissary and help unload and store away provisions. So I couldn't write that day. Then yesterday I was on guard, didn't sleep any till after three o'clock last night and I wouldn't be surprised if I didn't finish this letter for a day or two. I recieved Sybil's letter dated Sept 18th a few days ago I was a little surprised at the date of it, for I had got one a week before from Abi dated Oct 7th I believe, which stated that you were going to send me a pair of socks soon, and from the date of this I see that you had sent them a month before, for I received the package with the letter. (the last letter) But it dont make any difference when you wrote or when you sent the things for I got them all right and am very thankful for them. I had drawn two pair of socks about a month ago

---

[13] See letter of November 8, 1863, n. 12.

and worn holes in both, then drew two more pair a day or two before yours came, so I am pretty well supplied with that article of clothing. I wore that pair you sent me last fall nine months and then loaned them to Thom Sinclair[14] and never saw them again, they had been worn through and mended several times, I have some of the yarn yet that mother gave me when I left home. I dont know what I would have done if I had not had it last winter at Sweetwater, We wore our socks out and had none in the quarter-masters department nor any way to get any from the fort, till along in the summer. That is why I lent them. I hear that the mail has just now arrived I will wait till I see if there is any thing for me before I write more.

I have just been out to see and I find it is a mistake about the mail coming in. It has been due though since day before yesterday. something has happened along the road I recon to detain it. The mail from Laramie was captured by the red skins a few days ago near the south platte and the escort had a narrow escape from being taken also. I dont know whether any letters I had written was in that mail or not. The indians have been so troublesome down there lately that I am at a loss about sending money home. Perhaps I need not be uneasy though for I may not get any yet. The Pay Master payed off the troops up the road before he went to Powder River. He only gave them two months pay, if he pays us that way we wont have enough to pay our Sutler Bills It will be ten days before he will be here as he left Platte Bridge only a week ago for Fort Conner. Dinner is now ready and I will have to suspend again for awhile.

Dinner is over, we had bacon, bean soup bread and tea. We had a big indian scare in the Fort a few days ago, we were all sitting around our fires enjoying ourselves perfectly oblivious to everything without when we were suddenly startled by the shrill blast of the bugle sounding "to arms." Every fellow sprang for his "shooting irons" wondering what could be in the wind. We were out in line in nearly no time, The artilery was flying about over the parade and being got into position, and "there was mounting in hot

---

[14] Private (Corporal) Thomas C. Sinclair, a native of Highland County, Ohio, enlisted in Company G, Eleventh OVC, on February 24, 1864, and served at Three Crossings, Sweetwater, South Pass, and Fort Laramie. His principal duties were herder, teamster escort, and hospital attendant. He was discharged at Fort Leavenworth on July 14, 1866. Private Thomas C. Sincliar, CMF.

haste the steed," by those who had steeds, and while we were yet in line and awaiting orders, we were informed what the rumpus was. One of the infantry boys was up the river shooting ducks, he was surprised and fired upon by a party of five indians which his fertile imagination magnified to a hundred. He put dirt between them and himself and was soon in the post and gave the alarm. After the boy ran the reds lit into a small mule train that was corralled about a quarter of a mile from the post but it was too hot for them there and they got out of that and made tracks for the bluffs, by this time the cavalry was after them, but the reds were too well mounted. Our boys couldn't gain a rod on them, so after a chase of fifteen miles they gave up the pursuit and returned to the fort. In the evening Col. Maynadier[15] comander of the post sent over a note complimenting us highly for the promptness with which we fell out at the sound of alarm — saying that it augured well for the future, should there be occasion of the like again. Major General Wheaton the commander of the District of the Plains is going to establish his Headquarters at Omaha. He left here yesterday accompanied by his Staff and all the clerks. He took Co. "F." of our regiment for his escort. It has been reported here and is pretty generally beleived that the 11th Ohio will leave here by the first of March to be mustered out of service. I dont know how true it is but I understand that the General pledged his word and honor to Major Marshal[16] commander of the 11th that we should leave here in four months. He told the major that the 12th Missouri and 16th Kansas would go out before we did. The Major wanted to know why the 16th Kansas would go out before we did when they had more than a year to serve yet and we had only eight months. The Gen. told him that our officers had not worked for it and that was the reason. I will try and let you know

---

[15] A native of Virginia and graduate of West Point, Colonel Henry Eveleth Maynadier assumed command of Fort Laramie in the fall of 1865. Prior to his assignment as commander of the Fifth United States Volunteer Infantry, Maynadier had seen extensive service with the Tenth and Twelfth Infantry, mainly in the Mississippi River campaigns during the Civil War. He was mustered out on August 30, 1866, with the rank of Brevet Brigadier General. Heitman, *Historical Register*, vol. 1, p. 699.

[16] Major Levi Marshall was the former commander of Company E, Eleventh OVC. J. W. Vaughn, *The Battle of Platte Bridge*, p. 14.

about things as they transpire. I guess I'll get my letter finished without as much effort as I at first anticipated. No more. Write often

Hervey

Fort Laramie, [Dakota Territory]
Dec. 31st. 1865

Folks at home.

You are by this time no doubt wondering why Hervey dont write! I will tell you I think to your satisfaction why I have not written for some time past. It was the next day I believe after I had written my last letter about the middle of November, that an order came for me to take a small detachment and escort a Gov't Train to Fort Casper. We started with fifteen days rations expecting to be back at Laramie by the last of Nov. but as it was an ox train we were with and were making from two and a half to seven miles per day, we found ourselves at the end of fifteen days one hundred miles from Laramie and thirty miles yet from our destination, five days more brought us to the end of our trip, the day after our arrival we unloaded. I drew fifteen days rations for my men and we started back; our progress homeward not being any faster than it was going out, we reached Laramie after an absence of thirty-seven days.

I might write much that would be of interest concerning the incidents of the trip and may before I finish, but will now talk about something else. On my arrival here I found eight letters for me and have received two since, six from home and four from other places. The last one was from Warren and Sybil, at the time it was written, judging from the date, (Dec. 5th) I was more than a hundred miles from here trying to keep myself comfortable by a little cottonwood fire. We were mustered for pay today and, as the Paymaster arrived yesterday from Denver and the rolls are being made out, we will probably be paid off tomorrow or next day. Four months pay is due us, and as we settle up all our clothing and equipment accounts, some of us will come out considerably behind. As for myself I find in looking over the papers, under the head of — "The United States in Account with Hervey Johnson", the following: $54,00 for clothing, which being deducted

304

from the allowance ($93,00) leaves a balance of thirty-nine dollars, which will be marked on the payroll as "due soldier", making my pay amount to something over one hundred dollars.

Five indians came into the fort yesterday, have not yet fully learned the object of their visit, but I suppose it is concerning arrangements for a treaty. The Officers here receive orders from thier superiors at Washington, and *they*, of course through prejudice or false notions of philanthropy give orders that are not applicable. Every soldier who is acquainted with "indian hospitality" considers an indian his common enemy. Yet from orders we receive we are to consider ourselves the aggressors and sue to the savages for peace, at the very time they are committing depradations on the road. Some indians came in some weeks ago and were sent back to their tribe loaded with presents from the Officers and carrying back our protestations of peacable intentions, they were siezed and confined by their red brethren, so we were informed by those that came in yesterday — and are being kept as hostages till these return with satisfactory proofs of our sincerity. While we were on the road to Fort Casper and back the horses were stolen from two of the stations, Horse Shoe and Labonte. Fort Casper is the name of a new fort that is being erected at Platte Bridge. The party that I was with and myself had a very agreeable time on our way to that Post, the train traveled so slow that we had all the time we wanted to hunt, sometimes we were seven or eight miles from the road, in the mountains and scarcely a day passed that we did not have fresh meat of some kind, either rabbits sage hens or prarie chickens. We saw plenty of deer and antelope and got some shots at them, but being on foot we never succeeded in capturing one.

Between Horse Shoe and Laramie on our way up we met the Pay master and his escort returning from Powder river. Fifty miles from Laramie we camped on a creek called Elkhorn. We set about getting our supper, just as it was ready and we were about eating a most furious wind storm arose, which covered our meat and gravy with sand, we could'nt drink our tea for the wind would blow it out of the cups as fast as we would pour it in, we had to make our supper of bread alone, The "Bull whackers" as we call the cattle drivers, were less fortunate than us soldiers. They were behind us in getting their fire started, and when the wind came on it blew it every-where so they did not even get to make bread but came and stood around us like a

305

pack of hungry wolves while we were eating ours. It may be supposed that they ate a hearty breakfast next morning, having had nothing since the morning before. We frequently did with but one meal a day ourselves and that was breakfast which we generally got about the middle of the day. We got into camp at Laprelle one day about noon and after getting our breakfast the most of us sauntered off into the mountains. About three miles from camp at the northern base of the mountains, we found a natural arch of rock of about fifty feet span forming a bridge under which flows Laprelle creek. We worked our way down the almost perpendicular cliffs to the bottom of the channel and walked under the arch, it is about fifteen feet from the bottom of the channel to the roof of the arch, there is about ten or twelve feet of solid rock over the arch, and it is wide enough for three wagons abreast. As it is the first natural curiosity of the kind that I have ever seen, I might enlarge on it and say some thing "hyfalutin" but time and space forbids it. More anon   write soon

Hervey Johnson

Fort Laramie Dackotah Teritory
Jan 20th 1866

Sister Abi

The mail came in yesterday morning and brought me a letter dated Dec 24th and I thought this evening I would try and answer it. I was very glad to hear that you were all well. I dont wonder at you being surprised at not hearing from me for so long, and being anxious for fear something had befallen me, I know how it has been with me when the letters from home came few and far between, but you have before this learned why I had not written.

I am still in good health and most of the boys are the same, only one man from our company in the hospital, has the scurvy. One of our boys died a few days ago, at Fort Marshall while on his way to Laramie hospital, from St. Mary's a post near the south pass. His name is Chavil St Clair.[17] His parents live near Marshal-Highland Cy.

---

[17] See letter of July 25, 1866, n. 36.

The Sorgum business must have been quite remunerative the past season from the account abi gave of it. Well I am glad you are doing so well, I couldnt be there to help any, and perhaps if I had been, things would not have gone so well, I dont know what may happen, but I may be able to assist some next fall. . . . Did Jacob Kinzer say any thing about his son Sam? Where he was, or whether he had got back from the army or not. Did you tell him that Sam and I were corresponding with each other? It has been about six months since I heard from Sam and I dont know where he is. one company of his regiment is here in the same building we are in. . . .

Did you learn of Frank since he came home what part of Missouri he looked at? I understand there is now in that state over one million acres of land to be sold at $1.25 per acre. It is my opinion that missouri is going to be a great state at no distant day, and the abolition of slavery there was the first step towards it. It has been long known to be a rich agricultural country, but the presence of slavery as one of its institutions, prevented that *spirit* of *enterprise*, that characterizes the people of the northern states, from taking such hold of the inhabitants, as would be necessary to develope its vast resources. The doing away of the "institution" will bring men of enterprise, of all callings from the different northern states to settle in Missouri, and they are what will make it in a few years but little behind Ohio or Illinois. I think somewhere in Missouri I shall stop, perhaps not long, or not at all before I go home though, I would like to accept an invitation to come over and take dinner with you *any* day. I dont think New years is any better than other days. I hope you all enjoyed your chicken pie, sweet potatoes and canned fruits, I had boiled ox, bread and coffee that day, and dont remember that I envied any body else their dinner, or wished any body would "come over" and partake of ours.

I understand that Jim Patton reached Leavenworth on his way home and was there detained, and it is the opinion here that he will be sent back to the regiment.[18] We are about to have a new Captain over our company, his name is James Brown[19] He was orderly sergeant of the battery I belonged to winter before last. He was promoted to first Lieutenant and

---

[18] See letter of August 11, 1864, n. 40. Private Patton was detained because of illness.

[19] See letter of October 9, 1864, n. 55.

assigned to "K" Company when it was organized, from that he was promoted to Captain and assigned to our company. Our second lieutenant S. B. White[20] is promoted to first Lieutenant and assigned to Co "F". An orderly sergeant of Co "I" is to be our second Lieutenant. We have not now an officer who belonged to our company when it was organized. Rinehart Captain, and 2nd Lieut Collins both killed and first Lieut Bretney, dismissed from the service by order of a General Courtmartial.[21]

I got a letter from Tom Cooper[22] a few days ago, he is at Three crossings keeping the telegraph office, I discovered nothing in his letter that would lead me to suppose he was dissatisfied or discouraged about having to stay another winter. He had a great many questions to ask me, which I answered to the best of my ability. I dont remember of reading any thing in Abi's letter that sybil had written in hers I think sybil must have been mistaken. I am writing now by candlelight and as it is getting late I will quit and wait till tomorrow to finish.

Morning 21st This is a pleasant morning. the snow has all gone off, a soft breeze is blowing from the west, the ice on the Laramie is breaking up, and it seems almost like winter is breaking. The ice houses here have been undergoing repairs, and I suppose they will be filled as soon as the river freezes up again. I hope the weather will keep as it is now, as long as we stay here, I dont fancy working two or three weeks in the ice, like we did winter before last, and as soon as summer comes be moved away so we could get none of it. Our post sutler has just received a new stock of goods from St Louis. It almost breaks a man up to patronise him He sells hats at from seven to ten dollars. boots, sixteen to twenty dollars. I paid him five dollars for a military cap. Letter paper $1.00 per quire, envelopes fifty cents pack, lead pencil twentyfive cents, canned fruits $1.50 per can, ten cent bottle of ink, one dollar steel pens fifty cents a dozen, gloves from three to five and seven dollars raisins candies and nuts one dollar a pound. I am having me a cavalry jacket made that will cost when it is done $25.00. I am having it made of an infantry dress coat. I paid twelve and a half for

---

[20] See letter of October 9, 1864, n. 54.

[21] See letter of July 25, 1864, n. 35.

[22] See letter of August 29, 1863, n. 31.

the coat, the tailor chargs five and a half for cutting and making, and the lining buttons &c. will cost me over seven dollars.

Well as this sheet is nearly full I will quit.

Write soon —

Hervey

Fort Laramie [Dakota Territory]
Feb 1st 1866

Brother Warren

I concluded I would write again this morning, and maybe you will get my letter sometime. I cant imagine what is the reason you dont get my letters. Orpah said you saw an account in the "news,"[23] of the roads between Kearney and Laramie being blocked up with snow, and you thought that was the reason why my letters did not reach you, but I dont see what that has to do with it. In fact I think there is nothing of it, for we get our mail regularly twice a week, which could not be if the roads were blocked up as you suppose I received Warrens letter of Jan 11th by last mail. It was 16 days on the road, that dont look like there was any thing the matter with the roads.

I am in good health as usual, not a man from our company in the hospital. Our old captain Henry C. Bretney,[24] who received a dishonorable dismissal from the service, is lying dangerously sick at the hospital with the fever.

I quit writing this morning to attend to drawing rations for the prisoners. I have been detailed in the place of the Sergt who has been attending to that business, while he goes to Denver with the Paymaster. I have besides drawing rations for the prisoners, to see that they are kept at work hauling water for the garrisson, chopping wood and policeing. It is rather a disagreeable business to me but I have it to do. I am excused from all guard duty so when night comes I can go to bed, and not have to be up and running around all night.

---

[23] *Highland Weekly News*, Hillsboro, Ohio, December 23, 1865.
[24] See letter of July 25, 1864, n. 35.

Fort Laramie, Feb 1st 1866

Brother Warren

I concluded I would write again this morning, and maybe you will get my letter sometime. I cant imagine what is the reason you dont get my letters. Orpah s_____ an account in the "news" of the r____ Kearney and Laramie being _____ and you thought that w____ _____ _____ did not reach you ____ _____ with ____ we get ____ would not ____ I rec____ was 16 ____ any th____ good health ____ company in the M____ Henry C. Tretner who rece____ able dismissal from the service, is ____ dangerously sick at the hospital with the fever. I quit writing this morning to attend to drawing rations for the prisoners. I have been detailed in the place of the Sergt who has been attending to that business, while he goes to Denver with the Paymaster. I have besides drawing rations for the prisoners, to see that they are kept at work

A copy of one of Hervey Johnson's original letters. This one is addressed to his brother Warren and is dated February 1, 1866.
Courtesy of Mr. John J. Wassal, Jr., Wichita, Kansas.

Fort Laramie Feb 14th 1866
Brother Warren
I concluded I would
write again this morning, and maybe you will get
my letter sometime. I cant imagine what is the reason
you dont get my letters. Orpah said you saw an
account in the "news" of the roads between Kearney
and Laramie being blocked up with snow, and you
thought that was the reason why my letters did not
reach you, but I dont see what that has to do with
with it. In fact I think there is nothing of it, for we
get our mail regularly twice a week, which could
not be if the roads were blocked up as you suppose
I received Warrens letter of Jan 11th by last mail. It
was 16 days on the road, that dont look like there was
any thing the matter with the roads. I am in good
health as usual, not a man from our company
in the hospital. Our old captain Henry C. Cretney
who received a dishonorable dismissal from the
service, is lying dangerously sick at the hospital
with the fever. I quit writing this morning to
attend to drawing rations for the prisoners I have
been detailed in the place of the Sergt who has been
attending to that business, while he goes to Denver
with the Paymaster. I have besides drawing rations
for the prisoners, to see that they are kept at work

hauling water for the garrison, chopping wood and policeing. It is rather a disagreeable business to me but I have it to do. I am excused from all guard duty so when night comes I can go to bed, and not have to be up and running around all night.

I have not been able yet to see that map of lands in Missouri that you sent in a former letter, though I have been getting my mail very regularly. I have received a letter from you about every nine days since the twentieth of Dec. Perhaps the letter containing the map is somewhere on the road yet, and will reach me some time. I am glad to hear of the progress and improvement going on on the farm and I hope I will be there sometime to help. It seems to me that you have done extra well on the farm the past year. If I was to guess I would say that something over five hundred dollars have been cleared, how near have I guessed it?

About fourteen Big Indians came in this morning and have been holding a council all day with the Officers. I hope we will find out some time the result of these councils, they have been holding them and talking about them for a long time but we dont get to hear what conclusions they come to.

A few nights ago six men deserted, taking with them six of the best horses in the post, including some officers horses. An officer of the 12th Missouri with eight men went after them, but returned unsuccessful.

The deserters were from 11th Ohio, 2, 2 from 1st Missouri and two from the 6th U.S. Vols. It was reported by a Mexican that a man of Co. "F. 11th Ohio, was to pilot the deserters through to Denver, and that they were to pay him fifty dollars each for his services. This man was taken from his bed, on the night the men were discovered to be gone, and questioned by the commander of the post (Major Hughes of the 1st Missouri;) but he either knew nothing or would divulge nothing. The Major took his silence for obstinacy, and had him taken to the river which was full of mush ice, to be ducked. He ordered the sergeant of the guard (a little fellow of our company) to take the man into the river telling him that he would follow them in. the Sergt. refused to do it. So the Major took him in himself and kept him in till he was nearly drowned, but still he would tell nothing. There was a good deal of feeling manifest-ed among the Ohio and 6th U.S. men of the garrison on account of the proceeding. It was thought ~~that the~~ at one time that the men were going to turn out with arms and demand the release of the prisoner, who it was thought, would not survive his ducking long, but he got better, and the men quieted down. It is thought that charges will be preferred against the Major for such outrageous conduct. And Capt. Humfreville, commander of our regt. informed him that when any more Ohio men were to be ducked, he would do it himself. The Paymaster started this morning for Denver, he will pay off troops there on the first of March, then will return and pay off here.

Four of our boys went with him. As usual there are reports of us going home in two or three weeks, but as I have often told you, you needn't expect us till you see us. I can't promise Orpah that I will not be like him Patton, so bashful that I can't look at a woman. That hired hand of Bill Jones is David Cook. He belonged to our company and started for the states when Patton did, he was a queer sort of a fellow not fit for a soldier, but he did more work for the company than any other man in it, and made more money for himself. The way he acted when he got home is very characteristic of him. I suppose before this, Henry Wright and Mat Jones have entered the "bonds Matrimonial." I can't imagine where the six or seven couple are in our neighborhood that you are expecting to tie the knot soon, without including some of our folks, which Orpa asserts is not the case. I hope you ain't jealous or offended any, because Phebe didn't invite any of you to her wedding. I don't suppose you lost anything by not going. If I had been there, I don't think I would have considered it any honor to have attended myself. I received another letter from Thomas Cooper two or three days ago. He is enjoying himself hugely I should judge from his letter. Be says the Buffalo have come in near the road up in that country, and they have had fine sport hunting them, they have killed several. Enough for this time.

Write often   Hervey.

I have not been able yet to see that map of lands in Missouri that you sent in a former letter, though I have been getting my mail very regularly. I have received a letter from you about every nine days since the twentieth of Dec. Perhaps the letter containing the map is somewhere on the road yet, and will reach me some time. I am glad to hear of the progress and improvement going on on the farm and I hope I will be there sometime to help. It seems to me that you have done extra well on the farm the past year. If I was to guess I would say that something over fivehundred dollars have been cleared, how near have I guessed it?

About fourteen *Big Indians*[25] came in this morning and have been holding a council all day with the Officers. I hope we will find out sometime the result of these councils, they have been holding them and talking about them for a long time but we dont get to hear what conclusions they come to

A few nights ago six men deserted, taking with them six of the best horses in the post, including some officers horses. An officer of the 12th Missouri with eight men went after them, but returned unsuccessful. The deserters were from 11th Ohio, 2, 2 from 12th Missouri and two from the 6th U.S. Vols. It was reported by a Mexican that a man of Co. "I." 11th Ohio, was to pilot the deserters through to Denver, and that they were to pay him fifty dollars each for his services. This man was taken from his bed, on the night the men were discovered to be gone, and questioned by the commander of the post, (Major Hughes[26] of the 12th Missouri,) but he either knew nothing or would divulge nothing. The Major took his silence for obstinacy, and had him taken to the river which was full of mush ice, to be ducked. He ordered the sergeant of the guard (a little fellow of our company) to take the man into the river telling him that he would follow them in. the Sergt refused to do it, So the major took him in himself and kept him in till he was nearly drowned, but still he would tell nothing. There was a good deal of feeling manifested among the Ohio and 6th U.S. men of the garrison

---

[25] The Indians were probably Swift Bear, Standing Elk, and other leaders of the Brulé Corn Band who were coaxed to Fort Laramie by Colonel Maynadier and his Sioux envoy, Big Ribs. See George E. Hyde, *Spotted Tail's Folk*, p. 108; James C. Olson, *Red Cloud and the Sioux Problem*, pp. 28–29.

[26] Major A. J. Hughes of the Twelfth Missouri Volunteer Cavalry served as post commander at Fort Laramie from January 2, 1866, to March 3, 1866. Douglas C. McChristian, Acting Superintendent of the Fort Laramie National Historic Site, to the editor, May 6, 1977.

on account of the proceeding. It was thought at one time that the men were going to turn out with arms and demand the release of the prisoner, who it was thought, would not survive his ducking long, but he got better, and the men quieted down. It is thought that charges will be preferred against the major for such outrageous conduct, and Capt Humfreville[27] commander of our reg't, informed him that when any more Ohio men were to be ducked, he would do it himself.

The Pay Master started this morning for Denver, he will pay off troops there on the first of March, then will return and pay off here. Four of our boys went with him. As usual there are reports of us going home in two or three weeks, but as I have often told you, you neednt expect us till you see us.

I cant promise Orpah that I will not be like Jim Patton so bashful that I cant look at a woman. That hired hand of Bill Jones' is David Cook He belonged to our company and started for the states when Patton did. he was a queer sort of a fellow, not fit for a soldier, but he did more work for the company than any other man in it, and made more money for himself.

I received another letter from Thom Cooper two or three days ago. He is enjoying himself hugely I should judge from his letter. He says the Buffalo have come in near the road up in that country and they have had fine sport hunting them, they have killed several. Enough for this time.

Write often

Hervey

Fort Laramie, Dackotah Teritory
February 13th 1866

Sister Sybil.

It has been about two weeks since I have received a letter from home, and nearly that long since I wrote last. So I thought I would write again this morning. We have had some pretty fair weather since I wrote last and one very hard wind storm which lasted two nights and one day. I was relieved from acting police sergeant after acting three days. I got sick of it,

---

[27] See letter of October 18, 1863, n. 4.

and asked the Post Adjutant to detail some one else in my stead. He told me I would have to get some one to take my place before he would relieve me, so I went and talked with a corporal of the 6th Infantry, and got him to take my place, I went over and reported and was relieved immediately. You had better believe I was glad, It didnt suit me at all, the prisoners were all the time growling about their work and thier rations and I soon saw that I was not the man for the place. It needs to be some tyrant, some iron hearted fellow, some one who delights in seeing others punished, or rather one who is indifferent to the sufferings of others, for such a place as that.

A rather serious shooting affair occurred here yesterday, resulting in the death of one of the prisoners and slight wounding of another. I am more glad than ever now, for I felt that I should have to use something more than moral suasion in my own defence if I continued in my position, and the prisoners kept on as they had been. One of our company has been cooking for the prisoners, they abused him, called him all sorts of names, and even stole his carbine, revolver and cartridge box and threatened his life. He went day before yesterday to the Adjutant and asked to be relieved from cooking for them. They refused to relieve him and told him to try it two or three days longer, while at the same time the prisoners were ordered to be kept under stricter guard and made to march to their work and meals in ranks, when they found that the cook was the cause of this strictness, their indignation knew no bounds, they made no demonstrations at breakfast but told the guards that sebastian (the cook) would never come out of that cookhouse till he was carried out. Sebastian was informed of this talk and came up to the company before dinner to borrow a revolver of some of the boys, he got one and went back to the kitchen, got dinner ready and called the prisoners. They fell out in ranks to march down to dinner several of them picking up stones as they went down. The Sergt of the guard told the sentinel that was with them to shoot three of four of them if they went to raising any fuss. They went on down, and did not find the cook in the kitchen. He was sitting on a barrel outside with a sentinel who was guarding some prisoners that were washing. The foremost prisoner a big tall fellow wearing a ball and chain asked this sentinel where Sebastian was. The sentinel replied, "he is here." The prisoner said — "we want to clean out the bastard". Sebastian heard it and rushed into the kitchen with drawn

The "Ball and Chain" style for military prisoners at Fort Laramie and other federal military posts during the decade of the 1860's.
Courtesy of the Illinois State Historical Library.

revolver, which he discharged at the prisoner who had spoken. The sentinel tried to knock the pistol from his hand, but it was too late, the fatal ball had hit its mark, the man sunk into the arms of some of his fellow prisoners, exclaiming — "he has finished me". The ball entered his left side just below the ribs and came out on the right lower down, and took effect in the seat of another fellow's pants. McHenry (the prisoner that was shot) was taken to the hospital where he survived till seven oclock this morning. There was a general murmur of satisfaction throughout the fort when it was known that McHenry was fatally wounded. He belonged to Co. E. of our regt and had killed several of his own comrades in his drunken sprees, and was, at the time of this death, serving out a seven months imprisonment with ball & chain at hard labor, for an attempt upon the life of his captain. He was not fit to live, nor fit to die but the world is by far better off without him. His imprisonment would have terminated on the twentieth of April, when he was to receive a dishonorable discharge I have heard him say frequently that he was going to have his revenge on the officers of the regiment, and they all too well knew his character, to not know that it would be dangerous to turn him loose before the time of the regiment was out. Sebastian was disarmed and placed under guard by order of the commanding Officer, till an investigation of the affair could be made. Some of the Officers told him he "need not fear," "he would come out all right." It can be clearly proven that what he did was in self defence. There has more than a dozen men in this post carried concealed weapons for McHenry and it is very probable that, had not Sebastian killed him some one else would.

We had meeting here last first day, the first we have had since winter before last, The preacher is a chaplain of the regular army, he arrived here a few days ago in advance of his regiment which is somewhere on the Platte btween Julesburg and Cottonwood, on its way here. Orders have been issued to the Post Quartermaster to furnish transportation for our regiment. Co's. L. and I. are ordered down to Laramie. If all reports be true we will start by the middle of March for the states. We cannot go however till the regulars get here, and if the weather is bad they will be in no hurry. "Little priest," and his squaw are now attached to our company for messes. They are on their way from Fort Conner to the states on furlough. Priest is the chief of the Omaha scouts,[28] a company of indian soldiers who have been carrying the mail across from Laramie to Powder river   He was granted a furlough for distinguished bravery in a fight he had with the arappahoes, where he fought one hundred indians alone.   He had a Henry rifle[29] (sixteen shooter)   His clothes are full of bullet holes.   He was not hurt himself.

Write soon

Hervey

Fort Laramie D.T.
[Dakota Territory]
Mar 10th/66

Sister Abi.

The mail arrived last night bringing me a letter from home, dated Feb. 15th. I had begun to think that I had got my last letter from home, as for the last two or three mails there was but one or two letters for Co. G, besides the Post Master told it around that all mail for the 11th Ohio was ordered to be stopped at Omaha. That is a mistake I guess. We have had very fine weather here for the past two weeks till yesterday and today. we are now having real march weather, wind from the east cold and raw with dashes of snow.

We were paid off five or six days ago, two months wages. I received twenty dollars, the Sutler taking out his sixteen dollars first. The note I owe the 11th Kansas Sutler was not presented or I should have had but two dollars left, and I owed the tailor that. If the Kansas Sutler dont get his eighteen dollars he is out of luck. He has my note, and I cant pay it till it is presented. I've got eight dollars left of my twenty. I bought five dollars worth of butter, three pounds and a third I believe it was, I got for five dollars. That is pretty steep for butter aint it? I bought some in Kansas as

---

[28] The Omaha and Pawnee scouts provided valuable patrol service while Fort Connor was being constructed in the summer of 1865. See George E. Hyde, *A Life of George Bent Written from His Letters*, ed. by Savoie Lottinville, p. 227.

[29] The Henry was a .52 caliber rifle manufactured at the James Henry gun factory near Nazareth, Pennsylvania. Carl P. Russell, *Guns on the Early Frontiers*, pp. 136–37.

we came out her[e] at eight cents per pound, five dollars would have paid for over sixty pounds.

We dont know any nearer now, when we are going home than we did two years ago. The officers got up an indian scare two or three days ago and sent out scouts with five days rations. It was reported that the snake indians had taken the war-path against the Sioux, and were now somewhere in the vicinity of Laramie Peak. It is very necessary now that the Sioux shouldnt be hurt. There are to be two hundred of them here in a day or two, to have a pow-wow, and draw rations and clothes. These scouts were sent out to order the Snakes back to their own country   at least that is the report. But I think I can see further into a millstone than that. Orders have been received here for our regiment to report without delay to Tod's Barracks Columbus to be mustered out of service. The scouts were sent out I think so as to have a pretext for keeping us here. It will be reported to department headquarters, that hostile Snakes are on the war-path and the 11th Ohio cant be spared from the country. It is all the fault of the officers, that's the way they work it. They played that game on us last spring, or we would have been at home last may the first time we were ordered. Then again in the fall they played it, or we would have been home in October. We have been ordered home four or five times since last may, this I found out from the Sergeant Major only a few days ago. It will be impossible for me to let you know the exact time I will be at home, even if I knew when we would start. I can let you know when we start, but I will not have much chance to write while we are on the road. It is getting late, so I will quit for to night and finish tomorrow or some other time.

Morning, the 11th This is First day morning. The indian council is to be held to-day under the pavilion erected for the "Laramie Varieties." [30]

---

[30] The "Laramie Varieties" were colorful entertainments scheduled for festive occasions. Another enlisted man of the Eleventh OVC described the July 4, 1864, celebration as follows: "Boys were very busy putting up seats and canvas for the performance tonight. Copied programmes. Great rush around the door. Seats crowded. Performance good, consisting of pantomime [by minstrels], burlesque, songs, etc. Salute of fifteen guns fired after eleven. Fine sight." The performance was preceded by a fifty gun salute at noon, followed by a dinner composed of "roast beef, veal, mutton tongue, pies, cakes, etc." Myra E. Hull, ed., "Soldiering on the High Plains, The Diary of Lewis Byram Hull, 1864–1866." *Kansas Historical Quarterly*, vol. 7, no. 1 (February 1938), pp. 15.

All the soldiers in the garrison have the liberty to attend the council, provided there is room for them under the canvass after the Officers and indians get in. As I write this the white flag is being run up, while the Stars and Stripes are taken down to make place for the emblem of humiliation. As it is my intention to attend the council, I shall not finish my letter till that is over. Every soldier is seeing that his arms are in order for any emergency, and there wont be a man but will have a revolver some where about his clothes today. I know I shall. We dont want to be "slipped up on" like the garrison at Fort Larned[31] was last winter. The indians came in there, had a dance and pow-wow, had a lot of provisions and blankets given them, when all of a sudden there wasn't a squaw to be seen, while the indians set to work to murdering the unsuspecting soldiers who, of course were unarmed, and came very near being cleaned out. I dont think they'll get that advantage of us to-day, as we intend to profit by our own experience, as well as that of others. No more till after the council.

By candlelight. At twelve o'clock today, the indians could be seen crossing the river about a mile and a half from the fort, and forming a line along the bank. About a dozen men including officers, mountaineers and the chaplain, went down with a small flag to escort them up. when they reached the indians the latter set up a yell that we could hear distinctly. The indians

---

[31] Located on the south bank of the Pawnee River approximately eight miles west of present Larned, Kansas, this strategic post was established in 1859 as Camp on the Pawnee Fork (of the Arkansas River). Shortly thereafter it was renamed Camp Alert, and, on May 9, 1860, was permanently named after Colonel Benjamin F. Larned, then paymaster general of the U.S. Army. During the early years, Fort Larned served as a mail station and point of protection along the Santa Fe Trail, but, following the outbreak of the Civil War and Indian War of 1864, the post assumed a major role in the government's military operations in Indian country, as well as the headquarters for several important Indian agencies. With reference to the events in and around Fort Larned during the winter of 1865–1866, Johnson apparently was chronologically confused. In fact the situation at that upper Arkansas post was unusually stable, and doubtlessly Johnson has reference to the debacle in the spring of 1864. In late May 1864, while post commander Captain J. W. Parmeter was drunk, and while the majority of his garrison were being entertained by a group of Indian women, a combined force of Kiowas, Comanches, and Arapahoes stole 240 horses and mules from the Fort Larned stable. One of the best constructed federal installations west of the Missouri River, Fort Larned is presently being reconstructed as a National Historic Site. Robert W. Frazer, *Forts of the West*, p. 55; William E. Unrau, "The Story of Fort Larned," *Kansas Historical Quarterly*, vol. 23, no. 3 (Autumn 1957), pp. 257–80.

then separated themselves into three divisions, and started towards the fort advancing like a regiment in line of battle, the officers in advance of the center division. They marched this way till they came to the breastworks, when they drew in from the right and left and filed through the passage, then spread out again till they reached the entrance to the parade, where the main body of the warriors halted, while the officers and cheifs rode on in, to the front of Headquarters. The head chief was a gay looking chap, he was nearly covered with beads and gay feathers They all went into head-quarters, then at a word from Col. Maynadier the warriors dismounted and followed in, leaving their ponies in charge of the squaws, of whom there were thirty or forty. As the council was held in the headquarters build-ing, none of us buck soldiers could attend. I dont know what the council amounted to, but when it broke up, the red brethren all repaired to the commissary for thier grub, eight beeves were butchered for the occasion.

No more

Hervey

Fort Laramie D.T.
[Dakota Territory]
Mar. 19th 1866.

Sister Abi,

I have been waiting for two or three mails to get a letter from home and as none came for me, I concluded to write myself. I am well and have been since I wrote last, there are some pretty bad cases of scurvy, but as a general thing here, the health is very good. This is second day night, the mail came in this afternoon. There was but five or six letters for the company. A small detachment of men start out from here some time to night. they go south towards the "Cache a la Poudre" river. A part of the Quartermaster's herd was stolen some time yesterday and I suppose these men are going in pursuit Captain Childs the Post Quartermaster is going in command of the detach-ment. It is supposed that the stock was stolen by a squad of the 21st New York who left here, for Fort Collins a day or two ago. The squad that went out to order the Snake Indians back, have returned without seeing the

323

Snakes. They (the snakes) came down to within fifteen or twenty miles of the fort and stole a herd of ponies belonging to Charles Gueru the Post interpreter, thinking they were Sioux ponies. The ponies however were given up at Labonte. The snakes after they had stolen the ponies struck out and traveled right along in the road, driving the ponies before them. They came very near scaring one of Co Ls boys who was coming down from Deer Creek to Labonte They were the first indians he had seen making themselves so much at home on the road, and when he saw that they didnt try to skulk or take advantage of him he hardly knew what to make of it. But when he came up to them, they made him understand who they were, and what they were doing in the Sioux country.

The Sioux are in here every day buying notions and selling robes and moccasins to the soldiers. A small villag[e] came here a few days ago from the south, they have got their "teepes" stuck up just across the Laramie south west of the Fort. They are getting more familiar every day, and already the squaws smiling countenances are to be seen about the kitchen doors and windows at meal-times.

A squad of about thirty men have been drilling for a funeral escort. They are expecting the remains of Lieutenant Collins here soon from Platte Bridge. They are to be reinterred here with the honors of war. When the regiment leaves here they will be exhumed and taken to Hillsboro where there will be another military funeral.[32]

I have got what the soldier calls a "soft-snap," if I shall be fortunate enough to keep it I am detailed on daily duty in the Quartermasters office. I have a desk and secretary full of pigeon holes to keep books and papers in. There are four other desks in the room, but three of them ocupied. It is a very quiet place and suits me very well, nothing but writing to do, but it will take me some time to understand the routine of business. "Taps" has just now blowed and I must put out my light.

Morning, 21st I thought I would try to finish my letter this morning before I went to the office. There are two citizen clerks in the Department

---

[32] The remains of Lieutenant Caspar Collins were buried in the family plot at Hillsboro, Ohio, on July 24, 1866. Agnes W. Spring, *Caspar Collins: The Life and Exploits of an Indian Fighter of the Sixties*, p. 99.

and three soldiers. The hours for the soldier clerks is from nine to 12 and from one to four o'clock.

The Sioux had a dance yesterday on the parade in front of Head Quarters. While they were dancing and going on with their powwowing, the body of Lieut Collins arrived at the Post. They continued their dancing and noise as if in mockery while the remains were being conveyed to Head Quarters. The very same scamps had a war dance over his body once before, and no doubt they remembered it, when they saw the corpse yesterday and knew who it was. Some of the boys have been trying to learn more of the battle of Platte Bridge by asking of the indians, but as they understand each other's languages so imperfectly it is difficult to find out any thing. They said that the "Captain" meaning Collins "had a horse that ran a heap" a little ways, but their "ponies could run a heap a long ways" and the Captain could not get away. The Funeral takes place to-day at ten o'clock. An order was issued requiring all members of the regiment at the Post to be in attendance. I dont know whether I will get to go or not. I must quit and go to the office.

Afternoon. The head clerk gave me permission to attend the funeral this morning, so when I heard the bugle I came up on to the parade but I saw the procession had formed so I did not fall in with it. The Band went in advance playing a mournful air, then the Lieutenant in command of the escort, then came the escort in two platoons of eight men abreast in two ranks with arms reversed, two men between the two platoons, bore the regimental colors at a trail. Just in rear of the escort was the body, borne on a hand litter by six Lieutenants, the stars and stripes spread over the coffin. The Pallbearers and regimental Officers had each a strip of Black Crape on their arms, then came the members of the regiment in procession with side arms, in their rear citizens and soldiers mixed up promiscuously following to the graveyard Arrived there, the coffin was lowered and the Chaplain uttered a few imprescive remarks concluding with a prayer, When three volleys were fired over the grave by the escort and crowd dispersed. Inteligence was received here this morning by telegraph, of the uprising of fifty-thousand armed Fennians in Canada. The report may be premature, but it certainly wont be long before Canada will be invaded. There is a Fenian Circle here that meets once a week. The Commander of the Post

is a member   He wears a green rosette pinned to the breast of his coat.[33]
Well I must quit

Write soon

Hervey

Fort Laramie D.T.
[Dakota Territory]
April 1st 1866

Sister Sybil

Thy letter of March 3rd came to hand evening before last. I received one about a week ago from orpah & warren, but have been so busy that I could not answer it. It keeps four or five clerks busy all the time. Yesterday was monthly inspection, but the A.Q.M. had me excused so that I did not have to attend. Fort Laramie has been changed from Head Quarters, West Sub District of Nebraska, to Head Qrs, Dist of the Platte. I saw a printed order from Department Head Qrs, the other day, that stated there was to be 2 companies of cavalry and five of Infantry at this post this summer, and that on the receipt of the order all volunteers except the 5th & 6th Infantry were to be mustered out of service. The 7th Iowa started two days after the order came, the 6th Virginia was ordered to laramie to get ready to start. But the 11th Ohio is entirely forgotten. Well I dont mind it much   I have just three months from today yet to wear blue clothes   If we are kept till our time is out   It is all the work of the officers, we might have been four or five days on our road home if it hadn't been for them, about five or six have just got to wearing Scabs and it would be a pity now to muster them out of service. I believe if they had the say they would keep us six month over our time, they think it a "big thing" to be a commissioned officer. If you see us home before the first of July you may consider us "in luck." All the orders that have been sent here for us have been of no avail, and we dont look for any

---

[33] The Fenian Brotherhood was a society of militant Irish-Americans dedicated to the independence of Ireland and the annexation of portions of Canada to the United States. Armed parties crossed the Canadian border in 1866, but were easily turned back by Canadian militiamen. See D. F. Warner, *The Idea of Continental Union: Agitation for the Annexation of Canada to the United States, passim.*

better respect to be paid to future orders, but have made up our minds to remain three months longer, I am afraid it wont be healthy for some of our "Shoulder strap Men" to be along with us when we do start east. I believe half of them are afraid of us now.

This is morning 2*nd*. it is impossible for me to sit down and write a letter without stopping, I had to stop yesterday for want of something to write and this morning I dont think can write much. The weather here is warm and spring like, the biggest snow we have had this winter fell the fore part of last week. it was about five inches deep but it only laid in two days. We witnessed a total eclipse of the moon the night of the thirtieth of March it was the first total eclipse I had ever seen. I was highly amused at the remarks of some of the soldiers passed while watching the dark shadow steal over the surface of the moon. They betrayed brilliant ideas. Some were wondering what made the eclipse, one fellow explained it satisfactorily by saying that it was "a *pint* of the earth getting on this side of the moon," And even after the moon was wholly in the shadow of the earth, some of them maintained that it wasn't eclipsed yet, because we could see a kind of nebulous spot that indicated where the moon was, they said "it had to git as red as blood, and then it would git so we couldn't see it atall". It is highly entertaining to me to hear such bright ideas expressed, so I just stood back and listened, and let those that knew it all do the talking.

It is getting nearly time for me to go to the office, so I'll have to quit again. The mail dont go out for three days yet so maybe my letter will be done in time.

This is after dinner. 6 or 7 deserters from the 5*th* US Infantry were brought in here this morning, they deserted from Fort Reno[34] on Powder river the place where I went last fall. They have been at work this morning removing the benches and canvas from the ruins of a temporary Chapel that the wind had blown down. There are to be fifteen or twenty more of

---

[34] Fort Reno, established on June 28, 1866, and named after Major Jesse L. Reno, who was killed in the Battle of South Mountain in 1862, was located on the Powder River and the Bozeman Trail approximately sixty-five miles north of present Casper, Wyoming. It was abandoned by the federal government as a result of the Fort Laramie Treaty of August 29, 1868 and burned by the Sioux Indians immediately thereafter. Frazer, *Forts of the West*, p. 184.

them here tomorrow. The Pay Master arrived here yesterday from paying off the troops up the road. He will start to Denver in a few days. I heard another report to day. The Captain of Co K told his men that our reg't would leave here in three weeks, that's encouraging aint it. I saw some very pretty specimens of Moss Agate last evening. they were brought from near Sweet Water by some of the Pay master's escort. I want to try to get a specimen or two to bring home with me if I can. Indians are swarming about the fort now, they come and draw rations as regular as the soldiers. It looked like they were going to take the whole Commissary Department this morning. The squaws as usual do all the work loading the ponies they brought, there are some tolerably good looking squaws, but some of them are the embodiment of unearthly ugliness.

The mail will be here again this evening I dont look for any letter from home but there is one due me from a correspondent in Iowa. I have been saving all her letters I want to show some of them to you when I get home. I have a piece of Izinglass about two inches square that I am going to bring home with me. There are great solid banks of it in places out here I have seen it scale off in sheets like a pane of glass and just as clear. . . .

The bugle blows for roll call and I must quit

Write soon

Hervey

Fort Laramie D.T.
[Dakota Territory]
April 14th/66

Sister Abi

Thy letter of Mar. 28th came to hand by yesterdays mail and I thought I would try to answer it this evening. I am sitting in the Q.M. Office writing by candle light It is now nearly a month since I began to work here and it would suit me if I could stay here 'till the regiment leaves. I go to work at eight in the morning, quit at twelve, then work from one till four in the afternoon. I wish I could keep at it for about two months, I believe I would learn something in that time. We have a pet crow that stays in the room where we work and serves somewhat to break the monotony of our busy hours with his droll pranks, he is always hunting up some mischief to do, such as picking up a pen when it is dropped and hiding it in some crack or behind a box. One day I went out, I happened to leave my stool close to the table instead of slipping it under as I usually do, when I came back, Mr Crow had hopped on to the stool, (his wings are cropped) and from there to the table, where he deposited his *card*, pulled out all the papers as high up as he could reach and spattered ink all over them, and was down on the floor gawking around as if nothing had happened. He caught a mouse to day and had a big time with it and a heap of fun before he killed it. The 6th Virginia got here about a week ago from Platte Bridge. They do duty at the post, but are camped on the Laramie about half a mile below. I dont know when they will leave here for the states, I heard it reported that we would all go together. About forty of them passed the office awhile ago, starting on a scout. Somebody has invented another indian scare. I understand that they have stolen the Quarter Masters herd, and this party are going after them. It must come very natural to you when my letters come a long ways between, to think the reason you dont get any, is because I am on the way home. You will no doubt be gratified to learn that we —— havn't started yet, nor have any prospect of it till our time is out. I dont know what Tom Cooper[35] could have heard that was so encouraging, he is away up the road about two hundred and thirty miles from here, and hasn't been with the company for two years; but maybe he has a better way of finding out things than we have. The Pay master left a few days ago for Denver. He will be back here and pay us off again about the third or fourth of May. The bugle sounds for tatoo roll call and I must quit for to-night.

Morning 17th. I came down to the Office early this morning to try to finish my letter. It has been snowing now for two days but is so warm that it melts as fast as it falls. The sixth Va. leave this morning. They have a muddy disagreeable time for starting, but they dont care what kind of weather it is, so they get out of this country. The first emigrants passed here yesterday. They were going to Virginia City. The scout that I spoke of returned day before yesterday evening, having found every thing all right.

---

[35] See letter of August 29, 1863, n. 31.

The mail came in again yesterday but Brought me nothing. I dont think you need delay writing on account of hearing that we are coming home. I have been telling you this for the last six months, but still you are ready to believe any thing you hear from people who dont know any thing about it. I have an idea that we will find out when we are going home, as soon as any body else, and will be as competent authority as those one horse newspapers that you have been reading. Well enough for this time.

Write soon
Hervey.

Fort Laramie Dacotah Ter
May 1st 1866

Sister Orpah

The Mail arrived last night and brought me one letter from home dated April 4th and mailed the 12th. I was very glad to hear from home again for it seemed like it had been a month since I had heard. I am writing at my own table in the A.Q.M. Office. The soldiers are not stirring about the post much to day, having orders to remain in doors and be prepared for an out-break of the Indians. About five hundred of them came in this morning, most of them on foot. They make no hostile demonstrations but every one has his bow strung and his hand full of arrows. The larger number of them are formed in a semicircle Just back of the barracks and the Col and major are holding some kind of a conferrence with them, a few are straggling about over the Fort and as I write three or four are looking through the window at my back. I wish my table was differently arranged so I wouldn't have to turn around when they darken my window, but my rifle hangs on a nail within my reach and if any thing happens I think I am equal to the emergency. The Officers or some of them never went to bed at all last night. The Major made a bugler sleep with the guards so that he might be more readily awakened, to sound the assembly to arms in case the sentinels should smell a mice.

About one thousand indians are reported somewhere in the Platte just out of sight of the Fort, and for the last two or three nights indians have been seen skulking about the Fort as late as ten oclock in the night. Every fellow keeps his eyes peeled as it is our intention not to be "slipped up on" I dont know that the indians really meditate anything hostile, but if they have a right to carry thier bows strung and hands full of arrows we have a right to have something to shoot with close by us too. The Colonel[36] has been giving them provisions for two months with an unsparing hand. his object was to treat them well and get as many as he could collected about this post by the time the peace commissioners arrived from the states. The result is beyond his most sanguine expectations for they flock hither from the upper Missouri, from Minesota and from every where Sioux, Cheyennes and Arrapahoes, all apparently half famished from being so long on their Journey. The Col received a message from Department H^d Q^{rs} ordering him to stop issuing rations to the indians. He has been making them bland promises the most of which he is unable to fulfil, and in fact being drunk most of his time I guess he dont know half the time what he is promising.[37] When he received that order prohibiting the issue of rations he got scared, and ordered two companies to Laramie from up the road, one of them will be here to day the other tomorrow. I have for some time past entertained a sneaking idea that our officers here contemplated playing the Indians an indian game, and a little incident that occurred yesterday or rather a remark that was dropped by the Major rather strengthened that idea. I was over at the store, it was full of indians trading. The major was in there talking with an indian who could speak english a little. Through this fellow the major was carrying on a conversation with two Cheyenes who had just arrived from the southwest, from some where between Ft Halleck[38] and

---

[36] This was Colonel Henry E. Maynadier, commander of the Military District of the Platte. Olson, *Red Cloud and the Sioux Problem*, p. 28. See letter of November 10, 1865, n. 15.

[37] In early 1866 Colonel Maynadier had persuaded Big Ribs and several other "Laramie Loafers" (Indian leaders who lived off the military) to travel into the upper Missouri country for the purpose of announcing a major Indian treaty conference, to be held at Fort Laramie later that year. Distributing provisions and whiskey was an effective method of getting at least some Indian leaders to the treaty table. *Ibid.*, pp. 28–29.

[38] Fort Halleck was established on July 20, 1862, as a protective point on the Overland Trail and for the Pacific Telegraph. It was located on the west bank of Medicine Bow River approximately four miles west of present Elk Mountain, Wyo-

Greenriver. He was trying to find out something of the present whereabouts of a woman who was captured by them on the south road a few days after the battle at Platte Bridge. This Indian went out of the store pretty soon and I asked the Major who he was, he said he was Swift Bear[39] a sioux Chief, and then he went on to tell what he had been saying and then said, "we want to find out about this woman", in rather an undertone "and get them to bring her in — "Ah! the rascals we have not done with them yet by a —" I shant give the remainder of the sentence but it was sufficiently strong to give additional force to the whole. He had been drinking, or perhaps he would not have dropped such a remark in my hearing. What I had thought of was this, that they would get a large crowd of indians in the fort and have a big time issuing rations to them, and at a preconcerted signal have the garrison to light on them and wipe them out. it is a game of their own, one they have played frequently on the whites, and would be none too severe for them, but some how or other I dont feel as though I would like to have a hand in any thing of the kind especially at this stage of the game. I would have gone in for something of that kind Last summer when I had yet a year to serve in the army, but as I have but two months from today, I want as little to do with them as possible while I remain in this country. Some of the old mountaineers say there will be trouble again this summer, and I have no doubt of it myself, and if they will keep quiet till I get out of the country I will be very well satisfied. A good many of our company seriously contemplated staying in this country, and myself among the rest. We heard of the ravages of the cholera in the states and knew that it would not be healthy for us to go there especially at the time of year in which we will have to go. We wrote a petition asking to be discharged here and sent it to the Major, but he is an ambitious kind of a fellow and wants to create a sensation by bringing all the men back. We are still in the dark about the time we will leave this country, though numberless reports are going the rounds. I heard to day that our transportation would all be ready by tomorrow and that we

ming. It was named after Major General Henry W. Halleck and was abandoned on July 4, 1866. Frazer, *Forts of the West*, p. 181.

[39] Swift Bear was a Brulé leader who generally was friendly to the whites. Many of his followers, however, feared they would be killed if they came to Fort Laramie. Olson, *Red Cloud and the Sioux Problem*, p. 29.

would start by the fifteenth of May, but I dont believe it. I know we cant leave here till troops come to relieve us, and we still hear nothing ceartain of any being on their way here yet.

Yesterday was Inspection and muster, mustered for two months pay, but we will never be paid again in this country. The boys that went from here to Denver with the Pay master returned a few days ago but left the Paymaster there. The next time we are paid off will be at Columbus Ohio. The most of our company have been drawing horses to ride home on, they are all old broken down plugs that have been turned in from every regiment that has been in the country. I thought if I had to walk, I would rather walk alone, than to have a horse and have to walk and lead him. Sam Engle is going to drive the company wagon and I guess If I have more bed clothes than I can carry I will get on the good side of him and get him to haul some for me. You may think this is a curious piece of letter paper, but I think it is as good as any. It is what we call Folio Post. I have been making out some Inspection Reports and the sheet was this much too large. As it is about full I will have to quit. Write again

Hervey

Fort Laramie Dacotah Teritory
May 8th 1866

Brother Warren

I received thy letter of 15th last month this morning and was somewhat surprised at the opening Sentence which was in substance, that you scarcely — knew whether to write to me or not. From all the letters I have received from home for the past three or four months I have gathered the same, always at a loss whether to write or not, and I have been telling nearly as often as I have written that you neednt look for me till my time is out. it is strange, when you are told in nearly every letter you get, what our prospects of coming home are that you will still be in doubt, it is true I gave you the benefit of all the reports that were going the rounds some of which were encouraging, but at the same time I always gave my own opinion too. I have not quite seven weeks to serve from this date and if I get to leave here by the first of July I wont think any thing strange of it from the way things are drifting. I intend to let you know when we will start from here and when I do it will be time enough to think about not writing.

We have had some of the most disagreeable weather for the past 5 or six days that I have seen in this country, it rained nearly steady all yesterday morning, I never saw so much water on the ground before, it stood everywhere in great pools, even in side the Fort is a Pond now of about two acres. One who had never seen it would not believe that so much water would lay on the ground where it is nearly all sand or loose gravel, but what made it worse was the snow which began to fall yesterday morning and continued throughout the day, coming down in chunks something less than a wash board, everything was a perfect Slush. The sky has been fair to day so that the snow has all melted off except on the higher bluffs. Some of our boys were up the road with the mail, they got back this evening said the snow was two feet deep at Fort Marshall Sixty five miles from here.

I heard a new report about going home to day. I guess I'll have to tell it. One of the Clerks in the Commissary Office came in and told us that he heard the Post Adjutant say that the 11th Ohio would start tomorrow For the States, I cant see it. I dont want you to stop writing on the strength of it any how. A part of the regt was mustered out a few days ago at Leavenworth, the remainder is here. we do not know certain yet whether any troops for the plains have left the States or not, but I did hear on pretty good authority that a petition would be laid before next Congress, asking permission to recruit a regiment to relieve the 11th Ohio. The bugle sounds roll call and I must quit for to night.

Morning 9th I thought I [would] try to finish my letter this morning before business hours. The Post has been swarming with Indians since I last wrote A band of Cheyennes came in some days ago They have shown themselves a great deal better disposed than the Sioux, making themselves more familiar with the soldiers, coming among us with thier robes and skins to trade, many of them without weapons of any kind, and those who brought thier bows with them, had them unstrung and the arrows in the quivers. Many of the boys have bought seven or eight robes I dont know what they intend to do with so many I dont think they will get them hauled to the States for them. I have not bought any yet myself fearing I would have no way to take them home. I got three "Moss Agates" yesterday which I intend

334

to bring home with me. They are of a dove color, semitransparent and the moss can be seen all through the stone.

Last first day we had two funerals, one of a Captain of the 5th U.S. Vols. the other of Lieutenant Brown[40] of our regt who was killed summer before last while we were on an expedition to wind river, he was buried at Deer Creek when the expedition returned. He is to be taken to the states when the reg't goes home. It was an awful day the rain came down by bucketsfull the day of the funeral, but the boys stood it very well. They think they would be willing to attend a funeral every day rain or shine as long as the *officers* lasted.

I am glad to hear of the work on the farm going on so well, cant imagine what Warren is going to do with six acres of Flax. Have you any green apples yet? We have out here, at two dollars a dozzen or Sixty dollars a bushel, butter is $1.50 per pound, onions 50. cents, potatoes 30. We bought 4 or five sacks of potatoes for our company, have had two messes, they went first rate with $1.50 cent butter. Well it is now business hours. I will try to finish before the mail goes out tomorrow morning.

as I have a little liesure now I will write some more, a large emigrant train passed through this morning for Bannack City, there were a good many women with the train, one of our boys who was up the road with the mail came back snow-blind he is blind yet this morning. The boys who were with him prevented getting blind by rubbing powder over thier faces before they started out in the snow. The good effects of the big rain and snow are already becoming visible, the river bottoms and sides of the bluffs are begining to wear a greener hue. Nearly the middle of May and things beginning to look green!!! Astonishing early aint it? The Laramie river has begun to rise. The Platte has been past fording for some time. A ferry boat has been built and put on it so all the crossing is done that way, Well I will close, be sure and write. I dont hardly think we will start home to day

Hervey.

---

[40] He should not be confused with Lieutenant James A. Brown (see letter of October 9, 1864, n. 55) who was honorably discharged at Fort Leavenworth on July 14, 1866. Attempts to identify the Lieutenant Brown who died in 1864 were unsuccessful.

Fort Laramie D.T.
[Dakota Territory]
May 20th/66

Sister Abi

I received a letter from home by last mail which I suppose to have been written by thee as there was no Signature appended and all the family were mentioned except thyself. I am glad to learn that you are going to quit listening to tales you hear about me coming home, for if you dont quit pretty soon there will be none to listen to. I have 40 days to serve yet from to day. Some boys in "G" Co. have but 13 days. The 2nd day of June the first mans time is out, the others range from that on to the last of august. The mustering officer arrived here yesterday from Denver to muster us out of service, dont know when he will do it, but we know he cant do it till troops arrive here from the States, when that will be none of us know, though we hear where they are every few minutes. the latest was that they left Denver day before yesterday, would be here the last of this week. They came by Denver and the Smoky Hill road from Fort Riley[41] Kansas. Another report was that troops crossed the river at Julesburg several days ago for this place. Another that they camped at Mud Springs[42] a hundred miles from here a few nights ago, and a dozen others, for the reliableness of which we generally make the usual allowance, which is to believe none of them.

Today was the day set for the grand pow-wow, but as the commissioners have not arrived I suppose It will be postponed. The Sioux were thrown into a great excitement some time ago on account of the Utes who were supposed to be on the war path somewhere in this vicinity. (The name of the Utes is a terror to them) There was a small camp of the Sioux up the Laramie some distance above the Fort. the scare originated up there. two or three indians came down to the Fort and told that the Utes had attacked the

---

[41] Located on the north bank of the Kansas River just east of present Junction City, Kansas, this important post was established as Camp Center on May 17, 1853, and renamed Fort Riley on June 27, 1853, after Colonel Bennett Riley of the First U.S. Infantry. After 1855 it began its long history as the most important federal cavalry post west of the Mississippi. It continued to serve major military functions in the twentieth century and remains operative today. Frazer, *Forts of the West*, p. 57.

[42] See letter of January 1, 1864, n. 24.

village and killed five Sioux, the news soon spread to the other villages around the Fort and It wasnt long till Indians were seen everywhere on thier war ponies with thier bows arrows and other war rig. The men of the garrison crowded around on the banks of the river and on the upper porches of the buildings expecting to witness a genuine indian battle but were doomed to disappointment. The Post Interpreter who had gone up to the beleaguered village at the first alarm, soon returned and told us what the matter was. It was caused by a Cheyenne indian, the Sioux and Cheyennes are on friendly terms with each other, though the latter know the former to be the most cowardly tribe in this country notwithstanding thier superiority in numbers. Well this Cheyenne hid himself in a ravine near the Sioux camp and went to jabbering in his own tongue which the sioux could not understand, they took him at once for a Ute Spy or decoy placed there to take thier attention, while a larger party which they imagined concealed in the brush, would rush into camp and steal thier ponies and take off thier Squaws. That is all there was of it.

Major General Sherman's Inspector General[43] arrived here some days ago. He is a Major of the Regular Army and Colonel of Volunteers, was with Sherman all through the war. He inspected the troops yesterday, left this morning for Forts Mitchell and Sedgwick,[44] will be back here again in a week or two. Sherman himself was at Kearney a few days ago on his way to some of these western Posts,[45] he will be here some time during his round.

We had another indian scare in the Post day before yesterday though I guess there was no one scared but the officers. They had us to sleep with our arms by us on the strength of it any how with the admonition to "fall out, every one of us, armed, at the sound of the bugle" that is if it should sound that night. We went to sleep all ready but had no occasion to fall out during the night, only the night before one of the sentinels shot at an indian that was skulking about the Post, and the next day one of the Sioux bands got mad about thier beef of which they thought they were not getting enough. They wanted a whole ox on foot for each family or lodge; the Col would

---

[43] Robert G. Athearn, *William Tecumseh Sherman and the Settlement of the West*, p. 51.

[44] See letter of November 15, 1863, n. 14.

[45] For a detailed analysis of Sherman's tour of inspection, see Athearn, *William Tecumseh Sherman*, pp. 45–54.

not give it to them that way but ordered the butcher to kill three beeves and divide them by weight among the lodges equally. Heretofore the beef had been issued to them on foot and they killed it themselves, but they were getting too extravagant in thier demands and the Col. shut down on them. After the butcher had divided the three beeves around, the chief of the band said — the first man that took any of the beef should have his horse shot, so they left it all and went away with out any. they went over the river to where the man that keeps the ferry lives and got into a quarrel among themselves and threatened to destroy the ferry. I guess their quarrel nor threats either amounted to much but our officers thought we had better be prepared for a night attack.

the fore part of last week we witnessed a sight that is not often seen at Fort Laramie, it was that of "Drumming a soldier out of service." His name was Joseph Isaacs,[46] he is an Italian Jew, born in London, England, served in the rebel army during the rebellion, was taken prisoner, enlisted in the 6th U.S. Infantry, and was, at the time he was drummed out Serg't of Co "H" of that reg't. his offences were several, one of which was "uttering disloyal sentiments", The troops of the Garrison were formed on the parade, the prisoner was brought out to hear his sentence read, after first being marched along the line in front of the troops, after hearing his sentence, he was marched off out side the garrison the fife and drums playing the "rogues March". he was accompanied out of the garrison by the Serg't of the guard and four sentinels with bayonets fixed, two in advance of him with arms reversed, and two in the rear at a charge bayonet, some of our boys went down the river fishing that afternoon and found [him] sitting on the bank,

---

[46] Sergeant Isaac's real name was Emanuel H. Saltiel. Among other things, this remarkable individual was an English citizen, Officer of Cadets in the Tenth Tower Hamlet Rifleman (London), and former lieutenant and aide-de-camp to the Confederate command at Atlanta. Following his injudicious court-martial and humiliating discharge at Fort Laramie, he became a prominent mining engineer and businessman in Denver. Sergeant Joseph Isaacs, CMF, and Proceedings of the General Court-Martial Convened at Fort Laramie, D. T., Pursuant to S. O. No. 34, Headquarters, District of Nebraska, Dated Fort Laramie, D. T., November 8, 1865, Case File MM 3668, Sergt. Joseph Isaacs, Co. H, 6th U.S. Vols., Records of the Office of the Judge Advocate General, Army, RG 153, NA. For a detailed analysis of his military record and court-martial, see William E. Unrau, "Justice at Fort Laramie: The Trials and Tribulations of a Galvanized Yankee," *Arizona and the West*, vol. 15, no. 2 (Summer 1973), pp. 107–32.

some distance from the Post, they took him with them a piece and left him, when they came back, they found him walking about like a crazy man. They came on up to the Post and left him there and that was the last seen or heard of him. Well, this is already getting long enough and seems to me very uninteresting so I will close

Hervey

Fort Laramie [Dakota Territory]
May 30th 1866.

Folks at home.

I came down to the office pretty early this morning and having nothing to do I thought I would try to write a letter. It is drizzling rain now and every-thing forebodes a gloomy day. We have had two mails since I last wrote, the last one brought three letters for the 11th Ohio, none for me of course. Night before last we had a little excitement in the way of an indian chase, for a change. The last bugle for the night had sounded and all were in bed but the sentinels, when a shot was fired by the guard at the magazine. we were all out in an instant, wondering if the Post was attacked, we reached the door and could see men running, some in thier shirttails, some with thier pants on but no hat or shoes   (it was moonlight)   all intent to see the fun whatever it might be, in a few mo[m]ents the rattle and flash of rifle and pistol became generally promiscuous, mixed up with shouts of — halt! they're indians! shoot the red skins! we could see them making for the breastworks on the east side of the Fort and as they would near the "beat" of a sentinel, we could hear him open on them with his repeater. It sounded like a regular skirmish   The indians ran into a lodge a short distance from the fort and the firing ceased. they were followed into the lodge by the Provost Guard and brought out, they brought them up on the parade, and sent for the interpreter. there were four or five of them; one was killed in the skirmish and two wounded. the interpreter found out from them that they had been up the river to the village and were coming back to the lodge of a brother in law who lived just out side the fort, they said they had just come here and did not know they were not allowed inside the fort after dark. they were coming right through the Post when the sentinel at the

339

magazine challenged them, and they making no reply he fired at them, then they started to run, the report of his gun brought out the provost guard who followed the indians firing at them.

this morning the Indians were very mad over the affair, that is all of the band to which these belonged, thier Chief (Spotted Tail)[47] demanded restitution this morning, for the one that was killed. Two horses, ten beef cattle, and rations in proportion, they got all to day and the affair was amicably settled.

I forgot to say that I quit writing this morning, and it is evening now. I must quit again to attend evening roll call.

By candle light. Evening before last we had "dress parade" to hear the charges and sentence of John Grubbs[48] of the 6th West Virginia Cavalry, the man who killed his comrade last fall. I told you about him in one of my letters last fall. The Court Martial by which he was tried found him guilty of murder in the first degree, his sentence was "to be shot to death by musketry," the proceedings of the Court Martial were sent to Washington for the approval of the President. He approved all but the sentence, which he commuted to ten years imprisonment at hard labor in the Jefferson City Penitentiary Missouri. Captain Shuman[49] of Company "H" our reg't with five enlisted men started with him yesterday morning for his new home.

The long looked for Peace Commissioners arrived this evening from Julesburg There are three of them.[50] They will be assisted by the mountaineers. Col Maynadier the Commander of the District of the Platte, Head Quarters at Fort Laramie, is Chief of the commissioners. I understand that the treaty is to be made next sixth day (day after tomorrow.) But I dont think it will come off then, I think it will not take place till after the new garrison arrives here, three companies of the eighteenth Infantry will be

---

[47] Spotted Tail was chief of the Brulé Ring Band and Head Chief of the Brulés. Neither Olson nor Hyde mention the skirmish of late May 1866. Olson, *Red Cloud and the Sioux Problem*, pp. 32–35; Hyde, *Spotted Tail's Folk*, pp. 113–15.

[48] See letter of October 9, 1865, in which Johnson incorrectly associates Grubbs with the Second Virginia Cavalry.

[49] See letter of March 25, 1864, n. 4.

[50] The Commission was composed of E. B. Taylor, head of the Northern Indian Superintendency, R. N. McLaren of Minnesota, and Thomas Wistar of Philadelphia. Olson, *Red Cloud and the Sioux Problem*, p. 30.

U.S. Peace Commissioners at Fort Laramie holding a treaty meeting
with hostile Plains Indians in 1868.
Courtesy of the Nebraska Historical Society.

here in two or three days from denver, one company of the second dragoons arrived here yesterday afternoon, and the other company of the same reg't will be here in a few days. The company that came in yesterday will move into barracks today. The council is to be held on the north side of the platte about a mile from the Fort. The officers are afraid the indians will "play "dirt" on them if they hold it here; they are thinking of that Little affair that occurred recently in New Mexico, where two thousand Indians collected together and went to a fort somewhere down there for the purpose of making peace, They were received kindly and preparations made for the treaty, all was going on well, when all of a sudden the indians began their work of blood, the massacre was indiscriminate till not a man but one of the garrison of 150 was left alive, the man who escaped was out hunting and saw the whole affair from a hill some distance from the Fort. After the massacre the fort was set fire to and every building burned to the ground.[51]

All of our reg't will move out and camp at the place where the treaty is to be made. After the council is over we will take up our line of march for the east down the north side of the platte. I understand that Col. Maynadier says if the indians dont make peace when they get out there across the river, he is going to let them "go for" the 11th Ohio, he says they are all so keen to fight that he'll give them a chance if nothing happens, yet to "extinguish" themselves, now I'm not anxious for any of that in mine at all, not at this stage of the game. It would have suited last winter but the game is too near played out now. I think if such a thing should happen, and Colonel Maynadier should happen to be close around, that it is more than likely that he would be taken with a sudden and severe falling off his horse. In fact I think it would be unhealthy for several of our officers to be in the vicinity of a muss while it is going on. Three Ladies arrived here a few days ago, two of them are the wives of officers of the 5th U.S. Vols. the other is a single woman, she came out to assist the chaplain in teaching the white, half breed, and native children.

---

[51] None of the official forts in New Mexico were destroyed by Indians in 1866. See Frazer, *Forts of the West*, pp. 95–109. On the other hand, the Indians in New Mexico were very restive in 1866. Robert M. Utley, *Frontier Regulars, The United States Army and the Indians*, pp. 168–69.

Four boys of Company "K" are building a boat to go to the States in. All Johnson Kiah Sanders Sam Engle My Self and another fellow will go down the same way if we dont change our notions. We can get a boat, large enough for five men and thier baggage, built for fifty dollars, and about forty dollars would buy our rations, that would be $18.00 each, that the trip would cost us, and we would make it to St. louis Mo. in about twenty days. It may be though that we will not go that way

This sheet is not quite long enough so I'll have to quit

Hervey.

[Fort Laramie, Dakota Territory]
June 1st [1866]

As the mail dont go out till day after tomorrow I thought I would write some more. The mail came in this afternoon but brought me no letter from home as usual. Today is the day that I said the council was to be held but it hasnt come off yet, and when it begins I dont think it will end for a couple of weeks, I think it will take them that long at least to get through. Instead of crossing the river to hold the treaty as I said they were going to do, they are going to hold it in the Fort. workmen have been busy all day putting up an awning in front of Hd. Quarters for the the accomodation of the council. I got to see some of the commissioners yesterday, and was much surprised to see a gentleman with a hat, the crown of which was of camp kettle dimension and the brim of ample width, with white necktie and "shad belly" coat, in short, I was surprised to see a Quaker Preacher (as I learned he was) in this country. I have not learned his name nor spoken to him yet, but I intend to if opportunity offers, I have been [led to believe] too that he is from Philadelphia. He keeps rather secluded I have not seen him but twice since he came, I think he stays with Bullock the Post sutler.

Morning 2nd. the bugle sounded for tattoo roll call last evening so I didnt get to finish my letter. Three companies of the eighteenth U.S. Infantry arrived yesterday morning, one company of Cavalry is yet due here, and one company of the 6th U.S. Vols I understand that Col Carrington[52] of

---

[52] Under orders to fortify the Bozeman Trail in the middle Powder River country, Colonel Henry B. Carrington and approximately 1,000 troops of the Eighteenth

343

the 18th Infantry is crossing the river at Julesburg with seventeen hundred men recruits for his regiment, the ferry is such a poor affair that it will take them Several days to cross. Since the treaty is to be held in the Post I dont think we will move out as I stated in the fore part of my letter. The Peace commissioners brought out with them several artists, reporters and so forth. If you should see Frank Leslies illustrated News Paper[53] about the middle of July, you will perhaps see the pictures of all the principal Indian Chiefs at the council, and a great many other drawings of objects in this country, and a report of the council. The names of some of the Indian Cheifs will look well on paper, that is if they can be got on paper, especially the english translation of them, some of which I dont think will be translated at all. they will give the Indian names, in their reports I suppose and leave the english meaning for readers to guess at. The flag has been at half mast for three or four days in token of sorrow, for the death of General Scott.[54]

Captain Childs[55] the A.Q.M. was put under arrest this morning and the office was closed, so I have brought my material up to the Barracks to finish my letter. I could not learn positively for what the Captain was arrested. I was writing in the office this morning when George Childs the Captains Brother came in to the office in a terrible rage and told the first clerk to shut up office and not do another thing to day, he then came back into the other room where four or five of us were waiting and had all the window shutters closed before we could get our papers placed away. He told us there would be no business done there to day and that we might quit. It suits me very well. I will have nothing to do till I am returned to the company for duty, which wont be long.

Well I think my letter is long enough   Hervey

Regiment United States Infantry crossed the swollen South Platte near Julesburg May 30–June 14, 1866. At Fort Laramie, which Carrington and his men reached on June 14, the Third Battalion was severed for service on the Oregon Trail. Thus when the Eighteenth Regiment left Fort Laramie on June 17, its ranks included only eight companies — roughly 700 men. Dee Brown, *Fort Phil Kearny*, pp. 11–48.

[53] The pictures did not appear. See *Frank Leslie's Illustrated Newspaper*, New York, June–August 1866.

[54] This was General Winfield Scott, the unsuccessful Whig candidate in the presidential election of 1852.

[55] Captain Samuel Dearborn Childs, a native of Illinois, was honorably discharged on July 30, 1866. Heitman, *Historical Register*, vol. 1, p. 299.

Fort Laramie [Dakota Territory]
June 14th 1866

Sister Abi.

As this is probably the Last Chance I shall have to mail a letter I thought I would improve it by writing a letter home. The new Major of the 18th Infantry arrived and took command of Fort Larami yesterday. we moved out of the post this morning, are camped about a mile below on the river, The intention is to start tomorrow for Fort Leavenworth. Col Carringtons command is camped about three miles below us on the river, will come in to the fort tomorrow. The Indian treaty has not met since it adjourned.[56] A messenger who was sent out to bring in the Cheyennes, came back with his head and face all bruised up having barely escaped with his life. It seems that the old men and most of the Chiefs are in favor of peace, but the young men are in favor of war, this is why the messenger was handled so roughly. An old Chief who was with the messenger told him when they attacked him to shoot as many as he could and then run, I dont think he retaliated at all. The general opinion is that there be war again this summer. All I ask is for them to keep civil till we get to Kearney, I wont feel safe this side of there. Safe enough from the indians, but not safe from having to stop should any thing happen   I am writing on a box and sitting on the ground so you must excuse such scribbling as this and also the briefness of my letter.

Hervey

---

[56] The relationship between Carrington's arrival at Fort Laramie and the indecisive negotiations of 1866 is carefully discussed by Olson, *Red Cloud and the Sioux Problem*, pp. 35–40.

En Route to Highland County, Ohio

June 23, 1866

The music of brass bands, the waving of colorful banners, and the cheers for soldiers returning from the field of battle traditionally express some of the most profound sentiments of patriotism and nationalism. The Confederacy's capitulation at Appomattox Courthouse on April 9, 1865, led to hundreds of just such celebrations in the North. Virtually unnoticed shortly thereafter were the returning veterans of the Indian Wars of the 1860's, including those who had seen service in the Fort Laramie hinterland. Many, perhaps most, of these "buck soldiers" were obliged to find their own ways home, often at their own expense. To add insult to injury some were further humiliated by the actions of their superiors — those hated "shoulder strap men" — who saw nothing wrong in taking horses, saddles, weapons, and supplies from their tired and disillusioned subordinates. After all, the government was footing the bill.

To suggest that Hervey Johnson and his comrades were cynics by the time they were mustered out at Fort Leavenworth in the summer of 1866 is to underscore the larger moral ambivalence most Americans of that time entertained regarding the future of the Indian. Graycoats, secessionists, and slave-mongers were not difficult to categorize as certain enemies of the body politic, but such an analysis seemed inappropriate when applied to Native Americans. The ghosts of Uncas, Black Hawk, and the women and children at Sand Creek simply would not go away, nor would the distressing contradiction in concept of the Indian as a noble child of nature as opposed to a savage, bloodthirsty warrior. Perhaps Hervey Johnson, after he had returned to civilian life, better understood the paradox.

On the prarie, 16 miles from
Fort McPherson[1]
[Nebraska Territory]
June 23rd 1866.

Sister Sybil.

This is the first chance I have had to write since we left Laramie, and as there is a post office at the fort we will pass tomorrow I thought I would improve the opportunity. We are about two hundred and sixty five miles from Laramie, have traveled it in nine days, are getting along very well on the March, the fourth day on the march we had a hard wind and rain storm, some of the boys got wet but it didnt hurt them much The same day we camped near a telegraph office where there was no wood, some of the boys went to tearing the roof off a stable for fire wood, and it soon raised a muss the boys were ordered to carry back the wood they had taken off, and all of them done so but one man of Co "L", he was bull headed and refused to carry back a stick. His Lieutenant ordered him to be tied to a wagon wheel. Four men were ordered to tie him, and they declared they would not do it. The Lieut. had them tied up then for refusing to obey orders. They were soon cut loose by some one of the boys, the boy that cut them loose was tied then, and all five have been walking hand-cuffed and tied behind a wagon every day since The fellow that was the cause of it all got off without punishment. I could stand it to see him tied up to a wheel in the hot sun for a week. we were getting along so well, had no guards or any thing of the kind before the trouble happened, now the boys come on guard about every third night. When we got to Julesburg or Fort Sedgwick,[2] where we struck the south platte, the commanding officer tried to take our horses from us, our comd'g officer told him that we were ordered to take them to Leavenworth and we were going to do it, and if he went to forcing things, we would nt leave enough of his men to tell the tale. Our commander told us to shoot the first man that come after our horses, and I think we would have fought about as hard for our horses as we would for our lives, we could nt think of walking to the states at that stage of the game, but they beat us at

---

[1] See letter of October 24, 1863, n. 7.
[2] See letter of November 15, 1863, n. 14.

Fort Leavenworth, Kansas, in 1867. Here, at one of the most important federal military installations west of the Missouri, Hervey Johnson was mustered out in the spring of 1866. *Courtesy of the Kansas State Historical Society.*

last, by not giving us rations. They told us we would have to give up our horses or go without rations, we chose the latter, havent suffered any yet on account of it either, we only drew six days rations at Laramie but some of the companies had some ahead and they divided with the others, we will draw some tomorrow at McPherson to do to Kearney.

while we were in camp at Fort Sedgwick the most terrific hail storm I ever witnessed came upon us, the chunks of ice were as large as hen eggs, horses were knocked down, some had their eyes nearly put out, the hail beat right through wagon covers, gum blankets and everything that was put up for shelter, every horse that could break loose broke and stampeded, you ought to have seen the "walk a heaps" next morning; we went right ahead men were sent out and by ten o clock they found every horse and brought them to us on the road, I cant give all the particulars; if you will mention it when I get home I will tell all about it. It beat any thing I ever saw, I will never forget the day, it was the 20th of June.

Enough for the present excuse brevity and bad penmanship

Hervey.

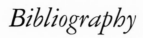

Bibliography

Brown, Charles H. Telegraph Trail of the Transcontinental Telegraph, 1861 (copy of the original in the Library of the Western Union, New York City). Hebard Collection, Western History Research Center, University of Wyoming Library, Laramie.

Company Order Books, Company G, Eleventh Ohio Volunteer Cavalry (copy of the original in the National Archives). Fort Laramie National Historic Site Library, Fort Laramie, Wyoming.

Dead Town Lists, vols. Lu-Ma and Sab-Sar. Manuscript Division, Kansas State Historical Society, Topeka.

Diary of Isaac B. Pennock, First Sergeant Company I, Eleventh Kansas Cavalry. Manuscript Division, Kansas State Historical Society, Topeka.

Fort Mitchell File. Western History Research Center, University of Wyoming Library, Laramie.

Fort Walbach File. Western History Research Center, University of Wyoming Library, Laramie.

Gunn, O. B. and D. T. Mitchell, "Gunn and Mitchell's New Map of Kansas and the Gold Mines." Lecompton: G. Sayres, 1862. Archives Division, Kansas State Historical Society, Topeka.

Letters from A. A. Provost Marshall General for Ohio, U.S. Provost General for Ohio, Official Circulars and Local Letters, 13th District 1863–1865. 3 vols. Archives Division, Ohio Historical Society, Columbus.

Muster Rolls of the Eleventh Regiment Ohio Volunteer Cavalry, United States Army, William O. Collins, Commander. Archives Division, Ohio Historical Society, Columbus.

Sweetwater Bridge Station. Western History Research Center, University of Wyoming Library, Laramie.

United States War Department. Case File MM 3668, Sergt. Joseph Isaacs, Co. H, Sixth United States Volunteers. Records of the Office of the Judge Advocate General, RG 153, Old Military Branch, Military Archives Division, National Archives, Washington, D.C.

————. Compiled Records Showing Service of Military Units in Volunteer Union Organizations, Ohio Cavalry. Records of the Adjutant General's Office, RG 94, Old Military Branch, Military Archives Division, National Archives, Washington, D.C.

————. Consolidated Military and/or Pension Files, Eleventh Kansas Volunteer Infantry, Eleventh Ohio Volunteer Cavalry, and Sixth United States Volunteers. Records of the Adjutant General's Office, RG 94, Old Military Branch, Military Archives Division, National Archives, Washington, D.C.

Adams, Herbert B., ed. *Contributions to American Educational History, No. 17.* Washington, D.C.: Government Printing Office, 1893.

Alter, J. Cecil. *James Bridger, Trapper, Frontiersman, Scout and Guide: A Historical Narrative.* Salt Lake City: Shepard Book Company, 1925.

Andreas, A. T. *History of the State of Kansas.* Chicago: A. T. Andreas, 1883.

Athearn, Robert G. *William Tecumseh Sherman and the Settlement of the West.* Norman: University of Oklahoma Press, 1956.

Bancroft, Hubert Howe. *History of Washington, Idaho, and Montana, 1845–1889.* Vol. 31 of the Works of Hubert Howe Bancroft. San Francisco: The History Company, 1889.

Brown, Dee Alexander. *Fort Phil Kearny, An American Saga.* New York: G. P. Putnam's Sons, 1962.

—————. *The Galvanized Yankees.* Urbana: University of Illinois Press, 1963.

Browne, J. Ross. *Resources of the Pacific Slope. A Statistical and Descriptive Summary of the Mines and Minerals, Climate, Topography, Agriculture, Commerce, Manufactures, and Miscellaneous Productions, of the States and Territories West of the Rocky Mountains.* New York: D. Appleton and Co., 1869.

Burton, Sir Richard F. *The Look of the West, 1860; Across the Plains to California.* Foreword by Robert G. Athearn. Lincoln: University of Nebraska Press, 1963.

—————. *The City of the Saints and Across the Rocky Mountains to California.* Edited and with an introduction and notes by Fawn M. Brodie. New York: Knopf, 1963.

Castel, Albert. *A Frontier State at War: Kansas, 1861–1865.* Ithaca: Cornell University Press, 1958.

—————. *William Clarke Quantrill: His Life and Times.* New York: F. Fell, 1962.

Clampitt, John W. *Echoes from the Rocky Mountains; Reminiscences and Thrilling Incidents of the Romantic and Golden Age of the Great West, with a Graphic Account of Its Discovery, Settlement, and Grand Development.* Chicago: Belford, Clarke & Co., 1889.

Connelley, William E. *The Life of Preston B. Plumb, 1837–1891.* Chicago: Browne and Howard Company, 1913.

Coutant, Charles G. *The History of Wyoming from the Earliest Known Discoveries. In 3 vols.* Vol. 1. Laramie: Chaplin, Spafford & Mathison, 1899.

Crawford, Samuel J. *Kansas in the Sixties.* Chicago: A. C. McClurg & Co., 1911.

Dodge, Grenville M. *The Battle of Atlanta and Other Campaigns, Addresses, Etc.* Council Bluffs: The Monarch Printing Company, 1910. Reprint, Denver: Sage Books, 1965.

Duke, Basil W. *A History of Morgan's Cavalry.* Edited and with an introduction and notes by Cecil Fletcher Holland. Bloomington: Indiana University Press, 1960.

Dunn, Jacob P., Jr. *Massacres of the Mountains: A History of the Indian Wars of the Far West, 1815–1875.* New York: Capricorn edition, 1970.

Ellis, Richard N. *General Pope and U.S. Indian Policy.* Albuquerque: University of New Mexico Press, 1970.

Frazer, Robert W. *Forts of the West.* Norman: University of Oklahoma Press, 1965.

Goetzmann, William H. *When the Eagle Screamed: The Romantic Horizon in American Diplomacy, 1800–1860.* New York: John Wiley, 1966.

Greeley, Horace. *An Overland Journey, from New York to San Francisco, in the Summer of 1859.* New York: C. M. Saxton, Barker & Co., 1860.

Hafen, LeRoy R. and Ann W. Hafen. *Powder River Campaigns and Sawyers Expedition of 1865.* Vol. 12 of The Far West and the Rockies Historical Sketches, 1820–1875. Glendale, Ca.: The Arthur H. Clark Company, 1961.

————, and Francis Marion Young. *Fort Laramie and the Pageant of the West, 1834–1890.* Glendale, Ca.: The Arthur H. Clark Company, 1938.

Hall, Jess A. and Leroy T. Hand. *History of Leavenworth County, Kansas.* Topeka: Historical Publishing Company, 1921.

Hawley, James H., ed. *History of Idaho, the Gem of the Mountains.* Vol. 1. Chicago: The S. J. Clarke Publishing Company, 1920.

Hebard, Grace Raymond and E. A. Brininstool. *The Bozeman Trail: Historical Accounts of the Blazing of the Overland Routes into the Northwest, and the Fights with Red Cloud's Warriors.* 2 vols. Glendale: The Arthur H. Clark Company, 1960.

Heitman, Francis B. *Historical Register and Dictionary of the United States Army, from Its Organization, September 29, 1789, to March 2, 1903.* 2 vols. Washington, D.C.: U.S. Government Printing Office, 1903. Reprint Urbana: University of Illinois Press, 1965.

Henderson, Paul C. *Landmarks on the Oregon Trail.* New York: Published by Peter Decker for the Westerners, 1953.

Hill, Edward E. *Historical Sketches for Jurisdictional Subject Headings Used for the Letters Received by the Office of Indian Affairs, 1824–1880.* Washington, D.C.: The National Archives and Records Service, 1967.

Hinshaw, William Wade. *Encyclopedia of American Quaker Genealogy.* Vol. 5. Ann Arbor: Edwards Brothers, Inc., 1946.

History of Ross and Highland Counties, Ohio. Cleveland: W. W. Williams, Printer, 1880.

Hoig, Stan. *The Sand Creek Massacre.* Norman: University of Oklahoma Press, 1961.

Humfreville, James Lee. *Twenty Years among our Hostile Indians.* New York: Hunter and Co., 1889.

Hyde, George E. *Life of George Bent Written from His Letters.* Edited by Savoie Lottinville. Norman: University of Oklahoma Press, 1968.

————. *Red Cloud's Folk: A History of the Oglala Sioux Indians.* Norman: University of Oklahoma Press, 1937.

————. *Spotted Tail's Folk, A History of the Brulé Sioux.* Norman: University of Oklahoma Press, 1961.

Ismert, Cornelius M. "James Bridger." In LeRoy R. Hafen, *The Mountain Men and the Fur Trade of the Far West.* Vol. 6. Glendale, Ca.: The Arthur H. Clark Company, 1968.

Jessee, Dean C., ed. *Letters of Brigham Young to His Sons.* Salt Lake City: Deseret Book Company in collaboration with the Historical Department of the Church of Jesus Christ of Latter-day Saints, 1974.

Johnson, Allen, and Dumas Malone, eds. *Dictionary of American Biography.* Vol. 4. New York: Charles Scribners Sons, 1930.

Johnson, Ludwell H. *Red River Campaign: Politics and Cotton in the Civil War.* Baltimore: The Johns Hopkins Press, 1958.

Kappler, Charles J., comp. and ed. *Indian Affairs: Laws and Treaties.* Vol. 2. Washington, D.C.: U.S. Government Printing Office, 1904.

Keim, De Benneville R. *Sheridan's Troopers on the Borders: A Winter Campaign on the Plains.* New York: G. Routledge, 1885.

Klement, Frank L. *The Copperheads in the Middle West.* Chicago: The University of Chicago Press, 1960.

Klise, Rev. J. W. *The County of Highland.* Madison, Wisc.: Northwestern Historical Association, 1902.

Larson, Taft A. *History of Wyoming.* Lincoln: The University of Nebraska Press, 1965.

LaTrobe, Charles Joseph. *The Rambler in North America; 1832–1833.* Vol. 2, 2nd ed. London: R. B. Seeley and W. Burnside, 1836.

Leckie, William H. *The Military Conquest of the Southern Plains.* Norman: University of Oklahoma Press, 1963.

McReynolds, Edwin C. *Missouri: A History of the Crossroads State.* Norman: University of Oklahoma Press, 1962.

Merk, Frederick. *Manifest Destiny and Mission in American History: A Reinterpretation.* New York: Knopf, 1963.

Mokler, Alfred James. *Fort Caspar (Platte Bridge Station).* Casper: The Prairie Publishing Company, 1939.

Monaghan, James, ed. *The Book of the American West.* New York: Messner, 1963.

Nadeau, Remi. *Fort Laramie and the Sioux Indians.* Englewood Cliffs, N.J.: Prentice-Hall, 1967.

Nibley, Preston. *Brigham Young: The Man and His Work.* Salt Lake City: Deseret Book Co., 1970.

Official Roster of the Soldiers of the State of Ohio in the War of the Rebellion, 1861–1866. Akron: Werner Printing and Lithograph Company, 1891.

Olson, James C. *Red Cloud and the Sioux Problem.* Lincoln: University of Nebraska Press, 1965.

Randall, James G., and David Donald. *The Civil War and Reconstruction.* Boston: D. C. Heath, 1961.

Reid, James D. *The Telegraph in America.* New York: Derby Brothers, 1879.

Rogers, Fred B. *Soldiers of the Overland, Being Some Account of the Services of General Patrick Edward Connor and His Volunteers in the Old West.* San Francisco: The Grabhorn Press, 1938.

Roseboom, Eugene H. *The Civil War Era, 1850–1873.* Vol. 4 of the History of the State of Ohio, edited by Carl Wittke. Columbus: Ohio State Archaeological and Historical Society, 1944.

361

Russell, Carl P. *Guns on the Early Frontiers: A History of Firearms from Colonial Times through the Years of the Western Fur Trade.* Berkeley: University of California Press, 1957.

Shalhope, Robert E. *Sterling Price: Portrait of a Southerner.* Columbia: University of Missouri Press, 1971.

Sheridan, Philip Henry. *Personal Memoirs of P. H. Sheridan, General, United States Army.* Vol. 2. New York: C. L. Webster & Co., 1888.

Shoemaker, Floyd Calvin. *Missouri and Missourians: Land of Contrasts and People of Achievements.* Vol. 1. Chicago: The Lewis Publishing Company, 1943.

Spring, Agnes W. *Caspar Collins, The Life and Exploits of an Indian Fighter of the Sixties.* New York: Columbia University Press, 1927.

Springer, Charles H. *Soldiering in Sioux Country: 1865.* Benjamin Cooling III, ed. San Diego: Frontier Heritage Press, 1971.

Stansbury, Howard. *An Expedition to the Valley of the Great Salt Lake of Utah.* Philadelphia: Lippincott, Grambo, & Co., 1852.

Thompson, Robert Luther. *Wiring a Continent, The History of the Telegraph Industry in the United States, 1832–1866.* Princeton: Princeton University Press, 1947.

Toole, Kenneth Ross. *Montana, An Uncommon Land.* Norman: University of Oklahoma Press, 1959.

Trenholm, Virginia Cole. *The Arapahoes, Our People.* Norman: University of Oklahoma Press, 1970.

Trollope, Anthony. *North America.* 3 vols. Leipzig: B. Tauchnitz, 1862.

United States War Department. *A Report on Barracks and Hospitals with Descriptions of Military Posts.* Surgeon General's Office Circular No. 4 (December 5, 1870). Washington, D.C.: U.S. Government Printing Office, 1870.

———. *Report on the Hygiene of the United States Army, with Descriptions of Military Posts.* Surgeon General's Office Circular No. 8 (May 1, 1875). Washington, D.C.: Government Printing Office, 1875.

Utley, Robert M. *Frontier Regulars: The United States Army and the Indians, 1866–1891.* New York: Macmillan, 1974.

Vaughn, Jesse W. *The Battle of Platte Bridge.* Norman: University of Oklahoma Press, 1963.

Vestal, Stanley [pseud.]. *Jim Bridger, Mountain Man, A Biography.* New York: W. Morrow and Company, 1946.

The War of Rebellion: A Compilation of the Official Records of the Union and Confederate Armies. Series I, vols. 22, pt. 1; 34, pt. 2; 41; 48, pt. 2. Washington, D.C.: U.S. Government Printing Office, 1888, 1890.

Ware, Captain Eugene F. *The Indian War of 1864.* Introduction and notes by Clyde C. Walton. Lincoln: University of Nebraska Press, 1960.

Warner, Donald F. *The Idea of Continental Union: Agitation for the Annexation of Canada to the United States, 1849–1893.* Lexington: University Press of Kentucky, 1960.

Weinberg, Albert K. *Manifest Destiny: A Study in Nationalist Expansionism in American History.* Baltimore: The Johns Hopkins Press, 1935.

Writers' Program of the Work Projects Administration in the State of Wyoming (WPA), comp. *Wyoming, A Guide to Its History, Highways, and People.* New York: Oxford University Press, 1941.

Wyandotte County and Kansas City, Kansas. Chicago: The Goodspeed Publishing Co., 1890.

Zornow, William F. *Kansas: A History of the Jayhawk State.* Norman: University of Oklahoma Press, 1957.

Newspapers and Articles

Barry, Louise. "The Ranch at Cow Creek Crossing (Beach Valley, P.O.)," *Kansas Historical Quarterly,* vol. 38, no. 4 (Winter 1972), pp. 416–44.

Carey, Raymond G. "The Puzzle of Sand Creek." *The Colorado Magazine,* vol. 41, no. 4 (Fall 1964), pp. 279–98.

Daily Union Vedette. Camp Douglas, Utah Territory, 1863–1866.

Frank Leslie's Illustrated Newspaper. New York, 1866.

Henderson, Paul. "The Story of Mud Springs." *Nebraska History,* vol. 32, no. 2 (June 1951), pp. 108–19.

Highland Weekly News. Hillsboro, Ohio, 1863–1866.

Hoopes, Alban W. "Thomas S. Twiss, Indian Agent of the Upper Platte, 1855–1861." *Mississippi Valley Historical Review,* vol. 20, no. 3 (December 1933), pp. 353–64.

Hull, Myra E., ed. "Soldiering on the High Plains, The Diary of Lewis Byram Hull, 1864–1866." *Kansas Historical Quarterly,* vol. 7, no. 1 (February 1938), pp. 3–53.

"Life of Oscar Collister, Wyoming Pioneer, as Told by Himself to Mrs. Chas. Ellis of Difficulty, Wyo." Pt. 1. *Annals of Wyoming*, vol. 7, no. 1 (July 1930), pp. 343–61.

"Life of Oscar Collister, Wyoming Pioneer, as Told by Himself to Mrs. Chas. Ellis of Difficulty, Wyo." Pt. 2. *Annals of Wyoming*, vol. 7, no. 2 (October 1930), pp. 369–78.

Mattes, Merril J. "Fort Mitchell, Scotts Bluff, Nebraska Territory." *Nebraska History*, vol. 33, no. 1 (March 1952), pp. 1–34.

————, and Paul Henderson. "The Pony Express: Across Nebraska from St. Joseph to Fort Laramie." *Nebraska History*, vol. 41, no. 2 (June 1960), pp. 83–122.

Pennock, Jake. "Diary," *Annals of Wyoming*, vol. 23, no. 2 (July 1951), pp. 4–29.

Sievers, Michael A. "Sands of Sand Creek Historiography." *The Colorado Magazine*, vol. 49, no. 2 (Spring 1972), pp. 116–42.

Unrau, William E. "A Prelude to War." *The Colorado Magazine*, vol. 41, no. 4 (Fall 1964), pp. 299–313.

————. "Justice at Fort Laramie: The Trial and Tribulations of a Galvanized Yankee." *Arizona and the West*, vol. 15, no. 2 (Summer 1973), pp. 107–32.

————. "The Story of Fort Larned." *Kansas Historical Quarterly*, vol. 23, no. 3 (Autumn 1957), pp. 257–80.

Weekly Rocky Mountain News. Denver, Colorado, 1863–1866.

Index of Subjects

Cattle, 139, 192, 212

Cavalry, disembarks at Omaha, 263; company of, due at Fort Laramie, 343. *See also* Troops

Cherry Creek, gold discovered at, 49

Cheyenne Indians, 101, 168, 143, 337; Hervey Johnson visits village of, 117–18, 121; fight at Fremont's Orchard, 101, 119–20, 119–20n; possible trouble with, 125; massacre of, at Sand Creek, 198–99; separate from Sioux Indians, 227; at an Arapaho village, 228; at the Battle of Platte Bridge, 273; at Fort Laramie, 331, 334, 335. *See also* Indians

Cheyenne Pass, 82, 82n, 89

Chimney Rock, 65, 65n

Cholera, 332. *See also* Health

Church of Jesus Christ of Latter-day Saints. *See* Mormons

Civil War, 127n; affects conscription in Ohio, 8–9; Indian country during, 23; affects Hervey Johnson's enlistment, 24; troop demands increased by, 49–50; Hervey Johnson speculates on end of, 80; disruption of communications during, 101; end of, 236

Coal, 116, 116n, 117

Comanche Indians, 168; at the Battle of Platte Bridge, 273. *See also* Indians

Company A. *See* Eleventh Ohio Volunteer Cavalry, Company A

Company B. *See* Eleventh Ohio Volunteer Cavalry, Company B

Company C. *See* Eleventh Ohio Volunteer Cavalry, Company C

Company D. *See* Eleventh Ohio Volunteer Cavalry, Company D; Seventh Iowa Cavalry, Company D

Company E. *See* Eleventh Ohio Volunteer Cavalry, Company E

Company F. *See* Eleventh Ohio Volunteer Cavalry, Company F; Seventh Iowa Cavalry, Company F

Company G. *See* Eleventh Ohio Volunteer Cavalry, Company G;

Sixth U.S. Volunteer Infantry, Company G

Company H. *See* Eleventh Kansas Cavalry, Company H; Eleventh Ohio Volunteer Cavalry, Company H; Sixth U.S. Infantry, Company H

Company I. *See* Eleventh Kansas Cavalry, Company I; Eleventh Ohio Volunteer Cavalry, Company I; Seventh Iowa Cavalry, Company I; Third U.S. Volunteer Infantry, Company I

Company K. *See* Eleventh Ohio Volunteer Cavalry, Company K; Third U.S. Volunteer Infantry, Company K

Company L. *See* Eleventh Ohio Volunteer Cavalry, Company L

Conscription, 8–9, 12

Conscription Act, 12

Copperheads, 8, 102, 119, 124, 179

Cottonwood Springs, 59, 59n

Courthouse Rock, 65, 65n

Court-martial, 57; of a sergeant, 103; of Captain Levi M. Rinehart, 207. *See also* Rinehart, Captain Levi M.

Cow Creek Station, 294

Coyote, 69

Crow Indians, 94, 94n, 107. *See also* Indians

Daily Union Vedette. See *Union Vedette*

Dakota Indians, 23. *See also* Indians

Dakota Territory, 16–17

Deer, 123, 131, 135, 233, 305

Deer Creek Station, 109, 109–10n; description of, 111, 140; Hervey Johnson assigned to, 101; Hervey Johnson arrives at, 106; work on quarters at, 167, 172; horses stolen at, 246; Eleventh Kansas Cavalry fights Indians near, 247

Denver City, 49, 82, 95, 96, 101, 119, 173, 296, 304, 316, 328, 329

Deseret News, report of polygamy in, 284

Eleventh Ohio Volunteer Cavalry, Company K, 298, 328

Eleventh Ohio Volunteer Cavalry, Company L, escorts telegraph repair train, 278; ordered to Deer Creek, 294; ordered to Fort Laramie, 319; man from, punished, 351

Elk, 109, 115, 123, 290

Emigration, amount of, 101, 119, 120, 124, 127, 128, 136, 157, 159, 160; effect of discovery of gold on, 177; discouraged by Indian attacks, 188

Emigrant Escort, 160

Emigrants, steal horses from the government, 139; leave mail at Deer Creek Station, 139; Indians steal stock of, 141, 154; increase size of trains for protection, 147; attacked by Indians, 147, 260; shooting game, 148–49; pressed to hunt Indians, 150; boots taken from, 173; safety of, crossing Plains, 214; theft of cattle from, 265; travel at night to avoid Indians, 277; pass Fort Laramie, 329, 335

Enlisted men, vs. officers, 4–5; written accounts by, 6–7. *See also* Officers; Troops

Europe, missionaries sent to, 128–29

Farm House, 89, 89n

Fenian Brotherhood, 325–26, 326n

Ferote's Ranch, 88, 88n

Fifth U.S. Volunteer Infantry, 326, 327, 335, 342

Firewood. *See* Wood

First Colorado Volunteer Cavalry, 101, 119, 119–20n

First Independent Battalion of Ohio Volunteer Cavalry, 10

First Missouri Cavalry, 293

First Nevada Cavalry, 252

First U.S. Volunteer Infantry, 262–63

Fish, 53–54, 60–61, 127–28, 171; catfish, 171, 178, 263; buffalo salmon, 263; hickory-shad, 263; pickerel, 107, 171,

178, 263; shovelheads, 61, 263; suckers, 263

Fishing, 53–54, 60–61, 106, 107, 130, 171, 178, 263–64

Five Civilized Tribes, 23

Food, 31, 35–36, 42, 44, 106, 109, 115, 117, 120, 123, 142, 160, 161, 170–71, 175, 179, 204, 208, 212, 219, 221, 233, 234, 236, 254, 265, 282, 296, 302, 305–306

Fort Alexander, 168, 168n

Fort Benton, 76, 76n

Fort Casper, 305

Fort C. F. Smith, 287

Fort Collins, 323

Fort Conner, 276, 276n, 297, 300, 302

Fort Cottonwood, 168

Fort Douglas. *See* Camp Douglas

Fort Halleck, 331, 331n

Fort Karney. *See* Fort Kearny

Fort Kearny, 45, 45n, 125, 168, 173

Fort Laramie, 53; description of quarters at, 54; description of surroundings of, 60; funerals at, 73, 325, 335; troops at, 75; erection of gymnasium at, 90; Indian parley held at, 101; post sutler at, 121, 296, 308, 320; Hervey Johnson journeys to, 173–74; Indians allowed liberties at, 214; wagons arriving at, 270; breastworks built at, 294; companies garrisoning, 298; Indian depredations at, 302–303, 337, 339–40; Indians arrive for council at, 315, 334; Indian council held at, 321–23; changed to Headquarters, District of the Platte, 326; troops at, 326; Indians draw rations at, 328; problems with Indians at, 330–31; peace commission at, 343, 345

Fort Laramie Treaty of 1851, 23, 49

Fort Larned, 322, 322n

Fort Leavenworth, 33, 34, 125; description of, 36–37, 36n; Hervey Johnson mustered out at, 13, 313

Fort McPherson, 59n, 353

Mail train, nonarrival of, 79, 80, 82; arrival of, 88

Massacres. *See* Ash Hollow; Lawrence, Kansas; New Ulm; Sand Creek

Mexico, possibility of troops being sent to, 127

Miamitown, Ohio, 28

Military campaigns, against Indians. *See* Indians, military campaigns against

Military desertion. *See* Desertion

Military encounters, with Indians. *See* Indians, and encounters with the military

Military funerals, descriptions of, 73, 193, 325, 335

Military posts, establishment of, 169, 182, 280

Military prisoners, 72, 81, 82–83, 89–91, 115, 292, 293, 309, 317

Military punishment, 57–58, 72, 82, 83, 87, 115, 315, 338–39, 351

Military routine, 63

Military, scouts for Indians. *See* Indians, soldiers in pursuit of

Military stock, stolen by Indians. *See* Indians, steal stock

Military supplies, 265–66

Military troops. *See* Troops

Military uniform, 67, 69, 72, 93–94

Missionaries, to Indians, 116; traveling East, 128–29

Mississippi River, 32

Missouri border, 169

Missouri River, 34, 35

Montana Territory, 16

Mormon refugees, trains of, 260–61, 277. *See also* Wagon trains

Mormons, 102, 126–27, 130, 165–67; emigration of, 101; traveling East, 127, 128–29, 260; and problems with the government, 76, 129–30, 260, 270, 284; William Boardman sent to write against, in *Union Vedette*, 297

Mormon telegraph operator, illness of, 126–27, 130

Mormon trains, horses stolen from, 165–67. *See also* Wagon trains

Mormon tyranny, 129

Mosquitoes, 261, 264

Moss agate, 328, 334–35

Mountain Battery, 59

Mountaineers, 80, 107–109, 110, 115, 178, 268, 332

Mountain howitzer. *See* Howitzer

Mountains, descriptions of, 122–23, 132–34, 180, 214, 235, 246, 283

Mountain sheep, 115

Mud Springs, 79, 79n, 187

Mules, price of, 194; stolen by Indians, 249–50

Mustered for pay. *See* Pay

Mustering officer, arrives at Fort Laramie, 336

Nebraska Territory, 16

New Orleans and Ohio Telegraph Lessees, 10

New Ulm massacre, 52

New York, Albany and Buffalo Telegraph Company, 10

Nineteenth Missouri Cavalry (?), 301

Officers, vs. enlisted men, 4–5; Hervey Johnson's opinion of, 326; disliked by enlisted men, 349. *See also* Drinking

Oglala Sioux Indians, 23, 101. *See also* Indians

Ohio Sixth Cavalry Regiment, formation of, 9; designation of First Independent Battalion of Ohio Volunteer Cavalry from, 10

Olatha, Kansas, 43, 44

Old Battalion, 64, 77–78, 97, 97n, 182, 183, 210, 218, 222

Omaha Scouts, 320, 320n

Ordnance, arrival of, at Fort Laramie, 297

Osage River, 41

Oskaloosa College, 33, 143

Overland Mail road, 260–61

Overland Stage Company, 103, 111
Overland Telegraph Company, 10–11.
    See also Telegraph

Pacific Railroad Bill, 52
Pacific Telegraph Act, 10
Pacific Telegraph Company, 10–12, 111,
    111n. *See also* Telegraph
Pawnee Indians, 278–79.
    See also Indians
Pawnee Scouts, 320, 320n
Pay, 27, 36, 45, 96, 199, 206, 234, 237,
    270, 271, 320; anticipation of, 72,
    297; arrives at Sweetwater Station,
    199; Hervey Johnson mustered for,
    267, 284, 304, 333; Hervey Johnson
    receives extra, for repairing telegraph
    line, 280; extra, given telegraph
    operators, 320
Paymaster, due at Fort Laramie, 270;
    arrives at Fort Laramie, 293, 296, 304,
    328; goes to Fort Conner, 297, 300,
    302; Hervey Johnson meets, 305;
    leaves for Denver, 316, 329
Payrolls, ordered to Fort Laramie, 239
Peace Commissioners, 287, 331, 336, 340
Peace treaties. *See* Treaties
Plains, description of marching across,
    53–58, 85–87, 88
Platte Bridge, tolls at, 123
Platte Bridge Station, 121, 122, 123;
    troops at, 106; Indians requesting food
    at, 155; encounters with Indians at,
    156, 169, 188; Indians, run off horses
    at, 157; Hervey Johnson travels to,
    from Sweetwater Station, 207, 231.
    See also Battle of Platte Bridge Station
Platte River, 60; level of, 90, 263, 335;
    fish in, 127–28. *See also* Fish
Porcupine, 295
Postage. *See* Mail
Posts. *See* Military posts
Post sutler, at Fort Laramie, 121, 296,
    308, 320
Powder River, 154–55, 188, 269,
    292–93, 296

Prairie dogs, 60, 65–66, 118–19
Prices, 45, 85, 159, 178, 179, 245, 296,
    299, 308, 320–21, 335
Prickly pear, 238
Prisoners, military. *See* Military prisoners
Punishment, military. *See* Military
    punishment

Quakers, and conscription, 8
Quarters. *See* Deer Creek Station;
    Fort Laramie; Sweetwater Station
Quartermaster, horses turned in to, 296;
    part of herd of, stolen, 323, 329;
    Hervey Johnson detailed to office of,
    324. *See also* Childs, Captain
    Samuel D.

Ranch, 88, 89
Rations, 233, 275, 283, 352–53.
    See also Food
Red Buttes, 123, 123n, 209, 215, 278,
    279, 280
Red fox, 162
Rocky Mountains, 60
Rocky Ridge telegraph station.
    See St. Mary's Station
Rush Creek, 187

Sagebrush, 107
Sage Creek, 243, 243n
Sage Creek Station, 243n
Sand Creek Massacre, 49, 94n, 187,
    198–99, 349
Saw mill, 172. *See also* Wood
Saints. *See* Mormons
Salt Lake City, possibility of troops being
    sent to, 127, 293
Santee Sioux Indians, 52.
    See also Indians; Sioux Indians
Scenery, descriptions of, 122–23, 132–34,
    142, 161, 180, 191, 214, 235, 246, 283
Scotts Bluffs, 64
Scouting, after Indians. *See* Indians,
    soldiers in pursuit of
Scurvy. *See* Health

374

Second California Volunteer Cavalry, 293, 297
Second U.S. Dragoons, 342
Second Missouri Light Artillery, 293
Second U.S. Volunteer Infantry, 262–63
Second Virginia Cavalry, 293
Second West Virginia Cavalry (?), 293
Seventh Iowa Cavalry, 169, 293, 326
Seventh Iowa Cavalry, Company D, 216
Seventh Iowa Cavalry, Company F, 298
Seventh Iowa Cavalry, Company I, 238
Seventh Michigan Cavalry, 282–83
Sickness. *See* Health
Silver, discovered at South Pass, 177
Sioux Indians, 17, 84, 94n, 101, 106, 115, 116n, 120, 122, 136, 169, 281; and the Fort Laramie Treaty of 1851, 23, 49; battle with Crow Indians, 94, 94n; parley at Fort Laramie, 101; attack Fort Pierre, 167; separate from Cheyenne Indians, 227; at Fort Laramie, 287, 324, 326, 331, 334, 336, 338. *See also* Brulé Sioux; Indians; Santee Sioux; Teton Sioux
Sixteenth Kansas Volunteer Cavalry, 293, 294, 303
Sixth Michigan Cavalry, 276, 282, 283, 293, 294
Sixth U.S. Regiment, 9–10
Sixth U.S. Volunteer Infantry, 281, 298, 315, 317, 326, 338–39, 343
Sixth U.S. Volunteer Infantry, Company G, 298
Sixth U.S. Volunteer Infantry, Company H, 338–39
Sixth Virginia Cavalry, 297, 326, 329
Sixth West Virginia Cavalry, 340
Snake Indians, 121, 168, 323–24
Snow-blindness, 110, 114, 335
Soapweed, 81
Soldiers. *See* Drinking; Indians; Military; Troops
Soldier's Reading Room, at Fort Laramie, 70, 77

Southern Cheyenne Indians. *See* Cheyenne Indians
South Pass Station, 106, 176, 176n, 177, 249
Sparksburg, Missouri, 35
Spencer Repeating Rifle, 92, 92n, 247
Stable, built at Sweetwater Station, 218
Stage line, 165. *See also* Overland Stage Company
St. Louis, Missouri, 32, 125
St. Mary's Station, 114, 114n, 306; burned by Indians, 226; repair of, 252
St. Marysville, Ohio, 42, 42n
Stockades, building of, 178, 182
Stone Ranch, 90, 103, 105
Store, at Deer Creek Station, 178
Supply trains, 76, 253
Sweetwater Station, 106, 114, 114n; Indians steal horses at, 249–50. *See also* Johnson, Private Hervey
Sweetwater River, 191
Sutler. *See* Post sutler

Tailor, 67, 135. *See also* Foote, ⸺
Talking wire. *See* Telegraph
Telegraph, 107; awarding of contract for, 11–12; disruption of, 12, 101, 110–11, 188, 226, 246, 247, 253, 268–69, 277, 292; effect of completion of, 50–51; repair of, 218, 247, 254, 262, 263, 271, 275–76, 277–81
Telegraph operators, 110–11, 178, 268, 281
Telegraph repair train, 278–80
Territories, changes in boundaries for, 16–17
Teton Sioux Indians, 23. *See also* Indians; Sioux Indians
Texas, possibility of troops being sent to, 127
Third U.S. Volunteer Infantry, 254, 255, 262–63
Third U.S. Volunteer Infantry, Company I, 263

375

Third U.S. Volunteer Infantry, Company K, 263
Three Crossings, 106, 226, 226n, 249, 308; attacked by Indians, 246
Timber. *See* Wood
Tobacco, 245
Tod's Barracks, Columbus, Ohio, 321
Treaties, 23, 49. *See also* Indians
Troops, 249, 263, 270; at Fort Laramie, 75, 234, 239, 326; at Deer Creek Station, 147; strength of, 239. *See also* Eighteenth U.S. Infantry; Eleventh Kansas Cavalry; Eleventh Ohio Volunteer Cavalry; Fifth U.S. Volunteer Infantry; First Colorado Volunteer Cavalry; First Independent Battalion of Ohio Volunteer Cavalry; First Missouri; First Nevada; First U.S. Volunteer Infantry; Fourteenth Pennsylvania Cavalry; Seventh Iowa Cavalry; Second California Volunteer Cavalry; Second U.S. Dragoons; Second Missouri Light Artillery; Second U.S. Volunteer Infantry; Second Virginia Cavalry (?); Second West Virginia; Seventh Michigan Cavalry; Sixteenth Kansas Volunteer Cavalry; Sixth Michigan Cavalry; Sixth Regiment; Sixth U.S. Volunteer Infantry; Third U.S. Volunteer Infantry; Twelfth Missouri Volunteer Cavalry; Twenty-first New York Light Artillery; Twenty-fifth New York Light Artillery
Twelfth Missouri Volunteer Cavalry, 293, 303, 305, 315
Twenty-fifth New York Light Artillery, 293
Twenty-first New York Light Artillery, 323

Union Pacific Railroad, 10
Union Vedette, 297, 297n
Uniform. *See* Military uniform
Upper Crossing, 106
U.S. Volunteers. *See* First U.S. Volunteer Infantry; Second U.S.

Volunteer Infantry; Third U.S. Volunteer Infantry
Ute Indians, 107, 168, 199, 336. *See also* Indians

Vincennes, Indiana, 32
Virginia City, 159, 329
Volunteering, vs. the draft, 12–13

Wabash River, 32
Wages. *See* Pay
Wagon trains, 76–77, 96, 127, 128, 141, 147, 148–49, 150, 154, 165–67, 260–61, 274, 277, 329, 335
Washington Territory, 16
Weather, 34–35, 41, 43, 58, 59, 63, 66, 69, 71, 77, 78, 79, 80, 82, 90, 93, 101, 108–109, 110, 124, 127, 131, 132, 134, 139, 143, 159, 173, 175, 200, 208, 211, 213, 219, 220, 226, 230, 231, 233, 238, 240, 249, 260, 284, 289, 300, 305–306, 308, 316, 320, 327, 329, 334, 339, 351, 353
Western Union Telegraph Company, 10, 11
Wheat, 158–59
Willow Spring, 189, 189n, 203, 205, 220–21, 277, 278, 280
Willow Spring Hill, 203, 215, 221, 277
Willow Spring Hollow, 204
Wind River, 155
Wind River expedition, 155, 240
Wind River Mountains, 123
Wolverine, 60
Wolves, 60, 71, 133, 147, 177, 183, 195, 200, 254; one as a pet, 112
Wood, 107, 172, 178, 195; supplies of, 79, 195, 198; hauling of, 140, 213; cutting of, 163, 200, 212, 234, 265
Wyandot, Kansas, 34, 34n
Wyoming Territory, 17

Yellowstone River, 62

376

Index of Names

sent to Missouri border, 169; sent to get cattle, 175; in charge of horse herd, 175; advanced to corporal, 188; ordered to Sweetwater Station, 189; in charge of Sweetwater Station, 195–96; sent for wagon, 198; sent for flour, 200; opinion of Lieutenant Caspar W. Collins, 211, 222, 237; opinion of Brigadier General Patrick E. Conner, 214, 281; death of horse of, 214–15; descriptions of mountains, 122–23, 132–34, 180, 214, 235, 246, 283; sent to dig out wagon, 220, 244–45; goods of, lost in Indian attack, 230; travels to Sweetwater Station, 231; correspondents of, 232; loneliness of, 235; attitude toward being a noncommissioned officer, 237–38; asks to be returned to ranks, 242; cares for John Hannaford, 245; possibility of reassignment of, 254; opinion of Colonel Thomas J. Moonlight, 261–62; sent to watch for stolen cattle, 265; supplies drawn by, 265–66; mustered for pay, 267, 284, 304–305, 333; tired of fighting, 267; draws horses, 269; sent for rations, 275–77; repairs telegraph line, 277–81; receives extra pay, 280; returns to Sweetwater Station to get belongings, 282; assigned to Fort Laramie, 289; leaves Sweetwater Station, 289; goes to Powder River, 292–93; detailed on duty at Fort Laramie, 292; attitude toward peace treaty, 296; turns in equipment, 296; acts as room orderly, 301; escorts government train, 304, 305; opinion of Missouri, 307; assigned to draw rations for prisoners, 309; relieved from acting as police sergeant, 316–17; describes Indian council, 321–23; detailed to Quartermaster's office, 324, 328; opinion of officers, 326–27; opinion of Colonel Henry Maynadier, 331, 342; possibility of, staying in the West, 332; expiration of term of service of, 336; possibility of, traveling to States by boat, 343; to start for Fort Leavenworth, 345; attitude toward punishment of a soldier, 351

Johnson, Orpah, 8, 171
Johnson, Semira, 8
Johnson, Sybil, 8
Johnson, Warren, 8

Kelley, ———, 108
Keelor, Tom, 291–92, 291n
King, Sergeant Thomas E., 28, 28n, 31
Kinzer, Sergeant Samuel O., 59, 59n, 67, 67n, 68, 95, 240, 294, 307

Lane, James Henry, 40, 40n
LaTrobe, Charles Joseph, 4
Lincoln, President Abraham, 50
Little Priest, 319–20
Little Shield, 228, 228n
Luptain, Ellis, 300, 300n

McHenry, ———, 319
McLaren, R. N., 287
Maberly, John, 54, 54n
Man-Afraid-of-His-Horses, 287
Marshall, Major Levi G., 169n, 303, 303n
Maynadier, Colonel Henry E., 303, 303n, 331n; and the Indian Peace Commission, 287, 323, 340, 342; gives rations to Indians, 331; drinking by, 331; Hervey Johnson's opinion of, 331, 342
Moellmann, Charles Frederick, 17–18
Merwin, Sergeant Hervey D., 38, 38n
Mitchell, Brigadier General Robert B., 101–102
Moonlight, Colonel Thomas J., 240n, 261–62, 261n
Morgan, General John Hunt, 27–32, 27–28n
Mulligan, Colonel James Adelbert, 34, 34n

Overman, Elias, 179

Page, Private John W., 108, 121, 121n